Watertown Rome

Routes and rates for summer tours

Watertown Rome

Routes and rates for summer tours

ISBN/EAN: 9783337145460

Printed in Europe, USA, Canada, Australia, Japan

Cover: Foto ©Andreas Hilbeck / pixelio.de

More available books at **www.hansebooks.com**

ROUTES AND RATES FOR SUMMER TOURS

1895

ROME · WATERTOWN · AND · OGDENSBURG · RAILROAD ·

N. Y. C. & H. R. R.R. CO., Lessee.

H. WALTER WEBB, THIRD VICE-PRESIDENT, N. Y. C. & H. R. R.R.

EDGAR VAN ETTEN, GENERAL SUPERINTENDENT.

THEO. BUTTERFIELD, GENERAL PASSENGER AGENT, SYRACUSE, N. Y.

PREFATORY.

THE object of this book is to furnish the patrons of the Rome, Watertown & Ogdensburg Railroad with a complete list of routes and rates for summer tours which shall include all pleasure resorts and places in the North and East that are of interest to the summer tourist. The unexaggerated description of places and regions, embellished with faithful reproductions of actual scenes and accompanied by accurate maps of the greatest summer resort region of America, and a full and reliable list of hotels and boarding houses, enables one easily to decide upon a pleasant place in which to spend the summer, or, if intent upon a summer tour, to select the particular route one has in mind.

This book contains more than six hundred summer tours, and the combinations that may be formed from the tickets are almost unlimited.

This book is carefully edited up to date. If any omissions are noted or if any corrections should be made, please advise the General Passenger Agent.

THE RIVER ST. LAWRENCE.

The River St. Lawrence, in its majestic sweep from the lake to the sea, offers more attractions than any other traveled route in the world. The route embraces the famed "Thousand Islands," the exciting Rapids, the awe-inspiring Saguenay, stately Canadian cities, and rugged and picturesque scenery without an equal in grandeur. The many charming pleasure resorts, including the favorite Canadian sea-bathing resorts, and the attractive fishing grounds near Cape Vincent and Clayton, and again below Quebec, present enticements not to be found elsewhere.

The business and professional men, scientists, scholars, literary workers, sportsmen, tourists and pleasure seekers find the highest gratification in contemplating the beauties of this peerless river. Throngs of people from nearly all parts of the world make this tour every summer. Competing in fashionable favor with a European trip, the tour of the St. Lawrence has become the popular summer trip for the American people. The Rome, Watertown & Ogdensburg Railroad is the direct and only all-rail route to the "Thousand Island" region, which properly is the starting point for the grand St. Lawrence River tour, Clayton being the gateway for the entire region.

The most elaborate description that can be written of the mighty St. Lawrence cannot convey a proper conception of its grandeur and beauty. The storied Rhine, with its legends and castle-crowned cliffs, loses all its charms after one has beheld in rapture the wonders of this most mighty river.

☞ This book is published for gratuitous distribution. Upon receipt of Ten Cents Postage it will be mailed to any address on application to THEO. BUTTERFIELD, G. P. A., Syracuse, N. Y.

A revised and enlarged edition of this book, describing routes and rates for the season of 1896, with new illustrations and maps, will be ready for circulation early in June, 1896. Send for a copy before deciding on your summer trip.

APPROACH TO THE CAVE OF THE WINDS, NIAGARA FALLS.—WESTERN TERMINUS R., W. & O. R.R.

IMPROVEMENTS.

ON March 14th, 1891, the Rome, Watertown & Ogdensburg R.R. was leased in perpetuity to the New York Central & Hudson River R.R., "The World's Greatest and Only Four-Track Railroad." The lessee company, appreciating the value of its new acquisition, and its capability of becoming the largest and most important summer resort and tourist traffic route in America, proceeded at once, with its usual enterprise, to raise to trunk-line standard that portion of the newly acquired property patronized by the summer travel. This has been accomplished by hard work and the outlay of a large sum of money—more than one million dollars—in permanent improvements and betterments, notably the relaying of the railway with the heaviest steel rails used north of the Trunk Lines, renewing and reballasting its road-bed, placing new ties and increasing the number of same per mile, replacing bridges with stronger new ones of steel and iron, and making various other improvements on the R., W. & O. System, all of which enable the Company to inaugurate a new era in Northern New York passenger train service. The improvement in equipment and service has kept pace with that of the road-bed and railway. Standard locomotives, capable of hauling the heaviest passenger trains at high speed, have been added to the motive power. The perfection and comfort of the new passenger equipment will elicit the admiration of our patrons. New trains, the counterpart in make-up of the famous Limited trains on the New York Central & Hudson River R.R., will run on fast schedule time and without stops from Syracuse and from Utica to Clayton for the Thousand Islands, the St. Lawrence River and Canada pleasure travel, also to Norwood for the White Mountains, Maine and New England sea-coast travel.

These trains will be perfectly appointed, solid vestibuled trains, and will carry new Day Coaches, new Wagner Sleeping Cars and Drawing-Room Cars and Café Smoking and Library Cars. All cars have Wagner Vestibules, and are mounted on steel wheels. In carrying out the policy of developing summer travel by offering every facility, the New York Central & Hudson River R.R. has placed in service new fast trains.

Complete trains will run at the speed of the New York Central Limited trains, and with the equipment above mentioned, between Suspension Bridge, Niagara Falls, Buffalo and Syracuse, stopping only at Rochester; and between New York and Utica the "Adirondack and Clayton Night Express" will carry new Vestibuled Buffet Sleeping Cars, and the "Adirondack and Clayton Day Express" will carry Wagner Vestibuled Drawing-Room Cars between New York and Clayton in connection with the above-mentioned trains on R., W. & O. R.R. No extra fare will be charged on these trains, a description of which will be found on pages 9, 10, 11, 13, 15 and 16 of this book.

R., W. & O. R.R. MILEAGE.

Niagara Falls to Massena Springs,	300.7 miles
Lewiston Junction to Lewiston,	3.6 "
Rochester, Windsor Beach and Ontario Beach,	9.3 "
Syracuse to Pulaski,	37.4 "
Richland to Rome,	41.1 "
Watertown Junction to Cape Vincent,	24.1 "
De Kalb Junction to Ogdensburg,	18.8 "
Syracuse to Oswego,	36.9 "
Utica (to Clayton 108.5 Miles) to Ogdensburg,	134.6 "
Carthage, Watertown and Sackett's Harbor,	29.9 "
Clayton to Theresa Junction,	15.8 "
Gouverneur to Edwards,	14.2 "
Total Rail Lines,	666.4 miles
Steamboat and Ferry Lines controlled by this Company,	84 "
Total,	750.4 miles

ILLUSTRATIONS OF PERMANENT IMPROVEMENTS.

SECTION OF DOUBLE TRACK IRON BRIDGE ACROSS OSWEGO RIVER AND OSWEGO CANAL AT OSWEGO.

Length of Bridge, 900 feet; height of track above water, 60 feet.

The Oswego section of the Rome, Watertown & Ogdensburg Railroad is double tracked and is operated as a double track road.

DOUBLE TRACK IRON BRIDGE ACROSS GENESEE RIVER AT CHARLOTTE.

Length of Bridge, 308 feet.

The Charlotte section of the Rome, Watertown & Ogdensburg Railroad is double tracked and is operated as a double track road.

Rome, Watertown & Ogdensburg R.R.

STUBBORN FACTS

FOR THE CONSIDERATION OF ST. LAWRENCE RIVER PASSENGERS.

THE public is respectfully informed that by taking the Rome, Watertown & Ogdensburg Railroad to Clayton (to which points solid trains are run from Niagara Falls, Suspension Bridge, Buffalo, Rochester, Oswego, Syracuse and Utica), from four to twelve hours in time, and from ten to fifty miles in distance, may be saved *en route* to St. Lawrence River points, the White Mountains, sea-coast resorts of Maine and Canada. These solid trains carry elegant vestibuled coaches and Wagner vestibuled buffet drawing-room cars, also vestibuled *café* smoking and library cars on day trains, and vestibuled sleeping cars on night trains. They run direct to steamboat dock at Clayton, and make immediate connections with the palace steamers of the Thousand Island Steamboat Company, known as the "White Squadron." This fleet consists of ten steamboats, the largest of which are the steamers "St. Lawrence," "Empire State" and "America." These three steamboats are the largest, swiftest and costliest, and most comfortable boats on the St. Lawrence River, and make immediate connections for Round Island, Thousand Island Park, Alexandria Bay, Westminster Park, and all resorts among the Thousand Islands. These boats are equipped with new and powerful electric searchlights of one million candle power, which dispel the darkness of night, and make it as clear and bright as noonday. Electric light excursions are run every night during the summer season. These steamers also make the Thousand Island Ramble, or Fifty Mile Tour of the Islands, and an excursion trip to Kingston. First class meals are furnished on these steamers at price of 50 cents each. Connection is also made at steamboat dock at Clayton, without transfer, with powerful steamers of the Richelieu & Ontario Navigation Company (Royal Mail Line Steamers) for Montreal, Quebec, the River Saguenay and Lower St. Lawrence, passing all the Thousand Islands and Rapids of the River St. Lawrence by daylight. We wish to emphasize the fact that the steamboats running in connection with the Rome, Watertown & Ogdensburg Railroad are staunch, safe boats, built expressly for, and adapted to, the waters they navigate; that they are not old boats remodelled, nor boats brought from calm and smooth river waters, and therefore unfit for navigation on such a large body of water as Lake Ontario, liable to sudden and violent storms.

By taking the Rome, Watertown & Ogdensburg Railroad to Clayton, the traveler avoids the unpleasant and monotonous trip over Lake Ontario, with its inevitable "mal de mer" when the lake is rough, and also the liability to delays and detentions when the lake steamers haul off from their regular trips and refuse to leave their moorings at Charlotte or Oswego on account of squalls on the lake or tempestuous weather. The fast trains of the Rome, Watertown & Ogdensburg Railroad run every day, unhindered by squalls or stormy weather, and passengers are always certain of making connections. These trains are run to Clayton expressly to avoid the lake trip, and to enable tourists and pleasure-seekers to enjoy among the Thousand Islands—the loveliest river resort in the world—the time thus gained, and which otherwise would be consumed in an uncertain and uninteresting lake passage.

The track has been re-laid with steel rails, the road-bed newly ballasted with gravel and stone, and the train service has been augmented and improved by the introduction of new, heavy and powerful locomotives, especially designed to haul heavy passenger trains at a high rate of speed.

In former years, before the construction of through rail lines to the River St. Lawrence, this business was compelled to go via lake ports; but the Rome, Watertown & Ogdensburg Railroad, realizing the great dissatisfaction occasioned by people being obliged to take the lake route, extended its rail line to Clayton, and established there the central point of the St. Lawrence River Steamboat System. Clayton at once became the great objective point for all travel destined to the St. Lawrence River, and the perfect train service, with its steamboat connections, maintained by the Rome, Watertown & Ogdensburg Railroad, meets the exacting requirements of all classes of travel.

· · · PALACE CAR SERVICE. · · ·

SEASON OF 1895.

Time-Table in effect from June 16 to September 21, 1895, inclusive.

EAST-BOUND AND NORTH-BOUND.

CHICAGO AND PORTLAND, ME.
(WAGNER BUFFET SLEEPING CARS.)

Lv. Chicago, Mich. Cent., daily, except Friday	11 30 p.m
" Detroit	9.40 a.m
Ar. Niagara Falls	5.37 p.m
Lv. Niagara Falls, N. Y. C. Depot, ex. Saturday	8.20 "
" Buffalo, "	9 15 "
" Rochester, "	11.00 "
" Syracuse, "	1.00 a.m
Ar. Norwood (Breakfast), except Sunday	6.00 "
" Fabyan's	4.35 p.m
" Portland, except Sunday	7.45 "

CHICAGO AND CLAYTON.
(WAGNER VESTIBULED SLEEPING CARS.)

Lv. Chicago, Mich. Cent., daily, ex. Saturday	3.00 p.m
" Detroit	11.25 "
Ar. Niagara Falls	6.53 a.m
Lv. Niagara Falls, daily, except Sunday	9.05 "
" Buffalo	10.00 "
" Rochester	11.50 "
" Syracuse	2.00 p.m
Ar. Clayton	5.20 "

NIAGARA FALLS AND CLAYTON.
(WAGNER VESTIBULED SLEEPING CARS.)

Lv. Niagara Falls, N. Y. C. Depot, daily	8.20 p.m
" Buffalo, " "	9.15 "
" Rochester, " "	11.00 "
" Syracuse, " "	1.00 a.m
Ar. Clayton (Thousand Islands), daily	5.45 "

Connects with steamer for Alexandria Bay daily, and for Montreal daily, except Mondays, until July 15th; after July 15th, Montreal steamer daily.

NIAGARA FALLS AND CLAYTON.
(WAGNER VESTIBULED DRAWING-ROOM CARS.)

Lv. Niagara Falls, week-days, N. Y. C. Depot.	9.05 a.m
" Buffalo, " "	10.00 "
" Rochester, " "	11.50 "
" Syracuse, " "	2.00 p.m
Ar. Clayton, " "	5.20 "

NEW YORK AND CLAYTON.
(WAGNER VESTIBULED SLEEPING CARS)

Lv. New York (Grand Central Station), daily	7.00 p.m
" Albany, daily	11.05 "
" Utica, "	1.35 a.m
Ar. Clayton, "	5.45 "

Connects with steamer for Montreal.

NEW YORK AND CLAYTON.
(WAGNER VESTIBULED DRAWING-ROOM CARS.)

Lv. New York (Grand Cent. Sta.), week-days,	8.33 a.m
" Albany	11.45 "
" Utica	2.10 p.m
Ar. Clayton	5.30 "

NEW YORK AND CAPE VINCENT.
(WAGNER SLEEPING CARS.)

Lv. New York (Grand Central Station), daily	9.15 p.m
" Utica	5.25 a.m
" Rome	5.50 "
Ar. Watertown	8.35 "
" Cape Vincent, daily	10.40 "

Car leaving New York Saturday night runs via Syracuse and arrives Cape Vincent 11.00 a.m. Sundays.

NEW YORK AND OGDENSBURG.
(WAGNER SLEEPING CARS DAILY.)

Lv. New York (Grand Central Station), daily	9.15 p.m
" Utica	5.50 a.m
Ar. Ogdensburg	11.20 "

Sunday's car arrives Ogdensburg 12.20 p.m.

UTICA AND CLAYTON.
(WAGNER DRAWING-ROOM CARS.)

Lv. Utica, week-days	2.10 p.m
Ar. Clayton	5.30 "

SYRACUSE AND CLAYTON.
(WAGNER DRAWING-ROOM CARS.)

Lv. Syracuse, week-days	2.00 p.m
Ar. Clayton	5.20 "

WEST-BOUND AND SOUTH-BOUND.

PORTLAND, ME., AND CHICAGO.
(WAGNER BUFFET SLEEPING CARS.)

Lv. Portland, daily, except Sunday	8.45 a.m
" Fabyan's	12.50 p.m
" Norwood	11.40 "
Ar. Syracuse	4.50 a.m
" Rochester, N. Y. C. Depot (Breakfast)	7.40 "
" Buffalo, "	9.45 "
" Niagara Falls, "	11.15 "
Lv. Niagara Falls, Michigan Central R.R	5.12 p.m
Ar. Detroit, " "	10.50 "
" Chicago, " "	7.50 a.m

CLAYTON AND CHICAGO.
(WAGNER VESTIBULED SLEEPING CARS.)

Lv. Clayton, daily, except Sunday	8.45 a.m
Ar. Syracuse	12.01 p.m
" Rochester	2.15 "
" Buffalo	4.15 "
Lv. Buffalo	4.25 "
" Niagara Falls	5.10 "
Ar. Detroit	10.50 "
" Chicago, Mich. Cent., daily, ex. Monday	7.50 a.m

CLAYTON AND NIAGARA FALLS.
(WAGNER VESTIBULED SLEEPING CARS.)

Lv. Clayton (Thousand Islands), daily	11.20 p.m
Ar. Syracuse, R., W. & O. R.R	4.50 a.m
" Rochester, N. Y. C. Depot (Breakfast)	7.40 "
" Buffalo, "	9.45 "
" Niagara Falls, "	11.15 "

This train leaves Clayton Sunday night 10.00 p.m.

CLAYTON AND NIAGARA FALLS.
(WAGNER VESTIBULED DRAWING-ROOM CARS.)

Lv. Clayton, week-days	8.45 a.m
Ar. Syracuse, R., W. & O. R.R	12.01 p.m
" Rochester, New York Central Depot	2.15 "
" Buffalo, " "	4.15 "
" Niagara Falls, " "	5.10 "

CLAYTON AND NEW YORK.
(WAGNER VESTIBULED SLEEPING CARS.)

Lv. Clayton, daily	9.00 p.m
Ar. Utica	1.00 a.m
" Albany	3.55 "
" New York (Grand Central Station)	7.45 "

CLAYTON AND NEW YORK.
(WAGNER VESTIBULED DRAWING-ROOM CARS.)

Lv. Clayton, week-days	12.01 p.m
Ar. Utica	3.20 "
" Albany	5.55 "
" New York (Grand Central Station)	9.40 "

CAPE VINCENT AND NEW YORK.
(WAGNER SLEEPING CARS.)

Lv. Cape Vincent, daily	5.20 p.m
" Watertown	6.30 "
Ar. Rome	9.20 "
" Utica	9.40 "
" New York (Grand Central Station)	6.30 a.m

Car leaves Cape Vincent on Sunday nights at 6.25 p.m. and runs via Syracuse to New York.

OGDENSBURG AND NEW YORK.
(WAGNER SLEEPING CARS DAILY.)

Lv. Ogdensburg, daily	3.40 p.m
Ar. Utica	9.50 "
" New York (Grand Central Station)	6.30 a.m

Sundays this train leaves Ogdensburg 4.50 p.m.

CLAYTON AND UTICA.
(WAGNER DRAWING-ROOM CARS.)

Lv. Clayton, week-days	12.01 p.m
Ar. Utica	3.20 "

CLAYTON AND SYRACUSE.
(WAGNER DRAWING-ROOM CARS.)

Lv. Clayton, week-days	8.45 a.m
Ar. Syracuse	12.01 p.m

NOTE.—Passengers will please consult official time-tables, as time here given may vary during the season, and the arrangement shown above is subject to change or modification after the season opens. Drawing-Room Cars will be run on various other day trains to and from Clayton, Utica and Syracuse.

THE ONLY ALL-RAIL ROUTE

TO THE

THOUSAND ISLANDS

DURING THE SEASON OF TOURIST AND PLEASURE TRAVEL

(JUNE 16TH UNTIL SEPTEMBER 21ST).

FAST EXPRESS AND SPECIAL TRAINS

ARE RUN TO AND FROM CLAYTON

The Gateway to all the Thousand Island Region.

These fast trains are run to Clayton expressly to avoid the slow lake trip with its many discomforts, and to enable tourists and pleasure-seekers to enjoy among the Thousand Islands the time thus gained (from 4 to 12 hours) which otherwise would be consumed in an uncertain and uninteresting lake passage.

TO THE THOUSAND ISLANDS.						STATIONS.	FROM THE THOUSAND ISLANDS.						
O	N	M	L	K	H Daily		A Daily.	B	C	D	E	F	G Daily.
......	......	9.00 AM	8.30 AM	......	8.15 PM	Lv....Suspension Bridge....Ar.	11.20 AM	......	......	5.15 PM	......	......	......
......	......	9.06	8.15	......	8.20	" ......Niagara Falls...... "	11.15	......	......	5.10	......	......	......
......	......	10.00	......	......	9.15	" ....Buffalo......... "	9.45	......	......	4.15	......	......	......
......	......	11.50	10.50 AM	......	11.00	" ....Rochester........ "	7.40	......	......	2.15	......	......	......
6.15 PM	......	2.00 PM	1.30 PM	5.40 AM	1.00 AM	Lv.........Syracuse.........Ar.	4.30 AM	......	12.35 PM	12.01 PM	......	9.30 PM	......
6.35 PM	......	......	1.50 PM	5.50 AM	......	Lv..........Rome..........Ar.	......	......	12.15 PM	......	......	9.20 PM	......
10.30 AM	8.33 AM	......	......	9.15 PM	7.00 PM	Lv.........New York.........Ar.	Leave Clayton daily, except Monday.	......	6.30 PM	......	9.40 PM	6.30 AM	7.45 AM
3.00 PM	11.45	......	......	2.00 AM	11.05	" ....Albany......... "		......	3.05	......	5.55	1.30 AM	3.55
5.55	2.10 PM	.....	1.40 PM	5.50	1.35 AM	Lv..........Utica..........Ar		......	12.30 PM	......	3.20 PM	9.50 PM	1.00 AM
10.25 PM	5.30 PM	5.20 PM	6.25 PM	10.20 AM	5.45 AM	Ar..........Clayton........Lv.	11.20 PM	......	8.30 AM	8.45 AM	12.01 PM	4.40 PM	9.00 PM
						Via Steamer							
......	6.00 PM	5.30 PM	6.50 PM	10.40 AM	6.00 AM	Ar.......Round Island..... Lv.	11.05 PM	......	8.10 AM	8.10 AM	11.25 AM	3.55 PM	8.25 PM
......	6.20	6.10	7.10	11.00	6.20	" . Thousand Island Park.. "	10.50	......	7.50	7.50	11.05	3.35	8.05
......	7.10 PM	7.00 PM	8.00 PM	11.50 AM	7.10 AM	Ar......Alexandria Bay.....Lv	10.00 PM	......	7.00 AM	7.00 AM	10.15 AM	2.45 PM	7.15 PM

Sunday trains arrive Clayton 5.45 a.m., 11.20 a.m.; leave Clayton 5.55 p.m., 9.00 p.m., 10.00 p.m.

For all trains except those in column L, the Suspension Bridge, Niagara Falls, Buffalo and Rochester, time given above is via N. Y. C. & H. R and such R., W. & O. trains run over N. Y. C. & H. R. R.R. tracks via Syracuse. Tickets reading over R., W. & O. R.R. to, from or via Lewiston or Rochester, are accepted on these trains via Syracuse.

Trains in columns L and O run over R., W. & O. tracks via Lewiston and Oswego.

Trains shown in columns headed A, D, E, G, H, M and N, have through Sleeping and Drawing-Room Cars. For Through Car Arrangement see page 9.

One of the palatial steamboats

"ST. LAWRENCE," "EMPIRE STATE" and "AMERICA,"

Queens of the River St. Lawrence,

Will make a complete tour of the Islands every day. Price for excursion tickets, 50 cents each. A delicious luncheon is served on the steamer, price 50 cents.

The Steamer "St. Lawrence" will run with an electric search-light excursion every night. Tickets 50 cents.

The Steamer "Empire State" runs excursions Thousand Islands to Kingston week-days. Tickets 50 cents.

The new Steamer "America" will run daily excursions.

FROM

NEW YORK

TO

THOUSAND ISLANDS.

WAGNER VESTIBULE DRAWING-ROOM CARS BETWEEN NEW YORK AND CLAYTON.

The Thousand Island Fast Line.

RUNS WEEK DAYS ONLY.

Train No. 553.

NEW YORK AND CLAYTON.

Lv. New York, week-days	8 33	AM
" Albany	11 45	"
Ar. Utica	2 00	PM
Lv. Utica	2 10	"
Ar. Clayton (Thousand Islands)	5 30	"
" Alexandria Bay (steamer)	7 10	"

Train No. 552.

CLAYTON AND NEW YORK.

Lv. Alexandria Bay (steamer) week-days	7 00	AM
" Clayton	12 01	PM
Ar. Utica	3 20	"
Lv. Utica	3 40	"
Ar. Albany	5 55	"
" New York	9 40	"

Magnificent new Vestibuled Buffet Drawing-Room Cars, New York and Utica; Through Coaches New York and Clayton.

The Thousand Island Fast Line is a train put on particularly by request of New York people who are summer residents of the Thousand Island region. This magnificent train makes the entire run by daylight in each direction, and is the fastest train ever run between New York and the Thousand Islands.

New York and Clayton Special.

RUNS EVERY DAY.

Train No. 555.

NEW YORK AND CLAYTON.

Lv. New York (daily)	7 00	PM
" Albany	11 05	"
" Utica	1 35	AM
Ar. Clayton	5 45	"
" Alexandria Bay (steamer)	7 10	"

Train No. 554.

CLAYTON AND NEW YORK.

Lv. Alexandria Bay (steamer) daily	7 15	PM
" Clayton	9 00	"
Ar. Utica	1 00	AM
" Albany	3 55	"
" New York	7 45	"

These Trains have Magnificent Through Sleeping Cars between New York and Clayton.

The time-table for the New York and Clayton Special is arranged to meet the requirements of summer residents of the Thousand Islands whose homes are in New York. By this train people can leave New York after dinner every day, at 7.00 p.m., and arrive at Alexandria Bay in time for breakfast; returning, leave Alexandria Bay, after dinner, 7.15 p.m., and arrive in New York in time for breakfast, 7.45 a.m. These trains are enabled to make the very fast schedule upon which they are run by the great improvements referred to on page 5 of this book.

Excursion Tickets will be sold at New York City offices on Saturdays at very low rates for the New York and Clayton Special. Passengers can leave New York after business hours on Saturday, spend Sunday among the Thousand Islands, and return to New York on Monday morning in time for business.

The Club Train

"The Niagara Falls and Thousand Islands Club Train."

THIS

Superbly Appointed Train

Runs over N. Y. C. & H. R. R.R Tracks from Niagara Falls via

BUFFALO AND SYRACUSE

Stopping only at Rochester.

Tickets reading via

: : R. W. & O. R.R. : :

to, from or via

LEWISTON OR ROCHESTER

are accepted on

N. Y. C. & H. R. R.R.

via

: : SYRACUSE. : :

N. Y. C. & H. R. R.R. and R. W. & O. R.R. Conductors on this Train and on the St. Lawrence Steamboat Express will lift such tickets and give interchange checks.

This Train consists of

WAGNER VESTIBULE CLUB CAR,
VESTIBULE DRAWING-ROOM CARS,
VESTIBULE SLEEPING CAR, TO AND FROM CHICAGO, AND
VESTIBULE COACHES.

COMPLETE TRAIN RUNS SOLID

BETWEEN

NIAGARA FALLS AND CLAYTON

VIA BUFFALO, ROCHESTER AND SYRACUSE.

This Train makes the Fastest Time ever made

BETWEEN

NIAGARA FALLS AND CLAYTON

AND STOPS ONLY AT

BUFFALO, ROCHESTER, SYRACUSE and WATERTOWN.

THE NIAGARA FALLS AND THOUSAND ISLANDS CLUB TRAIN.

FROM

NIAGARA FALLS.

EAST-BOUND.

Lve.	Suspen. Bridge, week days, N.Y.C.&H.R.Depot	9.00 AM
"	Niagara Falls	9.05 "
"	Buffalo	10.00 "
"	Rochester	11.50 "
"	Syracuse, R. W. & O	2.00 PM
Arr.	Clayton	5 20 "

THE NIAGARA FALLS AND THOUSAND ISLANDS CLUB TRAIN.

FROM

CLAYTON.

WEST-BOUND.

Lve.	Clayton, week days	8.45 AM
Arr.	Syracuse	12.01 PM
"	Rochester	2.15 "
"	Buffalo	4.15 "
"	Niagara Falls	5.10 "
Arr.	Suspension Bridge, N. Y. C. & H. R. Depot	5.15 PM

Immediate connections are made at Clayton with steamers of the Thousand Island Steamboat Company to and from all points in the Thousand Island region. Trains run solid to and from steamboat dock.

CHICAGO SLEEPING CAR

on this train runs via Michigan Central Railroad.

East bound—Leaves Chicago.... 3.00 p.m.
West-bound—Arrives Chicago.... 7.50 a.m.

ONLY 23 HOURS CLAYTON TO CHICAGO

Direct connections are made at Suspension Bridge and Buffalo with trains on the Michigan Central R.R., Grand Trunk R'y, Lake Shore & Michigan Southern R'y, Nickel Plate Line and "Big Four Route."

NEW 15 SECTION WAGNER VESTIBULED SLEEPING CARS RUN BETWEEN NIAGARA FALLS AND CLAYTON ON THIS TRAIN.

TIME-TABLE EAST-BOUND JUNE 16TH.

L've	Suspension Bridge (daily)	8 15	p.m.
"	Niagara Falls (daily)	8 20	"
"	Buffalo, N. Y. C. & H. R. R.R. (daily)	9 15	"
"	Rochester, N. Y. C & H. R. R.R. daily)	11 00	"
"	Syracuse, R. W. & O. R.R. (daily)	1 00	a.m.
Arr	Clayton (daily)	5 45	"
L've	Clayton daily T. I. S. B. Co	5 50	"
Arr.	Round Island	6 00	"
"	Thousand Island Park, T. I. S. B. Co.	6 20	"
"	Alexandria Bay, T. I. S. B. Co.	7 00	"
L've	Clayton, Rich. & Ont. Nav. Co. (daily after July 15th)	6 20	"
"	Alexandria Bay, "	7 15	"
"	Brockville, "	8 45	"
"	Prescott, "	9 30	"
"	Cornwall, "	12 45	p.m.
"	Coteau Landing, "	2 15	"
Arr.	Montreal (go alongside steamers for Quebec to transfer)	6 30	"
L've	Montreal, Rich. & Ont. Nav. Co.	7 00	"
Arr	Quebec connecting with steamer for Saguenay River	6 30	a.m.
L've	Quebec for Saguenay River, after July 15th, daily (except Sunday)	7 30	"

APPROACHING CLAYTON (THOUSAND ISLANDS).

THE . . . . . . CELEBRATED

St. Lawrence Steamboat Express

THE TOURIST'S FAVORITE TRAIN.

Leaves Niagara Falls 8.20 p.m. Every Day.

Arrives Clayton (Thousand Islands) 5.45 a.m. Every Day.

☞ Be sure your tickets read via R., W. & O. R.R. to Clayton, R. & O. Navigation Co. Clayton to Montreal, and avoid the lake ride and "mal de mer."

☞ It is positively the Only Comfortable Route.

☞ Montreal steamer leaves Clayton daily (except Mondays) until July 15th; after July 15th, daily.

R. & O. N. CO. BAPTISTE, THE INDIAN PILOT.

TIME-TABLE WEST-BOUND JUNE 16.

L've	Quebec, R. & O. N. Co. (Sundays excepted)	5 00	p.m
Arr.	Montreal next morning	6 30	a.m
L've	Montreal (Canal Basin) (Sundays excepted)	10 00	"
"	Lachine (connects with noon train)	12 30	p.m.
"	Valleyfield	6 00	"
"	Coteau connects 5 p.m. train from Montreal)	6 40	"
"	Cornwall	9 30	"
"	Dickenson's Landing	2 30	a.m.
"	Prescott	7 30	"
"	Brockville	8 30	"
"	Alexandria Bay.	10 30	"
"	Thousand Island Park	10 40	"
"	Round Island	11 00	"
Arr.	Clayton, R., W. & O. R R.	11 30	a.m.

A New Vestibuled Train, the "Niagara Falls and Thousand Islands Club Train," with Wagner Vestibule Club Car, leaves Clayton 8 45 a.m., arrives Syracuse 12.01 p.m., Rochester 2 15 p.m., Buffalo 4 15 p.m., Niagara Falls 5.10 p.m., Suspension Bridge 5.15 p.m., connects at Buffalo, Niagara Falls and Suspension Bridge with fast trains for all Western cities.

L've	Clayton (daily)	11 20	p.m.
Arr.	Syracuse, R., W. & O. R.R (daily)	4 50	a.m.
"	Rochester, N. Y. C. & H. R. R.R. (daily)	7 40	"
"	Buffalo (daily)	9 45	"
"	Niagara Falls (daily)	11 15	"
Arr.	Suspension Bridge, N.Y.C. & H.R.R.R.(daily)	11 20	a.m.

Niagara Falls, White Mountains, and New England Coast Line.

50 MILES SHORTEST LINE NIAGARA FALLS TO WHITE MOUNTAINS.

WAGNER BUFFET SLEEPING CARS

RUN THROUGH WITHOUT CHANGE BETWEEN

CHICAGO AND PORTLAND, ME. NIAGARA FALLS AND PORTLAND, ME.

This train, with Wagner Buffet Sleeping Cars attached, leaves Chicago, via Michigan Central R.R. daily, except Friday, at 11.30 p.m. and leaves Niagara Falls daily, except Saturday, at 8.20 p.m. West-bound it leaves Portland daily, except Sunday, at 8.45 a.m.

The run through the entire White Mountain Region is made in both directions by daylight. Observation Cars are attached for the passage through the famous "White Mountain Notch." The train stops directly in front of the principal hotels in the White Mountains. This is the only line running through cars, and is in every way the best and most comfortable route.

TIME-TABLE TAKING EFFECT JUNE 16, 1895.

EAST-BOUND.

L've	Chicago, Mich. Cent. R.R.	11.30	p.m
"	Detroit, Mich Cent. R.R.	9.40	a.m
"	Suspension Bridge	8.15	p.m
"	Niagara Falls	8.20	"
"	Buffalo	9.15	"
"	Rochester, N. Y. C. Depot	11.00	"
"	Syracuse	1.00	a.m
Arr.	Norwood (Breakfast)	6.00	"
"	Moira	7.24	"
"	Rouse's Point	9.40	"
"	Bluff Point	11.37	"
"	Swanton	10.20	"
"	Cambridge Junction	11.37	"
"	Hyde Park	12.05	p.m
"	Morrisville	12.10	"
"	St. Johnsbury	2.20	"
"	Lunenburg	3.45	"
"	Whitefield, Maine Cent. R.R.	3.57	"
"	Jefferson, Maine Cent. R.R.	3.45	"
"	Lancaster, Maine Cent. R.R.	3.30	"
"	Twin Mountain House, M C R.R.	4.23	"
"	Fabyan House, Maine Cent. R.R.	4.35	"
"	Bethlehem Junction, C. & M. R.R.	5.02	"
"	Maplewood, P. & F. N. R.R.	5.35	"
"	Bethlehem, P. & F. N. R.R.	5.40	"
"	Profile House, P. & F. N. R.R.	6.05	"
"	Summit Mt. Washington, Mt. W. R'y	6.30	"
"	Crawford House, Maine Cent. R.R.	4.47	"
"	Glen, Maine Cent. R.R.	5.47	"
"	North Conway, Maine Cent. R.R.	6.00	"
"	Boston		
"	Portland, Maine Cent. R.R.	7.45	p.m
"	Old Orchard Beach, B. & M. R.R.	9.15	"
"	Kennebunkport	9.50	"
"	Augusta, Maine Cent. R.R.	1.56	a.m
"	Bangor, Maine Cent. R.R.	4.50	"
"	Bar Harbor, Maine Cent R.R.	7.25	"
Arr.	St. Andrews, N. B., C. P. R'y	1.30	p.m
"	St. John, N. B., C. P. R'y	1.40	"
"	Halifax, N. S., Intercolonial R'y	11.20	p.m

Direct and immediate connections are made at Suspension Bridge and Niagara Falls, via Lewiston and steamer, to and from Toronto.

WEST-BOUND.

L've	Halifax, N. S., Intercolonial R'y	12.20	p.m
"	St. John, N. B., C. P. R'y	7.20	a.m
"	St. Andrews, N. B., C. P. R'y	7.40	"
L've	Bar Harbor, Maine Cent. R.R.	4.10	p.m
"	Bangor, Maine Cent. R.R.	8.00	"
"	Augusta, Maine Cent. R.R.	11.00	"
"	Kennebunkport	6.40	a.m
"	Old Orchard Beach	7.32	"
"	Boston	8.30	"
"	Portland, Maine Cent. R R	8.45	"
"	North Conway, Maine Cent. R.R.	11.00	"
"	Glen, Maine Cent. R.R	11.12	"
"	Bartlett	11.45	"
"	Crawford House, Maine Cent. R.R.	12.35	p.m
"	Fabyan House, Maine Cent. R.R.	12.50	"
"	Summit Mt. Washington, Mt. W. R'y	7.00	a.m
"	Profile House, P. & F. N. R R	10.45	"
"	Bethlehem, P. & F. N. R R	10.55	"
"	Maplewood, P. & F. N. R.R.	11.00	"
"	Bethlehem Junction, C. & M. R.R.	11.18	"
"	Twin Mountain House, Me. Cent. R.R.	1.02	p m
"	Lancaster, Maine Cent. R.R.	1.55	"
"	Jefferson, Maine Cent. R.R.	1.40	"
"	Whitefield, Maine Cent. R.R.	1.30	"
"	Lunenburg	1.45	"
"	St. Johnsbury	3.15	"
"	Morrisville (Supper)	5.35	"
"	Hyde Park	5.43	"
"	Cambridge Junction	6.20	"
"	Swanton	6.25	"
"	Bluff Point	6.23	"
"	Rouse's Point	7.10	"
"	Malone	9.23	"
"	Moira	9.40	"
"	Norwood	11.40	"
Arr.	Syracuse	4.50	a.m
"	Rochester (Breakfast)	7.40	"
"	Buffalo	9.20	"
"	Niagara Falls	11.15	"
"	Suspension Bridge	11.20	"
L've	Niagara Falls, Mich. Cent. R R.	5.12	p m
Arr.	Detroit, Mich. Cent. R.R.	10.50	"
"	Chicago, Mich. Cent. R.R	7.50	a m

☞ Make no mistake. Be sure your tickets read: R., W. & O. R.R. to Norwood, thence via Rouse's Point, Swanton and Lunenburg to Portland.

Niagara Falls, White Mountains, and New England Coast Line.

Rome, Watertown & Ogdensburg Railroad, Niagara Falls and Susp. Bridge to Norwood.
Central Vermont Railroad, - - - - - Norwood to Swanton.
St. Johnsbury & Lake Champlain Railroad, - - - Swanton to Lunenburg.
Maine Central Railroad, - - - - - - Lunenburg to Portland.

Wagner Buffet Sleeping Cars

COMMENCING JUNE 15th, 1895, WILL RUN THROUGH BETWEEN

Chicago (via Michigan Central R.R.) and Portland, Me.

Niagara Falls and Suspension Bridge and Portland, Me.

WITHOUT CHANGE.

THE

Union Station

AT

PORTLAND, ME.

is one of the handsomest and best appointed Railway Stations in America. Trains to and from Niagara Falls, Chicago, etc., via R., W. & O. R. R., make connections at this Station with through trains to and from all the famous sea-coast resorts of New England and the Maritime Provinces.

NEW UNION STATION AT PORTLAND.

THE

WAGNER

Palace Car Co.

recognizing the importance and popularity of this great highway of tourist travel, have placed new and elegantly appointed Buffet Sleeping Cars in the service.

These cars run through without change between Chicago and Portland, Maine.

This through line has been formed expressly for summer travel, and traversing the most interesting section of our country, offers greater inducements and better facilities for travelers to and from the eastern summer resorts than any other line. The route passes the principal tourist resorts in the East, including Niagara Falls, Buffalo, Rochester and Syracuse, the Thousand Islands, River St. Lawrence, Adirondack Mountains, Green Mountains and all resorts in the White Mountains, passing through the famous White Mountain Notch by daylight to Portland, Old Orchard Beach, Bar Harbor, St. Andrews, N. B., Provincetown, Plymouth, Falmouth, Chatham, Nantucket, Cottage City (Martha's Vineyard), Newport, Block Island, Narragansett Pier, Watch Hill, and other New England sea-shore resorts.

It is fifty miles the shortest line from Niagara Falls to the White Mountains, and passengers will find it to their interest and comfort to patronize this route.

TO TOURISTS AND PLEASURE SEEKERS

To All Points in Northern New York, River St. Lawrence, Canada and New England, the Rome, Watertown & Ogdensburg Railroad Presents Unequaled Advantages.

A BRIEF DESCRIPTION OF THE ROUTE.

ALL through trains of the Rome, Watertown & Ogdensburg Railroad, both east-bound and west-bound, allow ample time for passengers to view the beauties of Niagara Falls, the western terminus of this line. The Falls of Niagara are the grandest specimen of Nature's handiwork on this continent. At all seasons and under all circumstances, under all the varying effects of sunlight, or moonlight, or the dazzling glare of electric illumination, the scene is always sublime. The whirling floods, the ceaseless monotone of the thunderous roar, the vast clouds of spray and mist that catch in their depths the dancing sunbeams and transform them into hues of a thousand rainbows, seem striving to outvie each other in their tribute of homage to the mighty "Thunderer of the Waters."

The name Niagara is of Indian origin and signifies "Thunderer of the Waters." The whole region in the vicinity of the River and Falls is full of historical interest. From early times, when the Indian ruled supreme, through all the conflicts between the French and English down to the war of 1812, the region has been the scene of bloody strife and heroic engagements.

The waters of all the great lakes (excepting Ontario), with their numerous tributaries, draining an area of more than one hundred and fifty thousand square miles, flow through the Niagara River in their course to the sea.

In view of this immense supply, it is not surprising that the cataract pours its ceaseless flood year after year without diminution.

In its short course of thirty-six miles the river falls 336 feet. From Lake Erie to the Falls, a distance of twenty-two miles, the fall is fifteen feet. At the verge of the cataract, Goat Island, formerly called Iris Island, parts the channel into two courses, the larger of which with an average width of 2000 feet, plunges down 165 feet, and is known as the Horse-shoe Falls; while the other known as the American Fall is 800 feet wide, with a plunge of 159 feet. It is estimated that 100,000,000 tons of water pass over the Falls every hour. Besides the majestic cataract itself there are many other points of interest in the immediate neighborhood. Goat Island, already mentioned, is one mile in circumference, and has an area of sixty-one and one-half acres; it is accessible from the American side by a bridge 360 feet long. The island was once the favorite burying ground of the Indians; now it is handsomely laid out as a pleasure park. Lunar Island and the Three Sisters are connected by bridges with Goat Island, and from them fine views may be obtained of the rapids above the Falls. An enclosed stairway descends to the rocks below, where are pathways leading to the Cave of the Winds, a cavern excavated by the falling waters. Here, with suitable dresses and guides, one may pass under and behind the mighty sheet of descending water.

Two miles below the Falls the channel of the river turns abruptly at a right angle and throws the waters into terrific commotion. This boiling, turbulent pool is known as the Whirlpool. Beetling cliffs, 350 feet high, confine the howling flood within their narrowing limits, giving an outlet only twenty-five rods across to the confined torrent which pitches and rises to a height of from ten to forty feet. The depth of the narrow channel at the Whirlpool is estimated at 400 feet.

Prospect Park, comprising some twelve acres, adjoins the American Fall with a frontage of several hundred feet along the gorge, both above and below the American Fall. It commands a fine view of the Falls which is its chief feature Every facility is provided for a thorough enjoyment of the remarkable scene.

By means of an inclined railway one may descend to the water's edge, and, properly clothed, enter the Shadow of the Rock, as the space is called between the rocks and the sheet of water at the end of the American Fall.

NIAGARA FALLS—WESTERN TERMINUS R. W. & O. R.R.

A little steamer, the "Maid of the Mist," makes regular trips to the foot of the Falls, affording fine views of the cataract.

No charge is made for entrance to the Park.

The small fees asked at different points of interest, considering the convenience and protection offered, are just and reasonable. The appended list will show the ordinary charges.

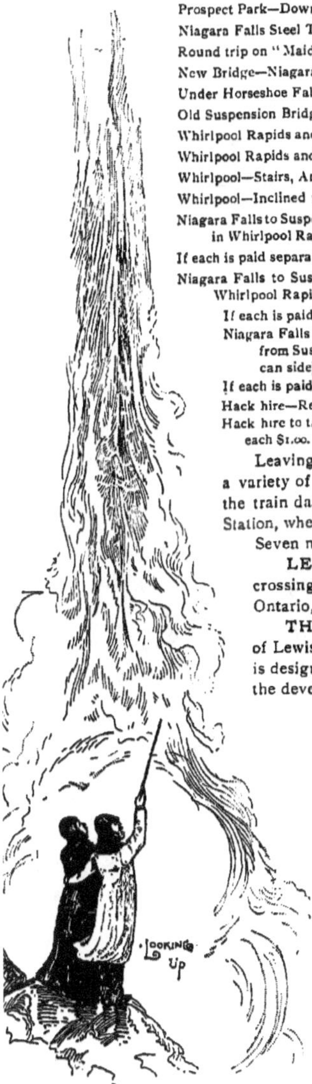

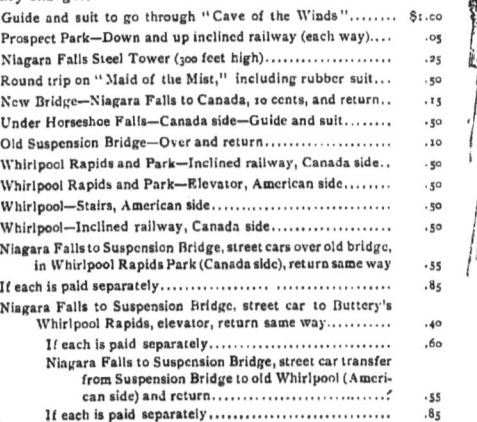

Guide and suit to go through "Cave of the Winds"........	$1.00
Prospect Park—Down and up inclined railway (each way)....	.05
Niagara Falls Steel Tower (300 feet high).....................	.25
Round trip on "Maid of the Mist," including rubber suit...	.50
New Bridge—Niagara Falls to Canada, 10 cents, and return..	.15
Under Horseshoe Falls—Canada side—Guide and suit........	.50
Old Suspension Bridge—Over and return.....................	.10
Whirlpool Rapids and Park—Inclined railway, Canada side..	.50
Whirlpool Rapids and Park—Elevator, American side........	.50
Whirlpool—Stairs, American side............................	.50
Whirlpool—Inclined railway, Canada side....................	.50
Niagara Falls to Suspension Bridge, street cars over old bridge, in Whirlpool Rapids Park (Canada side), return same way	.55
If each is paid separately..................	.85
Niagara Falls to Suspension Bridge, street car to Buttery's Whirlpool Rapids, elevator, return same way...........	.40
If each is paid separately.............................	.60
Niagara Falls to Suspension Bridge, street car transfer from Suspension Bridge to old Whirlpool (American side) and return...........................?	.55
If each is paid separately.............................	.85

Hack hire—Regular Rate,.......... $2.00 for first hour, $1.50 for each subsequent hour.
Hack hire to take in all places of interest for party of four (4) or more in each hack, each $1.00.

Leaving Niagara Falls and following the river, the tourist will enjoy a variety of wild and picturesque scenery. Passing Suspension Bridge the train dashes along the mountain, reaching the summit at River View Station, where a fine view is afforded of the river and the Canadian shore.

Seven miles below the Falls is the historic town of

LEWISTON, the point of arrival and departure of steamers crossing Lake Ontario. It is the head of navigation on Lake Ontario, and is beautifully situated on the Niagara River.

THE MODEL CITY, on the Niagara River, three miles east of Lewiston, chartered by special act of the New York Legislature, is designed to be the most perfect city in existence. The amount of the development fund is $25,500,000. This city will have unlimited water power; the Niagara water power will be doubled here, as there is a fall of 300 feet at the site of the city. Prospectus and full information can be obtained by addressing The Model Town Company, Lewiston, N. Y.

Directly opposite, on the Canadian side, is the interesting town of Queenston. It is well worth a visit, for it occupies an important place in history. Here the gallant General Brock and his aide-de-camp, McDonnell, fell, October 11, 1812. On the heights above the village is the monument erected to General Brock's memory, and from its commanding site it is a conspicuous object for several miles. It is 185 feet high, surmounted by a dome, which is reached by a flight of 250 steps on the inside.

After leaving Lewiston the road soon skirts Lake Ontario, passing through the finest farming section of the State. An almost continuous succession of peach orchards extends along the shore.

NEWFANE has a population of 800. Olcott, one mile distant, is a delightful resort on Lake Ontario.

R., W. & O. R.R.—ALONG THE NIAGARA RIVER, NEAR LEWISTON,

OAK ORCHARD-ON-THE-LAKE, two and a half miles from Carlton, is a beautiful resort on the wooded shores of Oak Orchard Harbor, with an unbroken sandy beach that allows unobstructed access to the waters of Lake Ontario. The air is cool and refreshing at all times. Bathing, boating, good fishing and cottage life in delightful summer homes, in the midst of beautiful scenery, are the attractive features of this resort. The Oak Orchard-on-the-Lake Company, incorporated in 1891, composed of prominent Buffalo gentlemen, is developing this place and has laid out attractive streets and avenues.

WATERPORT, a thriving village, is situated at the confluence of Orchard River and Otter Creek. Fruit-growing is a prominent industry in this vicinity. The village is fast becoming a large manufacturing centre. A number of Rochester gentlemen have formed a company with $500,000 capital to utilize the enormous water-power for manufacturing purposes. The great dam will be raised to the height of fifty-six feet. The surplus power will be utilized by a large electric plant and be transmitted for use in electric railways in neighboring cities and towns.

Two miles from **MORTON** is Troutburg, a pleasant summer resort on Lake Ontario, with good hotels, dancing and dining pavilions and other attractions.

CHARLOTTE (population 2000) the port of Rochester, is eighty-two miles from Suspension Bridge. The mouth of the Genesee River is crossed at this point on a magnificent iron draw-bridge, 300 feet long. In the vicinity are the very attractive lake resorts, Ontario Beach, Windsor Beach, Lake Bluff, Sea Breeze, Irondequoit Bay, Lake Beach and Lake View, which are yearly growing in popularity with residents of Northern and Western New York. These popular resorts on Lake Ontario are reached direct by trains of the Rome, Watertown & Ogdensburg Railroad. Every attraction is offered to the tourist or pleasure-seeker who delights in charming lake scenery. Comfortable and commodious hotels, with all modern improvements for the convenience and enjoyment of guests, offer superior advantages to families and all who delight in the beauties of natural scenery. Electric lights illuminate the beautifully arranged grounds and buildings;

R. W. & O. R.R.—MOUTH OF THE GENESEE RIVER, ONTARIO BEACH.

popular outdoor games of all kinds are provided; boating and sailing may be enjoyed without stint; bathing on the beach is not the least of the many attractions. Frequent trips are made *daily* by Rome, Watertown & Ogdensburg Railroad trains from Rochester to these delightful pleasure resorts, the fare for the round trip from Rochester being only twenty-five cents. Seneca Park is located on the east bank of the Genesee River, about four miles from Rochester, on the Rome, Watertown & Odgensburg Railroad, Rochester line. Trains stop at Seneca Park

R., W. & O. R.R.—WHIRLPOOL RAPIDS, NIAGARA RIVER.

R., W. & O. R.R.—WHIRLPOOL, NIAGARA RIVER.

Station. Trains east-bound and west-bound on the Niagara Falls line stop at Windsor Beach for breakfast and supper. At Windsor Beach connection is made for the large and handsome city of

ROCHESTER, seven miles distant, reached by a quick trip over the newly built track of the Rome, Watertown & Ogdensburg Railroad, which, on entering the city, crosses the Genesee River on a massive pier bridge of graceful proportions, a fine specimen of modern bridge building. The terminus of the Rome, Watertown & Ogdensburg Railroad in the city of Rochester is on State Street, a central and desirable site. The magnificent passenger station, a beautiful and massive

R. W. & O. R.R.—GENESEE RIVER BRIDGE—LENGTH, 705 FEET; HEIGHT ABOVE WATER, 102 FEET.

structure of stone, is occupied solely by the Rome, Watertown & Ogdensburg Railroad. The location is the finest and most central of any passenger station in Rochester, only five minutes from "the four corners" and the Powers Hotel. Street cars pass in both directions on State Street every few minutes, and no station in Rochester is so accessible to the various lines of street railways as the new station of the Rome, Watertown & Ogdensburg Railroad.

The city of Rochester is regularly laid out, the streets well paved and bordered with shade trees. The Genesee River passes through the city, and with its several falls furnishes a water-power without a rival. To this fine water-power is attributable much of the present prosperity of the city. Large flouring mills and manufacturing establishments are among the chief industries. Several large nurseries and seed farms are attractive objects of interest, and in the season of bloom are gorgeous sights, covering several acres with their brilliant flowers. Rochester contains many fine buildings and private residences. The Powers Block is a large and imposing fire-proof structure, containing a fine gallery of paintings; the Savings Bank building is an ornate

CITY OF ROCHESTER.

R. W. & O. R.R.—ONTARIO BEACH.

edifice, and many of the churches are noticeable specimens of fine architecture. The University of Rochester is an educational institution, occupying a massive building of red sandstone, surrounded by extensive grounds beautifully laid out. The Falls of the Genesee River, three in number, are among the natural attractions at Rochester. The first is ninety-six feet high, and from table rock in its centre Sam Patch made his last and fatal leap. The second fall is only twenty-five feet high, and a short distance below it is the third fall, which descends perpendicularly eighty-four feet. Rochester is an important station on the R., W. & O. R.R. and a large railroad centre. Connections are made at Rochester with N. Y. C. & H. R.R.; N. Y., L. E. & W. R.R.; B., R. & P. R.R. and the W. N. Y. & P. R.R. At

LAKESIDE is a beautiful summer resort on Lake Ontario; population 150. Occasional glimpses of Lake Ontario diversify the scene as we speed along from one thrifty village to another. **SODUS**, a beautiful village of 1200 inhabitants, has two good hotels.

WALLINGTON, thirty-two miles east of Charlotte, the Sodus Bay and Southern Division of the Pennsylvania R.R. connects for Sodus Point, a noted summer resort on the Lake, three miles distant. Sodus Point is delightfully situated on Lake Ontario and the west shore of Great Sodus Bay. The fishing is excellent, bass and pickerel being caught in abundance. Boating privileges are unsurpassed. Sodus Point and the Bluffs, a charming resort on the east shore of Sodus Bay, are also accessible from Sodus, only four miles distant, and

R. W. & O. R.R.—FULTON (OSWEGO FALLS).

ALTON Station, two miles from Wallington. Five miles beyond is **ROSE** Station. Lake Bluff, a pleasant lake resort, is reached by carriage to Port Glasco; thence by steamer.

WOLCOTT, five miles distant, is the stopping station for those who would enjoy the excellent fishing in Port Bay, where there is good fishing the year round. Pike, pickerel and black bass are taken in large quantities. At

STERLING, twenty-three miles from Wallington, the Lehigh Valley Railroad connects for Fair Haven on Lake Ontario and for all points in the enchanting Lehigh Valley region. Sixteen miles from Sterling, having passed Hannibal, we reach

OSWEGO, a city of about 21,000 inhabitants. The new Electric Street Railway has developed, and made easily accessible the popular Boulevard resort on the shore of Lake Ontario. A new summer hotel, with attractive cafés, is a feature of this popular resort. The pure air, excellent drainage, and other natural advantages of Oswego, contribute to its right to rank as the third healthiest city in the Union. The town is built on sloping ground on either side of the Oswego River, extending to the Lake, which at this point is seventy miles wide. A fine harbor affords facilities for an interchange of traffic with other lake ports; this, with three railroads, makes the city of considerable importance as a commercial centre.

The broad shaded streets, lined with handsome residences and business blocks, charm the eye and make Oswego one of the most attractive of lake cities. A fine boulevard extends along the lake shore a distance of three miles from the city, affording an unexcelled drive, with forest and fields on the one hand and the broad expanse of lake on the other.

Unrivaled facilities for pleasure are on every hand; white-winged yachts flit on the lake; steam launches plow its blue waters; graceful canoes skim the river. The sportsman will here find his paradise in casting the seductive fly in either the river or lake, both of which furnish an abundant supply of fish.

The city has one of the finest State Normal schools, eighteen churches, two daily and two weekly newspapers, an opera house, a public library containing twenty thousand volumes, and important manufacturing interests. The celebrated "Deep Rock" Spring is located here. The commerce with foreign countries is very heavy, the imports and exports aggregating six to eight millions of dollars annually. Oswego offers ample hotel accommodations for summer visitors. The Doolittle House and Lake Shore Hotel make special rates for summer guests.

Oswego is the diverging point of the New York, Ontario & Western Railway and the Delaware, Lackawanna & Western Railroad. The former connects with the Syracuse Division of the Rome, Watertown & Ogdensburg Railroad at Central Square.

At Oswego connection is made with the Phœnix Line of the Rome, Watertown & Ogdensburg Railroad, which is the popular route between Syracuse and Oswego via Phœnix and Fulton.

NEW HAVEN, eleven miles from Oswego and one mile and a half from Lake Ontario, affords fine opportunities for black bass fishing. Mexico Point and Ontario Park, four miles from **MEXICO** Station, are much frequented resorts, and offer excellent bass fishing.

SYRACUSE is an enterprising city of 100,000 inhabitants, situated at the south end of Onondaga Lake, an attractive sheet of water six miles long. This city is the seat of the most extensive salt producing industry in the United States. The streets are broad and beautifully shaded, and for the most part well paved. Many of the private residences are elegant and indicate the wealth and refinement of the place. The public buildings are fine and imposing structures, some especially being noteworthy for their striking architectural beauty. Syracuse University, under the patronage of the Methodist denomination, is a large and flourishing educational institution, occupying a commanding site on a hill to the east of the city. Its library contains the valuable collection of historical works once owned by the German historian Von Ranke. The Post-Office and Government Building and the new City Hall building are substantial and imposing specimens of architecture. The street railway service is first class and embraces the latest improved appliances and methods.

VIEW OF SYRACUSE FROM R. W. & O. TRAIN.

Five week-day trains and two Sunday trains connect here with the New York Central & Hudson River Railroad, West Shore Railroad, Delaware, Lackawanna & Western Railroad, and the Syracuse, Ontario & New York Railway from all points east, west and south to the Thousand Islands, St. Lawrence River, White Mountains and beyond; also to and from Oswego by the Phœnix Line.

Leaving Syracuse, on the Phœnix Line for Oswego, we pass the extensive salt works and run along the entire eastern shore of Onondaga Lake. This beautiful sheet of water is a favorite day pleasure resort for Syracusans and residents of Central New York. The resorts along its shore are numerous and attractive, the most prominent of which is the Iron Pier and Pavilion, located a few feet from the tracks of the Rome, Watertown & Ogdensburg Railroad. This pier is the gateway to Onondaga Lake, and the Iron Pier Company has invested more than $100,000 in specialties for the entertainment of the public. It is reached by People's Line street cars.

LIVERPOOL, with a population of 1500, is the seat of very extensive salt evaporating works and willow basket making, the latter industry amounting to $100,000 annually. At

BREWERTON, fifteen miles from Syracuse, connection is made with steamers for Frenchman's Island and South Bay, popular resorts five miles distant on beautiful Oneida Lake. Frenchman's Island and Hotel will be under popular and efficient management, and conducted in a first-class manner. This is a popular resort for Syracuse people. Boating, sailing, fishing, bathing, tennis, croquet, base-ball and good music are the attractions of this delightful place.

WOODARD, three miles north, is the junction point of the Phœnix Line with the Syracuse Division of the Rome, Watertown & Ogdensburg Railroad.

THREE RIVER POINT, the next station, is in the midst of attractive, natural scenery—the confluence of the Oneida, Seneca and Oswego Rivers—presenting a view at once striking and beautiful.

Messrs. Ramsay & Barnum, the new proprietors, have expended several thousand dollars in developing this resort, and have made Three Rivers one of the most attractive day pleasure resorts in Central New York. Every facility is found here for the entertainment of popular excursions, picnics and camping parties. Good fishing, row-boats, sail-boats, and steam yachts make water life at this place very attractive. Fine pavilions, dining rooms, dining tables, dancing platforms, croquet, tennis, and base-ball grounds, a beautiful grove and excellent music, together with various special entertainments, provided by the proprietors, are the features of this popular resort. Excursion trains are run from Syracuse, only thirteen miles distant, and excursion tickets are sold at the principal Rome, Watertown & Ogdensburg Railroad stations.

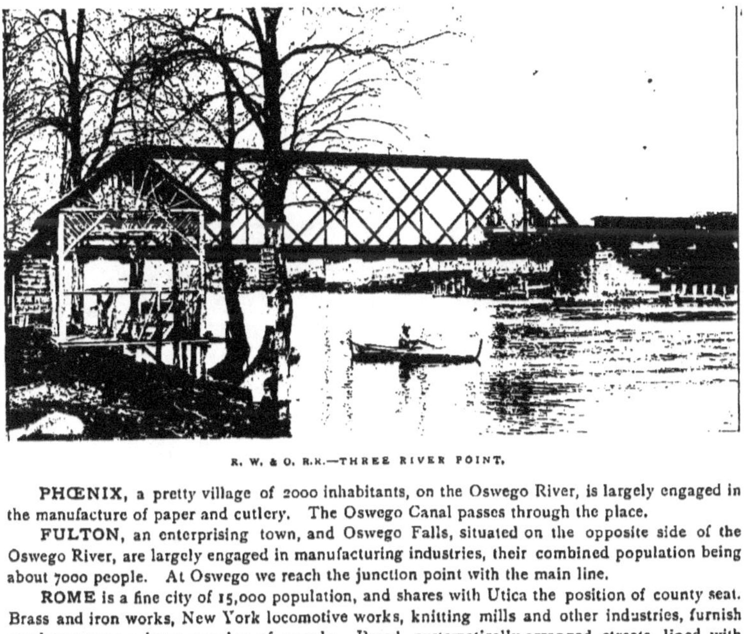

R. W. & O. R.R.—THREE RIVER POINT.

PHŒNIX, a pretty village of 2000 inhabitants, on the Oswego River, is largely engaged in the manufacture of paper and cutlery. The Oswego Canal passes through the place.

FULTON, an enterprising town, and Oswego Falls, situated on the opposite side of the Oswego River, are largely engaged in manufacturing industries, their combined population being about 7000 people. At Oswego we reach the junction point with the main line.

ROME is a fine city of 15,000 population, and shares with Utica the position of county seat. Brass and iron works, New York locomotive works, knitting mills and other industries, furnish employment to a large number of people. Broad, systematically arranged streets, lined with substantial business blocks and handsome private residences, indicate the prosperous character of the town.

McCONNELLSVILLE, thirteen miles north of Rome, is a small village of 200 inhabitants, largely engaged in the manufacture of chairs, distilling essential oils, and corn canning. Sylvan Beach and North Bay, resorts on Oneida Lake, are only five miles from this station. Passing

CAMDEN (population 3000) and **WEST CAMDEN**, places widely known for their chair factories and corn packing establishments, we reach

WILLIAMSTOWN.—Eight miles from the station is Redfield Square, where excellent trouting may be enjoyed, with good accommodations at reasonable rates. A run of nine miles brings us to

ALTMAR.—Salmon River Falls, 110 feet high, are only six miles distant, and well worth visiting. The place has a large tannery and extensive lumbering interests.

RICHLAND, twenty-nine miles east of Oswego, is the principal converging point of the Rome, Watertown & Ogdensburg Railroad system. There is fine trout fishing in the vicinity.

First class trout fishing will be found in the brook near the village of SANDY CREEK, six miles beyond Richland. Seven miles more, through a fine farming country, and the train halts at

PIERREPONT MANOR, a quiet village in the midst of picturesque scenery. Lake View, a resort on Lake Ontario, seven miles by stage, offers many attractions during the fishing and hunting season. The Big Sandy Life-Saving Station is near, and is interesting to the visitor.

ADAMS, the next station, is one of the oldest and most important towns in Jefferson County. Population, 1360. It has several churches and banks, and large manufacturing interests. Adams Collegiate Institute is located here. Adams was first settled in 1800, and named in honor of President John Adams. The town is pleasantly situated on the north branch of Sandy Creek, which passes through the town, and furnishes an important water power that is largely used.

ADAMS CENTRE, the next station, is a beautiful village of 500 inhabitants. It is very prosperous, being located in the midst of a rich farming country.

WATERTOWN is compactly built and has a population of 20,000. It is chiefly noted for the excellent water power furnished by the rock-bound Black River, which courses through the city, forming several cascades in its fall of 112 feet, within the corporation. A fine view of the cascades may be enjoyed by the tourist from the windows of the Rome, Watertown & Ogdensburg Railroad trains entering the city from the south. The surrounding country is fertile, and the products of the farm and dairy find ready market in the streets and on the Board of Trade. Watertown is extensively engaged in the manufacture of paper, carriages and wagons, steam engines, flour, etc., besides other industries. Watertown is the junction point for Sackett's Harbor, Cape Vincent and Kingston, Ont. After leaving Watertown, a ride of six miles brings us to

R. W. & O. R.R.—FRENCHMAN'S ISLAND.

BROWNVILLE, where the dark waters of the Black River, flanked by perpendicular rocky banks, twenty-five to fifty feet high, flow on soon to mingle with the green waters of Lake Ontario.

CHAUMONT, pleasantly situated on Chaumont Bay, possesses a mineral spring of much repute, and offers good fishing advantages. At

THREE-MILE BAY, three and a half miles beyond, is excellent bass fishing, besides good duck shooting in season. Forty-five minutes by rail from Watertown lands the passenger at

CAPE VINCENT, at the edge of the river where the lake pours its blue green waters into the archipelago of the St. Lawrence, with Canada across the island-dotted channel, a dozen miles away. Population 1500. Principal industry, seed raising.

It is at Cape Vincent that we first gain a glimpse of the clear waters, which, flowing down from the lake, here form the beginning of that peerless river, the St. Lawrence, coursing for hundreds of miles in alternate moods of calm and frenzied rapids, to the Canadian metropolis, where it is gathered into a deeper channel and flows on through the storied French-Canadian land, bearing great sea-going ships upon its bosom, until it is merged into the salt waters of the ocean.

SUSPENSION BRIDGE ACROSS BLACK RIVER AT WATERTOWN.

Undoubtedly the best bass and muskallonge fishing in the world will be found in the vicinity of Wolfe Island, just off Cape Vincent, the largest of the Thousand Islands, being thirty miles long and from seven to ten wide. The steamer "America" will land passengers at Marysville, a small village on the island opposite Kingston. At the west end of Simcoe Island, directly off the lighthouse, is deep water, which affords excellent bass fishing during July and August. At the head of Wolfe Island lies Horseshoe Island; between the two are many rocky shoals, where early fly-fishing for bass cannot be equalled on the St. Lawrence. The many bays along the island east of Marysville afford abundant opportunity for sport in trolling for pickerel, pike, muskallonge and other "gamy" fish.

Resuming our journey northward from Watertown, a run of ten miles, passing Sanford's Corners, brings us to **EVAN'S MILLS**, a pleasant village within three miles of the celebrated LeRay mansion (erected in 1809), where President Madison was once hospitably entertained. At

PHILADELPHIA, seven miles distant, a thriving village of 1300 inhabitants, with extensive lumbering interests, we cross the track of the Eastern Division, where a detour is made for Clayton, twenty-two miles distant, in the midst of the Thousand Island region.

ANTWERP AND KEENE'S are in the midst of valuable iron ore beds. The mines, once extensively worked, are now idle.

GOUVERNEUR, thirty-five miles north of Watertown, is a thriving place, largely engaged in lumbering, mining and marble interests. Quarrying and refining talc is an important industry. Excellent fishing is found in the numerous mountain brooks.

Connection is made here with the Gouverneur & Oswegatchie branch for **EDWARDS**, three miles from Trout Lake, in the midst of good fishing and hunting grounds.

One hundred and twenty-three miles from Rome we reach **DE KALB JUNCTION**, the diverging point for Ogdensburg to the north and Norwood to the east.

R. W. & O. R.R.—SUGAR RIVER BRIDGE—LOCKS ON BLACK RIVER CANAL.

Trout Lake and Cranberry Lake, favorite sporting resorts in the Adirondacks, are easily and comfortably reached from DeKalb Junction. Rensselaer Falls and Heuvelton, on the banks of the picturesque Oswegatchie, are soon passed, and we enter

STATE HOSPITAL FOR THE INSANE—UTICA.

OGDENSBURG, a city of 12,000 inhabitants, located on the River St. Lawrence. A steam ferry to Prescott connects the American and Canadian shores.

On the banks of the St. Lawrence River, two miles below Ogdensburg, is situated the St. Lawrence State Hospital, a group of handsome buildings with a capacity for 1500 patients. This institution represents the latest and most advanced ideas in regard to caring for the insane.

CANTON, a pleasant village of 3500 inhabitants, is located on Grass River. A small steam yacht plies between the town and a picnic grove, five miles away, which is fitted up for pleasure parties. From Canton a stage line runs to the Adirondack woods. Eleven miles beyond is

POTSDAM, a beautiful town with about 4400 population, built along the banks of the Raquette River. Potsdam is the seat of a State Normal School, and is also largely engaged in the manufacture of pulp, paper and dressed lumber.

A stage ride of twenty-one miles to the "Forest House" lands the traveler at the foot of the Adirondacks, where guides and boats can be procured for a trip on the lake, to hunting, fishing and camping grounds. Seven miles from Potsdam is

NORWOOD, the junction point with the Ogdensburg & Lake Champlain Railroad which forms, with the Rome, Watertown & Ogdensburg Railroad and their connections, the Niagara Falls, White Mountains and New England Coast line, over which are run through sleeping cars between Portland and Chicago, connecting directly to and from all places west. Connections are made at Portland, Union Station, with through trains for Bar Harbor and all places in the Maritime Provinces, and along the New England sea-coast. The population of Norwood is 2000. Thirteen miles beyond Norwood is

MASSENA SPRINGS, a noted health resort, where connection is made with the Grand Trunk Railway for Montreal, etc. A full description will be found on a subsequent page.

UTICA, the southern terminus of the Eastern Division of the Rome, Watertown & Ogdensburg Railroad, is a beautiful city of 44,000 inhabitants, and pleasantly situated in the fertile Mohawk Valley. It is one of the two seats of Oneida County, and is the centre of several railroad lines. The New York Central & Hudson River Railroad, the West Shore Railroad, the Delaware, Lackawanna & Western Railroad, the New York, Ontario & Western Railway, and the Rome, Watertown & Ogdensburg Railroad, besides the Erie Canal, are the chief outlets to the carrying trade of the city.

SOLDIERS' MONUMENT—UTICA.

The State Hospital for the Insane, a massive and imposing structure, occupies a commanding site in the western part of the city. Manufacturing interests are varied and extensive. Large woolen mills produce superior qualities of woolen cloth; two extensive cotton mills enjoy a world-wide reputation for the excellence of their products; another factory makes cotton yarn exclusively: farming and dairy interests are provided for by various establishments for the

EASTERN DIVISION OF THE ROME, WATERTOWN & OGDENSBURG RAILROAD.

manufacture of farming and dairy apparatus. Nearly all branches of industry are represented in the various other manufactories.

The new Masonic Home is located in the midst of beautiful natural scenery in the eastern part of the city, surrounded by a park disposed in the most beautiful style of landscape art.

The city is well built, and has many fine business blocks and public buildings. The post-office and government building is a substantial and handsome specimen of architecture. The streets are well laid out and shaded by rows of beautiful elms and maples, several avenues being bordered by double rows of trees and neatly kept lawns. Genesee Street, the main thoroughfare, is conceded to be one of the finest avenues in the United States. The many elegant private residences, environed by velvety lawns and blooming gardens, are evidences of the refinement and wealth which characterize the place. The city has forty-two churches, two opera houses, many excellent hotels, and a school system which has no superior in the State; three daily newspapers and a half dozen weeklies, besides several monthly publications. The street railway system of Utica is surpassed by few others, even in large cities. A belt line system and numerous spurs, comprising about twenty-five miles of road, operated entirely by electricity, together with two independent lines, furnish ample facilities for reaching different parts of the city and suburban villages.

Utica, aside from its wealth and culture, is noted for the many illustrious statesmen it has produced. The whole region is historic ground, and the tourist will be well repaid by a sojourn of a few days within its pleasant borders.

R., W. & O. R.R.—CROSSING BLACK RIVER AT CARTHAGE.

On leaving Utica and crossing the iron bridge which spans the Mohawk River at this point, we see on the right the Deerfield hills, overlooking the Mohawk and its valley, while on the left is presented a fine view of the entire city of Utica. A stretch of sixteen miles through a productive farming region brings us to

TRENTON, and from the train, 110 feet above Cincinnati Creek, we see on the one side the village of Trenton and the Cincinnati Creek; on the other the Cincinnati Creek and hills of the West Canada Creek. The view from this point is one of the finest on the line, and for scenic beauty is rarely surpassed in this country. One mile more brings us to

TRENTON FALLS station, about one-half mile from Trenton Falls. These remarkable curiosities, seven in number, are the most wonderful falls in America, and among the finest in the world; an extended description of them will be found in the following pages. From

PROSPECT, one mile beyond, another fine view of Trenton Falls presents itself. As we look from the train we see on the left, many feet below us, the Cincinnati Creek and Kamp's Mill. The view from this point, looking down the valley of the Cincinnati toward Trenton village, is considered one of the finest in the State of New York. At

REMSEN connection is made with the Adirondack & St. Lawrence line for points in the Adirondacks. Before this line was opened, **ALDER CREEK** and **BOONVILLE** were the favorite points of entrance to the Fulton Chain region and John Brown's Tract.

R., W. & O. R.R.—LYONS FALLS.

R., W. & O. R.R.—MILL CREEK NEAR LOWVILLE.

A few miles north of Boonville, from the bridge which spans Sugar River, seventy feet above the water, we obtain a good view of the Sugar River Falls and the viaduct of the Black River Canal, under which the Sugar River passes. The next point of interest is

LYONS FALLS, a wild, romantic and much frequented spot. The High Falls (seventy feet high), a glimpse of which is had from the train, are well worth visiting.

For the next thirty miles the route is through the beautiful valley of the Black River in full sight of the highlands of Brown's Tract. Just before reaching Lowville we see, seventy feet below us, Mill Creek, with its precipitous banks of solid rock, fifty feet high.

LOWVILLE is one of the most beautiful villages in Northern New York, and is noted for its fine drives, shady walks and excellent hotel accommodations. The population is 3500. A new and first-class eating house is conveniently located at this station. The North Woods and John Brown's Tract are easily reached from this point. The Lowville Mineral Springs, one mile from the station, offer many attractive features. Stages connect with all trains.

In the vicinity of Martinsburg and Lowville is some natural scenery of the grandest and most rugged description. Deep gorges or ravines, wrought out through centuries of time by the action of water, afford scenery that will compare favorably with the most noted of its kind in the State. Chimney Point is a huge, triangular pyramid of slate rock formed by the union of two gulfs in a rugged chasm 250 feet deep. Whetstone Gulf, about three miles south of Chimney Point, presents a greater amount and variety of scenery. The banks of the gorge are precipitous, with numerous sharp turns. The walls approach nearer in the upper portions, until both may be reached with the outstretched arms, and the torrent is compressed into a deep, narrow chasm. At one point a tiny cascade falls the whole distance from the top, like a white ribbon, which almost wastes itself in spray before reaching the bottom. From Lowville to Chimney Point is six miles; to Whetstone Gulf, seven miles. From the iron bridge crossing the Black River, near Carthage, a fine view of the river is obtained.

MILL CREEK AT LOWVILLE.

CARTHAGE is a large and important village, busy with many industries. This is the junction with the Carthage & Adirondack Railroad, which offers one entrance to the Oswegatchie region of the Adirondacks. The village is growing rapidly, and is already a large manufacturing centre. The population is about 5000.

Eighteen miles more, during which we catch another glimpse of Black River, and we reach the city of Watertown, which beautiful city has already been described in the trip over the Middle Division of the Rome, Watertown & Ogdensburg Railroad. Twelve miles beyond lies

SACKETT'S HARBOR, on Lake Ontario. This is one of the oldest places in the State, and is of considerable historical interest. Prominent among the interesting places to visit here are the Madison Barracks, a United States military station. Campbell's Point, a pleasant resort, and Henderson Harbor, a prominent summer resort on Lake Ontario, noted for its many excellent hotels and the finest bass fishing on Lake Ontario, are reached by steamer.

Leaving Carthage on the way to the River St. Lawrence we pass Philadelphia, and from the Indian River bridge just beyond, a beautiful scene presents itself as we trace the windings of the river, fifty feet below, whitened with foam from the tumbling waters of the falls, which come into full view on the right. Twenty miles distant lies

CLAYTON, in the midst of the Thousand Islands and fishing grounds of the River St. Lawrence. Connection is made here with the palace day steamers of the Richelieu & Ontario Navigation Company, the Royal Mail Line steamers, for Montreal, etc., passing through the Thousand Islands and rapids of the River St. Lawrence by daylight; also with steamers running in direct connection with trains of this road for Alexandria Bay—distance, twelve miles—passing through

MILLS AT THERESA, INDIAN RIVER.

the most beautiful and interesting portion of the Thousand Islands by daylight, and stopping at Round Island Park, Thousand Island Park, the International Camp-Meeting Grounds, at Fisher's Landing, and at Westminster Park.

Clayton, Alexandria Bay and the Island Parks are the most popular summer resorts in America. Crowds of people from all parts of the country throng these resorts during the pleasure season, enjoying the excellent fishing and the beauties of the wonderful Thousand Islands.

The hotel accommodations of these points are unsurpassed. At Clayton the Walton House, the Hubbard House, and the popular new Windsor Hotel furnish ample accommodations for all visitors. The new Frontenac Hotel on Round Island, one mile below Clayton, Grand View House, on Grand View Park, and the new Columbian Hotel, Thousand Island Park, four miles below Clayton, are among the most elegant hotels, both in appointments and surroundings, on the River St. Lawrence.

At Fisher's Landing the Grand Central Hotel, and at Alexandria Bay the Crossmon House, with accommodations for 500 guests, the Thousand Island House, with accommodations for 700 guests, and the Edgewood Park Hotel, are crowded during the entire summer season. The Westminster Park Hotel, directly opposite Alexandria Bay, is a favorite resort, its delightful location rendering it one of the pleasantest places on the river. Clayton, Alexandria Bay, Brockville and Prescott are the favorite points for taking the Royal Mail Line of Steamers, and the Rome, Watertown & Ogdensburg Railroad is the only all-rail route to Clayton, the shortest and only direct route to Alexandria Bay; also the shortest and only direct route to Brockville and Prescott.

Just before reaching Theresa Junction we have another view of Indian River, at the Indian River Water House. The High Falls of the Indian River have an altitude of eighty feet. Good fishing is found in Red and Muskallonge Lakes, a few miles from Theresa, in the midst of beautiful scenery. At

CROSSING INDIAN RIVER.

REDWOOD, six miles north, stages connect for Alexandria Bay, distant seven miles. Near

HAMMOND we see the Medina and Potsdam sandstone quarries. Large quantities of this stone, so popular for building and paving purposes, are shipped from this point. A ride of eleven miles brings us to

MORRISTOWN, on the River St. Lawrence, eleven miles from Ogdensburg. Directly opposite is the beautiful and picturesque Canadian city of Brockville. At Brockville connection is made with the Grand Trunk Railway, also with the Canadian Pacific Railway for Ottawa, the fishing and hunting grounds of the Ottawa River, and the great pine lumber region of Canada: and with the Brockville, Westport & Sault Ste. Marie Railway.

Terrace Park, one mile from Morristown, with its elegant new hotel, the Terrace House, situated on the river shore, is a delightful place. Trains stop directly in front of this hotel.

The route from Morristown to Ogdensburg runs along the south shore in full view of the River St. Lawrence. Trains pass in full sight of the Canadian cities of Brockville and Prescott. This is one of the most beautiful and picturesque routes in the country. At Ogdensburg connections are made with the Central Vermont Railroad; also with ferry for Prescott. At Prescott with Grand Trunk Railway; also with Canadian Pacific Railway for Ottawa.

R., W. & O. R R.—MORRISTOWN, OPPOSITE BROCKVILLE, ONT.

TRENTON FALLS, N. Y.

"Trenton is the summer song of rest."
"The most enjoyably beautiful spot among the resorts of romantic scenery in our country."

IN THE WOODS AT TRENTON FALLS.

"TRENTON," says George William Curtis in his "Lotus Eating," "is the summer song of rest. Beauty and grace are its praises. You hear them from those who are either hurrying to the grandeur of Niagara or from those who step aside to enjoy the music of the greater cataract softened into an exquisite echo. The charm of Trenton is unique, and in some choice niche of memory you will lay it aside, not as a sublime statue nor prophetic and solemn picture, but as a vase most delicate, and chased with pastoral tracery."

LOCATION.—Trenton Falls is situated in the central part of New York State, on the line of the Rome, Watertown & Ogdensburg Railroad, eighteen miles from Utica, ninety miles from Thousand Islands, seventy-four miles from Watertown, one hundred and sixteen miles from Ogdensburg. It is reached by four trains each day. The falls are a part of the West Canada Creek, which rises in the Adirondack region and is the principal supply of the Mohawk River.

THE HOTEL.—In the same delightful little volume from which we have already quoted, Mr. Curtis speaks these words of Moore's Hotel: "There is no better hotel than that at Trenton

MOORE'S HOTEL, TRENTON FALLS.

R. W. & O. R.R.—TRENTON FALLS.

Falls. It is spacious, clean and comfortable, and the table justifies its fame. It is by far the best hotel that I have met in my summer wandering." This is the universal testimony of travelers. Its proprietor is a man of rare culture, and the impress of his taste is upon his house and all that pertains to it. Comfort and refined enjoyment are placed first at Trenton, and nothing is allowed to usurp them.

THE FALLS.—In the following exquisite words Curtis paints the scenery: "Poets' fancies only should image the Falls, they are so rich and rare a combination of quiet picturesqueness of beauty and a sense of resistless force in the running water. You descend from a lofty wood into a long rocky chasm, which the Germans would call a *grund*, for it is not a valley. It is walled and paved with smooth rocks, and the thronging forest fringes the summit of the wall. Over this smooth pavement slips the river in those long, swift, still, foamless bounds, which vividly figure the appalling movement of a Titanic serpent. The chasm almost closes up the river, and you see a foamy cascade. Then, as if the best beauty and mystery were beyond, you creep along a narrow ledge on the rockside of the throat of the gorge and reach the first large fall. A slight spray enfolds you as a baptism in the spirit of the place. Before you is a level parapet of rock, and the river, after sliding very shallowly over the broad bed above, concentrates and plunges in a solid amber sheet. Close by the side of this you climb, and pass along the base of the over-hanging mountain, and stooping under the foot of an impending cliff, stand before the great fall, which has two plunges, a long one above, from which the river sheers obliquely over a polished floor of rock and again plunges. The river bends here, and a high, square regular bank projects from the cliff, smooth as a garden terrace, and perpetually veiled and softened by spray. It is one of the most beautiful and boldest points in the long ravine, and when the late light of afternoon falls soft upon it there is a strange contrast in your feelings as visions of Boccaccio's garden mingle with the wilderness of American woods.

BIRD'S-EYE VIEW FROM THE PINNACLE.

"You will recall the European falls of fame. The thousand Alpine cascades of Switzerland will flicker through your memory. Slight avalanches of snowdust shimmering into rainbow mist; and the Rhine will plunge once more over its little rocky barrier, sending its murmur far into the haunted depths of the Black Forest beside you. Or, farther on and fainter still, the rapids of the Nile and the rills of Lebanon will rush and gurgle as you did not dream to hear them again, nor will your fancy rest until it sinks in the Oriental languor of the banks of the Abana and Pharpar, rivers of Damascus."

Thus did Mrs. Kemble describe her impressions: "Presently we arrived at the first fall; I can't describe it; I don't know either its height or width; I only know it was extremely beautiful, and came pouring down like a great rolling heap of amber. The rocks around are high to the heavens, scooped and singularly regular; and the sides of the torrent are every now and then paved with large, smooth layers of rock, as even and regular in their proportions as if fairies had done the work. When we came to the beautiful circular fall we crept down to a narrow ridge and sat with our feet hanging over the black caldron, just opposite a vivid rainbow that was clasping the waterfall. We walked, I suppose, a mile and a half along the water's side, and in this distance its course is broken by six beautiful cataracts. The several falls are very various in their height and form, but they are all beautiful, most beautiful.

"Trenton is not a place to visit for a day, but to live the summer away in."

Among the most beautiful descriptions of this lovely place are those found in letters by N. P. Willis, which appeared in the *Home Journal*. Space permits only one short extract: "The most *enjoyably beautiful* spot among the resorts of romantic scenery in our country is Trenton Falls. To the lovers of Nature who visit it, the resemblance of its loveliness becomes the bright spot to which dream and reverie oftenest return.

ROCKY HEART.

"It seems to be curiously adapted to enjoy, being somehow not only the kind but the size of a place the arms of a mortal heart can enfold in its embrace. Trenton Falls is the place above all others where it is a luxury to *stay*—which one oftenest revisits—which one most commends to strangers to be sure and see."

SHERMAN FALLS.

NEW VIEWS.—The past three years have witnessed important changes at Trenton. Old paths have been widened, and new ones cut in the side of the ravine. New views have also been opened from the heights. One of these presents a scene that neither pen nor pencil can catch. The artist's admirable effort is only a *suggestion* of the view. The paths have been extended as well, till now about two miles of rocky wall stretch out from the foot of the stairs.

ITS CHARACTER.—In scenery Trenton Falls is the rarest combination of the beautiful and grand. It possesses the beauty and grace one misses at Niagara, and the grandeur and strength so lacking at Watkins and Havana.

THE SPORTSMAN'S PARADISE.

THE NORTH WOODS—GREAT NORTHERN WILDERNESS—JOHN BROWN'S TRACT—THE ADIRONDACK REGION.

THE gateways to this delightful region are reached only via the Rome, Watertown & Ogdensburg Railroad. The Empire State, although the most populous of any in the Union, contains a vast tract of land generally known as the Adirondack Region and John Brown's Tract. This great wilderness, although it has upon its borders ten of the most populous cities and as many large villages of the State of New York, and is bounded on the south by the great Mohawk Valley, with its immense manufacturing, transportation and farming interests—the Erie Canal and the four-track New York Central Railroad, the greatest of the Nation's highways; on the west by the Rome, Watertown & Ogdensburg Railroad, the Black River and the Black River Canal; on the north by the St. Lawrence River and the Ogdensburg & Lake Champlain Railroad; on the east by Lake Champlain, Lake George and is penetrated by the Mohawk & Malone Railway, being entirely surrounded both by rail and water-ways teeming with the immense travel and traffic of the Empire State, still retains all the characteristics of the primeval forest. A good idea of this whole region may be formed from the seventh annual report, dated March 7, 1879, to the Legislature of the State of New York, submitted by the Hon. Verplanck Colvin, Superintendent of the New York State Adirondack Survey. We quote from this report, in which Mr. Colvin says:

"I am now conducting a general geodetic survey of the whole of the region known as the Adirondack district of New York, including also the bordering settlements. The natural limits of this great topographical area are sharply defined. Geographically, its boundaries are Lake Champlain, the St. Lawrence, the Mohawk and the Black Rivers, into one or the other of which the mountain streams of the wilderness finally pour their waters. Geologically considered, the limits are almost identical with the geographical, and may be briefly said to be the outer line of the great central area of azoic or metamorphic rocks (granitic, feldspathic or crystalline) which give so marked a character to Adirondack scenery. Botanically, the borders of the wilderness region are indicated by the termination of the great forests of spruce, Canadian fir, beach and yellow birch, and vast peat mosses; while zoologically it may be designated as the region of wild game, or more accurately, at the present day defined as that portion of Northern New York contained within a line uniting these points along the borders of the great forest where men still at times trap the black bear *(Ursus Americanus)*. The last limit is much better marked than would at first thought seem possible, and follows very nearly the limits of the primitive rock. Each of these natural limits, when traced upon the ground, gives a very irregular figure, not unlike a great contour line surrounding the wilderness region, and owing to the rectangular form of maps, in order to properly inclose this very irregular area, and to show its relation to and connection with the remainder of the State, it is necessary to bring within the lines of latitude and longitude, which form the outer limits of the map, a great portion of the settled districts. This is important, in order that the approaches to the forest may be seen, so that those using the maps may be enabled to recognize points on the margin with which they are familiar, to get a general idea of directions and of distances; in the language of the topographer, to orient themselves. Viewed from the standpoint of my own explorations, the rapidity with which certain changes take place in the opening up to travel of the wild corners of the wilderness, has about it something almost startling.

"A few summers since I stood for the first time on the cool, mossy shore of the mountain springlet, Lake Tear-of-the-Clouds. Almost hidden between the gigantic mountain domes, this lovely pool, lifted on its granite pedestal toward heaven, the loftiest water mirror of the stars, beseeching, not in vain, from each low, drifting cloud some tribute for the sources of the Hudson; fresh, new, unvisited, save by wild beasts that drank, it was a gem more pure and more delightful to the eye than the most precious jewel. It is still almost as wild and quite as beautiful; but close behind our exploring footsteps comes the 'blazed line' marked with ax upon the trees; the trail, soon trodden into mire; the bark shanty, picturesque enough, but soon surrounded by a grove of stumps. And so glancing over the field of former labors I find following in the footsteps of my explorations the 'blazed line' and the trail, then the ubiquitous tourist, determined to see all that has been recorded as worth seeing. Where first comes one, the next year there are ten; the year after full a hundred. The woods are thronged; bark and log huts prove insufficient; hotels spring up as though by magic, and the air resounds with laughter, song and jollity. The wild trails, once jammed with logs, are cut clear by the axes of the guides, and ladies clamber to the summits of

From "OUTING." Copyrighted.

ADIRONDACK CAMP LIFE.

those once untrodden peaks. The genius of change has possession of the land; we cannot control it. When we study the necessities of our people we would not control it if we could.

"This change—this new revelation of fresh, exhilarating mountain summer life, is having too important and beneficial an influence upon society at present not to demand the sympathy of the government. To the wealthy dwellers of cities, debilitated by a tainted atmosphere, the breezes and the mountain springs bring life, while the free, joyous exercises of their children in these summer homes lay for them the foundations of continued health. But while these changes

SALMON FALLS, ADIRONDACK MOUNTAINS.

have opened to travel many of the most interesting nooks, they have only rendered more marked by contrast the wildness of the remainder, and the unvisited wilderness centres or cores are still left in all their sylvan purity. The bear and deer, though somewhat reduced in numbers, still haunt these remote places; panthers still roam untrammeled, and the wolf alone, persecuted by traps and poison, begins to be relatively scarce. Therefore, save to the hermits of the forest, whose semi-savage life cannot always be maintained, these changes are for the better, and no unselfish person will for a moment regret that his once solitary pleasures are now shared by the many. The sportsman has still a thousand unfrequented recesses—if he will seek them—where he may travel unmolested. Though the waters of the Raquette now flash responsive to the oars and paddles of ten boats where they once saw but one, and though its shores, once rendered less desolate by even the howl of the wolf, are now dotted with the summer cabins of the new dispensation, the panther and the bear still visit it; the deer, also, still driven by the hounds, seek a false safety in its waters, and to my own knowledge (the summer song and camp-fire long departed) in mid-winter the wolf does not disdain to travel on its ice. Though a wee steamer now plows the water of the Saranac, the huge lake trout—*salmonidæ*—still leap at evening from the surface; deer still drink at its shores, and once, not very long ago, the little steamer had its first adventure chasing a party of four bears that were swimming in the lake.

"The region is already the summer home of untold thousands—a public pleasure ground—a wilderness park to all intents and purposes, safe from human savages, and without a harmful serpent within its borders.

"Already private clubs have separated large areas. The moose (*Alce Americanus*, Jardine), by importation from Maine and Nova Scotia, have been restored to the grounds of the Adirondack Club, near Lake Santford, and the lakes re-stocked with choicest fish. So elsewhere in the forest the task of preservation is beginning, and only the luckless bears, wolves and panthers, etc., hiding from the uproar of invading civilization, find themselves without protection. A region of mystery,

From Harper's Magazine. Copyright, 1881, by Harper & Brothers.

A SWIM FOR LIFE.

over which none can gaze without a strange thrill of interest and of wonder at what may be hidden in that vast area of forest, covers all things with its deep repose. It is not the deer of which we think, treading the deep, rich moss among the stately tamaracks; nor the bear, luxuriating in the berry patches on the mountain side; nor the panther, nor the wolf, in their lonely and desolate wilds, seeking their feast of blood. We gaze downward from the mountain heights on thousands upon thousands of square miles of wilderness, which was always one—since forest it became—and which hides to-day, as it has hidden for so many ages, the secrets of form, and soil, and rock, and history on which we ponder.

"Few fully understand what the Adirondack wilderness really is. It is a mystery even to those who have crossed and re-crossed it by boats along its avenues—the lakes—and on foot through its vast and silent recesses, by following the long line of 'blazed' or ax-marked trees which the daring searcher for the fur of the sable or the mink has chopped, in order that he may find his way again in that deep and often desolate forest. In these remote sections, filled with rugged mountains, where unnamed waterfalls pour in snowy tresses from the dark, overhanging cliffs, the horse can find no footing, and the adventurous trapper or explorer must carry upon his back his blankets and a heavy stock of food. His rifle, which affords protection against wild beasts, at times replenishes his well-husbanded provisions, and his ax aids him in constructing, from bark or bough, some temporary shelter from storm, or hews into logs the huge trees which form the fierce, roaring, comfortable fire of the camp. Yet, though the woodman may pass his lifetime in some section of the wilderness, it is still a mystery to him. Following the line of ax marks upon the trees venturing along the cliff-walls of the streams which rush, leap on, leap downward, to form haughty rivers; climbing on the steep wooded slopes which never knew form or name on maps, he clings to his trapping line, and, shrouded and shut in by the deep, wonderful forest, emerges at length from its darkness to the daylight of the clearings, like a man who has passed

DEER HUNTING. From "OUTING."

under a great river or arm of the sea through a tunnel, knowing little of the wonders that had surrounded him. It is a peculiar region; for, though the geographical centre of the wilderness may be readily and easily reached in the light, canoe-like boats of the guides, by lakes and rivers which form a labyrinth of passages for boats, the core, or rather cores, of this wilderness extend on either hand from these broad avenues of water, and, in their interior spots remain to-day as untrodden by man and as unknown and wild as when the Indian paddled his birchen boat upon those streams and lakes. Amid these mountain solitudes are places where, in all probability, the foot of man never trod; and here the panther has his den among the rocks and rears his savage kittens undisturbed, save by the growl of bear or screech of lynx, or the hoarse croak of raven taking its share of the carcass of slain deer."

Copyrighted.

Much interesting and valuable information in regard to this region will be found in Mr. Colvin's reports.

To the uninitiated such a description of the Adirondack wilderness might seem a superfluity of words, with no other object than to create a popular interest in this great natural park. To the sportsman, however, it strikes the keynote to some of the rarest delights which can crown an experience with rifle or rod. Nearly every stream, fed by cool mountain springs, is alive with the daintiest and choicest fish that the most exacting angler could desire. The trout which abound in all these streams, and in the crystal, forest-fringed lakes, furnish just the kind of sport and excitement in which the expert angler most delights to exercise his skill. Speckled beauties, weighing from four ounces to as many pounds, and lake trout, often exceeding thirty pounds in weight, are quite enough to arouse the admiration and enthusiasm of Walton's most fastidious disciple. "One season of such sport is but the prelude to an annual visit to the same enchanting place, and the melting snows of spring barely uncover the mountain peaks before the impatient fisherman is wending his way to his favorite haunt in this wonderful region of mountain, forest, lake and stream. The lover of hunting, no less than the lover of fishing, finds here his choicest sporting-ground. The timorous and graceful deer abounding in these wilds yield sport in unmeasured degree, and he who has once tasted the pleasure of such sport, needs no spur to urge him again to its enjoyment. A savory steak of venison, hot from the coals of a camp-fire, or a toothsome trout, broiled in the true primitive style, is more to be coveted than the ambrosia of the gods.

Much has been said and much has been written about the great healthfulness of this charming country. The pure mountain air, fragrant with the balmy odors of cedar and spruce; the cool, sparkling water, bubbling from a thousand hidden springs, the freshness and charm of Nature unsullied by the art of man, are here offered as a free gift to any who will enjoy them. Truly, here is the fountain of perennial youth! Many who have tasted its joys can bear glad testimony to the benefits derived from a temporary sojourn in this wilderness. Constitutions enfeebled by too close application to the common affairs of every-day life, and brains exhausted by excessive mental work, are here speedily restored to health and vigor. Pulmonary complaints are greatly relieved by the soothing properties of the balsamic air.

To those who have not yet visited this entrancing region, our advice is that if you have a week or two to spare during the spring or summer months, engage a good guide and take a trip into the wilderness. This trip, once made, will surely be repeated at first opportunity, and we feel confident that every one will agree with the author of "Camps and Tramps in the Adirondacks," who, in describing his trip to the Beaver River waters, says: "One afternoon late in May found us four at Utica, waiting for the train on the Rome, Watertown & Ogdensburg Railroad. That road is associated in many minds with the opening scenes of the delightful vacation months. When the summer days come, and one has a fish-rod in his hand, then 'Rome, Watertown & Ogdensburg Railroad' is a phrase to conjure with. The brain of the happy sportsman, at the sound of these magic words, is filled with pictures of camp, stream and lake, for this road for many miles skirts the wilderness, and almost every station is the gateway to Paradise. And by connecting railroads one may, indeed, sweep northward, eastward and southward again, pretty much around the entire Adirondacks. I trust, then, that the ties of that road may never decay, and its rails never wear out, and that it may always pay good dividends, for it is, *par excel ence*, the highway to the gates of the Sportsman's Paradise."

From Harper's Magazine.

A CARRY—"THE START."

7

THE NORTH WOODS AND THE ADIRONDACKS.

FOR a complete and detailed description of all resorts and places in the great Northern Wilderness, the reader is respectfully referred to "Wallace's Guide to the Adirondacks," which book is generally recognized by sportsmen and guides as the standard guide for all this region. It is edited and published by E. R. Wallace, Syracuse, N. Y. We quote from this book by permission.

From Trenton Falls, Prospect, Remsen, Alder Creek, Boonville, Port Leyden, Lyons Falls, Glendale, Martinsburg, Lowville, Castorland, Carthage, Gouverneur, Canton and Potsdam, a short day's journey conveys the tourist into an unbroken wilderness; or via Remsen and the Mohawk & Malone Railway, Adirondack & St. Lawrence Line, the sportsman, tourist or pleasure seeker may reach direct almost any place in the Adirondacks. The Mohawk & Malone Railway is a magnificent, first-class railroad, fully up to the standard of the best trunk lines, and was opened for business in 1892. Solid trains start from Union Station at Utica and run to Malone, and through to Montreal, Quebec, via the R., W. & O. R.R. and Remsen. The Mohawk & Malone Railway is leased to and operated by the New York Central & Hudson River R.R. It has stations at Kent's for Lake Honnedaga; at Honnedaga for Little Moose Lake; at White Lake Corners for Bisby Lakes; at McKeever's for the Moose River region; at Fulton Chain for Old Forge House, one and a half miles distant, and with steamers for all points on the Fulton Chain of Lakes, with connections for Raquette Lake, Forked Lake, Blue Mountain Lake, Loon Lake, Utowana Lake and Eagle Lake by small boats and short portage; at Horseshoe Pond for Big Tupper Lake and Little Tupper Lake, Long Lake, Blue Mountain Lake and Raquette Lake; at Childwold for Childwold Park House; at Tupper Lake Junction for Tupper Lake and all points on the Raquette River; at Saranac Inn with steamer for all points on Upper Saranac Lake; at Saranac Junction for Lake Clear; at Saranac Village for all points on Lower Saranac Lake, Lake Placid, etc.; at Paul Smith's for all places on St. Regis Lake, Osgood Pond, Spitfire Pond and Meacham Lake; at Loon Lake for Loon Lake House, and all places in that vicinity. Connection is made at Remsen with this road in union station.

The Fulton Chain can be reached via Boonville, and twenty-six miles stage, or via Remsen and the Mohawk & Malone Railway direct. At Boonville, guides, horses and conveyances, and all supplies can be obtained. The men found here have passed the greater part of their lives in the woods, and know exactly what the tourist needs, and what he should leave behind. Persons desiring to have horses, guides, and supplies ready on arrival at Boonville or at Remsen, can address B. P. Graves or C. Phelps, Boonville, N. Y.

Moose River (Indian, *Te-ka-hun-di-an-do*, "clearing an opening") is twice as large as West Canada Creek, and is very rapid. The scenery along the most of its course is celebrated for its wildness and beauty. The angler might spend several days to advantage at Moose River, whipping that and the neighboring waters for trout.

At Old Forge, on a slight elevation that slopes gradually to the water—an extended reach of which it pleasantly overlooks—stands the large and commodious Forge House (P. O. "Old Forge"). When tourists are reminded that they are here afforded ten or twelve miles of boating in either direction, that they can descend the Moose River some ten or eleven miles before they encounter any serious falls or rapids, or can pass upwards from one beautiful lake to another, until the farther extremity of Fourth Lake is reached, and twelve delightful miles are passed with no interruption to the even tenor of their meditations by a single unromantic carry, none will fail to pronounce this location a most appropriate one for a forest inn. Ladies, especially, will note its superior attractions as a summer resort. The steam yachts *Fulton*, Captain Jack Sheppard, and *Hunter*, Captain Jonathan Meeker, make two daily trips through the first four lakes, landing at the different private and public camps located on their shores; fare $1.00 for the entire trip.

Where within the limits of the Adirondacks can be found a brighter array of glittering links than the Fulton Chain? Where a more lovely sheet than Lake Lila or the ideal Canachagala? Headley manifested his true appreciation of this section when he wrote the following:

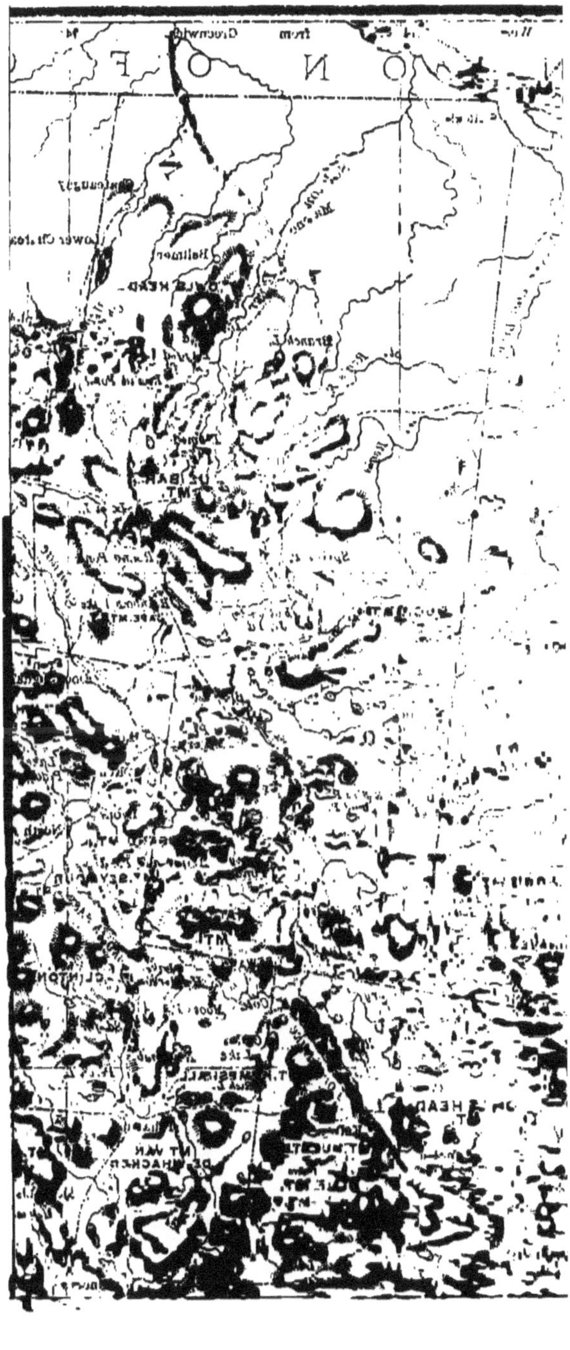

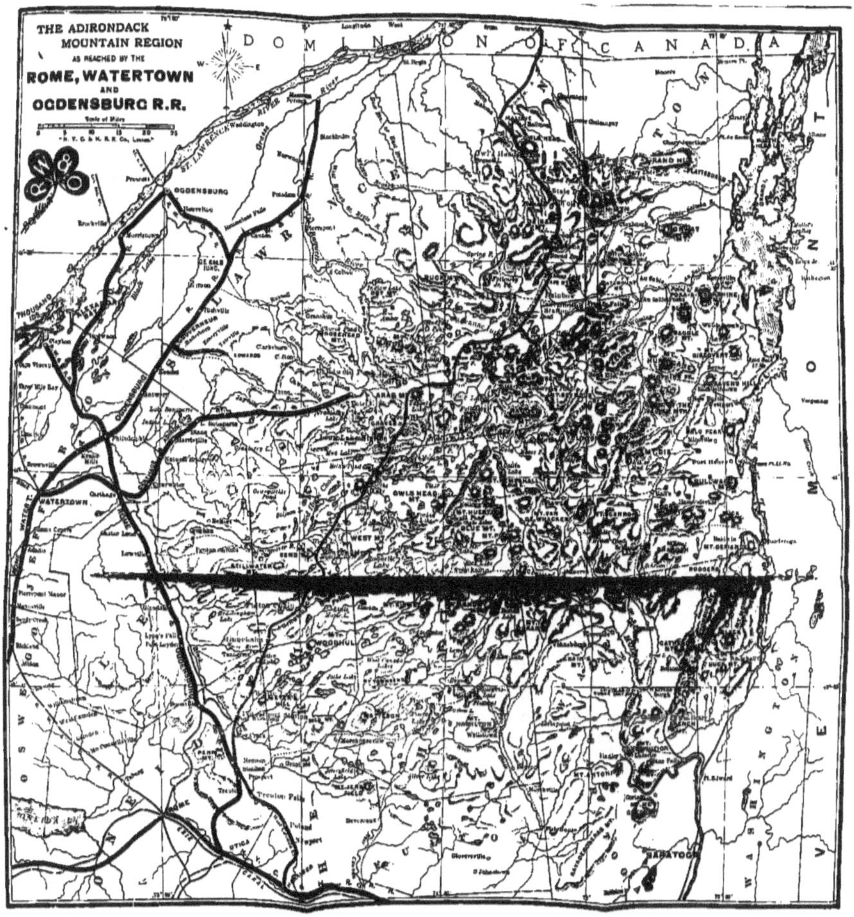
THE ADIRONDACK
MOUNTAIN REGION
AS REACHED BY THE
ROME, WATERTOWN
AND
OGDENSBURG R.R.
DOMINION OF CANADA
OGDENSBURG
WATERTOWN
SARATOGA

THE ADIRONDACK
MOUNTAIN REGION
AS REACHED BY THE
WATERTOWN
AND
R.R.
WATERTOWN

"The Eight Lakes are connected by streams, and form a group of surpassing beauty. They vary, both in size and shape, each with a different framework of hills, and the change is ever from beauty to beauty.

"There they repose like a bright chain in the forest, the links connected by silver bars. You row slowly through one to its outlet, and then entering a clear stream overhung with bushes, or fringed with lofty trees, seem to be suddenly absorbed by the wilderness. At length, however, you emerge as from a cavern, and lo! an untroubled lake, with all its variations of coasts, timber and islands, greets the eye. Through this you also pass like one in a dream, wondering why such beauty is wasted where the eye of man rarely beholds it."

From "OUTING." Copyrighted.

ON THE WAY TO A NORTH WOODS CAMP.

Brantingham! pleasing name of a lovely lake lying on the border of the Great Forest, perhaps 350 feet above the Black River valley, and 1400 feet above the level of the sea. Its banks, richly wooded, rise in gentle slopes to a moderate height, and with its various features it presents a scene charmingly wild and picturesque. Two islands, "Round" and "Dark," adorn its waters, the former rising abruptly in mound-like form, on whose elevated ground is perched a little cottage, embowered by evergreens, which is rented during the season to the different parties who apply. Dark Island, mostly clothed with *dark* green pines, and but a short distance away, is a very popular camping place.

Long Point, a narrow, rounded promontory entirely forest-clad, extends nearly one-half mile into the lake, and forms one of its most attractive features. Indeed, it would be difficult to exaggerate the charms of this favored spot. It affords fine sites for camps or cottages, as well as delightful rambles over its smooth, clean grounds, with the bewitching waters of the lake glittering on either side. The constant breeze, laden with sweet, balsamic odor of the prevailing tree, and

SYLVAN FALLS—SEVENTEEN MILES FROM POTSDAM.

the dense shade of these pines furnish delicious coolness even in the hottest days. On the lake near this point, there is a remarkable echo which repeats itself seven times.

The lake (1½ x 1¼) is so serrated with capes and bays, occasionally rimmed with golden sand, that it is said to have ten or twelve miles of coast. Brantingham, though a sheet of rare beauty, makes no pretension to the grandeur of the *mountain* scenery witnessed from many of the Adirondack lakes.

The Lake House is admirably situated on a pine-crowned bluff at the termination of the branch road. It is an unpretentious structure of home-like character, and the table is excellent, while the terms for entertainment are so reasonable that nearly all can afford to tarry here for days or weeks. It is now under the management of Mr. Leon Graves, a son of the owner of the property. He contemplates building a new hotel or greatly enlarging the present structure, a change made necessary by the increasing number of visitors to this beautiful place. Each year Brantingham is becoming more and more attractive as a summer resort, and includes among its most enthusiastic admirers a large number of New York people.

In 1887 the point opposite the hotel, formerly known as Smith's Point, was purchased by a gentleman from New York, who changed its name to "The Pines." The following spring he built a cottage on his possession, and since then ten or more cottages have been erected on the shores of the lake. Among the present owners of summer homes may be named the Rev. D. E. Lorenz, Ph.D., Mr. Joseph Kunzmann and the Rev. James H. Hoadley, D.D. of New York City; Mr. C. D. Manville, Mr. H. S. Lanpher and Mr. W. H. Greeley of Lowville; Mr. H. G. Emm, of Turin, N. Y.; Mr. Hedges of Elizabeth, N. J., and Mr. P. L. Hoadley of Newark, N. J.

Among the rambles and excursions that may be taken from the hotel are the following:

To the Mineral Spring, two-fifths mile southeast by road. Its waters are strongly impregnated with iron and contain some magnesia and a trace of sulphur.

It is two miles thence by this road, which is a branch of the main road, through the woods to Palen's Mills on Fish Creek. This excellent trout stream may be reached *en route* three-fifths mile beyond the spring (one mile from the hotel) by diverging to the right twenty-five or thirty rods; in the opposite direction—passing Round Pond, right—Lake Pleasant (one mile from the hotel) is reached. It may also be visited from the hotel by two other routes: 1. Boat to "The Pines" forty or sixty rods, thence road through the woods and across the fields three-quarters mile. 2. Boat to head of Sunset Bay just beyond "The Pines" one-quarter mile, thence good path one-quarter mile.

Lying one-eighth mile southeast of the hotel is Lily or Beaver Pond, the path to which leads through a handsome grove (Brower's Point) which offers delectable views of both lake and lakelet, in opposite directions. Its surface is generously mantled with the pure and odorous white water-lily. This little loch is an offshoot of the outlet of Brantingham Lake, flowing into Fish Creek

From "OUTING." Copyrighted.

A SURE CATCH.

(one mile). Again, from Brantingham Lake it is one mile north to Otter Creek, one of the best natural trout streams in this section; and two and one-half miles northeast (road) to Crooked Creek, also a very fine trout resort.

On Crooked Creek, one and one-half miles from Partridgeville, begins a series of beautiful waterfalls. There are three within a space of two miles, one of which descends twenty feet. This stream is very clear, and produces trout of silvery hue.

From the upper fall it is three-quarters mile by good path to Stony Lake, which is also reached by trail from Partridgeville, three miles. This picturesque sheet is fitly named. It is long (one mile) and narrow, and nearly encompassed by rocky shores. It contains one island, and several huge boulders dot its surface. It affords good deering and trouting, and flows into Independence River.

Little Otter Lake (½ x ⅓) lies three miles northeast of Brantingham Lake, and is reached by way of a road through the woods from the dam at Partridgeville. This attractive water is surrounded by a luxuriant growth of evergreens, and is gilded at its upper end by a sand beach. It is very pleasing, and needs only mountains to make it really beautiful. It is noted also for both deer and trout. Its inlets and its outlet—Little Otter Creek—are *all* good trout streams.

Brantingham Lake is well adapted as headquarters for excursions to other yet more distant lakes, streams and waterfalls, among which the following are recommended: It is eleven and one-half miles to Big Otter Lake, and ten miles to Big Pine Lake via the Otter Lake route; the road branching right at Botchford's Tannery, from which it is three miles of rough traveling. A commodious hotel, capable of accommodating fifty or more guests, has been built at Big Otter

From "OUTING." Copyrighted.

TROUT FISHING—LANDING THE PRIZE.

Lake. It is under the management of Mr. D. E. Burdick, proprietor of the Higby House at Glendale, from which point conveyances can always be secured both to Big Otter and Brantingham. Big Pine is a beautiful water, adorned by a single island, and a densely wooded mountain rises from its shore. It is admirable sporting ground for deer or trout. Distance thence to Big Otter Lake one and one-quarter miles northeast (trail to the dam). From Big Pine it is four miles east by blazed line to Middle Settlement Lake ($\frac{1}{3}$ x $\frac{1}{8}$) (two and one-half miles by trail from Brown

Tract Road) which takes its name from a clearing once made near it midway, on the Deacon Abbey road. It is long and narrow and of peculiar shape, and is nearly surrounded by bold mountain scenery. Its marshy borders furnish good feeding ground for deer, and it is also productive of trout. Thence it is one and one-half miles east by line to Cedar Pond. Near this carry (midway) rises a cavernous mountain, whose rocky ledges present an interesting spectacle. Thence by trail three-quarters mile northeast to Spring or Gibbs Lake (⅓ x ¼) from which a trail leads one and one-half miles to northeast corner of Middle Settlement Lake. Spring Lake is good ground for deer and trout. From Cedar Pond it is two and one-half miles to East Pond, and one and one-half miles west (line) to Middle Branch Lake. This sheet has bold and rocky shores, and near its outlet an immense boulder fifty feet in diameter lifts its summit above the water. Thence through the trackless woods south of west it is about five miles to Palen's Mills, from which it is two and one-half miles by plank road to Brantingham Lake House. Again, from Big Pine Lake it is two and one-quarter miles south (trail) to Little Pine Lake. From Lake Pine it is one and one-half miles south (trail) to Copper Lake (¾ x ½) famed for its large speckled trout. Copper Lake—in beauty rarely surpassed—contains one pretty island, and outlets into Pine Creek. It may be reached by road from Brantingham Lake, distance about eight

AMBER TRAIL SHANTY.

miles. From Glendale, a little village pleasantly situated on Black River, to Greig, three and one-half miles; Brantingham, P. O. three miles; Brantingham Lake by *branch* road one mile. The road from Glendale traverses a picturesque and undulating section of the country for a large portion of the route, skirting Black River in a long, pleasant reach, and nearly touching the noted Brantingham Lake.

Lowville, charmingly situated upon a bright little stream, whose miniature cañons and silvery cascades form many a romantic scene, is one of the tidiest, loveliest and wealthiest villages in Northern New York. Its broad and cleanly streets, adorned with handsome business blocks and tasteful residences, are richly shaded with the stately elm and sugar maple.

Chase's Lake, ten miles southeast of Lowville (good road), is noted for its pleasant scenery, and is often visited by pleasure parties. Hotel accommodations and boats for visitors are found at the lake.

Two routes extend from Lowville to Number Four: one uniting with the Martinsburg route, at Watson, three miles distant; and the other leading via Smith's Landing, two miles distant, and thence to Dayansville, three miles; Crystal Lake, eleven and a half miles; Number Four, four and a half miles; merging into the Martinsburg route, seven miles from Watson—total twenty-one miles. The latter road, though the longer of the two (three miles), is smoother and less sandy. Entering the clearing and passing on three-quarters of a mile, we arrive at the Fenton House, which is a most suitable resort for those not desirous of camping out, and yet who enjoy all the advantages in the way of the "line and the chase," which first-class sporting grounds afford, without leaving the railroad more than a score of miles behind. This explains why Number Four has become such a popular rendezvous.

POTTER POND.

The Fenton House, from a small and rude beginning, has grown into an extensive villa. In addition to the main structure, a large building (60 x 32), two and a half stories high, has recently been erected, the entire lower floor of which serves as a grand drawing-room for the guests. In this great hall, which is warmed by a huge fire-place and lighted by showy chandeliers, various kinds of amusements are gotten up by the visitors, including dancing and dramatic performances, which are greatly enjoyed. Connected with the house are supplementary buildings, including a store (well stocked with all kinds of supplies) and a post-office; and clustered near are several substantial cottages, offering pleasant accommodations. Charles Fenton, an accomplished sportsman, reliable woodsman, and a true lover of Nature, is eminently qualified for managing such an establishment. (P. O. Number Four, Lewis Co.)

There are many delightful places of interest within easy reach of Fenton's, among which the following should be noted:

Beaver Lake (1½ x ¼), an expansion of Beaver River, is attained by a pleasant descending path, partially shaded by evergreen and other wild trees (half a mile). Although in full view of the hotel, it is the frequent resort of deer. Near it (south) are Woodwardia and Beaver Ponds.

By rowing down the lake to its outlet, northwest, and following thence right north a path one and three-quarters miles, Crooked Lake or Lake Agan is reached; distance from Fenton's, three and a quarter miles. This is an unattractive sheet, as far as beauty of surroundings is concerned, but it has long been famed for the quantity and quality of the trout it yields.

To visit Sand Lake, a charming little pond (¾ x ⅓) lying one and three-quarters miles farther north, and a favorite locality for deer hunting, row the length of Crooked Lake and follow the trail leading from the head of that sheet.

Those who would "float" with almost certain success, will paddle down Beaver River to the large rock just below the portage to Crooked Lake, bridge their boats from the rock to another a few feet away, shoot the little rapids thence to the still water beyond, and there obtain their venison.

Francis Lake (1¼ x ¾), one mile southeast of Fenton's, is still quite a deer haunt; not noted for trout. In Burnt Creek, about three miles southwest of Fenton's, via the *old* Watson road, two and one-half miles and path (left) one-half mile, there is a remarkable trout resort called "Burnt Spring-Hole."

From "Outing." Copyrighted.

FISHING FROM RAFTS IN THE ADIRONDACKS.

From a point about four miles above Beaver Lake, a blind trail extends from the river, north, three miles to the four Mosher Ponds. These waters, being seldom disturbed, are the common resort of deer. This is equally applicable to numerous other lakes and lakelets usually well supplied with trout, lying still deeper in the wilderness. Hence the peculiar attractiveness of this particular section as a sporting territory.

Perhaps seven miles farther up the stream (three-quarters of a mile below Stillwater), a path is also taken north to another and larger group of ponds, styled the "Eleven Lakes" from one to five miles distant. These include the North Creek Chain, embracing Lower North Lake, Big or Upper North Lake, and others, forming the pretty little stream, North Creek flowing into the Beaver.

Stillwater-on-the-Beaver is really where navigation commences with parties passing up toward the head-waters of the stream. At this important point, on a commanding plateau, is located the Beaver River Club House for many years successfully run as a hotel. It is now open to members of the Club and their guests only. Stillwater is a fine sporting centre, and here we reach the boundaries of the magnificent forest domain of Dr. W. Seward Webb, Ne-ha-sa-ne Park.

Carthage, finely situated upon Black River, furnishes prime accommodations and ample facilities for reaching the sporting grounds.

Carthage is the western terminus of the "Old State Road," opened through the Wilderness to Crown Point in 1841-47. The magnitude of this "forest waste" becomes manifest when the length of this road is taken into consideration. From a point about twenty miles east of this place, to Schroon River (Root's) ninety-four and one-half miles, with the exception of the Number Four, Long Lake, Newcomb and several minor clearings, the route lies through a wilderness not yet invaded by civilization.

Portions of this road are not now traveled by wagon, viz.: Belfort to Number Four (it is passable two or three miles east of Belfort), and from Little Rapids road (branching left two miles east of south branch) to Brandreth's Lake.

In entering the woods from Carthage, parties may choose either of two general routes: one by way of Belfort, fifteen miles, and thence to the Oswegatchie Ponds, nine miles, or to Sand and Little Crooked Lakes—following the Oswegatchie road from Belfort, five miles, thence a path five miles to the former, whence it is one and three-quarters miles south to Crooked Lake; the other leading to Harrisville, twenty miles distant, passing through the village of Natural Bridge, nine miles.

The Carthage & Adirondack Railroad is leased to the New York Central & Hudson River Railroad. This is the route from Carthage to Harrisville and Benson Mines. By this line the distances from Carthage are as follows: Carthage to Natural Bridge, ten miles; thence to Harrisville, eleven miles; thence to Benson Mines, twenty-two miles.

Natural Bridge is a pleasant little place situated on Indian River (Indian, *Ojequack*, "Nut River") which here runs under the ground in two different places, and emerges a few rods below, forming a natural bridge six feet above the water and fifteen feet wide, a curiosity of considerable interest. The thriving village of Harrisville, situated on the west branch of Oswegatchie River is easily and conveniently reached. There is a good hotel at Harrisville (Kenwood Hall, E. P. Lake, Proprietor).

About four miles this side of Harrisville, and seventeen miles beyond Carthage, the route passes near and in sight of Lake Bonaparte (a wagon road extending to its margin, one-half mile) which is surpassed in beauty by but few of the Wilderness waters. It is five miles in length and averages two miles in width, encircles several wild rocky islands, and is environed by bold, precipitous shores. Lake Bonaparte is within easy reach of some of the best sporting grounds of the great Wilderness, notably the Oswegatchie waters, now conveniently accessible via the Carthage & Adirondack Railroad.

In addition to Lake Bonaparte and its surrounding waters, others of easy access from Harrisville are the Jayville Lakes, eight miles northeast; Jennie Creek Lake, six miles; South Creek Lake, six miles southeast; Liger's Lake near that, southeast, and the "rising star" of the Adirondacks, Star Lake, twenty-one miles east of Carthage.

Oswegatchie is the present railway station for Star Lake, some two and one-half miles distant. A new railroad station will be established within a mile of that beautiful resort. The stage ride from Oswegatchie to Star Lake Hotel is over a good highway, mostly through a magnificent forest. (Benson Mines is the terminus of the C. & A. R.R.)

Star Lake, one mile by three-quarters, star-like in form, purity and brightness, is one of the fairest of all that galaxy of gems adorning the Adirondack Wilderness. On the early maps it appeared as "Point Lake," having been thus designated from its curiously scalloped shores; and it has but recently received its more appropriate name. Its waters are as clear as crystal, objects being discernible at a great depth. It is apparently one vast spring-hole, having no visible inlets or outlet. This many-armed, islet-adorned, and hill-encircled little loch, fringed with beaches of golden sand, presents a lake-picture of peculiar and entrancing loveliness. Indeed it may well be termed, Blue Mountain Lake in miniature.

Until the completion of the Carthage & Adirondack Railroad to this locality, but few were aware of the existence of this veritable dream of beauty; but since becoming so easily accessible, rapidly increasing numbers of visitors have been attracted thither and, as a natural result, cottages are being rapidly built on the border of the lake, and sites for numerous others are in great demand. Residents of Utica, Rome and Syracuse, by the admirable train service offered, are enabled to breakfast at home and dine the same day at Star Lake. No other Adirondack resort offers equal accessibility and none greater attractions.

On a commanding site, at a convenient distance from the lake (elevation above the sea, 1850 feet), stands the commodious Star Lake House, a three-story structure, which offers the usual accommodations to tourists. The Edgewood House and the Cottage Hotel also furnish good entertainment. (P. O. Oswegatchie, St. Lawrence Co., N. Y.) All visitors will be richly repaid by ascending Bald Mountain, near the hotel.

Several sparkling streams within one-half to three-quarters of a mile of the hotel, and Little River, one to two and a half miles away, afford fine trouting; and still more distant, various other sequestered waters offer abundant sport.

Twin Lakes, lying about one mile northeast of the hotel by road, are peculiarly attractive and charm every visitor.

Again from Harrisville we may proceed by good road to Fine, twelve miles (via Pitcairn, three miles, and East Pitcairn, seven miles); thence eleven miles by poor road to "Landing," whence it is good boating up the east branch (interrupted only by three easy portages of forty rods, one-half mile and one mile) through a dense forest to Cranberry Lake, ten and one-half miles – total, thirty-five miles. Harrisville is connected with Gouverneur by a fair road, twenty miles. Stage daily; fare, $1.50. Telegraphic station at this place for all points.

About three miles above Harrisville the west and middle branches of the Oswegatchie unite their waters. Five miles up the latter stream where the road terminates is located the home of the noted hunter and woodsman, Warren Hume. We have now reached the borders of a district whose dense and undisturbed woods may truly be styled "the forest primeval." From Hume's place rare sporting grounds and picturesque resorts are generally of easy access.

At Jayville, on the Carthage & Adirondack Railroad, five miles distant, and three miles northeast of Round Lake, extensive mines are worked with good success. The iron produced is of the best quality.

The farm hostelry of Warren Hume, styled "Forest Home," (P. O. Harrisville, N. Y.) has recently been greatly enlarged and refurnished, and now offers attractive and home-like quarters to visitors. It is a model of neatness and comfort; and the table is supplied with the products of the farm, forest and stream.

Cranberry Lake, well in the heart of the Wilderness, is the chief resort for hunting parties starting from Gouverneur. To Hailesboro the distance is two miles; thence to Fowler, four miles; Fullerville, two and a half miles; Edwards, five and three-quarter miles; Fine, nine miles—total, twenty-three and one-quarter miles. Stages daily from Edwards to Fine; fare, 75c. The Gouverneur & Oswegatchie R.R. (N. Y. C. & H. R. R.R. Co. Lessee), now operated between Gouverneur and Edwards, renders staging unnecessary, at least part of the way.

From Fine we have a choice of two routes to Cranberry Lake. 1st. Five miles main road to "Griffin's," then six miles poor woods road to "Landing" at foot of the Stillwater, from which, by boat, it is ten and one-half miles up the Oswegatchie to the foot of the lake—encountering three portages *en route* one-eighth, one-half and one mile each respectively. This route is rarely traveled. 2d. And now the favorite route—nine miles from Fine, good road to Star Lake House; thence woods road, six miles, to the old "Albany" bridge across the "Big Inlet" of Cranberry Lake, Sternburg's (passing Lost and Hicks Ponds on the way), whence it is three miles along the rapids to the "flow" (river), and three miles farther to Cranberry Lake. A steamer meets parties at head of "the flow" and conveys them to Harewood Park Hotel, at the foot of the lake.

The route from DeKalb Junction to Cranberry Lake is popular and easy to travel: DeKalb Junction to Hermon, five miles; Russell, six miles; Clarksboro, eleven miles; Clifton Iron Mines, two miles; thence to Cranberry Lake, eleven and one-half miles; total, thirty-five and one-half miles.

"PAUL SMITH'S."

PAUL SMITH'S HOTEL is pleasantly located on the Lower St. Regis Lake, in the heart of the Adirondack Mountains, 2000 feet above tide-water, amidst a dense growth of pine and balsam forest, and in the immediate vicinity of the best fishing and hunting grounds to be found in the Adirondacks. The house, which is one of the largest hotels north of Saratoga, is situated 100 feet from and thirty feet above the lake, and has accommodations, with its cottages, for 350 guests. Rooms are large and well ventilated, single and *en suite*, two to ten communicating. The hotel is elegantly furnished throughout, and supplied with all modern improvements. The dining hall and service will be kept up to the usual high standard of excellence, and the table supplied with the delicacies of the season. The richest milk and cream from the proprietor's herd of select Alderneys is one of the principal features of fare; also fresh vegetables from the hotel garden.

THE TENNIS COURT.

Lower St. Regis Lake is one of the many beautiful bodies of water that are found in the Adirondacks, and is about one mile in width by one and a half in length. Its shores are high or gently sloping and well wooded. High hills seclude and protect it from strong winds, making it unusually safe and pleasant for boating and fishing. It is connected by navigable streams with several other pretty lakes, giving it unsurpassed advantages for delightful excursions, etc.

Good fishing is to be had in Lower St. Regis and the brooks emptying into it; also in the many lakes and ponds in its vicinity. Waters are stocked yearly with brook and lake trout from the Adirondack State Hatchery. The extensive addition recently built contains forty elegant sleeping rooms, large parlor, ladies' billiard room and a dance hall. General improvements have also been made on the premises and grounds, offering increased advantages for the amusement and comfort of guests.

Of the climate and its wonderful benefits to those afflicted with pulmonary diseases, enough has already been written to make mention of it unnecessary.

A first-class livery is connected with the house, where carriages and horses can be had at all hours, also saddle horses. Many beautiful drives over good roads can be taken from here.

A general store in the hotel contains all necessaries for supplying camping parties, excepting tents and blankets, at reasonable prices, including fishing tackle, ammunition, etc.

THE START OF THE TALLY-HO.

Telegraph and post-offices (daily mail) in the house, also telephone connection with all principal resorts in the Adirondacks. Amusements: boating, shooting, fishing, hunting, driving, billiards, bowling, lawn tennis, etc. Brook-trout fishing is best in May and June; fly fishing in July, August, and to September 15th. Deer can be killed from August 15th to November 1st. Hounding deer is permitted between September 1st and October 5th.

LAKE KUSHAQUA.

NESTLING among the verdant hills lies Lake Kushaqua—"beautiful resting place," as its Indian name signifies—the sinuous curves of its shore line making here a little bay, and there a small promontory, disclosing a constant succession of beautiful scenes.

On a bluff, commanding a view of the entire lake, stands Kushaqua Lodge, a family hotel, built for comfort. The water supply comes from mountain springs a mile distant, and is always pure, cool and sparkling. The sanitary arrangements are unsurpassed, the balsamic odor of evergreens is especially noticeable, and health is synonymous with Kushaqua.

Adjacent points of interest are conveniently reached at small expense. Paul Smith's can be reached in two hours, by driving, or in considerably less time by rail. Loon Lake is within easy walking distance. Saranac, Lake Placid, the Ampersand, all may be visited in a day's trip. An excursion can be made to Montreal and return in the same day, allowing five hours to visit the points of interest in and about the city. Malone, one of the prettiest villages in the picturesque valley of the St. Lawrence, offers another opportunity for a day's outing. To those who prefer to spend their summer days in the rest and quiet of this beautiful place, Kushaqua Lodge offers many inviting pleasures in boating, tennis, fishing and all forms of out-door, healthful recreation. To the sportsman Kushaqua is also enticing. It is a fine place for lake trout, and the surrounding brooks furnish some of the best sport for fly fishing to be enjoyed anywhere in the Adirondacks. Whether one be tourist, sportsman or a summer idler, Kushaqua Lodge offers many attractions.

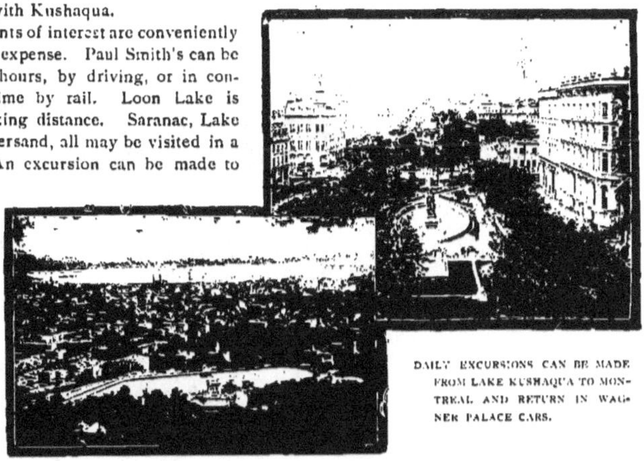

DAILY EXCURSIONS CAN BE MADE FROM LAKE KUSHAQUA TO MONTREAL AND RETURN IN WAGNER PALACE CARS.

SARANAC INN.—On the northerly limits of Upper Saranac Lake, amidst picturesque mountain and water scenery, the Saranac Inn is situated, with accommodations for 125 guests. (D. W. Riddle, Manager, P. O. Saranac Inn, N. Y.) From this point the lake travel is accomplished in small boats, or canoes, from the St. Regis to Blue Mountain Lake, Tupper to Raquette Lakes, and the Bog River country, going over a hundred miles or more, through lakes and connecting streams, disembarking only to cross the portages. From the Inn excursions may be made to recesses so deep and wild, and to lakes and ponds so primitive, that no trace of human life is visible. Boats, supplies, camp outfits and livery may be had at the Inn, kept for the accommodation of guests and travelers.

CHILDWOLD PARK HOUSE. Childwold lies 1450 feet above tidewater level, in a grove of majestic forest trees. It has within its boundaries, besides those preserved in its park, many favorite resorts of sportsmen, abounding in deer, duck and the dainty trout. The

KUSHAQUA LODGE, LAKE KUSHAQUA.

proprietors of the south half of this township, extending nine miles north and south, have preserved a small portion (5000 acres) embracing Lake Massawepie, the source of the Grass River, and a silvery chain of seven contributing lakelets, as a forest, game and pleasure park, to be ever kept as such in a wild, wooded state, for hotel and cottage sites. Lake

CHILDWOLD PARK HOUSE, FROM LAKE MASSAWEPIE.

Massawepie is but a small part of an ancient lake of large extent, the wave-worn shores of which can be traced for several miles, elevated from 150 to 200 feet above its present level.

The Childwold Park House (Wm. F. Ingold, Manager, P. O. address, Massawepie, N. Y.) can comfortably accommodate 300 guests. Cottages can be rented by those who prefer that charming way of living in the mountains. A skillful and successful physician resides in a pretty log cabin within the park grounds.

THE WAWBEEK—UPPER SARANAC LAKE.

WAWBEEK LODGE.—The name Wawbeek (Indian, meaning *big rock*) was suggested by a very large boulder, lying in front of the place, above the shore of the lake. Longfellow uses the name in several passages of his "Hiawatha":

"See the masses of the Wawbeek
Lying still in every valley."

"Nothing but the black rock yonder,
Nothing but the fatal Wawbeek."

Wawbeek Lodge is located on one of the most charming spots on the west shore of the Upper Saranac Lake, one hundred feet above the level of the lake, commanding an extensive lake and mountain view, and is reached by stages from Tupper Lake Station, eight miles, over a good wagon road, or via Saranac Inn and steamer. The house, a commodious new structure, is one of the best finished in the Adirondacks, and so designed that most of the rooms command a view of the lake. No pains have been spared to make it one of the most comfortable hotels in the Adirondacks. (F. W. Foster, Manager, Wawbeek, N. Y.) Tents will be placed within easy reach of the house, for the convenience of those desiring outdoor life. A physician will be in attendance at the house, and the comfort of guests will be looked after in every way. Telegraph and daily mail in the house. Terms, $3.50 per day; special rates by the week.

THE AMPERSAND is situated at the extreme northerly end of Lower Saranac Lake. It is roomy and artistic. From its picturesque and commanding position on a slight eminence, it overlooks the lake, surrounded by pines, spruce, hemlock and balsams. The name chosen for the

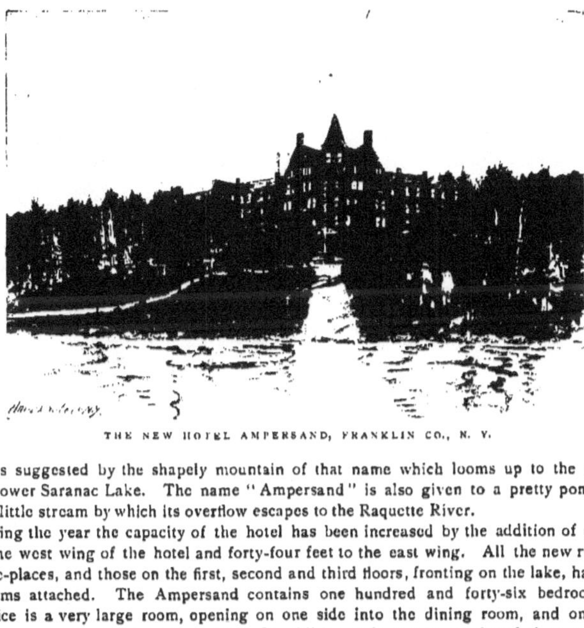

THE NEW HOTEL AMPERSAND, FRANKLIN CO., N. Y.

hotel was suggested by the shapely mountain of that name which looms up to the southward across Lower Saranac Lake. The name "Ampersand" is also given to a pretty pond, and the devious little stream by which its overflow escapes to the Raquette River.

During the year the capacity of the hotel has been increased by the addition of eighty-two feet to the west wing of the hotel and forty-four feet to the east wing. All the new rooms have open fire-places, and those on the first, second and third floors, fronting on the lake, have private bath-rooms attached. The Ampersand contains one hundred and forty-six bedrooms. The main office is a very large room, opening on one side into the dining room, and on the other through a reception room into the parlor. In addition to the rooms mentioned, there are a general reading room, writing rooms, card room, smoking room and ladies' and gentlemen's billiard parlors, while in the basement is a playroom for children, guides' rooms, barber shops, bath-room, a general store and post-office, and telegraph office. The piazzas are broad and extend along the entire front and ends of the house. The Ampersand offers special attractions to young people; music, afternoon and evening; tennis court; ball field; boating and sailing and walks in the woods, with seats scattered here and there. Good trout fishing and deer hunting in their season. This region is noted for its beautiful drives. The Ampersand has won an enviable reputation. Its generous fare, lavish comforts and varied means of enjoyment, have combined to make the enterprise a notable success. The hotel is situated a mile from the railroad station. The Ampersand is managed by Eaton & Young.

MASSENA SPRINGS.

MASSENA SPRINGS, a station on the Rome, Watertown & Ogdensburg Railroad, thirteen miles east of Norwood, is a resort which has enjoyed more than local fame for upwards of half a century. It is the connecting point between the Rome, Watertown & Ogdensburg Railroad and the Grand Trunk Railway.

The Springs (Indian, *Kan-a-swa-stak-e-ras*) are situated on Raquette River, one mile from Massena village, located on Grass River. These waters (consisting of five springs, not essentially different in their properties, of which "St. Regis" is the most important) have acquired a wide reputation for their medicinal qualities, and this celebrity is rapidly increasing. The early surveyors noticed them in 1799, when a copious volume of clear cold water was thrown up, strongly charged with sulphur; and the earth around trodden into a mire-hole by deer and moose, which frequented the spot on account of the saline qualities of the water. The Indians here found an abundance of game at all seasons, and vague traditions exist that they used the waters medicinally. (*Dr. Hough.*) The surroundings of the Springs are extremely beautiful, and the climate in this locality is very healthful. There are other attractions besides the Springs. To the piscatorial tourist this section is full of interest. Here he is within striking distance of three rivers which furnish fish in rich variety and profusion, including bass, pickerel and the celebrated muskallonge. Putting his boat in the lovely

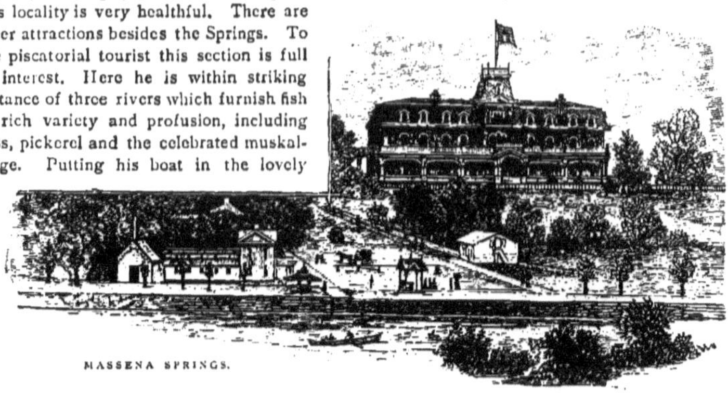

MASSENA SPRINGS.

Raquette, which sweeps along within a few miles of the Hatfield House, he can pass to the St. Lawrence (twelve miles), shooting like an arrow down the exciting but not dangerous rapids that intervene; thence up the St. Lawrence (three miles), or much farther if he desires; thence up Grass River to the dam (eight miles) which is only one mile below White's Hotel, at Massena village—a short mile from the Springs. What a delightful trip for a day! The Long Sault Rapids, one of the most attractive scenes on the St. Lawrence, four miles from here, can be run safely with small boats; and in the eddies below is the finest of muskallonge fishing. The Long Rapids on the Raquette, nine miles below the Springs, are the special haunts of legions of white-fish rarely found elsewhere in the vicinity. Trout also are caught in the neighborhood. Up Earl Creek, a short distance, which empties into the river four miles above these rapids, a noted angler captured one hundred and eighteen bass, two pickerel and one pike—averaging over two pounds each—in three or four hours' fishing. Similar examples, illustrating the fruitfulness of these streams, might be multiplied to any extent.

The Hatfield House is a fine brick structure, furnished with all modern improvements and conveniences for the comfort of its guests. It is a model establishment having few equals in Northern New York. At White's Hotel—a thoroughly built and spacious edifice—the traveler will find everything in the way of courteous attention, pleasant apartments, and well furnished tables that the most exacting could require, and the charges are very reasonable for a house of this class. The well kept and comfortable Harrowgate House is located on the spring grounds, and has lawn running down to the Raquette River. For information write to Sheddon & Stearns.

HENDERSON HARBOR.

THIS beautiful place is situated at the foot of Lake Ontario, eight miles above Sackett's Harbor, and is one of the most delightful spots on the great lakes. Henderson Bay is a very beautiful sheet of water, six miles long and from two to three miles wide. It is almost completely land-locked by high, wooded bluffs, and smooth, grassy, receding shores, with stretches of gravelly beach, making charming spots everywhere for camping, bathing and boating.

The waters are pure and clear, and abound in all kinds of fish, especially black bass. Muskallonge and pickerel of large size are frequently taken. Gull, Stony, Calf, Little and Big Galoup Islands, within easy rowing distance from the harbor, are especially fine fishing grounds. Parties frequently go over to these places in the morning and return at night with loads of bass.

Highland Park is the charming resort of families from Adams, who spend the summer in their own cottages. Paradise Park and Snowshoe Parks are attractive and popular. The surrounding country is everywhere beautiful and the roads and drives are delightful. Henderson Bay is in every respect a fine place for a summer outing. "Gill House," with spacious verandas, is the largest house at Henderson Harbor, open May 20; "Tyler's," with fine water front; "Frontier House," "Warner's," "Brooklyn," "Johnson's," "Paradise," are the names of places finely situated and popular. Boats, guides, and fishing outfits are easily procured.

Rates are reasonable and accommodations good. Henderson Harbor is reached by steamer from Sackett's Harbor, connecting with trains on the Rome, Watertown & Ogdensburg Railroad. The trip from Sackett's Harbor is interesting and attractive.

TYLER'S—HENDERSON HARBOR.

CAPE VINCENT, N. Y.

R., W. & O. R.R. DOCK AND STATION, CAPE VINCENT.

THIS delightful summer resort lies at the head of the St. Lawrence River, the beginning of the Thousand Island Region, and within sight of the sparkling blue waters of Lake Ontario. It is one of the most popular resorts on the St. Lawrence River, and is the terminus of a branch of the Rome, Watertown & Ogdensburg Railroad, twenty-six miles from Watertown. A comfortable steamer makes daily round trips between Cape Vincent, Carleton Island and Thousand Island Resorts.

Julian Ralph says: "If all mankind could be made conversant with the attractions of a summer vacation at Cape Vincent, the place would become a great city."

The fishing in the vicinity of Cape Vincent and Carleton Island is very good and of easy access, the fishing boats and guides being among the best in the Thousand Island Region.

Cape Vincent has long enjoyed the reputation of having few superiors as a place of summer rest. The sweep of the broad river and the nearness of the blue waters of Lake Ontario give to the air a delightful coolness and exhilarating freshness, without the humidity and extreme changes in temperature often felt at watering-places.

Carleton Island, three miles from Cape Vincent, is the summer home of the Carleton Island Club and Ithaca Club. Carleton Park, a beautiful plot of land on Carleton Island, has been mapped and surveyed; a large number of lots have already been sold and cottages erected by prominent people who have chosen this delightful spot for summer homes. Information relative to purchasing lots in Carleton Park may be obtained of Henry Folger, Kingston, Ont.

Opposite Cape Vincent is Kingston, Ont., a Canadian military post, and the most important city between Toronto and Montreal. A day may be pleasantly spent in Kingston visiting the Provincial Military Academy, the Fortress, Insane Asylum, and other public institutions. The steamer "America" makes two round trips daily between Cape Vincent and Kingston. First-class meals are served on the steamer. Daily excursions are run by the steamers of the Thousand Island Steamboat Company. Kingston is encircled by a fine electric street railway.

CITY AND HARBOR OF KINGSTON, CANADA, FROM THE FORT.

AQUATIC LIFE AT THE THOUSAND ISLANDS.

THE THOUSAND ISLANDS.

SCATTERED in prodigal profusion along the noble St. Lawrence River, from Cape Vincent and Clayton to Alexandria Bay and beyond—the channel in some places being twelve miles broad—are the island gems, more than 1800 in number, known collectively as the Thousand Islands. They vary in size from a small mass of rock, seemingly burdened to lift its bosky crest above the clear, deep water, to picturesque islands miles in extent, overspread with a rich and luxuriant vegetation. Nearly every island, large or small, is the pleasant summer home of its fortunate owner. The many beautiful cottages, of quaint and elegant design, or the more pretentious and stately castle-like structures of enduring stone, resplendent in gay streamers and pennants of every color, add to the natural loveliness of the scene an attractiveness that is bewitching, yet indescribable. The refined taste which has transformed these island wilds into pleasant haunts is nowhere more noticeable than in the many provisions for comfort and enjoyment which surround these summer homes, and make them pictures of delight and real contentment. The whole insular region is one of incomparable beauty, and just the place one seeks for rest and refreshment during the warm days of summer.

From Harper's Magazine. Copyright, 1881, by Harper & Brothers.

ENTRANCE TO LAKE OF THE ISLES—THE SENTINEL.

Laved by the clear, blue waters of the St. Lawrence, and fanned by gentle breezes which come laden with the balmy odors of balsam, pine and cedar, the Islands are at all times delightfully cool and refreshing, and invite one to enjoy, *per otium*, the rare pleasures they offer. A spirit of rest and freedom from all care seems to pervade the place, while the charm and fascinating beauty of the scene give it the semblance of a spectacle in fairyland or the beautiful vision of a dream; unlike a dream, however, the charm remains and the delights are real. As a resort, the Thousand Islands grow more popular every year, and the many improvements made each season have added so much to the natural attractions of the Islands that the transformed scene now appears more like the creation of romance. Every isle and dancing ripple pulsates with the breath of true poetry, and only a poet should sing the praises of the Thousand Islands.

During the summer season the Islands teem with life, and the reticulated channel of the sparkling blue river is flecked with the white wings of little sailing yachts and pleasure boats which, like birds of passage, flit hither and thither among the Islands, in search of pleasure and new delights. Pleasure cruising in canoe or boat is charming and always romantic; now floating in some sequestered bay, redolent of perfume from numberless water-lilies, whose pure white blooms dot the surface in grand profusion; now resting leisurely on the oar in the shade of some mysterious island, one listens in dreamy expectancy to catch the luring voice or seductive song of a Lorelei or some invisible siren, from the quiet repose of the wood-embowered isles, until the

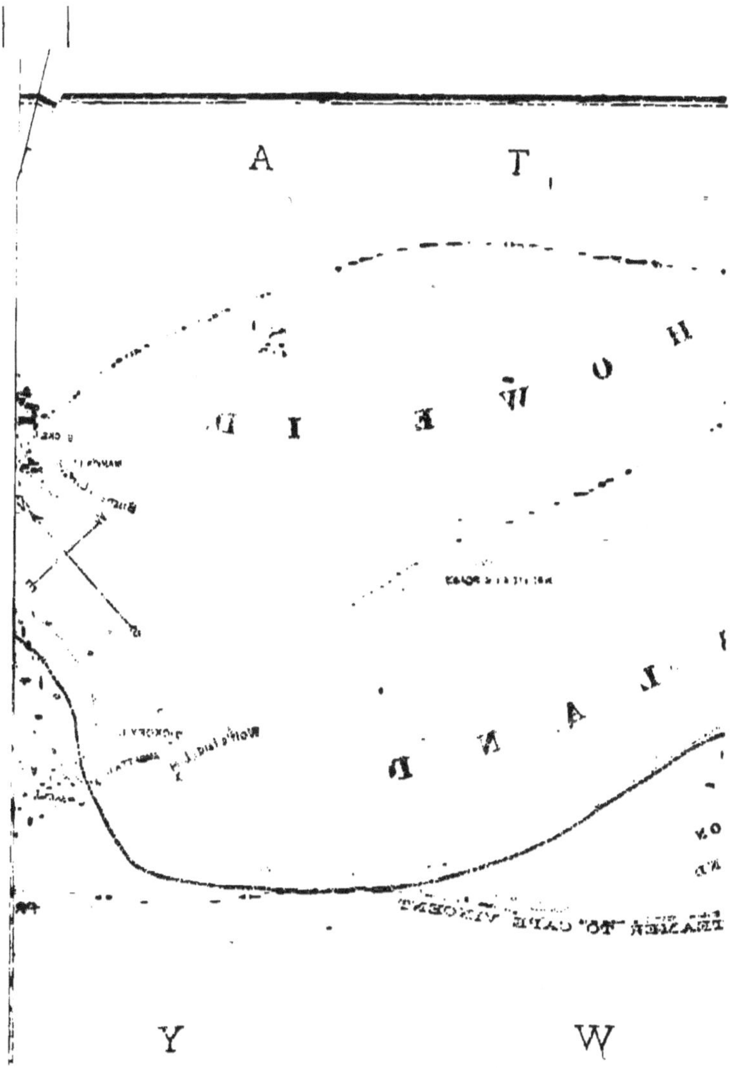

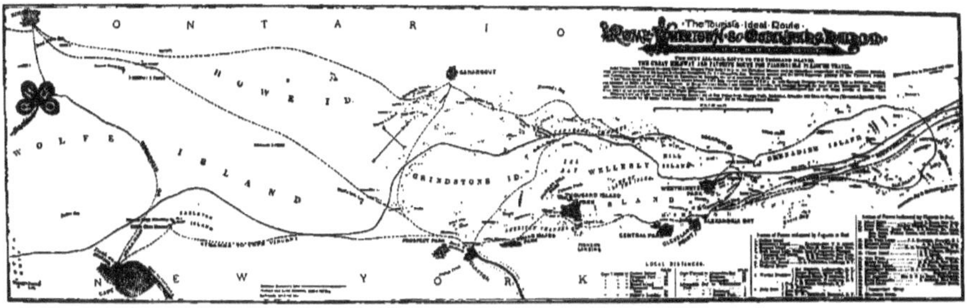

O N T A R I O
N E W Y O R K
W O L F E I S L A N D
H O W E I D.
GANANOQUE
GRINDSTONE ID.
WELLESLEY ISLAND
The Tourist's Ideal Route
ALEXANDRIA BAY
CENTRAL PARK
PROSPECT PARK
LOCAL DISTANCES.

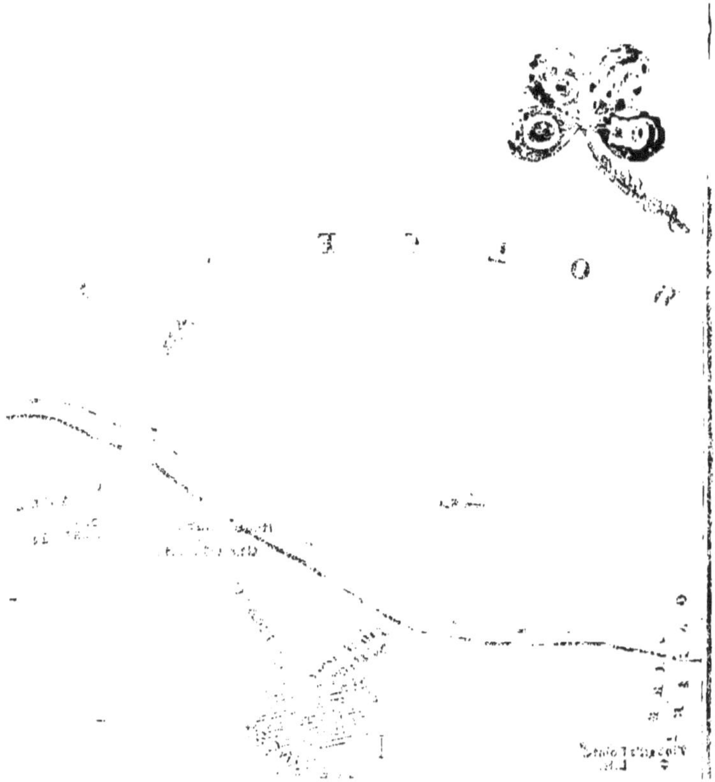

MOONLIGHT AMONG THE THOUSAND ISLANDS.

deep, sonorous whistle of a passing steamer, or the shrill screech of a steam launch breaks the spell and disturbs momentarily the reverie. The scene does not close with the wane of day. As the setting sun gilds the nestling isles with his parting ray, and the lengthening shadows of evening slowly enfold all in gentle embrace, the glow of lights from one island is soon followed by the bright response from another, then another—each island marked by a distinctive device arranged in brightly colored lights peculiar to itself—until the illuminated spectacle rivals even Venice herself in the splendor of a carnival dress.

Sporting in all its variety, both with the rod and with the gun, is unsurpassed, the excellence and variety of the game yielding the tourist, as well as the sportsman, rare returns. To the invalid and to all afflicted with hay fever, the pure, salubrious and invigorating atmosphere renders this place of resort a delightful sanitarium. The hotels at Cape Vincent, Clayton, Round Island, Thousand Island Park, Westminster Park, Grinnell Island, Alexandria Bay and Edgewood Park are modern in style, and offer accommodations equal to any at the oldest and most frequented pleasure resorts. The conventionalities of ultra-fashionable resorts are not imperative in their demands here, and a sojourn of a few weeks or months among the Thousand Islands will be a season of pure enjoyment and refreshment.

From Harper's Magazine.

ENTRANCE TO LOST CHANNEL—THE LIGHT-HOUSE.

CLAYTON, N. Y.

THE PRINCIPAL GATEWAY AND CHIEF DISTRIBUTING POINT FOR THE GREAT ST. LAWRENCE RIVER AND THOUSAND ISLAND REGION.

CLAYTON is situated directly in front of the upper group of the Thousand Islands, and is a delightful place of resort. It contains five churches, two banks and three telegraph offices. There are three celebrated hotels here—Hubbard House, Walton House and New Windsor Hotel. The finest fishing on the River St. Lawrence is found in the immediate vicinity of Clayton; pike, black bass, pickerel and muskallonge of extraordinary size are easily caught here. Experienced and attentive oarsmen, the best of boats, and splendid hotel accommodations render this the favorite resort for fishing parties.

R., W. & O. R.R.—APPROACHING CLAYTON.

All trains run solid to the R. W. & O. R.R. Steamboat dock at Clayton. Thirteen magnificently equipped trains arrive at and depart from Clayton daily, except Sunday, and five fast express trains are run on Sunday. Through Sleeping Cars are run from New York, Chicago, Niagara Falls, Buffalo, etc. Day trains have magnificent Wagner Vestibule Drawing-Room Cars, and night trains have Wagner Vestibule Palace Sleeping Cars.

The train service has been improved by the addition of the famous Club Train, which is the finest and fastest train that has ever been run to and from the St. Lawrence River. This Vestibule Train is run between Niagara Falls and Clayton, via Buffalo, Rochester and Syracuse, and comprises a Wagner Club Car, Vestibule Coaches and Wagner Buffet Drawing-Room Car; it also carries a Wagner Sleeping Car, which runs to and from Chicago.

Clayton is a base of supplies for the cottage population all along the river. Beautiful Round Island, with its handsome summer residences, is only one mile below. The Thousand Island Park, with its summer population of 10,000 people, is only four miles from Clayton; Central Park is eight miles; Alexandria Bay, the great resort of the Thousand Islands, is only ten miles; Edgewood Park is nine miles; Westminster Park is eleven miles; in fact, all principal resorts and summer homes in the entire Thousand Island region are easily and quickly reached from Clayton.

THE "EMPIRE STATE."

Direct and immediate connections are made, to and from all these places, without transfer. The steamers of the Thousand Island Steamboat Company, the "White Squadron," which run in connection with the R., W. & O., carry the United States mails. These steamers have made an international reputation by punctual service and perfect management in all details. The steamer "Empire State," the largest of the fleet, has a capacity of 1000; steamer "St. Lawrence," capacity 860; new steamer "America," capacity 600. Each has a powerful electric searchlight, which is of great value in navigating at night; the searchlight of the steamer "St. Lawrence" being of one million candle power, and one of the most powerful lights in the world. First-class meals are served on these boats; price, fifty cents.

The steamers of the Richelieu & Ontario Navigation Company also arrive at and depart from the R., W. & O. R.R. dock, bound to and from Montreal, Quebec, and the River Saguenay.

Famous Fishing Grounds of the River St. Lawrence.

Located in the Immediate Vicinity of Cape Vincent, Clayton and Alexandria Bay.

THE fisherman's sport is thus graphically described by Mr. Howard Pyle, himself an adept with the rod as well as the pen:

"One of the great features of enjoyment to the casual visitor to the Thousand Islands consists in occasional picnic dinners; not the ordinary picnic dinner where a table-cloth is spread upon the ground, and cold meats and sundries upon the table-cloth, where long-legged spiders or centipedes career across the viands or drop into one's cup of luke-warm coffee, but dinners

CATCHING MUSKALLONGE.

as luxurious in their bill of fare as any of the hotels can afford, combined with all the unfettered gaiety incident to such an *al fresco* meal. A day's fishing is nominally the back-bone of the expedition, around which the day's pleasure is actually built. We will suppose that the party of a dozen ladies and gentlemen is formed, and the day planned for the expedition arrived—a clear, sunny one, with not a ripple stirring the glassy surface of the stream. Six boats are hired, a gentleman and lady going in each under the superintendence of a fisherman. Perhaps, if the fishing-ground be distant, a steam yacht is engaged, the boats, stretching in a long line, are taken in tow, and off the jolly party starts, with flags flying merrily.

"At length the desired spot is reached, and the sport begins, each party fishing as if their lives depended upon it, and all internally praying that if a monster pickerel or muskallonge is caught, they may be the particular ones selected by Fortune as the catchers thereof. But whether such a capture is made or not, the fishing is sure to be fine, and so exciting that the

From Harper's Magazine.—Copyright, 1881, by Harper & Brothers.

THE RIFT—LAKE OF THE ISLES.

dinner hour approaches without notice, until warned by the shrill whistle of the little steam yacht, the boats wend their way from all quarters to the 'dinnerin'' place.

"The luncheon, mind you, is not made up according to the simple bill of fare presented at the desk of the hotel, composed of mere necessaries, such as eggs, bread and butter, coffee and fat pork; but under the supervision of the overseer of the luncheon room at the hotel, it crops out in various 'extras' and 'sundries,' in the shape of a tender chicken or two, juicy steaks and chops, green corn, tomatoes, and the like. The fishermen—excellent cooks, deft and cleanly—perform the task of preparing the meal with wonderful dispatch, and in a short time a royal repast is laid before the hungry anglers, whose appetites, whetted by healthful exercise and invigorating air, do ample justice to the feast. After dinner, while the fishermen are packing away the dishes and other etcetera, the ladies retire for a short nap and the gentlemen for a social cigar; then, as evening approaches, back to the hotel, there to doff the flannel shirts and fishing dresses, and once more to assume society clothes and manners.

"Many, however, prefer solitary sport, or with a company of two or three gentlemen only; and by starting in the early morning, long trips can be made far down below Grenadier Island. There, in the more shallow portions of the river, striped with long beds of water-grasses, green and purple, undisturbed by the turmoil and commotion of passing steamboats, the indolent pickerel lies tranquilly in the secluded tangle of his own especial retreat; or huge black bass, reaching sometimes to the weight of five or

FIDDLER'S ELBOW.

THE DEVIL'S OVEN.

six pounds, stand guard along the edge of the grass, waiting for some unwary minnow or perch to pass. At rare intervals are spots where the savage muskallonge, the tiger of fresh-water fish, lies hidden among the water-grasses in solitary majesty. Sluggishly he lies, glaring with his savage eyes to right and left of him, watching for his prey. He sees a minnow in the distance, apparently twitching and wriggling in a very eccentric course; a moment the monarch poises himself, with waving fins, then, a sudden sweep of his majestic tail, and he darts like a thunderbolt upon his intended victim. The next moment the sharp agony of the fisherman's hook is in his throat. For a moment he lies in motionless astonishment, then as he feels the line tighten, and discovers that he is indeed caught, he struggles with rage, making the water eddy and swirl with the sweeps of his powerful tail, and causing the rod to bend almost double. This way and that he darts, mad with rage and pain, while the line hisses as it spins from the reel, but in vain; in spite of all his endeavors he feels the tightening line drawing him nearer and nearer to the surface. Again and again he is brought to the side of the boat, only to dart away once more, until at last, sullen, exhausted and conquered, he lies motionless in the water beside the victorious fisherman's skiff. A moment more and the gaff strikes his side, and he is landed safely in the bottom of the boat.

"In the early spring, when the shallows of Eel Bay or other sheets of water of the same kind become free from ice, the water, not being deep, becomes warm much more quickly than elsewhere, and here the half-frozen fish congregate in great quantities. The professional fisherman in the bow of the boat holds a spear in shape like a trident, but with an alternate sharp iron prong

4 From Harper's Magazine.

GENERAL VIEW OF THE THOUSAND ISLANDS.

between each barbed shaft, the whole fixed upon a long, firm handle. Immediately upon seeing a fish he darts this gig at him, fixing the barb so effectually in his victim that to strike is to capture him. The weapon used is called a jaw-spear from its peculiar form, being a jaw-shaped piece of wood, with a sharp iron barb firmly fixed in the angle, against which the eels are forced, and pinned fast, until they are safely landed in the boat. Eel spearing is generally pursued at night, not only because the water is usually more quiet than during the day-time, but also because the light of the blazing pine chunks in the 'jack' or open brazier fixed in the bow of the skiff makes objects on the bottom more apparent by contrast with the surrounding gloom. The means employed by sportsmen are more legitimate, although, be it mentioned, it requires in no mean degree a quick eye and a ready hand to strike a pickerel upon the run in eight or ten feet of water.

"In June fly-fishing is employed, and fine sport it is to cast a dainty green or peacock fly so adroitly as to tempt a plump bass, in the seclusion of his rocky retreat beneath the overhanging birches along the bank, and fine sport to land him, too, for the bass, lusty and strong through good living and pure water, will battle vigorously."

INLET TO THE LAKE OF THE THOUSAND ISLANDS.

From "OUTING." Copyrighted.

CANOEING ON RIVER ST. LAWRENCE.

PROSPECT PARK.

THE wave of enterprise rolls high along the mighty St. Lawrence. Each year brings fresh evidence of the growing popularity of the many parks already established in the vicinity of Clayton and Alexandria Bay.

The site chosen for Prospect Park is the projecting point of mainland, one mile above Clayton, formerly known as Bartlett's Point. Its peculiar configuration gives it advantages which are not possessed by any other park on the St. Lawrence River. Projecting into the water, it commands an unbroken view in either direction of the river and its scenery. It rises as a bluff in one place to a height of eighty-five feet, and in another spot attains an altitude of one hundred feet above the water. The view from this bluff on a clear day is enchanting in its loveliness. To the westward, Lake Ontario, seventeen miles distant, and Carleton Island, may be seen in pale outline; looking down the river, Alexandria Bay and the miniature world of parks, hotels and island homes are within the range of vision; to the north the spires of Gananoque, and farther west those of Kingston stand in sharp relief against the cloudless sky. Turning from all this, a glance southward captivates the beholder with the beauty of the land scape, gentle slopes, wooded hills and fruitful fields indicating thrift and intelligent husbandry, spread out before him. The glow of sunset is the finishing touch which Nature gives to this delightful picture. The visitor at the park will soon make this elevated spot his favorite haunt.

From "OUTING." Copyrighted.

CANOEING ON RIVER ST. LAWRENCE.

ROUND ISLAND AND "THE FRONTENAC."

ROUND ISLAND is situated in the American channel of the River St. Lawrence, one and one-half miles below Clayton, the nearest terminus of the Rome, Watertown & Ogdensburg Railroad. The island is about one mile long and 1400 feet wide. It is undoubtedly the gem of the Thousand Islands, and with its elegantly appointed first-class hotel, and the many beau-

"THE FRONTENAC."

tiful cottages along the shore, beautiful grounds, luxuriant foliage, substantial docks and peerless water front, there is no doubt that it will be the favorite resort among the Thousand Islands.

The great charm of Round Island is its freedom from repressive conventionalities. Guests at the hotel and cottages vie in the general effort to promote the enjoyment of all. The popularity of this favored place among summer tourists and families is an assured fact, and many seeking picturesque sites for permanent summer homes, under the assurance of stability of the affairs of the island, find it desirable to locate here, where so many have already found delightful homes and a refuge from the heat of the cities. The cool, dry, bracing air, free from fogs, dust and mosquitoes, is highly recommended to those afflicted with hay fever, malaria, insomnia, pulmonary and kindred affections.

SUMMER HOME OF HON. JAMES J. BELDEN.

"The Frontenac" is a hotel of superior excellence, whose appointments, conveniences and management are the best. For health, rest or pleasure its location and surroundings have no superior. Camp-fires are a feature of evening life at Round Island. The popularity of the extemporized entertainments around the blazing logs beneath the trees will be recalled by all who have ever participated. The following gentlemen are officers and trustees: A. C. Belden (of Syracuse), President; C. A. Johnson (New York), Vice-President; H. Van Wagenen (New York), Treasurer; Chas. A. Myers (New York), Secretary; Jacob Hays, E. D. Dickinson and F. H. Taylor.

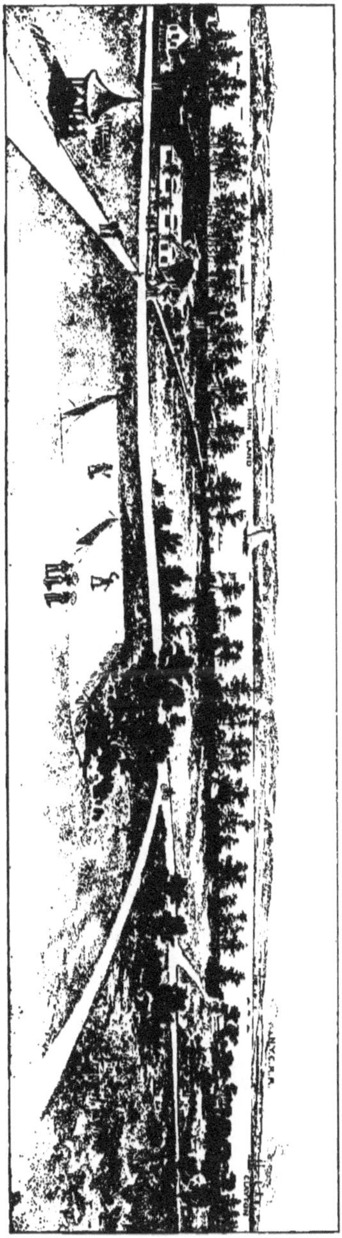

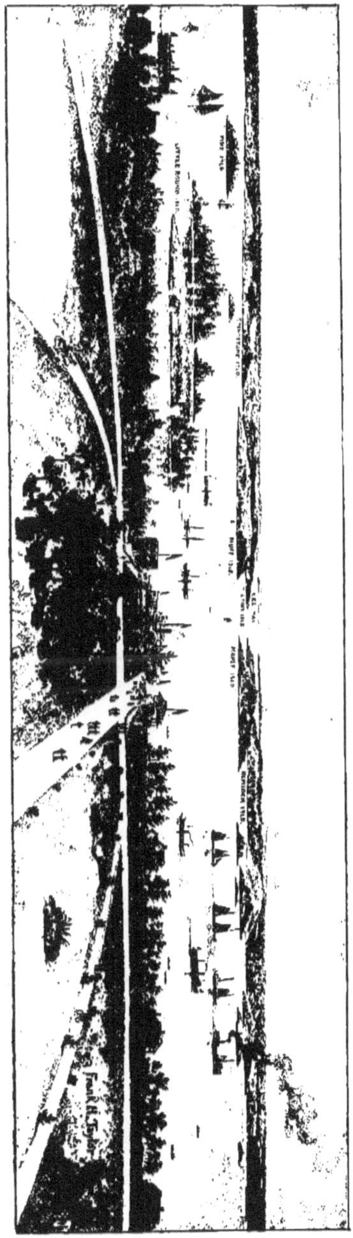

VIEWS FROM THE FRONTENAC HOTEL, ROUND ISLAND, LOOKING NORTH AND SOUTH.

THOUSAND ISLAND PARK.

THE NEW HOTEL "THE COLUMBIAN."

THOUSAND ISLAND PARK, at the head of Wellesley Island, is the most extensive summer resort on the river, covering about one thousand acres, laid out in smaller parks and avenues and already occupied by five to six hundred beautiful cottages. Originally established as a denominational park, it is now conducted by business men as a strictly undenominational resort where, as at Chautauqua, the best speakers of all denominations are heard, and summer schools and University Extension lectures are available at moderate charges. Rev. Wm. Searles, D.D. of Auburn, N. Y., is the director of services.

The large and fine hotel in this Park was destroyed by fire in 1890, and the "Columbian" (a cut of which appears above) has been erected in its place. It is open to early summer travel. It is finely furnished, replete with every modern convenience, and under the management of experienced proprietors. Built in the form of a Greek cross, it has no inside rooms or poorly ventilated apartments, and combines safety with elegant views from every room. It is lighted by electricity, and its kitchens are in brick fire-proof buildings, while the laundries are one block away.

The large tabernacle, capable of seating 3500 people, is a vast structure designed for the convenience and comfort of the large assemblages that meet beneath its roof for services, lectures or entertainments. The tabernacle, chapels, stores, and other public buildings, as well as the Park itself, are lighted by electricity.

A new water supply and reservoirs, of better quality and capacity, have been provided for this season. The sanitary conditions of the Park are excellent.

The facilities for boating, fishing, driving or horseback riding are unsurpassed. Concerts and other entertainments fill up the week-day evenings for those who desire them.

There is much that appeals to the visitor's sense of the picturesque at this Park.

The beautiful avenue along its water front gives far-reaching views of the flowing river upon one hand, and leafy vistas along the side avenues which lead into the heart of the Park domain.

All steamers in going up or down the river stop at the wharf of Thousand Island Park. It is a truly International Park, for many Canadian families come here annually to fraternize with their American cousins. As a health and pleasure resort it is unexcelled by any other in the world.

GRAND VIEW PARK.

THIS mid-river resort is located on the most westerly point of Wells or Wellesley Island, in the very centre of the famed fishing waters, where bass, pickerel and muskallonge abound. From the broad piazzas of the Grand View House, or from the lawn in front, one may look southeasterly across Round Island to the American main shore and thence, from the same standpoint, as far as the vision can reach, southerly, westerly and northerly to the Canadian shore—taking in the entire sweep of the St. Lawrence, which is here seven miles wide, with its many islands of emerald spread about in panoramic splendor. High and dry and free from dust or malaria as this park is, the prevailing westerly breezes daily invigorate the work-worn denizens of city and town who come here for rest, health, recreation and pleasure. Hay fever subjects have found at this park complete exemption from this troublesome complaint when arriving prior to the period of its annual recurrence and remaining until the period is passed.

Surrounded on almost every side by stretches of water, this favored location has attracted many purchasers of lots, and the building of cottages has increased year by year.

PIAZZA GRAND VIEW HOUSE, GRAND VIEW PARK.

The finest bathing beach among the Thousand Islands is located here, its smooth, sandy bottom reaching far out, with a gradual slope, into deep water; and with the added accessories of toboggan slide, bathing suits for adults of both sexes and for children, and life-preservers for those learning to swim, great sport is had every fine day during the season.

The erection of a chapel is contemplated this year; a lot centrally located has already been selected by a committee of clergymen, with the assurance that it is to be donated for that purpose.

The Grand View House, with its annex cottages, at present affords accommodations for about 125 guests, and its capacity is expected to grow with the needs of the location. In the broad expanse of the river the current here is not rapid, and the exercise of rowing is a favorite pastime even of women and children; a boat livery is connected with the park, and experienced oarsmen will pilot guests for fishing when desired.

The steamer "St. Lawrence" makes this landing on her afternoon trip and search light rambles among the islands, and the almost hourly steam ferry throughout the day, to and from Thousand Island Park, transfers guests and the mails arriving by the line steamers from Clayton and other points. Special inducements are offered to persons desiring to purchase lots and build cottages.

Application for board, rental of cottages or otherwise, should be made to HAMILTON CHILD, Superintendent, Grand View Park, Thousand Islands, N. Y. during the season; at other times, Syracuse, N. Y.

THE THOUSAND ISLAND HOUSE,

ALEXANDRIA BAY, N. Y.

OPEN FROM JUNE UNTIL OCTOBER. THE LARGEST AND MOST ELEGANT HOTEL ON THE RIVER ST. LAWRENCE.

THE THOUSAND ISLAND HOUSE commands from its site many of the grandest views of the river, in both directions, that are gained from any point, and from its airy tower the eye takes in a vision which, for extent and variety of scenery, is rarely equaled. To those who have never been guests at this house, and who have never visited these scenes, some statistics concerning this king of all summer resort hotels will be interesting.

THE LAWN—THOUSAND ISLAND HOUSE.

ITS DIMENSIONS.—The main building is 276 feet long and 66 feet wide; the eastern portion is five stories high and the western four stories, this difference being occasioned by the unevenness of the rock on which it is erected. From the centre of the main part a wing of the same height, and 40 feet wide, extends back 100 feet. A tower, 24 by 27 feet, rises 160 feet above the foundation. Under the end is a natural cellar in the solid rock, 150 feet long.

EXTERIOR FEATURES.—The hotel is built on the solid rock, which slopes from its front to the river and steamboat landing, only three rods distant. A veranda 13 feet wide shadows the first and second stories along the front and ends, the entire length being 376 feet. The office and connecting rooms of the east end also have a veranda, as shown in the engraving. Balconies ornament the tower, affording the guests opportunities to extend their views at pleasure along and across the river. The tower and Mansard roof, with arched windows, give to the upper part of the structure a most elegant appearance, and harmonize pleasingly with the rest of the building. The hotel will accommodate 500 guests. Hay fever and malaria are unknown here.

The cuisine, always noted, will this year be under the direction of a *chef* with large experience in New York. The hotel has all conveniences and latest improvements, including gas and electric lighting throughout. A full orchestra of first-class musicians will give three concerts daily. This admirably equipped hotel will be most ably managed by Mr. J. B. Wistar, for many years with the Hotel Brunswick, New York. Special rates for families and season guests. Tourists must not forget during their stay at the Thousand Island House while out fishing to enjoy one of the famous Island Dinners.

CENTRAL PARK.

CENTRAL PARK is one of those choice spots in nature whose charms never appeal in vain to the lover of beautiful scenery. The Park lies on a projecting point of the mainland, midway between Thousand Island Park and Alexandria Bay. Beautiful groves invite one to rest in their shade; pleasant walks tempt one to saunter through the lovely glades and enjoy the rest and quiet of this peaceful place. A fine roadway leads to the mainland and affords delightful drives in the country.

CENTRAL PARK AND THE STEAMER "ST. LAWRENCE."

The Central Park Hotel, an attractive and homelike house, stands on the margin of the river in the midst of mighty forest trees. Beech, oak, maple, pine and hemlock trees spread their shade over the capacious grounds and fill the air with fragrance and delicious coolness. Broad verandas command an unobstructed view of the majestic river and afford unbounded enjoyment to guests who can sit here and leisurely survey the wondrously beautiful panorama.

The conveniences for boating and fishing at Central Park have no superior on the river. Fishing parties will be provided with every requisite for a fishing excursion; boats with experienced oarsmen are obtainable at all times. Everything needed for the popular outdoor sports, such as lawn tennis, croquet, etc., will be found here. Telegraph and telephone connection.

"THE WHITE SQUADRON."

The steamer "St. Lawrence," which is shown in the illustration on this page, at the Central Park dock, is one of the fleet of steamers owned and operated by the Thousand Island Steamboat Company, known collectively as the "White Squadron." Reference to these steamers is made on page 70. The fleet consists of ten steamers, namely: the "Empire State," capacity 1000; "St. Lawrence," capacity 860; new steamer "America," capacity 600; "Islander," capacity 500; "Jessie Bain," capacity 150; "J. F. Maynard," capacity 125; "Pierrepont," capacity 420; "Princess Louise," capacity 240; "Lorelei," capacity 125, and "Junita," capacity 45.

The "Empire State," "St. Lawrence," "America" and "Islander" are electrically lighted, and each has a powerful electric searchlight.

The "America" is of steel frame and hull, to match the "St. Lawrence." It is finished in carved wood, luxuriously furnished, and illuminated with 250 incandescent electric lights. Its searchlight (1,000,000 candle power) is the most powerful that can be used for the purpose. Among other unique features the wheels deserve special mention. Through panels of heavy plate glass the revolutions of the feathering bucket wheels may be watched, and at night varicolored electric lights placed within the paddle boxes, illuminate the spray and splash from the wheels, producing a novel and fascinating sight.

These steamers make also the following daily excursions, calling at Central Park: The famous Island Ramble every afternoon; the wonderful electric searchlight trip every evening, and the trip to Kingston, Ont., daily, except Sundays. Price fifty cents each trip.

SITUATED IN THE MIDST OF THE THOUSAND ISLANDS OF THE RIVER ST. LAWRENCE.

ALEXANDRIA BAY is one of the most famous and fascinating summer resorts in America, and is, without doubt, the loveliest river resort in the world. It is the gem of all the resorts in the Thousand Island region. In the immediate vicinity of hundreds of lovely islands, upon which the owners have erected their beautiful summer homes, its situation is not surpassed by that of any other resort in America. Its elegant and unrivalled hotel accommodations, its location and its many unequalled attractions, all combine to render it the most popular of summer resorts. Thousands of people from all parts of the world visit this place annually, and it is the place of all places in which one delights to linger, enjoying as one may the beauties of the wonderful Thousand Islands, the famous fishing, the pure air for which this region is noted, the delightful society, and the exhilarating pastime of boating.

Alexandria Bay has hotel accommodations now for upwards of two thousand people. The beauties of this place and the fame of its wonderful fishing grounds have been known and appreciated for many years. In the early part of the present century, before the days of the

ALEXANDRIA BAY.

railroad and steamboat, people journeyed by stage to Alexandria Bay to enjoy the delightful climate and famous fishing. It was visited by the celebrated statesmen and men prominent in the commercial and political world of that day.

In 1848 the first hotel, for the accommodation of tourists and fishermen, was erected, and from this small beginning the present great resort has grown. Water life is seen in perfection, and at its best, at Alexandria Bay. Hundreds of row-boats, canoes, sailing yachts, steam yachts, and various other craft of all kinds congregate at Alexandria Bay daily, making this place their headquarters. Many of the island residents in the vicinity of Alexandria Bay have magnificent steam yachts, fitted and furnished in the most luxurious style. Others have sailing yachts or row-boats, which offer a pleasant and easy means for the islanders to reach Alexandria Bay to enjoy the evening festivities at the principal hotels, where hops or grand balls are given nearly every evening during the season, the music being especially fine.

The illuminations at night at Alexandria Bay are strikingly beautiful. Electric and colored lights in profusion illuminate the hotels and cottages, and the effect on the water, with its myriad of shimmering reflections, is grand and beautiful.

The view from the verandas of the hotels broadens into a magnificent panorama of the countless features of the St. Lawrence River scenery. The Royal Mail Line of steamers, en route to and from Toronto, Montreal, Quebec and the River Saguenay, ride by in stately majesty. At intervals the steamers of the "White Squadron," to and from Clayton, Cape Vincent and Kingston, and daily lines of steamers to Clayton, Morristown, Brockville, Ogdensburg, and various other ports along the river, pass in review as they speed along on their way from resort to resort or from the Great Lakes to the Lower St. Lawrence.

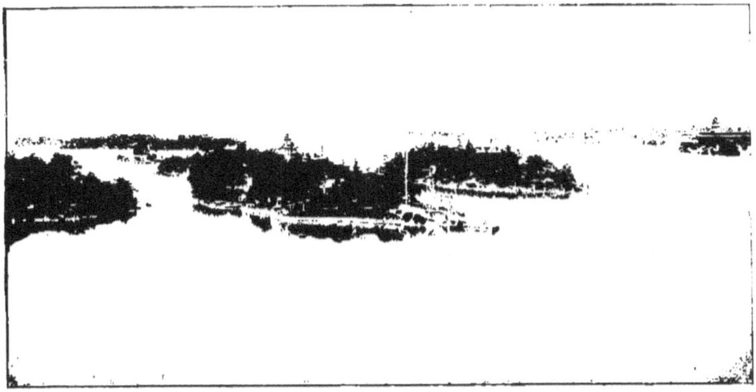

THOUSAND ISLANDS—NEAR ALEXANDRIA BAY.

Alexandria Bay is a favorite port for taking the Richelieu & Ontario Navigation Company's steamers for Montreal. Many passengers who arrive at Clayton on the Steamboat Express, prefer to go from Clayton to Alexandria Bay by a steamer of the Thousand Island Steamboat Company, and there change to the Richelieu Line steamers, as the steamers of the Thousand Island Steamboat Company, en route from Clayton to Alexandria Bay, pass through the most interesting portion of the St. Lawrence.

Alexandria Bay is one of the favorite resorts on the St. Lawrence River for fishermen. The luncheon put up at the hotels at this point is delicious and satisfying, and fully carries out the idea expressed in the description of the fishing trip on page 72 of this book. The oarsmen at Alexandria Bay are expert and courteous. Particular attention is given by the hotel proprietors to all minor details pertaining to fishing parties and island picnics.

ENTRANCE TO THE LOST CHANNEL.

THE CROSSMON, ALEXANDRIA BAY, N. Y.

THE PIONEER OF SUMMER RESORT HOTELS ON THE ST. LAWRENCE.

THE old Crossman House, under the same management as the new, had for over a quarter of a century been the resort of all fishing parties and tourists visiting Alexandria Bay. During this time, numbering, as it did, among its guests such prominent gentlemen as Governor Seward, Martin Van Buren, John Van Buren, Silas Wright, Frank Blair, Preston King, Gen. Dick Taylor, Rev. Dr. George Bethune, and many others, the house acquired a national reputation, which, owing to the elegant entertainment and careful attention paid to the guests by the proprietor and his estimable wife, was well deserved, and has ever since been maintained. As the wonderful beauties of this region became known throughout the land, and the influx of visitors during the summer season, ever increasing, began to assume its present gigantic proportions, the proprietor, to keep pace with the times and to relieve in a measure the pressure for hotel accommodations, determined in 1872 to erect a new hotel. The new Crossmon, as the illustration shows, is an elegant five-story building, constructed in the most substantial manner, and is unsurpassed in arrangement and pleasing effect by any hotel on the St. Lawrence. It is most charmingly situated close to the river on the north, with the little gem of a bay, from which the village takes its name, on the east, thus having two water sides. The south side of the hotel fronts the principal street of the village, which gives the hotel, in reality, two fronts with their entrances: the one being towards the river, where boat passengers enter, and the other on the street, where carriages are the mode of conveyance. The irregular formation of the rock foundation upon which the building stands allows the hotel to be five stories high at one end and four stories at the other. It has verandas around the second and third stories, and is topped by seven towers. The grounds about the hotel consisting of three acres, are nicely graded, having a tennis court, etc., and at

the Crossmon docks plenty of good boats are always in readiness for fishing parties. The hotel will accommodate 300 guests. It is supplied with gas, water, electric bells, etc.; has telegraph office, and the table service will be found all that could be desired. A most pleasing feature, in which the Crossmon has always taken a leading part, is in the display of lanterns at night. No visitor who has ever witnessed the dazzling effect of hundreds of colored lights arranged amidst the shrubbery or along the margin of the still waters, as viewed from a boat, will ever forget the beauty of the spectacle. The majority of the most ornate and costly island properties, which have made the Thousand Islands so famous, are located in the immediate vicinity of the Crossmon. This house has for many years been a favorite summering place with the distinguished representatives of several foreign nations resident at Washington.

WESTMINSTER PARK.

SOME of the most prominent gentlemen of the Presbyterian denomination, noting the wonderful beauties of the lower portion of Wellsley Island, and with the idea (which has proved so true) that where Nature had done so much, art could easily produce perfection, met together in 1878, and effected the organization of the Westminster Park Association, which association is regularly chartered under the laws of the State of New York. The association purchased the lower portion of Wellsley Island, directly opposite Alexandria Bay, which is only one-fourth of a mile distant. The portion of the island included in the park grounds consists of 200 acres of ground, in formation an irregular neck of upland, rising to a mean elevation above the water of about forty feet, with rounded heights lifted to extremes of 150 feet. From these summits, which are reached by easy slopes, either in carriages or on foot, the whole group of the Thousand Islands, extending along the river for a distance of twenty miles, are brought into full view. Nothing of the camp meeting enters into this association. A large portion of the park has been subdivided into building lots, many of which were quickly purchased by people from different sections of the country, and tasteful cottages erected thereon, making delightful summer homes for their occupants.

NOBBY ISLAND—ARBOR.

There are still many desirable lots which may be purchased at reasonable prices. Special inducements are offered to persons desiring to purchase lots and build cottages. Application for information should be made to Hon. A. Cornwall, President, Alexandria Bay, N. Y., or to G. R. Hanford, Secretary, Watertown, N. Y.

WESTMINSTER PARK, NEAR ALEXANDRIA BAY.

THE THOUSAND ISLANDS.

NAMES OF ISLANDS AND OWNERS.

LINLITHGOW.

THE rapid development of the Thousand Island Region, the loveliest river resort in the world, is largely due to the fact that, aside from the peerless beauty of the natural scenery, many of the more eligible islands have been purchased by prominent persons, who have improved them and erected thereon picturesque summer residences, in many cases even elegant and luxurious ones. A few of these delightful island homes are illustrated on the pages of this book, and will give an idea of the refinement and taste which characterize them, and the charm of gaiety and life which they lend to this fascinating region. The pursuit of rest and recreation is the one aim of the dwellers in these water-environed homes; and when the community is settled for the summer, a more animated picture of genuine enjoyment can not be found. Below is given a list, alphabetically arranged, of the names of the principal islands, together with the names of their owners:

Alice—Two acres....................................Col. A. J. Casse, New York.
Allegheny Point (main-land)—Two acres..............J. S. Lancy, Cleveland, O.
Anjier—One acre....................................J. B. Hamilton, New York.
Antoine—One-quarter acre...........................Mrs. Sarah and George Walter, Alexandria Bay, N. Y.
Arcadia and Ina—Five acres.........................S. A. Briggs, Pasadena, Cal.
Atlantis—Twenty-five acres.........................Dr. G. W. Bailey, Elizabeth, N. J.
Aviglon—One acre...................................Mrs. E. D. Becra, Washington, D. C.

Basswood—One acre....Thos. A. Gillespie, Pittsburg, Pa.
Bay Side—One acre....H. F. Mosher, Watertown, N. Y.
Bay View—Two acres....J. Y. Chapin, Ogdensburg, N. Y.
Belden Cottage (head of Round Island)....Hon. J. J. Belden, Syracuse, N. Y.
Belle Vista Lodge (main-land)—Five acres....Wm. Chisholm, Cleveland, O.
Belle Isle—Ten acres....Dr. Bell, Ogdensburg, N. Y.
Beera—One-half acre....Mrs. E. D. Beera, Washington, D. C.
Berkshire—Twenty acres....Hon. S. G. Pope, Ogdensburg, N. Y.
Bill—One acre....Rev. Walter Ayrault, Geneva, N. Y.
Bingham—Seven acres....Andrew Devine, Washington, D. C., and Fred. J. Warburton, New York.
Birch—Seven acres....W. J. Lewis, Pittsburg, Pa.
Bixby Point....F. M. Bixby, Jr., New York.
Bluff or Crawford -Seventy-five acres....E. R. Washburn, New York.
Bok View—Four acres....J. Y. Chapin, Ogdensburg, N. Y.
Bonnie Castle Point (main-land)—Fifteen acres....Mrs. J. G. Holland, New York.
Bonnie Eyrie (Wells's Island)....Mrs. Peck, Boonville, N. Y.
Boscobel—One-half acre....G. L. Hopkins, Kansas.
Brooklyn Heights (foot of Round Island)....C. A. Johnson, Brooklyn, N. Y.
Brown's Bay Point (Wells's Island)—Twenty acres....Mrs. Mary Friedman, New York.
Buffalo Point (Wells's Island)—One acre....Mrs. —— Sherman, Buffalo, N. Y.
Calumet—Three acres....Chas. G. Emery, New York.
Calumet—One-half acre....Oliver H. Green, Boston, Mass.
Camp Royal (Wells's Island)—Three acres....Rev. R. H. Pullman, Baltimore, Md.
Castle Rest—Three acres....Geo. M. Pullman, Chicago, Ill.
Cedar—One acre....J. M. Curtis, Cleveland, O.
Cedar—Thirty-five acres....M. J. Phillips, Cedar Island Hotel.
Cement Point (head Grindstone Island)—Eighty acres..W. F. Ford, Lafargeville, N. Y.
Center—One acre....E. R. Washburn, New York.
Charrie — ....J. W. Taylor and L. Hasbrouck, Ogdensburg, N. Y.
Chillom—Four acres....Mrs. A. H. Grunolt, Pittsburg, Pa.
Chippewa Point—Eighty acres....Chippewa Investment Co.
Cleopatra—Three acres....H. R. Heath, Brooklyn, N. Y.
Clinton's No. 1—Fifteen acres....N. Scely, New York.
Clinton's No. 2—Three acres....N. Scely, New York.
Cloud Rest—Four acres....Mrs. A. H. Grunolt, Pittsburg, Pa.

BONNIE CASTLE, THE ELEGANT SUMMER RESIDENCE OF MRS. J. G. HOLLAND.

Comfort—Two acres....................................A. E. Clark, Chicago, Ill.
Coral Isle—Two acres....................................C. Wolfe, New York.
Craig Side (Wells's Island)....................................H. A. Laughlin, Pittsburg, Pa.
Crescent Cottage (main-land)—Ten acres....................................Mrs. John T. Howe, Troy, N. Y.
Cuba—One acre....................................Michael Chauncey, Brooklyn, N. Y.
Dark—Three acres....................................Wm. H. Harrison, Canton, N. Y.
Davitts One-quarter acre....................................H. G. Davitts, New York.
Deer—Forty acres....................................Geo. D. Miller, Albany, N. Y.
Delft Haven (Wells's Island)—Two acres....................................Gen'l J. B. Van Petten, Claverack, N. Y.
Deshler—Fifteen acres....................................W. G. Deshler, Columbus, O.
Devil's Oven—One acre....................................H. R. Heath, Brooklyn, N. Y.
Dewey—Three acres....................................E. W. Dewey, New York.
Dinglespiel—Six acres....................................Hugo Meyer, New York.
Douglass—Five acres....................................Douglas Miller, New Haven, Conn.
Edanista (Wells's Island)—Two acres....................................Thomas Wilson, M.D., Claverack, N. Y.
Edgewood Park (main-land)—Thirty acres....................................J. P. Sampson, Cleveland, O.
Edgewood Point (mainland)—One acre....................................G. C. Martin, Watertown, N. Y.
Elephant Rock—One-eighth acre....................................T. C. Chittenden, Watertown, N. Y.

DIXIE—SUMMER HOME OF COL. D. W. WRENN.

Ella—One-fourth acre. R. E. Hungerford, Watertown, N. Y.
Elsinore—Seven acres. Prof. Wm. McAfee, Claverack, N. Y.
Ethelridge (head of Round Island). Dr. Geo. D. Wheelen, Syracuse, N. Y.
Excelsior Group—Five acres. C. S. Goodwin, New York.
Fair View Park — Three acres. Jas. A. Cheney, Syracuse, N. Y.
Fairy Land—Twenty acres. Chas. H. Hayden and Wm. B. Hayden, Columbus, O.
Felseneck (Wells's Island) Two acres. Prof. A.G. Hopkins, Clinton, N.Y.

Fern—One acre....................................N. & J. Winslow, Watertown, N. Y.
Fern Cliff (Wells's Island)....................................Latimer Bros., New York.
Fisher's Landing (main-land)—Two acres....................................Mrs. R. Gurnee and Miss Newton, Omar, N. Y.
Flora Island—One-half acre....................................Flora Wilson, Watertown, N. Y.
Florence—Two acres....................................H. S. Chandler, New York.
Frederick's—Two acres....................................C. L. Frederick, Carthage, N. Y.
Gipsy....................................J. M. Curtis, Cleveland, O.
Goose—Two acres....................................E. S. Hicks, Brooklyn, N. Y.
Goose—One-quarter acre....................................Mrs. L. Simonds, Watertown, N. Y.
Governor's—Two acres....................................C. G. Emery, New York.
Grenell—One hundred acres....................................E. P. Gardner, Syracuse, N. Y.; Jno. Rogers and Mrs. Julia W. Haskell, Passaic, N. J.; L. J. Burdett, Otsego Camp Club, Caleb Clark, Cooperstown, N. Y.; Miss E. M. Griswold, Adams, N. Y.; Wesley M. Rich, Jos. Sayles, Rome, N. Y.; Reuben Fuller, Chas. Ellis, Clayton, N. Y.; Chas. Chickering, Copenhagen, N. Y.; C. O. Pratt, Syracuse, N. Y.
Half-way—Three acres....................................Frank Chapman, Ogdensburg, N. Y.
Harmony—One-fourth acre....................................Mrs. Celia Burger, Syracuse, N. Y.

Hart's—Five acres....................................Hon. E. K. Hart, Albion, N. Y.
Hatnell Point—One-half acre..........................Dr. H. D. Payne, Watertown, N. Y.
Hay's Cottage (head of Round Island).................Jacob Hays, New York.
Helena—One-half acre.................................Mrs. Helen Taylor, New York.
Helen's—Ten acres....................................O. G. Staples, Washington, D. C.
Hen—One-quarter acre.................................W. F. Morgan, New York.
Hill Crest (Wells's Island)—One acre.................Gen'l J. H. Shields, Washington, D. C.
Holloway's Point (main-land)—One acre................Nathan Holloway, Clayton, N. Y.
Hopewell Hall (Wells's Island)—One hundred acres....W. C. Browning, New York.
Hub—One-half acre....................................G. W. Best, Oswego, N. Y.
Hub Clarke...W. S. Clarke, New York.
Huguenot—Two acres...................................Levi Hasbrouck, Ogdensburg, N. Y.
Idlewild—Four acres..................................Mrs. R. H. Eggleston, New York.
Indolence—One acre...................................Mrs. Elizabeth Skinner, Brooklyn, N. Y.
Ingleside..Mrs. G. B. Marsh, La Porte, Ind.
Ingle Nook—Five acres................................G. B. Shepard, Ogdensburg, N. Y.
Island Frances—Three acres...........................Mrs. W. H. Weston, New York.
Island Gracie—One acre. J. T. Savey, Cleveland, O.
Island Home—One acre. Mrs. S. D. Hungerford, Adams, N. Y.
Island Kate—One acre. G. W. Lascell, Lynn, Mass.
Island Mary—Two acres. Wm. L. Palmer, Carthage, Dak.
Island Royal—One acre. Royal E. Dean, New York.
Islandula—One-quarter acre. Mrs. Evelyn Daws, Buffalo, N. Y.
Isle Imperial—One acre. G. T. Rafferty, Pittsburg, Pa.
Isle of Pines—Two acres. R. McCord, New York.

ISLAND ROYAL.

Jersey Heights (Grenell Park). Mrs. L. L. Carlisle, Newark, N. J.
Jolly Oaks (Wells's Island)—Two acres. Prof. A. H. Brown, Dr. N. D. Ferguson, Jno. Norton, O. T. Green, Carthage, N. Y.; Hon. W. W. Butterfield, Redwood, N. Y.
Josephine—Two acres. Mrs. A. M. Kenyon, Watertown, N. Y.
Keewayden (main-land)—Ten acres. J. W. Jackson, Plainfield, N. J.
Keplar's Point (main-land)...........Frank Ritter, Rochester, N. Y.
Killien's Point (main-land)—One acre..—— Killien, Lockport, N. Y.
Kittie Harrison—One-half acre........J. B. Hamilton, N. Y.
Kit Grafton—One-half acre............Mrs. S. L. George, Watertown, N. Y.
Lady of the Lake—Three acres.........Mrs. S. H. White, Alexandria Bay, N. Y.
Lakewood (Wells's Island)—Twenty acres...H. R. Heath, Brooklyn, N. Y.
Lattimer—One-quarter acre............Mrs. C. E. Lattimer, Syracuse, N. Y.
Ledges...............................Mrs. Sarah E. K. Hudson, New York.
Lindenhof (main-land)—One acre.......................Frank Ritter, Rochester, N. Y.
Lindner's—One acre...................................Jno. Lindner, Jersey City, N. J.
Lindsley—One-quarter acre............................Mrs. L. B. H. Morrison, Erie, Pa.
Linlithgow—One-fourth acre...........................Mrs. R. A. Livingstone, New York.
Little Angel—One-eighth acre.........................W. A. Angel, Chicago, Ill.
Little Charm—One-eighth acre.........................Mrs. F. W. Barker, Alexandria Bay, N. Y.
Little Delight—One acre..............................Louis W. Morrison, New York.
Little Fraud—One-half acre...........................R. H. Pease, San Francisco, Cal.
Little Gem—One-half acre.............................Mrs. Fred. W. Thomson, Syracuse, N. Y.
Little Lehigh—One acre...............................W. A. & Rollin H. Wilbur, Bethlehem, Pa.

Little Round Island—Five acres........................John B. Cass and Audrey J. Mooney.
Little Witherby—One-half acre........................Mrs. L. E. B. Bow, Wilburnham, Mass.
Lackey Point (main-land)............................Geo. C. Ball, Chicago, Ill.
Lone Pine—One acre.................................W. M. Comstock and W. Rulison.
Long Rock—One acre.................................W. F. Wilson, Watertown, N. Y.
Long Branch Point (main-land)—Ten acres.............Mrs. C. E. Clark, Watertown, N. Y.
Lookout—Two acres..................................Thos. H. Borden, New York.
Lotos Land—Seven acres.............................G. H. Robinson, New York.
Louisiana Point (Wells's Island)....................Hon. D. C. LaBatt, New Orleans, La.
Madeleine—One acre.................................J. B. Hamilton, New York.
Manhattan—Five acres...............................J. L. Hasbrouck and Hon. J. C. Spencer, New York.
Maple—Ten acres....................................Mrs. Jos. Atwell, Syracuse, N. Y.
Maple—Six acres....................................J. L. Hasbrouck, New York.
Manzanita—Twelve acres.............................J. G. Knapp, Ogdensburg, N. Y.
Melrose Lodge (Cherry Island)—Nine acres............A. B. Pullman, Chicago, Ill.
Minnesetah—One and one-half acres...................Mrs. A. H. Lord, Ogdensburg, N. Y.
Minnow...Rev. W. W. Welch, Medina, N. Y.

NOBBY ISLAND—RUSTIC BRIDGE.

Murray Hill Park—380 acres. Thousand Island Investment Co.
Myers—Five acres. P. T. Dodge, New York.
Nemah-Bin—Two acres. Jas. H. Oliphant, Brooklyn, N. Y.
Netts—One acre. Wm. B. Hayden, Columbus, O.
Nirvana—Ten acres. Dr. J. H. Brownlow, Ogdensburg, N. Y.
Nobby—Three acres. H. R. Heath, Brooklyn, N. Y.
No Name—One-quarter acre. J. B. Hamilton, New York.
Number 3—One acre. C. L. Frederick, Carthage, N. Y.
Nut Shell—Four acres. Mrs. C. W. Crossmon, Alexandria Bay, N. Y.
Oak—525 acres. St. Lawrence Improvement Co.

Occident and Orient—Three acres.....................E. R. Washburn, New York.
One Tree—One-half acre.............................Rev. M. W. Chase, Ogdensburg, N. Y.
Oriole—Two acres...................................Miss H. I. Pope, Alexandria Bay, N. Y.
Ours—Three acres...................................Mrs. M. Carter, Poughkeepsie, N. Y.
Owl's Nest—One-half acre...........................Rev. D. A. Ferguson, Hammond, N. Y.
Palisades (Wells's Island)—Seven acres..............Mrs. A. C. Beckwith, Utica, N. Y.
Peel—Two acres.....................................Mrs. Sarah Lake and M. Parker, Watertown, N. Y.
Pike—One acre......................................A. F. Dickinson, New York.
Pine or Beckwith—Nine acres.........................C. G. Emery, New York.
Pine—Five acres....................................J. B. Hamilton, New York.
Point Avelon—Three acres...........................Geo. L. Ryon, Ogdensburg, N. Y.
Point Lookout—One acre.............................Miss L. J. Bullock, Adams, N. Y.
Point Marguerite (main-land)—Thirty acres...........Mrs. E. Anthony, N. Y.
Point Vivian (main-land)—Ten acres..................Rezot Tozer, J. J. Kinney, F.O. Hungerford, Geo. Ivers, Evan's Mills, N. Y., and others.
Ponemah—Two acres..................................J. C. Howard, Ogdensburg, N. Y.
Porter's—One-half acre.............................C. G. Porter, Watertown, N. Y.
Rabbit—Twelve acres................................Marian Holmes, Morristown, N. Y.

Ragnarock—Two acres ....S. S. Thompson, Elizabeth, N. J.
Resort—Three acres...................................W. J. Lewis, Pittsburg, Pa.
Rest Haven (Wells's Island)—One acre...............John Calkins, Alexandria Bay, N. Y.
Riverside (main-land)—One acre......................Jas. C. Lee, Oswegatchie, N. Y.
Robbins—Fifty acres..................................C. T. Emery, New York.
Rob Roy—Two acres....................................A. H. Greenwault, Pittsburg, Pa.
Rob Roy—Eight acres..................................Dr. J. R. Dixon, Ogdensburg, N. Y.
Rose Island—Two acres................................Hudson P. Rose, Cleveland, O.
Rock Island..United States Government Lighthouse.
St. Elmo—Three acres. Nathaniel W. Hunt, Brooklyn, N. Y.
St. Helena—Two acres. H. Stillman, Oswego, N. Y.
St. John's—Six acres. Hon. Chas. Donahue, New York.
St. Peter's—One-half acre. G. S. Dorwin, Ogdensburg, N. Y.
Schooner—Six acres. J. Norman, Whitehouse, N. Y.
Seven Isles—Five acres. Hon. Bradley Winslow, Watertown, N. Y.
Seven Oaks—Two acres. G. S. Dorwin, Ogdensburg, N. Y.

ST. ELMO ISLAND.

Shady Covert (Wells's Island)........................B. J. Maycock, Buffalo, N. Y.
Shady Ledge (foot of Round Island)...................Frank H. Taylor, Philadelphia, Pa.
Snug Harbor—Two acres................................E. L. Strong, Ogdensburg, N. Y.
Sophia—One-half acre.................................C. L. Frederick, Carthage, N. Y.
South Side...H. R. Clark, Jersey City, N. J.
Spinster—One-half acre...............................Lydia M. Hastings and Mary Ellen Campbell, Alexandria Bay, N. Y.
Sport—Four acres.....................................E. P. Wilbur, Bethlehem, Pa.
Spuyten Duyvil—One acre..............................Alice P. Sargent, New York.

FAIRY LAND—SUMMER HOME OF C. H. & W. B. HAYDEN.

Stanley Heights—Two acres.......................... H. R. Heath, Brooklyn, N. Y.
Stuyvesant Lodge.................................... J. T. Easton, Brooklyn, N. Y.
Summer Land—Ten acres.............................. Summer Land Association.
Sunbeam Group—One acre............................ Odd Fellows, Watertown, New York.
Sun Dew—One acre................................... C. M. Slanen, Paymaster U. S. Navy.
Sunnyside—Two acres................................ W. Stevenson, Sayre, Pa.
Sunnyside (Cherry Island)—Five acres............... Rev. Geo. H. Rockwell, Tarrytown, N. Y.
Sylvan and Moss—Three acres........................ S. T. Woolworth, Watertown, N. Y.
Tacony Point (Wells's Island)—One acre............. J. B. Hamilton, New York.
Two in Eel Bay—Two acres........................... Dr. E. L. Sargent, Watertown, N. Y.
Twin—One acre...................................... I. L. Huntington, Watertown, N. Y.
Valhalla—Two and one-half acres.................... G. S. Dorwin, Ogdensburg, N. Y.

WARNER'S ISLAND.

Vanderbilt—One acre................................ J. B. Hamilton, Brooklyn, N. Y.
Van Wagenen Cottage (head of Round Island)......... H. Van Wagenen, New York.
Vilula Point (main-land)—One-half acre............. Frank Dana, Alexandria Bay, N. Y.
Walton—Seven acres................................. G. H. Robinson, New York.
Warner—One acre.................................... Mrs. H. H. Warner, Rochester, N. Y.
Watch—One acre..................................... Mrs. Elizabeth Skinner, New York.
Watch—Eight acres.................................. W. M. Perkins, New York.
Wau Winet—One-half acre............................ C. E. Hill, Chicago, Ill.
Waving Branches (Wells's Island)................... D. C. Graham, Stone Mills, N. Y.; A. Snell, Lafargeville, N. Y.; J. Petrie, Watertown, N. Y.; J. B. Loucks, Lafargeville, N. Y.; Isaac Mitchell, L. Hughes, Stone Mills, N. Y.; L. Ainsworth, F. Smith, H. S. Tolles, Ira Traver, Watertown, N. Y.

Welcome—Three acres. W. C. Browning, New York.
West Point—W. C. Browning, New York.
West View Point (main-land) Thousand Island Club—One acre. Hon. S. G. Pope, Ogdensburg, N. Y.
Whitney—Colden, Rhine, Ga.
Wild Rose—One acre. Hon. W. G. Rose, Cleveland, O.
Wildwood (Wells's Island) — Two acres. Dan'l C. McEwen, Brooklyn, N. Y.
Windecot—One acre. W. F. Sudds, Gouverneur, N. Y.
Woodlands—Ten acres. Mrs. Alex. Mitchell, Milwaukee, Wis.
Wynoke—C. P. Olcott, Elizabeth, N. J.

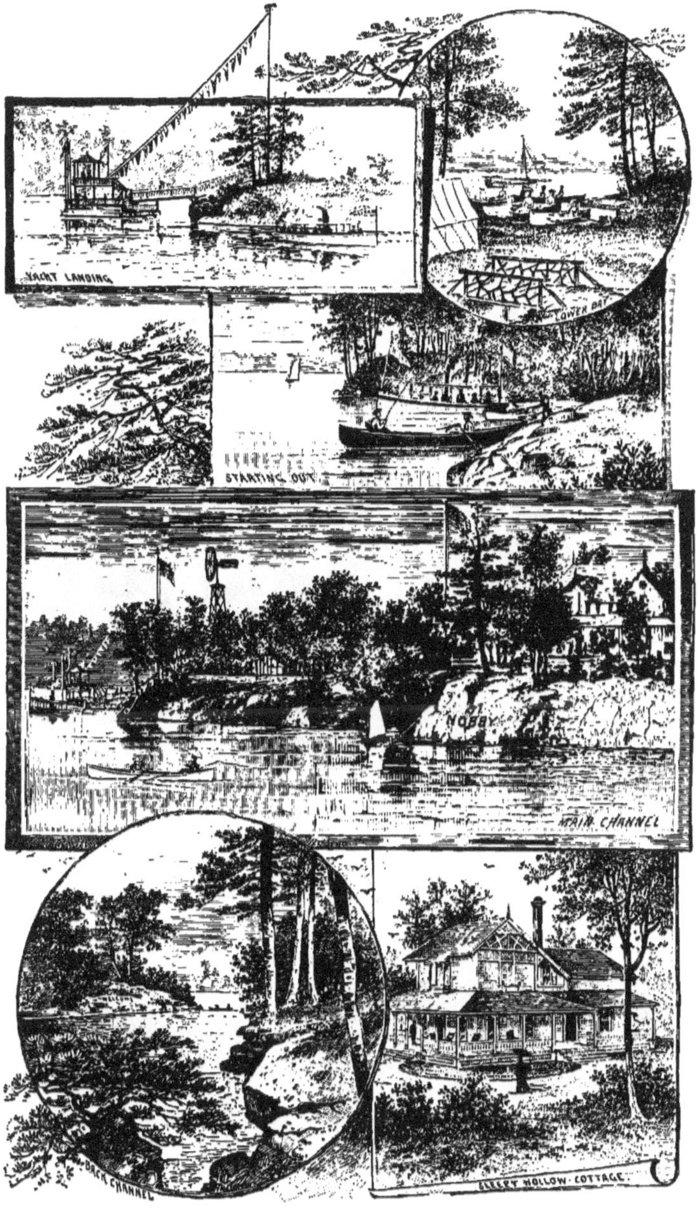

NOBBY ISLAND—THE SUMMER RESIDENCE OF H. R. HEATH, ESQ

CANOEING ON THE ST. LAWRENCE.

From "OUTING." Copyrighted.

PORTION OF A. C. A. CAMP, GRINDSTONE ISLAND, 1884.

CANOEING is one of the most exciting, as well as delightful, sports of water life on the River St. Lawrence, and this pastime is indulged in to a great extent among the Thousand Islands. An idea of the pleasures of the daring canoeist may be obtained from the illustrations on page 75, which are realistic scenes, and faithfully portray different positions of canoes of the American Canoe Association, full-rigged and under sail. These are actual scenes taken from the 1889 annual meet on the St. Lawrence River. The American Canoe Association, appreciating the many great advantages of the Thousand Island waters, have had several annual meets here.

From "OUTING." Copyrighted.

PORTION OF A. C. A. CAMP, SUGAR ISLAND, 1889.

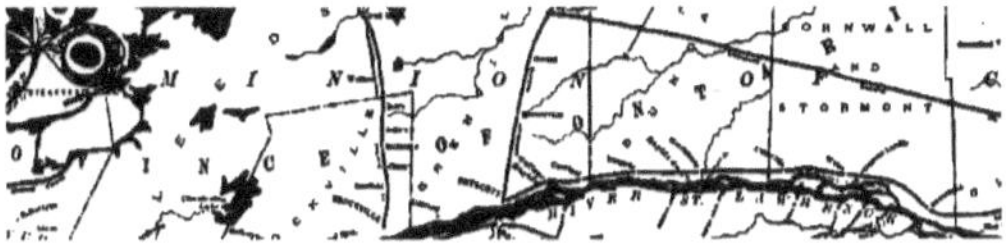
STORMONT

SHOOTING THE RAPIDS.

ON leaving Alexandria Bay by the palace day steamers of the Richelieu & Ontario Navigation Co's Royal Mail Line, the tourist enjoys a view of all the Thousand Islands, which, commencing at Cape Vincent, end at Brockville, or Morristown. The picturesqueness of this trip is almost indescribable. Although the islands are not as attractive as those between Clayton and Alexandria Bay, the scenery, generally speaking, is of a wild and interesting nature. The last of the Thousand Islands are called the Three Sisters from their resemblance to each other. They are situated equi-distant from each other and in nearly a direct line between Brockville—the terminus of the eastern division of the Canadian Pacific Railway—and Morristown, on the Rome, Watertown & Ogdensburg Railroad; and it has often been remarked, it seems as if Nature had placed them there as natural abutments of a bridge to connect these railway lines, which must eventually carry all the traffic from the Upper Ottawa Valley, the Hudson's Bay region and the far Northwest to the Atlantic seaboard. Brockville is called the Queen City of the St. Lawrence, and is the prettiest city between Montreal and Toronto. It received its name in honor of General Brock. The trip from Brockville or Morristown to Ogdensburg or Prescott is quickly made. Ogdensburg, called the Maple City on account of its beautiful foliage, is situated at the junction of the Oswegatchie and St. Lawrence Rivers. It is a curious sight here to notice the deep brown water of the Oswegatchie commingle with the clear green water of the St. Lawrence. Ogdensburg is a beautiful city. Besides being a very important railway centre, it is quite a place of resort for tourists, the excellent hotel accommodations and the beauties of the St. Lawrence and Oswegatchie presenting attractions which cannot well be resisted. Directly opposite is the Canadian city of Prescott, the terminus of the St. Lawrence and Ottawa Division of the Canadian Pacific Railway, and quite an important junction point.

DESCENDING THE RAPIDS.

The whole region in the vicinity of Prescott, Ogdensburg and below, is possessed of great historical interest, owing to the many battles fought in this section of the country between the French, English, Americans and Indians. History locates and describes these so well that an extended description of them here may be omitted. From Prescott to Morrisburg the sail is uneventful. Just below Morrisburg is Chrysler's Farm, where, in 1813, the Americans and English fought a battle.

R., W. & O. DOCK AT MORRISTOWN.

Soon after passing Morrisburg the increasing speed of the steamer indicates that the most exciting and fascinating portion of the St. Lawrence River is near at hand, and with eager expectancy the exhilarating, exciting and never-to-be-forgotten descent of the rapids is commenced.

The first rapid, or series of rapids, is known as the Long Sault. This is a continuous rapid for nine miles. The river is divided in the centre by an island. In former years the descent of this rapid was made through the south channel only, the north channel being considered too dangerous, but recent examinations have proved that either channel can be descended with safety. The south channel is very narrow, and the swiftness of the current is so great that a raft will drift nine miles in forty minutes, which, comparatively speaking, is as fast as the speed of the fastest steamboats in still water. The rapids of the Long Sault rush along at a speed of twenty miles per hour. The sensation while in this rapid is unlike that when descending its successors. The Long Sault reminds one of the ocean in a storm, except that the swift going downhill in a steamboat is, to most persons, an entirely new experience, and the steep descent is fully realized if one has neglected to take hold of some stationary portion of the steamer. The terrific roar and seething violence of the river are intensely fascinating. Great nerve and power are required in piloting the steamer so as to keep her straight ahead and in the channel, as a slight deviation would turn the steamer sideways, in which case she would be instantly capsized and submerged; but the discipline and system of the Richelieu & Ontario Navigation Company's steamers are so perfect that such a calamity is utterly impossible. While descending the rapids a tiller is attached to the rudder as an extra precaution, and the force required to keep the steamer straight in her course is so great that four men are kept constantly at the wheel and two at the tiller.

A SKIFF IN THE LACHINE RAPIDS.

After leaving the Long Sault Rapids we pass several Canadian villages, and enter Lake St. Francis, which begins near Cornwall and extends a distance of forty miles to Coteau du Lac. Just below this village are the Coteau Rapids, then come the Cedars, Split Rock and Cascade Rapids. The passage through the Cedars is very exciting. There is a peculiar motion of the steamer, which, in descending, seems like settling down as she glides from one ledge of rocks to another. This is supposed to be owing to the existence of a strong undercurrent. It was in these rapids that a detachment of three hundred men, under Gen. Amherst, was lost in 1759.

R. & O. N. CO. STEAMER AT QUEBEC.

The passage of the Split Rock Rapids is full of interest and excitement, intensified by the apparent danger in the steamer's course as she comes near to a threatening ledge of rock. Danger seems imminent. The speed of the vessel and the character of the surroundings add little pleasure to one's reflections; but at the proper moment the skillful pilot causes the boat to

SHOOTING THE LACHINE RAPIDS.

swerve a little, and the dangerous ledge is safely passed. The next series of rapids, from their resemblance to a succession of short leaping falls, are very appropriately named the Cascades. After passing the Cascade Rapids the steamer enters Lake St. Louis, a broadened expanse of the St. Lawrence at the *embouchure* of the Ottawa River.

The quiet passage of twelve miles through Lake St. Louis serves to stimulate curiosity in regard to the Lachine Rapids, which are nine miles from Montreal, and are the last rapids of importance on the St. Lawrence. The velocity and fierceness of the current are so great that to avoid the rapids the Lachine Canal was constructed, and during stormy weather is used for passage from Lachine to Montreal. The Lachine Rapids are the most difficult of navigation of any on the St. Lawrence. Baptiste, an Indian pilot, has made it his business for over forty years to pilot steamers down these rapids. During the summer season he is exclusively in the service of the passenger steamers shooting these rapids, and under his skillful guidance there is no danger in passing through Lachine Rapids. But if the day is stormy, or a south wind prevails, the tourist leaves the rapids behind him with a grateful sense of relief, especially if his point of observation has been the bow of the boat. With rocks ahead and rocks beneath, asserting their presence by impudent thumps against the steamer's keel, the experience is seasoned with just enough thought of danger to give it zest; and when one is assured beyond doubt that there is not the least real danger the excitement becomes a pleasure. The pilots of the Richelieu & Ontario Navigation Company (Royal Mail Line), a different set of whom are employed for each series of rapids, have made their business the study of their lives. They are in the exclusive service of this company, and know every current and rock in their respective portions of the voyage

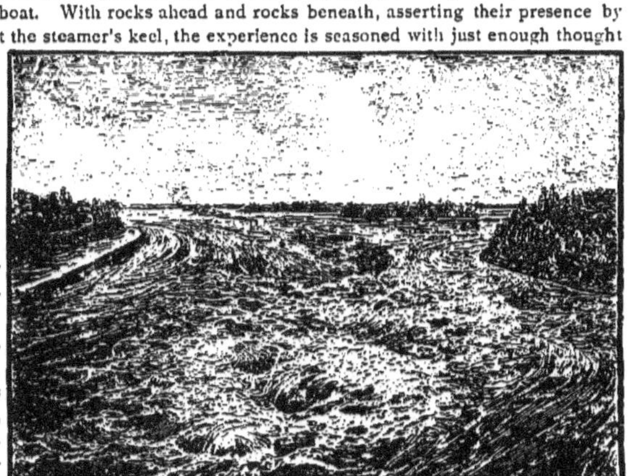

IN THE LONG SAULT RAPIDS.

CITY OF MONTREAL.

MONTREAL, the metropolis of British North America, stands at the head of ocean steamship navigation and is situated on an island of the same name. Mount Royal, which gives the city its name, affords beautiful drives and views. Montreal has many attractions in its beautiful churches and public buildings.

The French Parish Church, or Cathedral of "Notre Dame," is capable of seating 10,000 people. Its two large towers are 220 feet high, and command a view of the city and surrounding country, the vista extending for miles in all directions. The view of the St. Lawrence from

ALONG THE RIVER FRONT, MONTREAL.

the right tower is especially fine. This tower contains the immense bell, weighing nearly 30,000 pounds, which is used also for the fire alarm. The left tower contains a musical chime of bells. The interior decorations of this church are exceedingly fine, and include numerous valuable paintings and statues. The other churches in Montreal noted for beauty of design and decoration are the Church of the Gesu, the English Cathedral, and several Presbyterian churches. The new Roman Catholic Cathedral, in process of erection, will be after the style of St. Peter's, Rome. The principal buildings of Montreal are noted for the substantial manner in which they are constructed, and for their architectural beauty. Among these may be noted the Court House, new Post-Office, Merchants' Exchange, Mechanics' Institute, Bank of Montreal, Bank of British North America, Molson's Bank, Merchants' Bank, Albert Buildings, Custom House and many others. Among the other objects of interest may be placed the Bonsecours Market, the Government House, Hotel Dieu Hospital, McGill College, and various other institutions of learning, the different nunneries, the statue of Her Majesty, Nelson's Monument, the Young Men's Christian Association Building, Mount Royal Cemetery, and the Wonderful Reservoirs, excavated out of solid rock, located 206 feet above the river and twenty-five feet deep. The drives around Montreal are exceedingly pleasant, the enjoyment of the beautiful scenery being enhanced by the splendid carriage roads, which have few equals in this country. The wharves of the city of Montreal are not equaled in America.

CITY OF QUEBEC.

QUEBEC—LOWER TOWN.

KENT GATE—QUEBEC.

QUEBEC, founded in 1608, is one of the oldest cities in America, and also one of the most interesting. In population and maritime commerce it is third among the chief cities of Canada, ranking next after Montreal and Toronto. The form of the city is nearly a triangle, the Plains of Abraham forming the base, and the Rivers St. Lawrence and St. Charles the sides. The city is divided into two parts, known as the upper town and the lower town. The upper town is strongly fortified, and includes within its limits the citadel of Cape Diamond, which covers the entire summit of the promontory and embraces an area of more than forty acres. St. John and St. Louis, suburbs, are also included in the upper town, although outside the line of fortification. The citadel occupies a commanding site 345 feet above the river, and is the strongest fortress in America. Quebec is pre-eminently the stronghold of Canada, and is called the "key of the St. Lawrence." The citadel, from its great elevation, affords a fine view of the river and surrounding country. The line of fortifications inclosing the citadel and upper town is nearly three miles in length. There were formerly five gates, now, however dismantled, opening from the city, three of which, Prescott, Palace and

Hope gates, communicate with lower town, and two, St. Louis and St. John gates, communicate with the suburbs of the same names. Dufferin Terrace, in upper town, is a well-constructed promenade, occupying the site of the old castle of St. Louis. It is the fashionable and favorite place of resort for the people of Quebec. Its elevation, 245 feet above the river, affords a splendid view of the lower town, the fertile island of Orleans and the shipping at anchor. From the ramparts between St. Louis and St. John gates, and also from the balconies of the University, the prospect is almost without a rival. The lower town, the oldest part of the city, is built upon the narrow strip of land encircling the promontory, from Cape Diamond to the mouth of the St. Charles River. Its limits embrace the suburbs of St. Roch, St. Sauveur and Boisseauville. The streets are very irregular. The activity of the city centers in lower town and St. Roch.

Eight miles below the city are the celebrated Falls of Montmorenci. As is well known, these falls are only fifty feet wide, but descend in a perpendicular sheet more than 250 feet. The place is much frequented. The Chaudiere Falls on the river Chaudiere, nine miles above Quebec, and the Falls of St. Anne on the river of the same name, twenty-four miles below the city, are wild and beautiful, both in themselves and in their immediate neighborhood. Among the objects of interest in and about the city, besides those already mentioned, are the Governor's Garden, Grand Battery, English Cathedral, French Cathedral, Hotel Dieu Convent and Hospital, the University, Jail, Court House, City Hall, Custom House, Lunatic Asylum at Beaufort, Wolfe's Monument, Plains of Abraham, where Wolfe and Montcalm fell; Lake St. Charles and Lake Beauport, abounding with trout, new fortifications at Pt. Levis, etc. The churches and conventual establishments are principally in the upper town, the mercantile buildings in the lower.

CITY OF OTTAWA.

THE trip down the St. Lawrence and through Canada is incomplete without a visit to Ottawa. Since the day that Ottawa was designated by Her Majesty as the capital of the Dominion it has continued to increase in prosperity and population, until now it ranks as one of the most important and interesting cities in British North America. The public buildings erected here by the Government for the use of the Dominion Parliament and the different department offices of the general Government, reflect great credit both upon the Government liberal enough to provide for their erection and the architect capable of designing such models of beauty. The buildings are located upon a bluff overlooking the Ottawa River and its valley, and the view from this spot is one of the finest in Canada. The library, one of the largest, most interesting and valuable in the world, contains over 100,000 volumes. It has a large building of superb design and finish, devoted to its exclusive use, and to many a visit to this library will well repay a

RIDEAU FALLS, OTTAWA.

RIDEAU HALL, RESIDENCE OF HIS EXCELLENCY, THE GOVERNOR-GENERAL OF CANADA.

trip to Ottawa. The location and design of both buildings and grounds are unsurpassed in America. Cards of admission and well-informed guides (persons in Her Majesty's service) will be furnished to tourists without charge, on application. Rideau Hall, the residence of His Excellency, the Governor-General, is an interesting place to American tourists, and all are allowed to visit the beautiful grounds during the summer season. Information as to reception days may be obtained at the Canadian Pacific Railway offices. The scenery in and around Ottawa will be found grand and impressive. One of the principal attractions is the Chaudiere Falls, which are 200 feet wide and forty feet deep, and, next to Niagara, are not excelled in importance, beauty and grandeur by any in this country. On the northern side the Little Chaudiere Falls, after their leap, go into a subterranean passage, and are found again at a place called "The Kettles," half a mile lower down. Below the falls the river is spanned by a suspension bridge, from which an excellent view of them is had. The Rideau Falls, about one mile eastward from the city, are remarkably graceful and picturesque. The water power of Ottawa is one of the finest on the continent. It furnishes the power for an excellent electric-light system, as well as many industries and manufactories.

The immense tract of country drained by the Ottawa River and its tributaries supplies an almost inexhaustible quantity of lumber, which is one of the largest sources of the wealth of Ottawa, and its development has made the city one of the largest lumber marts in the world. One of the large experimental farms, established by the Dominion Government in 1887 for research in economic matters pertaining to agriculture, is situated about two miles from the city.

The Rideau Canal enters the Ottawa River at Ottawa, the descent being made by a series of eight massive stone locks. The military bridges, constructed of stone and iron, are splendid specimens of engineering skill. The population of the city is about 50,000, not including the city of Hull, on the opposite side of the river. French and English are spoken with equal fluency by many of the inhabitants. Ottawa is very easy of access, being an important station on the Canadian Pacific Railway. The Ottawa River Navigation Company's steamers run to Montreal, passing through the Lachine Rapids of the St. Lawrence River by daylight. The famous Caledonia Springs are easily reached from Ottawa. The arrangement in this book of tours via Ottawa will be found very attractive, while the rates are so reasonable as to be within the reach of all.

THE PARLIAMENT BUILDINGS AT OTTAWA.

LAKE ST. JOHN

AND THE

NEW ROUTE TO THE FAR-FAMED SAGUENAY.

THE Quebec & Lake St. John Railway extends northward 190 miles from the ancient walled city of Quebec straight through the virgin wilderness, to Lake St. John, P. Q., from which reservoir the Saguenay River derives its waters. Fast trains with elegant parlor cars leave Quebec at 8.30 a.m., daily except Sunday, for Roberval and Chicoutimi, connecting at Chicoutimi with the Saguenay steamers for Tadousac, Cacouna, Murray Bay and Quebec, passing down the Saguenay by daylight, making a trip unequalled in the grandeur of its scenery.

At St. Ambroise is the Indian village of Lorette, alongside the beautiful falls of that name. Valcartier is beautifully situated in the lovely valley of the Jacques Cartier River, hemmed in by the mountains. Lake St. Joseph is a charming lake, with delightful scenery, eight miles long and twenty miles in circumference. A summer hotel and the cottages of several citizens of Quebec are pleasantly situated here. A little steamer makes the tour of the lake. St. Raymond is a very pretty village on the River St. Anne, which here widens out into a most beautiful valley.

Since the construction of the railway a number of fishing clubs have been formed, and have leased lakes from the Government for fishing purposes.

Lake Edward, a beautiful sheet of water, twenty-one miles in length, and full of picturesque islands, has been leased by the railway company and fishing permits may be obtained from the tourist agent by all patrons of the railway. This lake is noted for its large, red trout.

Lake Bouchette and the adjoining large Lac des Commissaires are charming sheets of water, well worthy of a visit by tourist or sportsman.

Passengers leaving Quebec or Lake St. John in the morning will be served with a comfortable luncheon, at a moderate price, at the new hotel adjoining the station at Lake Edward. Dinner for passengers for Lake St. John will be served at the Hotel Roberval.

Lake St. John is a magnificent sheet of water, abounding in fish, such as the "ouananiche," weighing from five to fourteen pounds. Only on a fine day can the other side of the lake be seen; at all other times it conveys the impression of an inland sea. Following up the west shore of the lake the scenery is very fine. A distant blue point, hardly visible at first, gradually resolves itself into a long coast line, dotted with farms, villages and churches, reminding one of the St. Lawrence below Montreal. A steel-framed steamboat, the "Mistassini," capable of accommodating 400 passengers, gives all tourists to the lake rare opportunities of novel sight-seeing such as they never enjoyed before.

An elegant new hotel, The Hotel Roberval, Lake St. John, has first-class accommodation for 300 guests, having been recently enlarged. This hotel has been built on a commanding site, affording a magnificent view of the whole expanse of Lake St. John. Almost in front of the hotel is the steamboat wharf, where tourists may embark on the passenger steamer making daily trips and excursions to all points on Lake St. John during the season of navigation.

A new hotel, the Island House, has been built on an island at the Grand Discharge of Lake St. John, in the centre of the "ouananiche" (fresh-water salmon) fishing grounds, and is in daily communication with Hotel Roberval by new fast steamer across the lake. These hotels control the fishing rights of Lake St. John and tributaries, all of which are free to their guests.

The region now opened up by this railway affords, probably, the best sporting ground in America. In all the innumerable lakes and rivers touched by the road, fish of all kinds abound, including the "ouananiche," or the fresh-water salmon.

W. H. H. Murray's legend of the Saguenay, called "The Doom of Mamelons," gives a full description of the many attractions of the Saguenay region. Copies of a beautifully illustrated guide-book can be obtained by writing to Mr. Alex. Hardy, General Passenger Agent of the Q. & L. St. J. R'y, Quebec, P. Q.

MONTMORENCI FALLS—CITY OF QUEBEC IN DISTANCE.

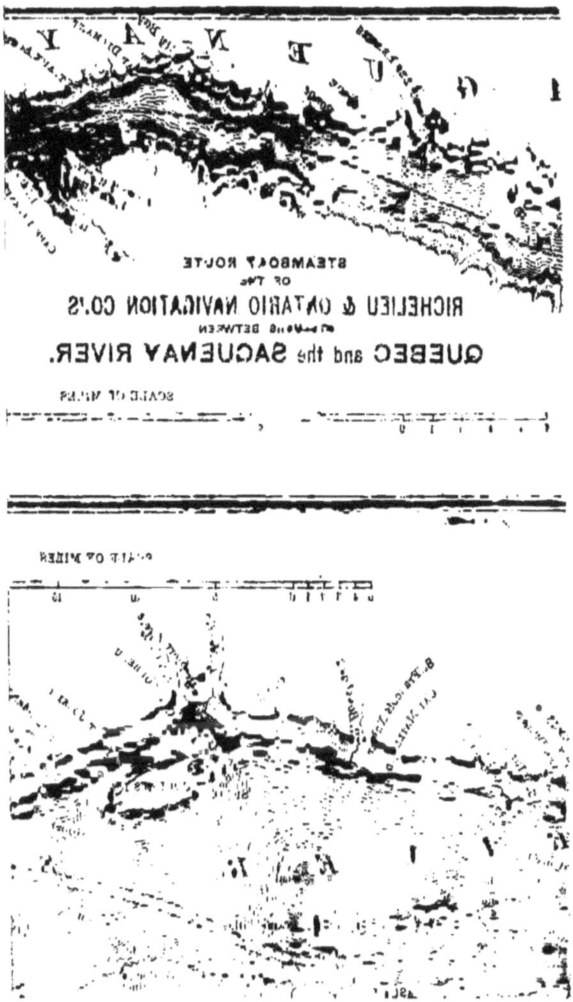
STEAMBOAT ROUTE
OF THE
RICHELIEU & ONTARIO NAVIGATION CO.'S
BETWEEN
QUEBEC and the SAGUENAY RIVER.
SCALE OF MILES

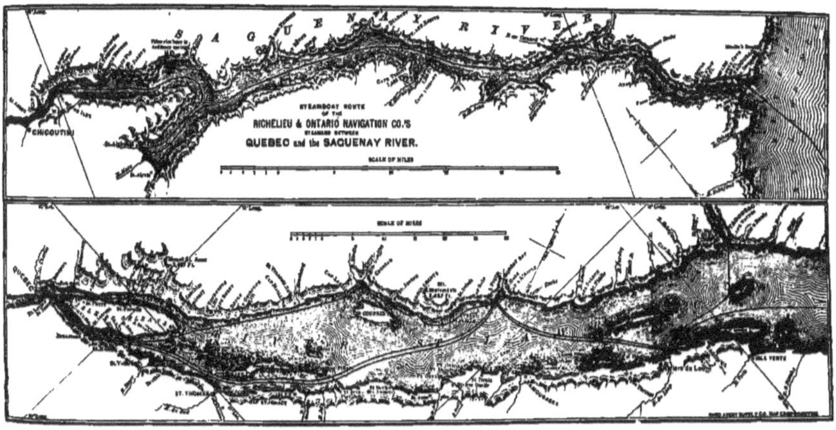
SAGUENAY RIVER
STEAMBOAT ROUTE
OF THE
RICHELIEU & ONTARIO NAVIGATION CO.'S
STEAMERS BETWEEN
QUEBEC and the SAGUENAY RIVER.
SCALE OF MILES
CHICOUTIMI
QUEBEC
ISLE VERTE

THE RIVER SAGUENAY.

A TOUR of the St. Lawrence is not complete unless it includes the wealth of wonders offered by the remarkable Saguenay River. Leaving Quebec, a slight detour of a couple of days affords the opportunity for viewing the grandest and most striking river scenery on this continent. At Tadousac, 120 miles below Quebec, the Saguenay empties into the St. Lawrence, and from the moment the channel is entered the beholder is impressed with the grandeur of the

TRINITY COVE—RIVER SAGUENAY.

prospect before him. Almost breathless with wonder, as though spell-bound by some guardian spirit of the mysterious place, the charmed observer gazes in awe at the sublime spectacle spread before him. On either side perpendicular cliffs of granite and syenite in solemn majesty rise abruptly from the water's edge to a height of nearly 2000 feet. The quiet flow of the river in its deep and rock-bound channel is in perfect accord with the wondrous charm of the situation. The depth of this river is something remarkable; at its mouth a line of 330 fathoms could not sound bottom; at St. John's Bay, twenty-eight miles above Tadousac, the water is one mile and a half deep. Six miles beyond St. John's Bay is Eternity Bay. Two majestic promontories, like gigantic sentinels, guard its entrance—Cape Trinity, 1500 feet high, on the left; Cape Eternity, 1900 feet high, on the right. At this point the river is a mile and a quarter deep. Sixty miles above Tadousac is Grand or Ha-Ha Bay, nine miles long and six miles wide. It affords good

CAPE ETERNITY AND CAPE TRINITY—RIVER SAGUENAY.

CHICOUTIMI, SHOWING STE. ANNE, SAGUENAY RIVER.

anchorage for the largest vessels, the average depth being from fifteen to thirty-five fathoms. The attractions of this place are many and very inviting. Its name is said to come from the joy it afforded the first navigators of the river, who found here their first landing place, and expressed their delight by a hearty Ha! Ha!

After "doing" Quebec, the excursion up the Saguenay is a fitting sequel to a visit to the ancient citadel, and will give an opportunity for enjoying the attractions of several of Canada's most famous watering-places, and also the grand and rugged scenery of the Lower St. Lawrence. The citadel of the old town looks down in silent majesty as the steamer glides slowly away on its course down the broad river. Passing the Island of Orleans on the right, a glimpse of Ste. Anne and its noted shrine on the left, Cacouna, the Newport of Canada, comes into view as the steamer approaches the opposite shore. Twenty miles across the river again and the steamer is at the entrance to the mysterious Saguenay region.

TADOUSAC, FROM SAGUENAY RIVER.

Near the mouth of the Saguenay is Tadousac, a small village. It has, with Cacouna and Murray Bay, the reputation of a popular watering-place, and is a favorite resort for the people of Quebec and other places up the river. The scenery is wild and striking, and the waters abound in excellent salmon. The village contains the oldest church in America north of Florida. The steamer stops long enough at Tadousac to give ample opportunity for seeing the sights and enjoying the natural attractions of the place. Chicoutimi, sixty-five miles from the mouth of the Saguenay, stands at the head of navigation on the river. It contains a population of 700 inhabitants, and boasts of a few interesting buildings of some pretension. The scenery here lacks the grandeur of the Lower Saguenay, being less rugged. The margins of the river are low, and offer few attractions compared with Eternity Bay

or other points down the river. The fishing is excellent, not only in the Saguenay, but also in the Chicoutimi River, and is extensively carried on. The immense forests of this region, as yet only partly explored, furnish an important industry to the place, the lumber trade being very large and important. Being accessible to the largest vessels, it possesses natural facilities for the shipment of lumber, which add greatly to the trade and importance of the place. Lake St. John, a fine body of water, fifty miles long and nearly as wide, is reached from Chicoutimi by trains on the Quebec & Lake St. John Railway. The Lake St. John region is destined to become popular not only to the tourist, but also to the sportsman, its many attractive resorts being easily accessible also by rail from Quebec. Though fed by eleven large rivers, the waters of Lake St. John find their only outlet through the channel of the majestic Saguenay.

ENTRANCE TO HA-HA BAY.

Unusual attractions for the tourist and others visiting the far-famed River Saguenay, are offered this season by the Richelieu & Ontario Navigation Co. This enterprising company will put in service on the Saguenay route the large and commodious steel steamer "Canada," having numerous state-rooms, new furniture, large, airy dining-room, new carpets, new draperies, and is complete in every respect, affording passengers every degree of comfort. This popular route is growing in greater favor each season with all classes. The sportsman and the angler have here an unlimited field to practise their art, the salmon and lake trout being found in abundance.

The Saguenay Line of the Richelieu & Ontario Navigation Co. is composed of the beautiful iron steamer "Carolina," the splendid steel steamer "Canada" and the fine steamer "Saguenay." Steamers leave Quebec for the River Saguenay on the mornings of Tuesday, Wednesday, Friday and Saturday at 7.30 a.m., arriving at Ha-Ha Bay or Chicoutimi between 4.00 a.m. and 8.00 a.m. the following morning, according to the tide.

TO THE OCEAN VIA THE GULF OF ST. LAWRENCE.

THE most fascinating trip for summer tourists is by steamer from Quebec to the principal cities and towns of the lower Maritime Provinces of the Dominion. The route traversed by the steamers of the Quebec Steamship Co., from Montreal and Quebec to Pictou, N. S., is over 1000 miles, rich in historic associations, and abounds in grand and picturesque scenery. Leaving Quebec and passing down the St. Lawrence the eye catches a succession of views which, in beauty and grandeur, are nowhere surpassed on this continent. Notable places between Quebec and Father Point are Cacouna and Murray Bay—two famous Canadian watering-places. Father Point, nearly 200 miles below Quebec, is where European steamers leave their pilots, and, being a marine telegraph station, the passing of steamers and vessels is telegraphed to all parts of the world. Below the Point the voyager gets the last glimpse of the headlands on the north shore of the mighty river. The coast is everywhere indented with beautiful bays and rivers, abounding in salmon and other fish. Gaspe, where Jacques Cartier landed in 1534, is 450 miles from Quebec, and has special attractions in its situation, inhabitants and industries. A little farther on is Perce, which derives its name from the wonderful pierced rock in front of it, and about which cluster a myriad of curious legends; then come in succession the beautiful Bay of Chaleur and the famous fishing and lumbering stations—Paspebiac and Dalhousie. Steaming down the bay and over the waters of the broad gulf, the mouth of the beautiful Miramichi River is soon reached. The steamer passes down the Northumberland Strait, with the bright shores of Prince Edward Island on the one hand and the shores of New Brunswick and Nova Scotia on the other, calling at Summerside and Charlottetown, and after a few hours' pleasant sail the harbor of Pictou, 1050 miles from Montreal, is reached. Pictou is a place of considerable importance as a coal shipping port, and a visit to the coal mining region of Nova Scotia in this vicinity will prove interesting and instructive. The journey may be broken here and continued by rail, or taking the steamers of the North Atlantic Steamship Line, the water course may be resumed. Leaving Pictou and following the coast, the steamer enters the Gut of Canso, which separates Cape Breton Island from Nova Scotia. The strait is from one mile to one mile and a half broad. At Port Hawkesbury a delightful side trip may be made to the attractive resorts of Cape Breton. Comfortable steamers ply the waters of the Bras d'Or, a land-locked sea whose rugged and picturesque scenery has no equal this side of Scotland. A round trip through the Bras d'Or to Sydney, the principal place in Cape Breton, will be a memorable experience, full of surprises and delights. Boarding the steamer again the journey is resumed, the grand and imposing scenery of the Strait of Canso merges into the boundless expanse of the open sea. Passing Cape Canso, the extreme northeastern point of Nova Scotia, the course of the steamer is along the rugged coast of Halifax. Leaving Halifax, a delightful sail of 400 miles through the open sea occupies thirty hours, and lands the tourist in Boston.

From "OUTING."

ALONG THE COAST. Copyrighted.

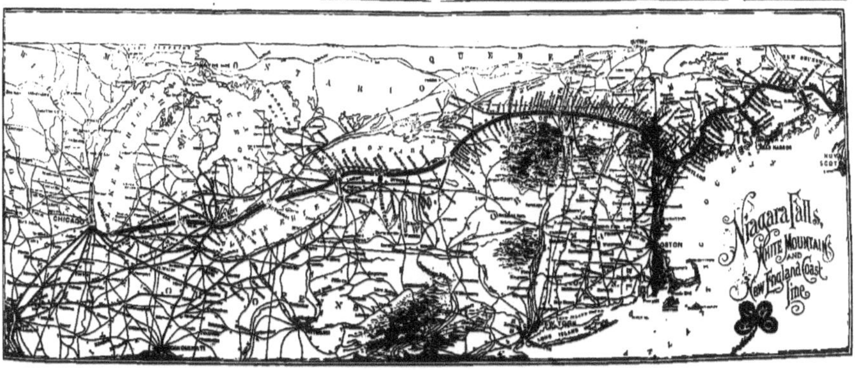
Niagara Falls,
White Mountains
and
New England Coast
Line
CHICAGO
BOSTON

TO THE WHITE MOUNTAINS AND THE SEA-SHORE.

THE mountain and sea-shore resorts of New England are best and most quickly reached from the West via the Rome, Watertown & Ogdensburg Railroad, the short line, and part of the Niagara Falls, White Mountains and New England Coast Line, which carries Wagner Buffet Sleeping Cars from Niagara Falls via Fabyan's, White Mountains, to Portland, Maine, without change. Wagner Buffet Sleeping Cars are also run from Chicago, via Michigan Central R.R., to Portland, via this route. The train runs via Rome, Watertown & Ogdensburg Railroad, Niagara Falls to Norwood, thence via Rouse's Point, Swanton and Lunenburg, passing through the heart of the White Mountains, to Portland, Maine.

MAINE CENTRAL R.R.—THROUGH THE NOTCH.

The route eastward from Norwood is over the tracks of the Central Vermont Railroad, which passes along the great plateau to the north of the Adirondacks, and looks down upon the valley of the St. Lawrence. At Norwood, a side trip may be made to Massena Springs, as noted elsewhere. At Malone connection is made with the Mohawk & Malone Railway.

At Rouse's Point connection for Montreal, Saratoga and New York is made. From Swanton the train passes eastward over the rails of the St. Johnsbury & Lake Champlain R.R., surmounting the elevated region bordering the Green Mountains, passing St. Johnsbury (with connection to all points north and south) to Lunenburg in the White Mountains. Side trips are made to summit of Mount Washington, Maplewood, Bethlehem, Profile House, etc. Lake Winnipesaukee is best reached by continuing on the Boston & Maine R.R., to Weir's, where connection is made with steamer "Lady of the Lake" for Centre Harbor and Wolfboro.

From Fabyan's the trip to the sea-shore is made via the Maine Central Railroad passing the Crawford House, and through Crawford Notch down the grand White Mountain Notch in view of

THROUGH THE HEART OF THE NOTCH.

ASCENT OF MT. WASHINGTON.

the Willey House, and through North Conway. Observation cars are used upon this portion of the trip.

At Portland one may choose between the near-by shore resorts of Old Orchard and Kennebunkport and a trip to Mount Desert, or the resorts hidden away in the Maine forests. Lake Winnipesaukee is also reached by leaving the Maine Central Railroad route at North Conway, there taking the Boston & Maine R.R. to Wolfboro.

The White Mountains have been aptly styled the "Switzerland of America" and have long been a favorite resort for summer travelers. These mountains are situated in Coos County, New Hampshire, and consist of a number of peaks from 4000 to 6000 feet high—the most elevated being Mount Washington, which rises to an altitude of 6243 feet above the level of the sea. It is the centre of attraction for tourists in the region, and around it are clustered many points of interest, each having a peculiar charm. "The Notch" is a narrow gorge, the entrance being but twenty feet wide — between two enormous cliffs, and extends a distance of two miles, abounding in cascades and precipices. "Franconia Notch" contains several natural curiosities, among which is the "Flume," a waterfall of 250 feet. "The Old Man of the Mountains" is a profile of the human face, delineated with striking exactness by a peculiar combination of the surfaces and angles of five massive granite blocks, at the height of 1000 feet, on the summit of a bold, jutting cliff. "Tuckerman's Ravine," the "Gulf of Mexico," and "Oake's Gulf" are deep ravines, in which snow and ice remain until late in summer. The "Devil's Den," "Gibbs' Falls," "Falls of the Ammonoosuc," and other well-known attractions, are all crowded in this wonderful region, and are accessible to visitors without danger or serious inconvenience. Excellent hotels are located in the immediate vicinity of most of the places enumerated. The ascent of Mount Washington is now made by a peculiarly constructed railway, and the journey is entirely safe, while it certainly

FRANKENSTEIN TRESTLE—MAINE CENTRAL R.R.

supplies all the elements of the picturesque and exciting. From the top, where a house is erected for the accommodation of tourists, a wonderful view is enjoyed, embracing the Green Mountains of Vermont on the west; the White Mountains and Franconia Range on the southwest; the distant mountains of Canada on the north; the Atlantic Ocean on the east, and Lake Winnipesaukee and the mountains surrounding it on the south; while various rivers, small lakes, towns and hamlets fill in and complete the picture. The house on the summit is used as a signal station throughout the year by the United States Government. The sea-shore resorts of Maine merit more than a passing notice. Old Orchard Beach has long been known among leading centres of social life in the summer. Within a few years the beautiful location of Kennebunkport has brought it into prominence. A branch railroad connects with the main line of the Boston & Maine R.R. at Kennebunk Station. Kennebunkport is twenty-five

"OLD MAN OF THE MOUNTAINS,"
Near Profile House, Franconia Notch, White Mountains, N. H.

MOUNT WASHINGTON, AS SEEN FROM MAINE CENTRAL R.R. AT FRANKENSTEIN, N.H.

From "OUTING." Copyrighted.

MAINE COAST, NEAR KENNEBUNK.

miles west of Portland. The Ocean Bluff Hotel, conducted by Messrs. Stimpson & Devnell, is one of the largest and finest houses in the State. Excellent boating may be enjoyed in smooth water; surf-bathing is a leading attraction. There are several pleasant drives—one to the quaint old fishing village of Cape Porpoise, two miles to the east, one through Kennebunk Village to the Falls and one of three or four miles at low tide to the west, along Wentworth's and Parson's Beaches and through Hart's Woods to Lord's Beach in Wells. Along the latter drive are the summer cottages of President Clark, of the New York, New Haven & Hartford Railroad; ex-President Lord, of the Boston & Maine Railroad, and Charles Parsons, ex-President of the Rome, Watertown & Ogdensburg and New York & New England Railroads.

PROFILE HOUSE AND ECHO LAKE, FRANCONIA NOTCH, WHITE MOUNTAINS, N. H.

From "OUTING." Copyrighted.

OFF THE MAINE COAST.

Portland's harbor is the garden-spot of Casco Bay, which, in its magnificent sweep from the headlands at Cape Elizabeth to the long peninsulas of Harpswell, holds—so says popular fable—365 islands, one for each day of the year.

Cushing's Island, three miles from the city, is the most exclusive of Casco's isles, as well as one of the most beautiful. It is for the most part covered with an ancient forest growth, and its seaward shore rises in the bold cliffs which are so characteristic of the rugged Maine coast.

"White Head," familiar to poet and painter, one of the finest examples of *the marine*, is there.

Chebeague Island, farther down the bay, nine miles from the city, is a delightful little resting retreat in the lower bay, from which the charming cyclorama of the sea is spread.

AM.BK.NOTE.CO.N.Y.
CRESCENT SURF
KENNEBUNK, ME.

BAR HARBOR, MT. DESERT ISLAND, MAINE.

CATHEDRAL ROCK.
"THE OVENS."

DURING the last twenty years Mount Desert has been transformed from a comparatively uninteresting place into one of the most delightful and popular resorts on the Atlantic coast. Bar Harbor is most comfortably reached by the Niagara Falls, White Mountains and New England Coast Line, which runs through Wagner Buffet Sleeping Cars from Niagara Falls; also from Chicago over the Michigan Central R.R. and connecting lines, to Portland, Me., where connection is made with trains of the Maine Central R.R. for Bar Harbor. Mount Desert, which is so prominent among the many attractive summer resorts on the coast of Maine, is an island averaging twelve miles in length and nine in width, named by the French navigator Champlain, who visited it in 1604, "Isle of the Desert Mountains," which name has been shortened to "Mount Desert." The Indians called it "Pemetic (at the head)," and justly esteemed it a place of importance. The coast outline is extremely irregular and broken, being indented by numerous coves and bays, some almost bisecting the island; towering above all are the mountain peaks, which mark the island as a striking and conspicuous object in the coast scenery.

Bar Harbor, the chief resort on the island, is delightfully situated on the eastern shore overlooking Frenchman's Bay, and is conveniently reached by the Niagara Falls, White Mountains and New England Coast Line, in connection with the Maine Central R.R., and a ferry which affords a half hour's delightful sail across the bay. The first cottage erected at Bar Harbor as a summer residence was built in 1867, and since that time numerous cottages and elegant summer homes have been established, broad avenues and streets laid out, costly and beautiful residences built on the bluffs and cliffs, transforming the "desert" into a large and charming village, with churches and all the requirements exacted by a refined and intelligent community. Bar Harbor owes its name to the sand bar which in times of low water is exposed, and connects the island with Bar or Rodick's Island, affording a passage between the two islands.

Aside from the gaiety and refined society of Bar Harbor there are many natural attractions reached by pleasant drives, which lend a peculiar charm to the resort. Schooner Head Cliffs, about four miles from Bar Harbor, cleft by a deep fissure called "Spouting Horn," is a spot much visited. Sand Point and the "Ovens" are the objective points of another favorite drive. The "Ovens" are bold and frowning cliffs, whose bases have been hollowed and worn by the ceaseless beating of the waves into caverns simulating curious architectural forms. The advice of persons familiar with the turns of the tide should be sought before one ventures to explore the "Ovens."

The natural feature of the island and the one which suggested its name is the mountains, of which there are thirteen principal peaks and many others of less importance. Green Mountain is the chief of the group, and its ascent affords a delightful trip to the tourist. The route from Bar Harbor is by carriage drive to Eagle Lake, a beautiful pond two and three-quarters miles in length by three-quarters in width, thence by steamer to the foot of the Green Mountain Railway, a work of wonderful engineering skill, which runs to the summit of the mountain. The grade is steep, but the ascent is safely and quickly made. The view from the summit on a clear day

AT ANCHOR OFF BAR HARBOR.

is remarkably fine. While the ascent of some of the mountains is comparatively difficult and fatiguing, all are accessible and afford magnificent views of the grand and bold rock scenery of the Maine coast, which has ever been the favorite haunt of the marine artist and the lover of grand ocean scenery.

Bar Harbor offers superior hotel accommodations for summer visitors, and no summer itinerary should be considered complete which does not include Bar Harbor among its attractions.

Time-tables for Niagara Falls, White Mountains and New England Coast Line, giving full particulars as to time and train service, may be obtained of all principal railway ticket agents.

ST. ANDREWS, N. B.

On a jutting point of land that pierces the waters of Passamaquoddy Bay, nestles the quaint village of St. Andrews. The charm of the situation is heightened by the wondrous beauty of the Bay. This magnificent sheet of water, stretching out seventeen miles long by six miles broad, has often been likened to the Bay of Naples.

No point along the coast of Maine and New Brunswick has a more favored location than St. Andrews. The old place has been a sort of "Sleeping Beauty" of the seaside for generations, and its attractions were known long before vacation trips were made a necessary part in the plan of summer life, as a respite from toil. With each recurring year it grows in popularity as a restful summer resort, and constantly draws back the visitors of past years, who have been won by the charms of the place.

On an elevation overlooking the village is situated "The Algonquin," a modern summer resort hotel, replete with every luxury and comfort. The hotel has been enlarged and improved for the season of 1895; the capacity of the house has been doubled, offering guests the choice of rooms *en suite*, with private bath, or single rooms, as desired. "The Algonquin" is under American management, and it has acquired such an enviable reputation that guests who have once enjoyed the comforts it offers, make arrangements a year in advance for the next season's accommodations.

The entire vicinity is traversed by the finest roads for cycling or pleasure riding. Private horses and carriages may, *for the season's use*, be taken into St. Andrews from the United States free of duty, through the courtesy of the Canadian Customs.

St. Andrews is reached by direct rail lines from the West via Niagara Falls, thence by Niagara Falls, White Mountains and New England Coast Line, in Wagner Buffet Cars, through the White Mountains to Portland, where connection is made twice daily with express trains over the Maine Central and Canadian Pacific Railways for St. Andrews. From Boston double daily through trains to St. Andrews, via Boston & Maine R.R. in 13 hours, or by International Steamers in 17 hours.

Descriptive books, maps and views will be found at principal ticket offices in the West, or by addressing Mr. O. E. Jenkins, General Western Agent of Rome, Watertown & Ogdensburg Railroad, 95 Clark Street, Chicago, Ill. For rooms, rates, etc., address previous to June 15th, Albert Miller, Manager of "The Algonquin," Room 39 B, Equitable Building, Boston, Mass.

SUMMER EXCURSION TICKETS.

SPECIAL INFORMATION FOR TOURISTS—SEASON 1895.

Tickets herein described are good until November 1st, and entitle holders to all privileges of regular first-class tickets.

Children between five and twelve years of age, half fare; over twelve, full fare; under five, free.

Richelieu & Ontario Navigation Co.—Commencing June 15, Rich. & Ont. Nav. Co. steamers leave R., W. & O. R.R. dock, Clayton, daily, except Monday, until July 15; after July 15, steamers leave Clayton daily for Montreal. After September 15 and until September 30 steamers will leave tri-weekly—Tuesdays, Thursdays and Saturdays—at the same hour. Steamers leave Montreal for Quebec daily, except Sunday, at 7.00 p.m.; Sundays, 3.00 p.m. Steamers for the River Saguenay leave Quebec, from June 15 until July 15, on Tuesdays, Wednesdays, Fridays and Saturdays, at 7.30 a.m.; after July 15, until further notice, daily, except Sunday, at 7.30 a.m. Between Clayton and Montreal, and also between Clayton and Brockville or Prescott, meals and berth are extra. On return trip, Montreal to Clayton, meals and berth are included. Between Montreal and Quebec, meals and berth are extra; supper, 50c.; state-room berth, 50c., 75c. or $1.00, according to location; whole state-room, $1.00, $1.50, $2.00 and $3.00, according to location. Between Quebec and the Saguenay River, meals and berth are extra: breakfast, 50c.; dinner, 75c.; supper, 50c.; open berth, day or night, 50c.; day and night, $1.00; the trip, $2.00; half a state-room, day or night, $1.00; day and night, $2.00; the trip, $2.00; whole state-room, day or night, $2.00; day and night, $3.00; the trip, $4.00.

Ottawa River Navigation Co.—Meals and berth are extra. Train leaves Bonaventure depot, Montreal, 8.00 a.m., *daily*, to connect with steamer at Lachine, for Ottawa and intermediate ports. Steamer leaves Queen's Wharf, Ottawa, for Montreal, *daily*, at 7.30 a.m., shooting the Rapids, arriving at Montreal 6.30 p.m.

Charlottetown Steam Navigation Co. (Limited).—Meals and state-rooms are extra. Steamers for Summerside and Charlottetown make close connection at Pt. du Chene, every day except Sunday, with Intercolonial Railway morning train. Steamers leave Charlottetown for Pictou, and Pictou for Charlottetown, every morning, except Sunday, at 6.00 a.m.

Quebec Steamship Co.—Meals are included; berth extra. During season of 1895 steamers leave Quebec at 2.00 p.m. on the following dates: May 14 and 28, June 11 and 25, July 9 and 23, August 6 and 20, September 3 and 17, October 1 and 15.

Canada Atlantic & Plant Steamship Co.—Meals extra: dinner, 75c.; breakfast and supper, 50c. each. Tickets entitle holders to berth in cabin. State-room berth, Halifax to Boston, $1.50 to $3.00, according to size and location; Charlottetown to Boston, $2.00. On and after June 27, 1895, the steamers "Olivette" and "Halifax" will leave Halifax for Boston Tuesdays and Thursdays at 8.00 a.m. and Saturdays at 10.00 p.m.; time to Boston, 27 hours. Commencing June 29, 1895, the steamship "Florida" will leave Charlottetown Tuesdays at 7.00 p.m.; Hawksbury, Wednesdays at 10.00 a.m.; due at Boston Fridays at 9.00 a.m.

The Yarmouth Steamship Co. (Limited).—Tickets include berth in cabin. About June 15 a fast steamship, "Yarmouth" or "Boston," leaves Lewis's Wharf, Boston, for Yarmouth, N. S., every Monday, Tuesday, Thursday and Friday at 12.00 m.; returning, leave Yarmouth for Boston every Tuesday, Wednesday, Friday and Saturday evening. Carries a regular mail to and from Boston.

International Steamship Co.—Summer arrangement July 1 to September 9, 1895. State-rooms, $1.00, $1.50 and $2.00 each. Meals extra: dinner, 75c.; breakfast or supper, 50c. Steamer leaves St. John for Eastport and Portland Tuesday and Friday at 7.00 a.m. Steamer leaves St. John for Eastport and Boston direct, Mondays, Wednesdays, Thursdays and Saturdays at 7.00 a.m. Going East, steamer leaves Boston at 5.00 p.m. for Eastport and St. John Mondays, Tuesdays, Thursdays and Fridays. No steamer from Boston on Wednesdays and Saturdays.

Bay of Fundy Steamship Co. (Limited).—Between St. John, Digby and Annapolis. Until June 20 a steamer leaves St. John Monday, Wednesday, Thursday and Friday at 7.30 a.m., local time; after June 20, during July and August, and until September 9, steamer leaves St. John daily, except Sunday, at 7.30 a.m., local time; returning, leaves Annapolis and Digby, until June 20, on Tuesday, Wednesday, Thursday and Saturday on arrival of express train from Halifax; after June 20, and during July and August, daily, except Sunday, due at St. John about 7.00 p.m. After September 9 consult local time-tables for changes.

Bras d'Or Steam Navigation Co. (Limited).—Steamer "May Queen" makes two trips daily, Sundays excepted, between Grand Narrows and Baddeck. Steamer "Blue Hill" runs daily between Mulgrave and St. Peter's. Steamer "Marion" leaves Port Mulgrave Tuesdays and Fridays for Sydney, passing through Lennox Passage and St. Peter's Canal, calling at Grand Narrows, Baddeck and Boularderie Island.

People's Line Steamboats.—Between Albany and New York, state-room, $1.00, $2.00 or $3.00, according to location; cabin berth, 50c.; fare, $1.50; round trip, $2.50.

Fall River Line.—Passengers holding tickets reading via the Fall River Line, in either direction, are privileged to stop over at Newport, R. I., on application to purser. Tickets reading between New York and Boston include a berth on steamer. State-rooms are $1.00 and $2.00 extra, according to location, and accommodate two persons. Meals are not included in price of tickets.

Lake Champlain Transportation Co.
Lake George Steamboat Co. } Tickets reading over these lines are good via D. & H. C. Co.'s R.R., and will be accepted for passage via rail.

Travelers will please note that many of the Steamboat and Stage lines discontinue their regular trips about October 1, and run irregularly thereafter.

C. T. Co. steamers on Lakes Champlain and George cease running about October 1. Hudson River Day Line steamers cease running about October 15. Rich. & Ont. Nav. Co. steamers between Clayton and Montreal cease running September 15. Mt. Washington Railway trains are discontinued September 20.

Tickets for all routes described herein, and full information, can be obtained of the following agents of the Rome, Watertown & Ogdensburg R.R. Co.:

B. B. Denison, No. 6 Cataract House, Niagara Falls.
B. B. Denison, N. Y. C. & H. R. Station, Niagara Falls.
J. C. Kalbfleisch, 11 East Main Street, Rochester.
W. E. Brown, Larned Block, Syracuse.
T. M. Petty, R., W. & O. Station, Oswego.
H. I. Fay, No. 1 Bagg's Hotel, Utica.
M. W. Campbell, Depot Ticket Office, Utica.
At Principal Stations of the Company, and also of
E. N. Blood, N. Y. C. & H. R. R.R., Buffalo Depot.
H. Parry, City Ticket Office, 1 Exchange Street, Buffalo.

Tourist tickets for many of the principal routes described herein may be obtained at principal ticket offices of the following transportation lines:

N. Y. Central & Hudson River R.R.
Pennsylvania R.R.
N. Y., Lake Erie & Western R.R.
West Shore R.R.
Philadelphia & Reading R.R.
Central Vermont R.R.
Boston & Maine R.R.
Boston & Albany R.R.
Fitchburg R.R.
Michigan Central R.R.
Lake Shore & Michigan Southern R'y.
Wabash R.R.
"Big Four Route," C. C. C. & St. L. R'y.
N. Y., Chicago & St. Louis R.R.
New York, Pennsylvania & Ohio R'y.
Louisville & Nashville R.R.
Pittsburg & Lake Erie R'y,
Allegheny Valley R. R.
Lake Superior Transit Co.
Hudson River Day Line.
People's Line Steamboat Co.
Northern Steamship Co.
Cook's Tourist Ticket Office.
World Travel Co. Ticket Offices.
H. Gaze & Sons' Ticket Office.

And Other Principal Railway Lines.

SPECIAL NOTICE.—If passengers are unable to purchase, at the offices of connecting lines, a through ticket by just the route desired, they are requested, in the West, to buy excursion tickets to Niagara Falls only; and in the East to buy to Utica only, or to nearest junction point on R., W. & O. R.R., and then purchase through tickets of any of the above-named R., W. & O. R.R. agents. Information as to minor details, expenses, etc., etc., cheerfully furnished. Letters asking for information should be addressed to

THEO. BUTTERFIELD, General Passenger Agent, Syracuse, N. Y.

Or to **O. E. JENKINS, General Western Passenger Agent, 96 Clark St., Room 15, Chicago, Ill.**

ROUTES AND RATES

FOR

Summer Excursion and Tourist Tickets.

IN EFFECT JUNE 1st TO SEPTEMBER 30th, 1895, INCLUSIVE.

STOP-OVERS AT ALEXANDRIA BAY.—The Coasting Law will not permit the Richelieu & Ontario Navigation Company to carry passengers between two American Ports: i.e., from CLAYTON to ALEXANDRIA BAY. Therefore, passengers desiring to stop at Alexandria Bay must take the steamers of the THOUSAND ISLAND STEAMBOAT COMPANY at CLAYTON. Coupons reading via the Richelieu & Ontario Navigation Company will be accepted by the Thousand Island Steamboat Company. Passengers destined to points east of Alexandria Bay who do not desire to stop at Alexandria Bay may take the Richelieu & Ontario Navigation Company's Steamers at Clayton.

Rates from Oswego, N. Y.—Via CLAYTON—One way 40 cents; round trip 50 cents less than Syracuse. Via MORRISTOWN, OGDENSBURG, NORWOOD or MASSENA SPRINGS—One way 35 cents; round trip 60 cents less than Syracuse.

Rates from Rome, N. Y.—Are same as from Syracuse, except ONE WAY rates via Clayton which are 5 cents less.

Rates from Watertown, N. Y.—Via CLAYTON—One way $2.20; round trip $3.80 less than Syracuse. Via MORRISTOWN, OGDENSBURG, NORWOOD or MASSENA SPRINGS—One way $2.20; round trip $3.95 less than Syracuse.

SPECIAL LIMITED TICKETS To **Clayton and return; Cape Vincent and return; Carleton Island and return; Round Island and return; Thousand Island Park and return; Alexandria Bay and return; Westminster Park and return; Central Park and return**, are on sale at all stations of the Rome, Watertown & Ogdensburg Railroad, at reduced rates.

Thousand Island and Adirondack Tour. See Route 530.

FOR RATES, APPLY TO ANY ROME, WATERTOWN & OGDENSBURG RAILROAD TICKET AGENT.

Route 1—Childwold Station (Adirondacks).
Form G 1.
R., W. & O. R.R.....to Remsen
N.Y. C. & H. R. R.R. Childwold Sta.
Through Rates.
Limited to continuous passage.
Clayton..........$4.51 | Watertown $4.46

Route 2—Childwold Station (Adirondacks) and Return.
Form G 2 R.
R., W. & O. R.R.....to Remsen
N.Y. C. & H. R. R.R. Childwold Sta.
RETURNING SAME ROUTE.
Through Rates.
Limited to thirty days from date of sale.
Clayton..........$6.65 | Watertown. ...$6.65

Route 3—Lake Kushaqua (Adirondacks).
Form G 1.
R., W. & O. R.R.....to Remsen
N.Y. C. & H. R. R.R. Lake Kushaqua
Through Rates.
Limited to continuous passage.
Clayton........ ..$4.51 | Watertown.....$4.46

Route 4—Lake Kushaqua (Adirondacks) and Return.
Form G 2 R.
R., W. & O. R.R.....to Remsen
N.Y. C. & H. R. R.R. Lake Kushaqua
RETURNING SAME ROUTE.
Through Rates.
Limited to thirty days from date of sale.
Clayton..........$6.65 | Watertown.....$6.65

Route 5—Loon Lake Station (Adirondacks).
Form G 1.
R., W. & O. R.R.....to Remsen
N.Y. C. & H. R. R.R. Loon Lake Sta.
Through Rates.
Limited to continuous passage.
Clayton..........$4.51 | Watertown.....$4.46

Route 6—Loon Lake Station (Adirondacks) and Return.
Form G 2 R.
R., W. & O. R.R.....to Remsen
N.Y. C. & H. R. R.R. Loon Lake Sta.
RETURNING SAME ROUTE.
Through Rates.
Limited to thirty days from days of sale.
Clayton...... ....$6.65 | Watertown.....$6.65

Route 7—Paul Smith's Station (Adirondacks).
Form G 1.
R., W. & O. R.R.....to Remsen
N.Y. C. & H. R. R.R. Paul Smith's Sta.
Through Rates.
Limited to continuous passage.
Clayton..........$4.51 | Watertown.... $4.46

Route 8—Paul Smith's Station (Adirondacks) and Return.
Form G 2 R.
R., W. & O. R.R.....to Remsen
N.Y. C. & H. R. R.R. Paul Smith's Sta.
RETURNING SAME ROUTE.
Through Rates.
Limited to thirty days from date of sale.
Clayton..........$6.65 | Watertown.....$6.65

Route 9—Saranac Inn Station (Adirondacks).
Form G 1.
R., W. & O. R.R.....to Remsen
N.Y. C. & H. R. R.R. Saranac Inn Sta.
Through Rates.
Limited to continuous passage.
Clayton..........$4.51 | Watertown.....$4.46

Route 10—Saranac Inn Station (Adirondacks) and Return.
Form G 2 R.
R., W. & O. R.R.....to Remsen
N.Y. C. & H. R. R.R. Saranac Inn Sta.
RETURNING SAME ROUTE.
Through Rates.
Limited to thirty days from date of sale.
Clayton...... ...$6.65 | Watertown.....$6.65

Route 11—Saranac Lake (Adirondacks).
Form G 1.
R., W. & O. R.R.....to Remsen
N.Y. C. & H. R. R.R. Saranac Lake
Through Rates.
Limited to continuous passage.
Clayton..........$4.69 | Watertown.....$4.64

Route 12—Saranac Lake (Adirondacks) and Return.
Form G 2 R.
R., W. & O. R.R.....to Remsen
N.Y. C. & H. R. R.R. Saranac Lake
RETURNING SAME ROUTE.
Through Rates.
Limited to thirty days from date of sale.
Clayton..........$7.01 | Watertown.....$7.01

SEE ABOVE NOTE REGARDING STOP-OVER AT ALEXANDRIA BAY.

Route 13—Albany, N. Y.

Forms Ex. 254 and Ex. 641.

R., W. & O. R.R.	to Clayton
R. & O. Nav. Co.	Alexandria Bay
R. & O. Nav. Co.	Montreal
N. Y. C. & H. R. R.R.	Albany

Through Rates.

Niagara Falls	$19 10	Syracuse	$16.25
Rochester	17.85	Utica	16.10

Route 14—Albany, N. Y.

Form Ex. 250.

R., W. & O. R.R.	to Clayton
R. & O. Nav. Co.	Alexandria Bay
R. & O. Nav. Co.	Prescott
Ferry	Ogdensburg
C. V. R.R. (O. & L. C. Div.)	Rouse's Point
D. & H. R.R.	Plattsburg
D. & H. R. R. or Cham. Trans. Co.	Ft. Ticonderoga
D. & H. R.R.	Baldwin
L. Geo. St'mb't Co.	Caldwell
D. & H. R. R. (via Saratoga)	Albany

Through Rates.

Niagara Falls	$18.60	Syracuse	$15 65
Rochester	17.25	Utica	15.50

Route 15—Albany, N. Y.

Form Ex. 251.

R., W. & O. R.R.	to Clayton
R. & O. Nav. Co.	Alexandria Bay
R. & O. Nav. Co.	Prescott
Ferry	Ogdensburg
C. V. R.R. (O. & L. C. Div.)	Rouse's Point
D. & H. R R.	Plattsburg
D. & H. R.R. or Cham. Trans. Co	Ft. Ticonderoga
D. & H. R.R. (via Saratoga)	Albany

Through Rates.

Niagara Falls	$17.10	Syracuse	$14.15
Rochester	15.75	Utica	14.00

Route 16—Albany, N. Y.

Forms Ex. 254 and Ex. 321.

R., W. & O. R.R.	to Clayton
R. & O. Nav. Co.	Alexandria Bay
R. & O. Nav. Co.	Montreal
Grand Trunk R'y.	Rouse's Point
D. & H. R.R.	Plattsburg
D. & H. R.R. or Cham. Trans. Co.	Ft. Ticonderoga
D. & H. R.R.	Baldwin
L. Geo. St'mb't Co.	Caldwell
D. & H. R.R.	Albany

Through Rates.

Niagara Falls	$20.60	Syracuse	$17.75
Rochester	19.35	Utica	17.60

Route 17—Albany, N. Y.

Forms Ex. 254 and Ex 322.

R., W. & O. R.R.	to Clayton
R. & O. Nav. Co.	Alexandria Bay
R. & O. Nav. Co.	Montreal
Grand Trunk R'y.	Rouse's Point
D. & H. R.R.	Plattsburg
D. & H. R.R. or Cham. Trans. Co.	Ft. Ticonderoga
D. & H. R.R.	Albany

Through Rates.

Niagara Falls	$19.10	Syracuse	$16.25
Rochester	17.85	Utica	16.10

Route 18—Albany, N. Y.

Forms Ex. 254 and Ex. 323.

R., W. & O. R.R.	to Clayton
R. & O. Nav. Co.	Alexandria Bay
R. & O. Nav. Co.	Montreal
Grand Trunk R'y.	St. John's
Cent. Vermont R.R.	Burlington
Cham. Trans. Co.	Ft. Ticonderoga
D. & H. R.R.	Albany

Through Rates.

Niagara Falls	$19.10	Syracuse	$16.25
Rochester	17.85	Utica	16.10

Route 19—Albany, N. Y.

Forms Ex. 254 and Ex. 324.

R., W. & O. R.R.	to Clayton
R. & O. Nav. Co.	Alexandria Bay
R. & O. Nav. Co.	Montreal
Grand Trunk R'y.	St. John's
Cent. Vermont R.R.	Burlington
Cham. Trans. Co.	Ft. Ticonderoga
D. & H. R.R.	Baldwin
L. Geo. St'mb't Co.	Caldwell
D. & H. R.R.	Albany

Through Rates.

Niagara Falls	$20.50	Syracuse	$17.75
Rochester	19.35	Utica	17.60

Route 20—Alexandria Bay, N. Y.

Form Ex. 122.

R., W. & O. R.R.	to Clayton
Thous. Isl. St'b't Co.	Alexandria Bay

Through Rates.

Niagara Falls	$6.85	Syracuse	$3.90
Rochester	5.50	Utica	3.75

Route 21—Alexandria Bay, N. Y.

Form Ex. 124.

R., W. & O. R.R.	to Ogdensburg
Ferry	Prescott
R. & O. Nav. Co.	Alexandria Bay

Through Rates.

Niagara Falls	$8.35	Syracuse	$5.55
Rochester	7.45	Utica	5.25

Route 22—Alpine House (Gorham).

Forms Ex. 254 and Ex. 546.

R., W. & O. R.R.	to Clayton
R. & O. Nav. Co.	Alexandria Bay
R. & O. Nav. Co.	Montreal
Can. Pac. R'y.	Newport
Boston & Maine R.R.	Lunenburg
Maine Central R.R.	North Conway
Maine Central R.R.	Glen
Stage	Glen Site
Stage	Alpine House (Gorham)

Through Rates.

Niagara Falls	$23.25	Syracuse	$20.40
Rochester	22.00	Utica	20.25

Route 23—Alpine House (Gorham).

Forms Ex. 254 and Ex. 547.

R., W. & O. R.R.	to Clayton
R. & O. Nav. Co.	Alexandria Bay
R. & O. Nav. Co.	Montreal
Can. Pac. R'y.	Newport
Boston & Maine R.R.	Lunenburg
Maine Central R.R.	Fabyan's
Con. & Mont'l R.R.	Base Mt. Wash.
Mt. Washington R'y.	Summit
Stage	Glen Site
Stage	Alpine House (Gorham)

Through Rates.

Niagara Falls	$25.90	Syracuse	$23.05
Rochester	24.65	Utica	22.90

Route 24—Alpine House (Gorham).

Forms Ex. 399 and Ex. 442.

R., W. & O. R.R.	to Clayton
R. & O. Nav. Co.	Alexandria Bay
R. & O. Nav. Co.	Montreal
Can. Pac. R'y or R. & O. Nav. Co.	Quebec
Ferry	Point Levis
Grand Trunk R'y.	Alpine House (Gorham)

Through Rates.

Niagara Falls	$21 85	Syracuse	$19.00
Rochester	20.60	Utica	18.85

Route 25—Bar Harbor, Me. (Mt. Desert I.)

Form Ex. 663.

R., W. & O. R.R.	to Norwood
Cent. Vermont R.R.	Swanton
St. J. & L. C. R.R.	Lunenburg
Maine Central R.R. (via Portland)	Bar Harbor

Through Rates.

	Unlim'd	Lim'd
Niagara Falls	$22 20	$17.15
Rochester	20.70	15.60
Syracuse	18.95	.....
Utica	17.95	.....

Limited Rates.

Good only for continuous passage east of Portland.

Niagara Falls	$21.20	Syracuse	$17.95
Rochester	19.70	Utica	16.95

Route 26—Bar Harbor, Me. (Mt. Desert I.) and Return.

Form Ex. 664.

R., W. & O. R.R.	to Norwood
Cent. Vermont R.R.	Swanton
St. J. & L. C. R.R.	Lunenburg
Maine Central R.R. (via Portland)	Bar Harbor

RETURNING SAME ROUTE.

Through Rates.

	Unlim'd	Lim'd
Niagara Falls	$38.00	$31.80
Rochester	35.75	29.95
Syracuse	33.15	.....
Utica	32.00	.....

Limited Rates.

Good only for continuous passage east of Portland.

Niagara Falls	$35.50	Syracuse	$30.65
Rochester	33.25	Utica	29.50

Route 27—Bar Harbor, Me. (Mt. Desert I.)

Form Ex. 548

R., W. & O. R.R.	to Norwood
Cent. Vermont R.R.	Swanton
St. J. & L. C. R.R.	Lunenburg
Maine Central R.R.	Rockland
Portland, Mt. D. & M. St'mb't Line.	Bar Harbor

Through Rates.

	Unlim'd	Lim'd
Niagara Falls	$19.70	$15.65
Rochester	18.20	14 10
Syracuse	16.45	.....
Utica	15.45	.....

Route 28—Bar Harbor, Me. (Mt. Desert I.) and Return.

Form Ex. 549.

R., W. & O. R.R.	to Norwood
Cent. Vermont R.R.	Swanton
St. J. & L. C. R.R.	Lunenburg
Maine Central R.R.	Rockland
Portland, Mt. D. & M. St'mb't Line.	Bar Harbor

RETURNING SAME ROUTE.

Through Rates.

	Unlim'd	Lim'd
Niagara Falls	$34.00	$30.30
Rochester	31.75	28.45
Syracuse	29.15	.....
Utica	28.00	.....

Route 29—Bethlehem, N. H.

Form Ex. 686.

R., W. & O. R.R.	to Norwood
Cent. Vermont R.R.	Swanton
St. J. & L. C. R.R.	Lunenburg
Maine Central R.R.	Zealand Jc.
Prof. & F. Notch R.R.	Bethlehem

Through Rates.

	Unlim'd	Lim'd
Niagara Falls	$13.15	....
Rochester	11.65	.....
Syracuse	10.05	....
Utica	9 05	.....

SEE NOTE ON PAGE 119 REGARDING STOP-OVER AT ALEXANDRIA BAY.

Route 30 – Bethlehem, N. H. and Return.

Form Ex. 686 R.

R., W. & O. R.R.....to Norwood
Cent. Vermont R.R.. Swanton
St. J. & L. C. R.R.... Lunenburg
Maine Central R.R... Zealand Jc
Prof. & F. Notch R.R. Bethlehem

RETURNING SAME ROUTE.

Through Rates.

Niagara Falls..$24.20	Syracuse......$13.15
Rochester 22.20	Utica........... 17.25

Route 31—Bethlehem, N. H.

Forms N 13 and Ex. 181.

R., W. & O. R.R.....to Norwood
Cent. Vermont R.R.. Swanton
St. J. & L. C. R.R.... Lunenburg
Maine Central R.R... Scott's
Con. & Mont'l R.R... Bethlehem Jc.
Prof. & F. Notch R.R. Bethlehem

Through Rates.

Niagara Falls..$13.15	Syracuse.......$10.05
Rochester...... 11.65	Utica............. 9.05

Route 32—Bethlehem, N. H. and Return.

Form Ex. 590.

R., W. & O. R.R.....to Norwood
Cent. Vermont R.R.. Swanton
St. J. & L. C. R.R.... Lunenburg
Maine Central R.R... Scott's
Con. & Mont'l R.R.. Bethlehem Jc.
Prof. & F. Notch R.R. Bethlehem

RETURNING SAME ROUTE.

Through Rates.

Niagara Falls..$24.20	Syracuse.......$19.15
Rochester...... 22.20	Utica............ 17.25

Route 33—Bethlehem, N. H.

Forms N 14 and Ex. 181.

R., W. & O. R.R.... to Norwood
Cent. Vermont R.R.. Montpelier
Mont. & W. R. R.R.. Wells River
Con. & Mont'l R.R... Bethlehem Jc.
Prof. & F. Notch R.R. Bethlehem

Through Rates.

Niagara Falls..$13.15	Syracuse.......$10.05
Rochester...... 11.65	Utica............ 9.05

Route 34—Bethlehem, N. H. and Return.

Form Ex. 589.

R., W. & O. R.R.....to Norwood
Cent. Vermont R.R.. Montpelier
Mont. & W. R. R.R.. Wells River
Con. & Mont'l R.R... Bethlehem Jc.
Prof. & F. Notch R.R. Bethlehem

RETURNING SAME ROUTE.

Through Rates.

Niagara Falls..$24.20	Syracuse.......$19.15
Rochester...... 22.20	Utica............ 17.25

Route 35—Bethlehem, N. H.

Forms Ex. 399 and Ex. 665.

R., W. & O. R.R.....to Clayton
R. & O. Nav. Co..... Alexandria Bay
R. & O. Nav. Co..... Montreal
Grand Trunk R'y or R. & O. Nav. Co. } Quebec
Ferry.............. Point Levis
Quebec Central R'y.. Sherbrooke
Boston & Maine R.R. Lunenburg
Maine Central R.R... Zealand Jc.
Prof. & F. Notch R.R. Bethlehem

Through Rates.

Niagara Falls..$22.20	Syracuse.......$19.35
Rochester 20.95	Utica 19.20

Route 36—Bethlehem, N. H.

Forms Ex. 400 and Ex. 665.

R., W. & O. R.R.....to Clayton
R. & O. Nav. Co..... Alexandria Bay
R. & O. Nav. Co..... Montreal
Can. Pac. R'y or R. & O. Nav. Co.. } Quebec
Ferry.............. Point Levis
Quebec Central R'y.. Sherbrooke
Boston & Maine R.R. Lunenburg
Maine Central R.R... Zealand Jc.
Prof. & F. Notch R.R. Bethlehem

Through Rates.

Niagara Falls..$22.20	Syracuse.......$19.35
Rochester 20.95	Utica 19.20

Route 37—Bethlehem, N. H.

Forms Ex. 400 and Ex. 747.

R., W. & O. R.R.....to Clayton
R. & O. Nav. Co..... Alexandria Bay
R. & O. Nav. Co..... Montreal
Can. Pac. R'y or R. & O. Nav. Co. } Quebec
Ferry.............. Point Levis
Quebec Central R'y.. Dudswell Jc.
Maine Central R.R... Zealand Jc.
Prof. & F. Notch R.R. Bethlehem

Through Rates.

Niagara Falls..$22.20	Syracuse.......$19.35
Rochester...... 20.95	Utica............ 19.20

Route 38—Bethlehem, N. H.

Forms Ex. 399 and Ex. 747.

R., W. & O. R.R.....to Clayton
R. & O. Nav. Co..... Alexandria Bay
R. & O. Nav. Co..... Montreal
Grand Trunk R'y or R. & O. Nav. Co. } Quebec
Ferry.............. Point Levis
Quebec Central R'y.. Dudswell Jc.
Maine Central R.R.. Zealand Jc.
Prof. & F. Notch R.R. Bethlehem

Through Rates.

Niagara Falls..$22.20	Syracuse.......$19.35
Rochester...... 20.95	Utica............ 19.20

Route 39—Bethlehem Junction, N. H.

Form Ex. 680.

R., W. & O. R.R.....to Norwood
Cent. Vermont R.R.. Swanton
St. J. & L. C. R.R... Lunenburg
Maine Central R.R... Zealand Jc.
Prof. & F. Notch R.R. Bethlehem Jc.

Through Rates.

	Unlim'd	Lim'd
Niagara Falls	$12.65	.....
Rochester..........	11.15	.....
Syracuse..........	9.55	.....
Utica..........	8.55	.....

Route 40—Bethlehem Junction, N. H. and Return.

Form Ex. 686 R.

R., W. & O. R.R.....to Norwood
Cent. Vermont R.R.. Swanton
St. J. & L. C. R.R.... Lunenburg
Maine Central R. R.. Zealand Jc
Prof. & F. Notch R.R. Bethlehem Jc.

RETURNING SAME ROUTE.

Through Rates.

Niagara Falls..$23.20	Syracuse.......$18.15
Rochester...... 21.20	Utica............ 16.25

Route 41—Bethlehem Junction, N. H.

Form N 13.

R., W. & O. R.R.....to Norwood
Cent. Vermont R.R.. Swanton
St. J. & L. C. R.R... Lunenburg
Maine Central R.R.. Scott's
Con. & Mont'l R.R.. Bethlehem Jc.

Through Rates.

Niagara Falls..$12.65	Syracuse........$9.55
Rochester...... 11.15	Utica............ 8.55

Route 42—Bethlehem Junction, N. H. and Return.

Form Ex. 577.

R., W. & O. R.R.....to Norwood
Cent. Vermont R.R.. Swanton
St. J. & L. C. R.R... Lunenburg
Maine Central R.R.. Scott's
Con. & Mont'l R.R... Bethlehem Jc.

RETURNING SAME ROUTE.

Through Rates.

Niagara Falls..$23.20	Syracuse.......$18.15
Rochester...... 21.20	Utica........... 16.25

Route 43—Bethlehem Junction, N. H.

Form N 14.

R., W. & O. R.R.....to Norwood
Cent. Vermont R.R.. Montpelier
Mont. & W. R. R R.. Wells River
Con. & Mont'l R.R.. Bethlehem Jc.

Through Rates.

Niagara Falls $12.65	Syracuse........$9.55
Rochester...... 11.15	Utica 8.55

Route 44—Bethlehem Junction, N. H. and Return.

Form Ex. 578.

R. W. & O. R.R.....to Norwood
Cent. Vermont R.R.. Montpelier
Mont. & W. R. R.R.. Wells River
Con. & Mont'l R.R... Bethlehem Jc.

RETURNING SAME ROUTE.

Through Rates.

Niagara Falls..$23.20	Syracuse.......$18.15
Rochester...... 21.20	Utica............ 16.25

Route 45—Bethlehem Junction, N. H.

Forms Ex. 254 and Ex. 325.

R., W. & O. R.R.....to Clayton
R. & O. Nav. Co..... Alexandria Bay
R. & O. Nav. Co..... Montreal
Grand Trunk R'y.... St. John's
Cent. Vermont R.R.. Montpelier
Mont. & W. R. R.R.. Wells River
Con. & Mont'l R.R... Bethlehem Jc.

Through Rates.

Niagara Falls..$17.35	Syracuse.......$14.45
Rochester. 16.05	Utica.... .... 14.30

Route 46—Bethlehem Junction, N. H. and Return.

Forms Ex. 255 and Ex. 326.

R., W. & O. R.R.....to Clayton
R. & O. Nav. Co..... Alexandria Bay
R. & O. Nav. Co..... Montreal
Grand Trunk R'y.... St. John's
Cent. Vermont R.R.. Montpelier
Mont. & W. R. R.R.. Wells River
Con. & Mont'l R.R... Bethlehem Jc.

RETURNING SAME ROUTE.

Through Rates.

Niagara Falls..$28.50	Syracuse.......$24.00
Rochester...... 26.50	Utica............ 24.00

Route 47—Bethlehem Junction, N. H.

Forms Ex. 254 and Ex. 687.

R., W. & O. R.R.....to Clayton
R. & O. Nav. Co..... Alexandria Bay
R. & O. Nav. Co..... Montreal
Can. Pac. R'y........ Newport
Boston & Maine R.R. Lunenburg
Maine Central R.R.. Zealand Jc.
Prof. & F. Notch R.R. Bethlehem Jc.

Through Rates.

Niagara Falls..$17.35	Syracuse $14.45
Rochester...... 16.05	Utica............ 14.30

SEE NOTE ON PAGE 119 REGARDING STOP-OVER AT ALEXANDRIA BAY.

Route 48—Bethlehem Junction, N. H. and Return.

Forms Ex. 285 and Ex. 688 R.

R., W. & O. R.R.....to	Clayton
R. & O. Nav. Co.....	Alexandria Bay
R. & O. Nav. Co.....	Montreal
Can. Pac. R'y........	Newport
Boston & Maine R.R.	Lunenburg
Maine Central R.R ..	Zealand Jc.
Prof. & F. Notch R.R.	Bethlehem Jc.

RETURNING SAME ROUTE.

Through Rates.

Niagara Falls	$28.50	Syracuse	$24.00
Rochester	26.50	Utica	24.00

Route 49—Bethlehem Junction, N. H.

Forms Ex. 399 and Ex. 689.

R., W. & O. R.R.....to	Clayton
R. & O. Nav. Co.....	Alexandria Bay
R. & O. Nav. Co.....	Montreal
Grand Trunk R'y or R. & O. Nav. Co.	Quebec
Ferry..........	Point Levis
Quebec Central R'y..	Sherbrooke
Boston & Maine R.R.	Lunenburg
Maine Central R.R..	Zealand Jc.
Prof. & F. Notch R.R.	Bethlehem Jc.

Through Rates.

Niagara Falls	$21.70	Syracuse	$18.85
Rochester	20.45	Utica	18.70

Route 50—Bethlehem Junction, N. H.

Forms Ex. 4.0 and Ex. 689.

R., W. & O. R.R.....to	Clayton
R. & O. Nav. Co.....	Alexandria Bay
R. & O. Nav. Co.....	Montreal
Can. Pac. R'y or R. & O. Nav. Co.	Quebec
Ferry................	Point Levis
Quebec Central R'y .	Sherbrooke
Boston & Maine R.R.	Lunenburg
Maine Central R.R..	Zealand Jc.
Prof. & F. Notch R.R.	Bethlehem Jc.

Through Rates.

Niagara Falls	$21.70	Syracuse	$18.85
Rochester	20.45	Utica	18.70

Route 51—Bethlehem Junction, N. H.

Forms Ex. 406 and Ex. 748.

R., W. & O. R.R.....to	Clayton
R. & O. Nav. Co.....	Alexandria Bay
R. & O. Nav. Co.....	Montreal
Can. Pac. R'y or R. & O. Nav. Co.	Quebec
Ferry................	Point Levis
Quebec Central R'y.	Dudswell Jc.
Maine Central R.R..	Zealand Jc.
Prof. & F. Notch R.R.	Bethlehem Jc.

Through Rates.

Niagara Falls	$21.70	Syracuse	$18.85
Rochester	20.45	Utica	18 70

Route 52—Bethlehem Junction, N. H.

Forms Ex. 399 and Ex. 748.

R., W. & O. R.R.....to	Clayton
R. & O. Nav. Co.....	Alexandria Bay
R. & O. Nav. Co.....	Montreal
Grand Trunk R'y or R. & O. Nav. Co.	Quebec
Ferry	Point Levis
Quebec Central R'y.	Dudswell Jc.
Maine Central R.R...	Zealand Jc.
Prof. & F. Notch R.R.	Bethlehem Jc.

Through Rates.

Niagara Falls	$21.70	Syracuse	$18.85
Rochester	20.45	Utica	18.70

Route 53—Block Island, R. I.

Form Ex. 550.

R., W. & O. R.R.....to	Norwood
Cent. Vermont R.R..	White River Jc.
Boston & Maine R.R.	Concord
Con. & Mont'l R.R...	Nashua
Boston & Maine R.R.	Boston
N. Y., N. H. & H. R.R.	Newport
Steamer..............	Block Island

Through Rates.

	Unlim'd	Lim'd
Niagara Falls	$18.90	$11.60
Rochester	18.55	11.30
Syracuse	16.95	....
Utica	16.85	....

Route 54—Block Island, R. I. and Return.

Form Ex. 551.

R., W. & O. R.R.....to	Norwood
Cent. Vermont R.R..	White River Jc.
Boston & Maine R.R.	Concord
Con. & Mont'l R.R...	Nashua
Boston & Maine R.R.	Boston
N. Y., N. H. & H. R.R.	Newport
Steamer..............	Block Island

RETURNING SAME ROUTE.

Through Rates.

	Unlim'd	Lim'd
Niagara Falls	$32 00	$22.30
Rochester	33.00	21.70
Syracuse	27.75	.....
Utica	26.50	.....

Route 55—Block Island, R. I. and Return.

Form Ex. 552.

R., W. & O. R.R.....to	Norwood
Cent. Vermont R.R..	White River Jc.
Boston & Maine R.R.	Concord
Con. & Mont'l R.R...	Nashua
Boston & Maine R.R.	Boston
N. Y., N. H. & H. R.R.	Newport
Steamer..............	Block Island
Steamer..............	Newport
N. Y., N. H. & H. R.R.	Boston
Boston & Maine R.R.	North Conway
Maine Central R.R. .	Lunenburg
St. J. & L. C. R.R....	Swanton
Cent. Vermont R.R..	Norwood
R., W. & O. R.R.....	starting point

Through Rates.

	Unlim'd	Lim'd
Niagara Falls	$37.50	$23.55
Rochester	35.50	21.70
Syracuse	33.25	.....
Utica	32.00	.....

Route 56—Bluff Point, N. Y. (Hotel Champlain).

Form Ex. 605.

R., W. & O. R.R.....to	Norwood
C. V. R.R. (O. & L. C. Div.)	Rouse's Point
D. & H. R.R..........	Bluff Point

Through Rates.

Niagara Falls	$10.35	Syracuse	$7.25
Rochester	8.85	Utica	7.15

Route 57—Bluff Point, N. Y. (Hotel Champlain), and Return.

Form Ex. 606.

R., W. & O. R.R.....to	Norwood
C. V. R.R. (O. & L. C. Div.)	Rouse's Point
D. & H. R.R.	Bluff Point

RETURNING SAME ROUTE.

Through Rates.

Niagara Falls	$19.80	Syracuse	$14.00
Rochester	17.00	Utica	14.00

Route 58—Bluff Point, N. Y. (Hotel Champlain).

Form Ex. 607.

R., W. & O. R.R.....to	Norwood
Cent. Vermont R.R..	Burlington
Cham. Trans. Co.....	Bluff Point

Through Rates.

Niagara Falls	$10 80	Syracuse	$7.85
Rochester	9.45	Utica	7.75

Route 59—Bluff Point, N. Y. (Hotel Champlain).

Forms Ex 254 and Ex 608.

R., W. & O. R.R.....to	Clayton
R. & O. Nav. Co.....	Alexandria Bay
R. & O. Nav. Co.....	Montreal
Grand Trunk R'y....	Rouse's Point
D. & H. R.R..........	Bluff Point

Through Rates.

Niagara Falls	$14.25	Syracuse	$11.40
Rochester	13.00	Utica	11.25

Route 60—Bluff Point, N. Y. (Hotel Champlain).

Forms Ex. 254 and Ex. 609.

R., W. & O. R.R.....to	Clayton
R. & O. Nav. Co.....	Alexandria Bay
R. & O. Nav. Co.....	Montreal
Grand Trunk R'y....	St. John's
Cent. Vermont R.R..	Burlington
Cham. Trans. Co.....	Bluff Point

Through Rates.

Niagara Falls	$15.45	Syracuse	$12.60
Rochester	14.20	Utica	12.45

Route 61—Boston, Mass.

Form Ex. 563

R., W. & O. R.R.....to	Norwood
Cent. Vermont R.R..	White River Jc.
Boston & Maine R.R.	Concord
Con. & Mont'l R.R ..	Nashua
Boston & Maine R.R.	Boston

Through Rates.

	Unlim'd	Lim'd
Niagara Falls	$17.70	$10.65
Rochester	16.35	9.10
Syracuse	14.75	.....
Utica	11.65	.....

Route 62—Boston, Mass. and Return.

Form Ex. 311.

R., W. & O. R.R.....to	Norwood
Cent. Vermont R.R..	White River Jc.
Boston & Maine R.R.	Concord
Con. & Mont'l R.R..	Nashua
Boston & Maine R.R.	Boston

RETURNING SAME ROUTE.

Through Rates.

	Unlim'd	Lim'd
Niagara Falls	$28.50	$20.05
Rochester	26.50	18.20
Syracuse	24.25	.....
Utica	23.00	.....

Route 63—Boston, Mass. and Return.

Form Ex. 569.

R., W. & O. R.R.....to	Norwood
Cent. Vermont R.R..	White River Jc.
Boston & Maine R.R.	Concord
Con. & Mont'l R.R ..	Nashua
Boston & Maine R.R.	Boston
Boston & Maine R.R.	North Conway
Maine Central R.R...	Lunenburg
St. J. & L. C. R.R....	Swanton
Cent. Vermont R.R..	Norwood
R., W. & O. R.R. ...	starting point

Through Rates.

	Unlim'd	Lim'd
Niagara Falls	$34.00	$20.05
Rochester	32.00	18.20
Syracuse	29.75	.....
Utica	28.50	.....

Route 64—Boston, Mass.

Form Ex. 229

R., W. & O. R.R.....to	Norwood
C. V. R.R. (O. & L. C. Div.)	Rouse's Point
D. & H. R.R.........	Plattsburg
D. & H. R.R. or Cham. Trans. Co.	Ft. Ticonderoga
D. & H. R.R.........	Baldwin
L. Geo. St'mb't Co...	Caldwell
D. & H. R.R. (via Saratoga)	Albany
Boston & Alb'y R.R.	Boston

Through Rates.

Niagara Falls	$20.90	Syracuse	$17.80
Rochester	19.40	Utica	17.70

Route 65—Boston, Mass.

From Ex. 791.

R., W. & O. R.R.... to	Norwood
C. V. R.R. (O. & L. C. Div.)	Rouse's Point
D. & H. R.R.	Plattsburg
D. & H. R.R. or Cham. Trans. Co.	Ft. Ticonderoga
D. & H. R.R.........	Baldwin
L. Geo. St'mb't Co...	Caldwell
D. & H. R.R.........	Saratoga
Fitchburg R.R.......	Boston

Through Rates.

Niagara Falls	$20.90	Syracuse	$17 80
Rochester	18.40	Utica	17.70

SEE NOTE ON PAGE 119 REGARDING STOP-OVER AT ALEXANDRIA BAY.

Route 66—Boston, Mass.
Form Ex. 690.

R., W. & O. R.R.....to	Norwood
Cent. Vermont R.R..	Swanton
St. J. & L. C. R.R....	Lunenburg
Maine Central R.R...	Fabyan's
Con. & Mont'l R.R...	Nashua
Boston & Maine R.R.	Boston

Through Rates.

Niagara Falls..$18.43	Syracuse.......$15.18
Rochester 17.23	Utica 14.18

Route 67—Boston, Mass. and Return.
Form Ex. 594.

R., W. & O. R.R.....to	Norwood
Cent. Vermont R.R..	Swanton
St. J. & L. C. R.R....	Lunenburg
Maine Central R.R...	Fabyan's
Con. & Mont'l R.R...	Nashua
Boston & Maine R.R.	Boston

RETURNING SAME ROUTE.

Through Rates.

Niagara Falls..$32.85	Syracuse......$28.60
Rochester...... 30.85	Utica........... 27.35

Route 68—Boston, Mass.
Form Ex. 681.

R., W. & O. R.R.....to	Norwood
Cent. Vermont R.R..	Swanton
St. J. & L. C. R.R....	Lunenburg
Maine Central R.R...	Portland
Boston & Maine R.R.	Boston

Through Rates.

Niagara Falls $18.43	Syracuse.......$15.18
Rochester 17.23	Utica 14.18

Route 69—Boston, Mass.
Form Ex 692.

R., W. & O. R.R.....to	Norwood
Cent. Vermont R.R..	Swanton
St. J. & L. C. R.R...	Lunenburg
Maine Central R.R...	North Conway
Boston & Maine R.R.	Boston

Through Rates.

Niagara Falls..$18.43	Syracuse.......$15.18
Rochester...... 17.23	Utica............ 14.18

Route 70—Boston, Mass.
Form Ex. 693.

R., W. & O. R.R.....to	Norwood
Cent. Vermont R.R..	Swanton
St. J. & L. C. R.R....	Lunenburg
Maine Central R.R. (via Portland)	Vanceboro
Can. Pac. R'y.......	St. John
International S.S. Co.	Boston

Through Rates.

Niagara Falls..$29.50	Syracuse.......$26.25
Rochester...... 28.00	Utica....... .... 25.25

Route 71—Boston, Mass.
Form Ex. 882.

R., W. & O. R.R.....to	Norwood
Cent. Vermont R.R..	Swanton
St. J. & L. C. R.R....	Lunenburg
Maine Central R.R. (via Portland)	Vanceboro
Can. Pac. R'y........	St. John
Bay of Fundy S.S. Co.	Annapolis
Dominion Atlantic R'y	Halifax
Canada Atlantic & Plant S.S. Co.....	Boston

Through Rates.

Niagara Falls..$37.30	Syracuse.......$34.05
Rochester...... 35.80	Utica....... .... 33.05

Route 72—Boston, Mass.
Form Ex. 793.

R., W. & O. R.R.....to	Norwood
Cent. Vermont R.R..	Swanton
St. J. & L. C. R.R....	Lunenburg
Maine Central R.R. (via Portland)	Vanceboro
Can. Pac. R'y........	St. John
Intercolonial R'y.....	Pt. du Chene
Charl't'n St. Nav. Co.	Summerside
P. E. Island R'y......	Charlottetown
Charl't'n St. Nav. Co.	Pictou
Intercolonial R'y	Halifax
Dominion Atlantic R'y	Annapolis
Bay of Fundy S.S. Co.	St. John
International S.S. Co.	Boston

Through Rates.

Niagara Falls..$44.55	Syracuse.......$41.30
Rochester...... 43.05	Utica. 40.30

Route 73—Boston, Mass.
Form Ex. 696.

R. W., & O. R.R.....to	Norwood
Cent. Vermont R.R..	Swanton
St. J. & L. C. R.R....	Lunenburg
Maine Central R.R. (via Portland)	Vanceboro
Can. Pac. R'y........	St. John
Intercolonial R'y.....	Pt. du Chene
Charl't'n St. Nav. Co.	Summerside
P. E. Island R'y......	Charlottetown
Charl't'n St. Nav. Co.	Pictou
Intercolonial R'y	Halifax
Canada Atlantic & Plant S.S. Co.	Boston

Through Rates.

Niagara Falls..$39.85	Syracuse.......$36.60
Rochester...... 38.35	Utica........... 35.60

Route 74—Boston, Mass.
Form Ex. 595.

R., W. & O. R.R.....to	Clayton
R. & O. Nav. Co.....	Alexandria Bay
R. & O. Nav. Co.....	Prescott
Ferry	Ogdensburg
Cent. Vermont R.R...	Swanton
St. J. & L. C. R.R....	Lunenburg
Maine Central R.R...	North Conway
Bost. & Maine R.R. (East'n Division)	Boston

Through Rates.

Niagara Falls..$21.90	Syracuse.......$16.95
Rochester...... 20.55	Utica....... .... 18.80

Route 75—Boston, Mass. (Adirondack Tour).
Forms Ex. 254 and Ex. 867.

R., W. & O. R.R.....to	Clayton
R. & O. Nav. Co.....	Alexandria Bay
R. & O. Nav Co.....	Montreal
N. Y. C. & H. R. R.R.	Albany
Boston & Albany R.R.	Boston

Through Rates.

Niagara Falls..$23.15	Syracuse.......$20.30
Rochester...... 21.90	Utica............ 20.15

Route 76—Boston, Mass. (Adirondack Tour).
Forms Ex. 254, Ex. 851, Ex. 179 and Ex. 214.

R., W. & O. R.R.....to	Clayton
R. & O. Nav. Co.....	Alexandria Bay
R. & O. Nav. Co.....	Montreal
N. Y. C. & H. R. R.R.	Albany
Day Line Steamers...	New York
Fall River Line.......	Boston

Through Rates.

Niagara Falls..$25.10	Syracuse.......$22.25
Rochester...... 23.85	Utica........... 22.10

Route 77—Boston, Mass. (Adirondack Tour).
Forms Ex. 254, Ex. 851, Ex. 180 and Ex. 214.

R., W. & O. R.R.....to	Clayton
R. & O. Nav. Co.....	Alexandria Bay
R. & O. Nav. Co.....	Montreal
N. Y. C. & H. R. R.R.	Albany
People's Line St'rs ...	New York
Fall River Line.......	Boston

Through Rates.

Niagara Falls..$24.60	Syracuse.......$21.75
Rochester...... 23.35	Utica 21.60

Route 78—Boston, Mass. (Adirondack Tour).
Forms 254, Ex. 851 and Ex. 214.

R., W. & O. R.R.....to	Clayton
R. & O. Nav. Co.....	Alexandria Bay
R. & O. Nav. Co.....	Montreal
N. Y. C. & H. R. R.R.	New York
Fall River Line.......	Boston

Through Rates.

Niagara Falls..$25.50	Syracuse.......$22.65
Rochester...... 24.25	Utica........... 22.50

Route 79—Boston, Mass.
Form Ex. 228.

R., W. & O. R.R.....to	Clayton
R. & O. Nav. Co.....	Alexandria Bay
R. & O. Nav. Co......	Montreal
Grand Trunk R'y....	Rouse's Point
D. & H. R.R.........	Plattsburg
D. & H. R.R. or Cham. Trans. Co.	Ft. Ticonderoga
D. & H. R.R.........	Baldwin
L. Geo. St'mb't Co...	Caldwell
D. & H. R.R. (via Saratoga)	Albany
Boston & Alb'y R.R.	Boston

Through Rates.

Niagara Falls..$24.65	Syracuse $21.80
Rochester... .. 23.40	Utica............ 21.65

Route 80—Boston, Mass.
Forms Ex. 254 and Ex. 788.

R., W. & O. R.R.....to	Clayton
R. & O. Nav. Co......	Alexandria Bay
R. & O. Nav. Co......	Montreal
Grand Trunk R'y....	Rouse's Point
D. & H. R.R.........	Plattsburg
D. & H. R.R. or Cham. Trans. Co.	Ft. Ticonderoga
D. & H. R.R.........	Baldwin
L. Geo. St'mb't Co...	Caldwell
D. & H. R.R.........	Saratoga
Fitchburg R.R......	Boston

Through Rates.

Niagara Falls..$24.65	Syracuse.......$21.80
Rochester...... 23.40	Utica 21.65

Route 81—Boston, Mass.
Forms Ex. 254 and Ex. 331.

R., W. & O. R.R.....to	Clayton
R. & O. Nav. Co......	Alexandria Bay
R. & O. Nav. Co......	Montreal
Grand Trunk R'y....	Rouse's Point
D. & H. R.R.........	Plattsburg
D. & H. R.R. or Cham. Trans. Co.	Ft. Ticonderoga
D. & H. R.R.........	Baldwin
L. Geo. St'mb't Co...	Caldwell
D. & H. R.R.	Albany
People's Line St'rs....	New York
Fall River Line......	Boston

Through Rates.

Niagara Falls..$25.95	Syracuse.......$23.10
Rochester...... 24.70	Utica 22.95

Route 82—Boston, Mass.
Forms Ex. 254, Ex. 355 and Ex. 221.

R., W. & O. R.R.....to	Clayton
R. & O. Nav. Co.....	Alexandria Bay
R. & O. Nav. Co.....	Montreal
Grand Trunk R'y....	Rouse's Point
D. & H. R.R.........	Plattsburg
D. & H. R.R. or Cham. Trans. Co.	Ft. Ticonderoga
D. & H. R.R.........	Baldwin
L. Geo. St'mb't Co...	Caldwell
D. & H. R.R.........	Albany
People's Line St'rs...	New York
Providence Line.....	Providence
N.Y., N. H. & H. R.R.	Boston

Through Rates.

Niagara Falls..$25.95	Syracuse.......$23.10
Rochester...... 24.70	Utica. 22.95

Route 83—Boston, Mass.
Forms Ex. 254, Ex. 355 and Ex. 219.

R., W. & O. R.R.....to	Clayton
R. & O. Nav. Co......	Alexandria Bay
R. & O. Nav. Co....	Montreal
Grand Trunk R'y....	Rouse's Point
D. & H. R.R.......	Plattsburg
D. & H. R.R. or Cham. Trans. Co.	Ft. Ticonderoga
D. & H. R.R.........	Baldwin
L. Geo. St'mb't Co...	Caldwell
D. & H. R.R.........	Albany
People's Line St'rs...	New York
Stonington Line......	Stonington
N.Y., N. H. & H. R.R.	Providence
N.Y., N. H. & H. R.R.	Boston

Through Rates.

Niagara Falls..$25.95	Syracuse.......$23.10
Rochester...... 24.70	Utica 22.95

SEE NOTE ON PAGE 119 REGARDING STOP-OVER AT ALEXANDRIA BAY.

Route 84—Boston, Mass.

Forms Ex. 254 and Ex. 333.

R., W. & O. R.R. ...to	Clayton
R. & O. Nav. Co.....	Alexandria Bay
R. & O. Nav. Co.....	Montreal
Grand Trunk R'y....	Rouse's Point
D. & H. R.R.........	Plattsburg
Cham. Trans. Co.....	Burlington
Cent. Vermont R.R..	Bellows Falls
Fitchburg R.R	Boston

Through Rates.

Niagara Falls	$20.90	Syracuse	$18.05
Rochester	19.65	Utica	17.33

Route 85—Boston, Mass.

Forms Ex. 254 and Ex. 338.

R., W. & O. R.R.....to	Clayton
R. & O. Nav. Co.....	Alexandria Bay
R. & O. Nav. Co.....	Montreal
Grand Trunk R'y....	St. John's
Cent. Vermont R.R..	Burlington
Cham. Trans. Co.....	Ft. Ticonderoga
D. & H. R.R.........	Baldwin
L. Geo. St'mb't Co...	Caldwell
D. & H. R.R.........	Albany
Day Line Steamers...	New York
Fall River Line.......	Boston

Through Rates.

Niagara Falls	$26.60	Syracuse	$23.75
Rochester	25.35	Utica	23.60

Route 86—Boston, Mass.

Forms Ex. 254, Ex. 375 and Ex. 221.

R., W. & O. R.R.....to	Clayton
R. & O. Nav. Co.....	Alexandria Bay
R. & O. Nav. Co.....	Montreal
Grand Trunk R'y....	St. John's
Cent. Vermont R.R..	Burlington
Cham. Trans. Co.....	Ft. Ticonderoga
D. & H. R.R.........	Baldwin
L. Geo. St'mb't Co...	Caldwell
D. & H. R.R.........	Albany
Day Line Steamers...	New York
Providence Line......	Providence
N.Y., N. H. & H. R.R.	Boston

Through Rates.

Niagara Falls	$26.60	Syracuse	$23.75
Rochester	25.35	Utica	23.60

Route 87—Boston, Mass.

Forms Ex. 254, Ex. 375 and Ex. 219.

R., W. & O. R.R.....to	Clayton
R. & O. Nav. Co.....	Alexandria Bay
R. & O. Nav. Co.....	Montreal
Grand Trunk R'y....	St. John's
Cent. Vermont R.R..	Burlington
Cham. Trans. Co.....	Ft. Ticonderoga
D. & H. R.R.........	Baldwin
L. Geo. St'mb't Co...	Caldwell
D. & H. R.R.........	Albany
Day Line Steamers...	New York
Stonington Line......	Stonington
N.Y., N. H. & H. R.R.	Providence
N.Y., N. H. & H. R.R.	Boston

Through Rates.

Niagara Falls	$26.60	Syracuse	$23.75
Rochester	25.35	Utica	23.60

Route 88—Boston, Mass.

Forms Ex. 254 and Ex. 329.

R., W. & O. R.R.....to	Clayton
R. & O. Nav. Co.....	Alexandria Bay
R. & O. Nav. Co.....	Montreal
Grand Trunk R'y....	St. John's
Cent. Vermont R.R..	Bellows Falls
Fitchburg R.R.......	Boston

Through Rates.

Niagara Falls	$20.50	Syracuse	$17.65
Rochester	19.25	Utica	17.50

Route 89—Boston, Mass.

Forms Ex. 254 and Ex. 339.

R., W. & O. R.R.....to	Clayton
R. & O. Nav. Co.....	Alexandria Bay
R. & O. Nav. Co.....	Montreal
Grand Trunk R'y....	St. John's
Cent. Vermont R.R	White River Jc.
Boston & Maine R.R.	Concord
Con. & Mont'l R.R..	Nashua
Boston & Maine R.R.	Boston

Through Rates.

Niagara Falls	$20.50	Syracuse	$17.65
Rochester	19.25	Utica	17.50

Route 90—Boston, Mass. and Return.

Form Ex. 307.

R., W. & O. R.R.....to	Clayton
R. & O. Nav. Co.....	Alexandria Bay
R. & O. Nav. Co.....	Montreal
Grand Trunk R'y....	St. John's
Cent. Vermont R.R..	White River Jc.
Boston & Maine R.R.	Concord
Con. & Mont'l R.R..	Nashua
Boston & Maine R.R.	Boston

RETURNING SAME ROUTE.

Through Rates.

Niagara Falls	$34.50	Syracuse	$30.00
Rochester	32.50	Utica	30.00

Route 91—Boston, Mass. and Return.

Form Ex. 596.

R., W. & O. R.R.....to	Clayton
R. & O. Nav. Co.....	Alexandria Bay
R. & O. Nav. Co.....	Montreal
Grand Trunk R'y....	St. John's
Cent. Vermont R.R..	White River Jc.
Boston & Maine R.R.	Concord
Con. & Mont'l R.R..	Nashua
Boston & Maine R.R.	Boston
Boston & Maine R.R.	Nashua
Con. & Mont'l R.R..	Fabyan's
Maine Central R.R...	Lunenburg
St. J. & L. C. R.R....	Swanton
Cent. Vermont R.R..	Norwood
R., W. & O. R.R.....	starting point

Through Rates.

Niagara Falls	$37.35	Syracuse	$31.65
Rochester	34.60	Utica	31.65

Route 92—Boston, Mass.

Forms Ex. 254 and Ex. 691.

R., W. & O. R.R.....to	Clayton
R. & O. Nav. Co.....	Alexandria Bay
R. & O. Nav. Co.....	Montreal
Can. Pac. R'y........	Newport
Boston & Maine R.R.	Wells River
Con. & Mont'l R.R..	Nashua
Boston & Maine R.R.	Boston

Through Rates.

Niagara Falls	$20.50	Syracuse	$17.65
Rochester	19.25	Utica	17.50

Route 93—Boston, Mass.

Forms Ex. 254 and Ex. 591.

R., W. & O. R.R.....to	Clayton
R. & O. Nav. Co.....	Alexandria Bay
R. & O. Nav. Co.....	Montreal
Can. Pac. R'y........	Newport
Boston & Maine R.R.	Lunenburg
Maine Central R.R..	Fabyan's
Con. & Mont'l R.R..	Nashua
Boston & Maine R.R.	Boston

Through Rates.

Niagara Falls	$20.50	Syracuse	$17.65
Rochester	19.25	Utica	17.50

Route 94—Boston, Mass. and Return.

Forms Ex. 255 and Ex. 598.

R., W. & O. R.R.....to	Clayton
R. & O. Nav. Co.....	Alexandria Bay
R. & O. Nav. Co.....	Montreal
Can. Pac. R'y........	Newport
Boston & Maine R.R.	Lunenburg
Maine Central R.R..	Fabyan's
Con. & Mont'l R.R..	Nashua
Boston & Maine R.R.	Boston

RETURNING SAME ROUTE.

Through Rates.

Niagara Falls	$34.50	Syracuse	$30.00
Rochester	32.50	Utica	30.00

Route 95—Boston, Mass. and Return.

Form Ex. 593.

R., W. & O. R.R.....to	Clayton
R. & O. Nav. Co.....	Alexandria Bay
R. & O. Nav. Co.....	Montreal
Can. Pac. R'y........	Newport
Boston & Maine R.R.	Lunenburg
Maine Central R.R..	Fabyan's
Con. & Mont'l R.R...	Nashua
Boston & Maine R.R.	Boston
Boston & Maine R.R	Nashua
Con. & Mont'l R.R...	Concord
Boston & Maine R.R.	White River Jc.
Cent. Vermont R.R..	Norwood
R., W. & O. R.R.....	starting point

Through Rates.

Niagara Falls	$37.35	Syracuse	$31.65
Rochester	34.60	Utica	31.65

Route 96—Boston, Mass.

Forms Ex. 254 and Ex 698.

R., W. & O. R.R.....to	Clayton
R. & O. Nav. Co.....	Alexandria Bay
R. & O. Nav. Co.....	Montreal
Can. Pac. R'y........	Newport
Boston & Maine R.R.	Lunenburg
Maine Central R.R...	Zealand Jc.
Prof. & F. Notch R.R.	Profile House
Stage.................	No. Woodstock
Con. & Mont'l R.R...	Nashua
Boston & Maine R.R.	Boston

Through Rates.

Niagara Falls	$23.40	Syracuse	$20.55
Rochester	22.15	Utica	20.40

Route 97—Boston, Mass.

Forms Ex. 254 and Ex. 601.

R., W. & O. R.R.....to	Clayton
R. & O. Nav. Co.....	Alexandria Bay
R. & O. Nav. Co.....	Montreal
Can. Pac. R'y........	Newport
Boston & Maine R.R.	Lunenburg
Maine Central R.R...	North Conway
Boston & Maine R.R.	Boston

Through Rates.

Niagara Falls	$20.50	Syracuse	$17.65
Rochester	19.25	Utica	17.50

Route 98—Boston, Mass.

Forms Ex. 254 and Ex. 602.

R., W. & O. R.R.....to	Clayton
R. & O. Nav. Co.....	Alexandria Bay
R. & O. Nav. Co.....	Montreal
Can. Pac. R'y........	Newport
Boston & Maine R.R.	Lunenburg
Maine Central R.R...	Portland
Boston & Maine R.R.	Boston

Through Rates.

Niagara Falls	$20.50	Syracuse	$17.65
Rochester	19.25	Utica	17.50

Route 99—Boston, Mass.

Forms Ex. 254 and Ex. 699.

R., W. & O. R.R.....to	Clayton
R. & O. Nav. Co.....	Alexandria Bay
R. & O. Nav. Co.....	Montreal
Can. Pac. R'y........	Newport
Boston & Maine R.R.	Lunenburg
Maine Central R.R...	Zealand Jc.
Prof. & F. Notch R.R.	Profile House
Prof. & F. Notch R.R.	Bethlehem Jc.
Con. & Mont'l R.R..	Base Mt. Wash.
Mt. Washington R'y.	Summit
Stage.................	Glen Site
Stage.................	Alpine House (Gorham)
Grand Trunk R'y....	Portland
Boston & Maine R.R.	Boston

Through Rates.

Niagara Falls	$34.75	Syracuse	$31.90
Rochester	33.50	Utica	31.75

Route 100—Boston, Mass.

Forms Ex. 254 and Ex. 700.

R., W. & O. R.R.....to	Clayton
R. & O. Nav. Co.....	Alexandria Bay
R. & O. Nav. Co.....	Montreal
Can. Pac. R'y........	Newport
Boston & Maine R.R.	Lunenburg
Maine Central R.R..	Portland
International S.S. Co.	St. John
Intercolonial R'y.....	Mulgrave
Bras d'Or S. Nav. Co.	Sydney
Bras d'Or S. Nav. Co.	Mulgrave
Intercolonial R'y. ...	Halifax
Canada Atlantic & Plant S.S. Co.	Boston

Through Rates.

Niagara Falls	$46.00	Syracuse	$43.15
Rochester	44.75	Utica	43.00

SEE NOTE ON PAGE 119 REGARDING STOP-OVER AT ALEXANDRIA BAY.

Route 101—Boston, Mass.

Forms Ex. 254 and Ex. 859.

R., W. & O. R.R.	to Clayton
R. & O. Nav. Co.	Alexandria Bay
R. & O. Nav. Co.	Montreal
Can. Pac. R'y	St John
Bay of Fundy S.S. Co.	Annapolis
Dominion Atlantic R'y	Halifax
Canada Atlantic & Plant S.S. Co.	Boston

Through Rates.

Niagara Falls	$37.30	Syracuse	$34.45
Rochester	36.05	Utica	34.30

Route 102—Boston, Mass.

Forms Ex. 254 and Ex. 859.

R., W. & O. R.R.	to Clayton
R. & O. Nav. Co.	Alexandria Bay
R. & O. Nav. Co.	Montreal
Can. Pac. R'y	St. John
Intercolonial R'y	Pt. Du Chene
Charl't'n St. Nav. Co.	Summerside
P. E. Island R'y	Charlottetown
Charl't'n St. Nav. Co.	Pictou
Intercolonial R'y	Halifax
Dominion Atlantic R'y	Annapolis
Bay of Fundy S.S. Co.	St. John
International S.S. Co.	Boston

Through Rates.

Niagara Falls	$42.20	Syracuse	$39.35
Rochester	40.95	Utica	39.20

Route 103—Boston, Mass.

Forms Ex. 254 and Ex. 330.

R., W. & O. R.R.	to Clayton
R. & O. Nav. Co.	Alexandria Bay
R. & O. Nav. Co.	Montreal
Grand Trunk R'y	Portland
Boston & Maine R.R.	Boston

Through Rates.

Niagara Falls	$20.50	Syracuse	$17.65
Rochester	19.25	Utica	17.50

Route 104—Boston, Mass.

Forms Ex. 254 and Ex. 701.

R., W. & O. R.R.	to Clayton
R. & O. Nav. Co.	Alexandria Bay
R. & O. Nav. Co.	Montreal
Grand Trunk R'y	Groveton
Con. & Mont'l R.R.	Nashua
Boston & Maine R.R.	Boston

Through Rates.

Niagara Falls	$20.50	Syracuse	$17.65
Rochester	19.25	Utica	17.50

Route 105—Boston, Mass.

Forms Ex. 254, Ex. 709 and Ex. 199.

R., W. & O. R.R.	to Clayton
R. & O. Nav. Co.	Alexandria Bay
R. & O. Nav. Co.	Montreal
Grand Trunk R'y	Groveton
Con. & Mont'l R.R.	Fabyan's
Con. & Mont'l R.R.	Bethlehem Jc.
Prof. & F. Notch R.R.	Profile House
Prof. & F. Notch R.R.	Bethlehem Jc.
Con. & Mont'l R.R.	Nashua
Boston & Maine R.R.	Boston

Through Rates.

Niagara Falls	$23.50	Syracuse	$20.65
Rochester	22.25	Utica	20.50

Route 106—Boston, Mass.

Forms Ex. 254 and Ex. 703.

R., W. & O. R.R.	to Clayton
R. & O. Nav. Co.	Alexandria Bay
R. & O. Nav. Co.	Montreal
Grand Trunk R'y	Groveton
Con. & Mont'l R.R.	Fabyan's
Con. & Mont'l R.R.	Bethlehem Jc.
Prof. & F. Notch R.R.	Profile House
Stage	No. Woodstock
Con. & Mont'l R.R.	Nashua
Boston & Maine R.R.	Boston

Through Rates.

Niagara Falls	$23.40	Syracuse	$20.55
Rochester	22.15	Utica	20.40

Route 107—Boston, Mass.

Forms Ex. 254, Ex. 104, Ex. 199 and Ex. 131.

R., W. & O. R.R.	to Clayton
R. & O. Nav. Co.	Alexandria Bay
R. & O. Nav. Co.	Montreal
Grand Trunk R'y	St. John's
Cent. Vermont R.R.	Montpelier
Mont. & W. R. R.R.	Wells River
Con. & Mont'l R.R.	Bethlehem Jc.
Prof. & F. Notch R.R.	Profile House
Prof. & F. Notch R.R.	Bethlehem Jc.
Con. & Mont'l R.R.	Fabyan's
Maine Central R.R.	Crawford's
Maine Central R.R.	Fabyan's
Con. & Mont'l R.R.	Nashua
Boston & Maine R.R.	Boston

Through Rates.

Niagara Falls	$24.00	Syracuse	$21.15
Rochester	22.75	Utica	21.00

Route 108—Boston, Mass.

Forms Ex. 254 and Ex. 343.

R., W. & O. R.R.	to Clayton
R. & O. Nav. Co.	Alexandria Bay
R. & O. Nav. Co.	Montreal
Grand Trunk R'y	Alpine House (Gorham)
Stage	Glen Site
Stage	Sum't Mt. Wash.
Mt. Washington R'y.	Base
Con. & Mont'l R.R.	Bethlehem Jc.
Prof. & F. Notch R.R.	Profile House
Stage	No. Woodstock
Con. & Mont'l R.R.	Nashua
Boston & Maine R.R.	Boston

Through Rates.

Niagara Falls	$34.25	Syracuse	$31.40
Rochester	33.00	Utica	31.25

Route 109—Boston, Mass.

Forms Ex. 254, Ex. 344 and Ex. 199.

R., W. & O. R.R.	to Clayton
R. & O. Nav. Co.	Alexandria Bay
R. & O. Nav. Co.	Montreal
Grand Trunk R'y	Alpine House (Gorham)
Stage	Glen Site
Stage	Sum't Mt. Wash.
Mt. Washington R'y.	Base
Con. & Mont'l R.R.	Bethlehem Jc.
Prof. & F. Notch R.R.	Profile House
Prof. & F. Notch R.R.	Bethlehem Jc.
Con. & Mont'l R.R.	Nashua
Boston & Maine R.R.	Boston

Through Rates.

Niagara Falls	$36.93	Syracuse	$34.08
Rochester	35.63	Utica	33.93

Route 110—Boston, Mass.

Forms Ex. 399 and Ex. 416.

R., W. & O. R. R.	to Clayton
R. & O. Nav. Co.	Alexandria Bay
R. & O. Nav. Co.	Montreal
Grand Trunk R'y or R. & O. Nav. Co.	Quebec
Ferry	Point Levis
Grand Trunk R'y	Portland
Boston & Maine R.R.	Boston

Through Rates.

Niagara Falls	$25.50	Syracuse	$22.65
Rochester	24.25	Utica	22.50

Route 111—Boston, Mass.

Forms Ex. 399 and Ex. 427.

R., W. & O. R.R.	to Clayton
R. & O. Nav. Co.	Alexandria Bay
R. & O. Nav. Co.	Montreal
Grand Trunk R'y or R. & O. Nav. Co.	Quebec
Ferry	Point Levis
Grand Trunk R'y	Groveton
Con. & Mont'l R.R.	Nashua
Boston & Maine R.R.	Boston

Through Rates.

Niagara Falls	$25.50	Syracuse	$22.65
Rochester	24.25	Utica	22.50

Route 112—Boston, Mass.

Forms Ex. 399 and Ex. 705.

R., W. & O. R.R.	to Clayton
R. & O. Nav. Co.	Alexandria Bay
R. & O. Nav. Co.	Montreal
Grand Trunk R'y or R. & O. Nav. Co.	Quebec
Ferry	Point Levis
Grand Trunk R'y	Sherbrooke
Boston & Maine R.R.	Lunenburg
Maine Central R.R.	North Conway
B. & M. R.R. (E. Div.)	Boston

Through Rates.

Niagara Falls	$25.50	Syracuse	$22.65
Rochester	24.25	Utica	22.50

Route 113—Boston, Mass.

Forms Ex. 399 and Ex. 706.

R., W. & O. R.R.	to Clayton
R. & O. Nav. Co.	Alexandria Bay
R. & O. Nav. Co.	Montreal
Grand Trunk R'y or R. & O. Nav. Co.	Quebec
Ferry	Point Levis
Grand Trunk R'y	Sherbrooke
Boston & Maine R.R.	Concord
Con. & Mont'l R.R.	Nashua
Boston & Maine R.R.	Boston

Through Rates.

Niagara Falls	$25.50	Syracuse	$22.65
Rochester	24.25	Utica	22.50

Route 114—Boston, Mass.

Forms Ex. 399 and Ex. 707.

R., W. & O. R.R.	to Clayton
R. & O. Nav. Co.	Alexandria Bay
R. & O. Nav. Co.	Montreal
Grand Trunk R'y or R. & O. Nav. Co.	Quebec
Ferry	Point Levis
Quebec Central R'y	Sherbrooke
Boston & Maine R.R.	Concord
Con. & Mont'l R.R.	Nashua
Boston & Maine R.R.	Boston

Through Rates.

Niagara Falls	$25.50	Syracuse	$22.65
Rochester	24.25	Utica	22.50

Route 115—Boston, Mass.

Forms Ex. 400 and Ex. 707.

R., W. & O. R.R.	to Clayton
R. & O. Nav. Co.	Alexandria Bay
R. & O. Nav. Co.	Montreal
Can. Pac. R'y or R. & O. Nav. Co.	Quebec
Ferry	Point Levis
Quebec Central R'y	Sherbrooke
Boston & Maine R.R.	Concord
Con. & Mont'l R.R.	Nashua
Boston & Maine R.R.	Boston

Through Rates.

Niagara Falls	$25.50	Syracuse	$22.65
Rochester	24.25	Utica	22.50

Route 116—Boston, Mass.

Forms Ex. 399 and Ex. 428.

R., W. & O. R.R.	to Clayton
R. & O. Nav. Co.	Alexandria Bay
R. & O. Nav. Co.	Montreal
Grand Trunk R'y or R. & O. Nav. Co.	Quebec
Ferry	Point Levis
Grand Trunk R'y	Sherbrooke
Boston & Maine R.R.	Wells River
Con. & Mont'l R.R.	Nashua
Boston & Maine R.R.	Boston

Through Rates.

Niagara Falls	$25.50	Syracuse	$22.65
Rochester	24.25	Utica	22.50

SEE NOTE ON PAGE 119 REGARDING STOP-OVER AT ALEXANDRIA BAY.

Route 117—Boston, Mass.

Forms Ex. 399, Ex. 761 and Ex. 131.

R., W. & O. R.R. ....to	Clayton
R. & O. Nav. Co.....	Alexandria Bay
R. & O. Nav. Co.....	Montreal
Grand Trunk R'y or R. & O. Nav. Co.	Quebec
Ferry...............	Point Levis
Grand Trunk R'y....	Sherbrooke
Boston & Maine R.R.	Lunenburg
Maine Central R.R...	Zealand Jc.
Prof. & F. Notch R.R.	Profile House
Prof. & F. Notch R.R.	Bethlehem Jc.
Con. & Mont'l R.R...	Fabyan's
Maine Central R.R...	Crawford House
Maine Central R.R..	Fabyan's
Con. & Mont'l R.R...	Base Mt. Wash.
Mt. Washington R'y.	Summit
Stage...............	Glen Site
Stage...............	Alpine House (Gorham)
Grand Trunk R'y....	Portland
Boston & Maine R.R.	Boston

Through Rates.

Niagara Falls..$39.35	Syracuse.......$36.50
Rochester...... 38.10	Utica........... 36.35

Route 118—Boston, Mass.

Forms Ex. 400 and Ex. 749.

R., W. & O. R.R. ....to	Clayton
R. & O. Nav. Co......	Alexandria Bay
R. & O. Nav. Co. ...	Montreal
Can. Pac. R'y or R. & O. Nav. Co.	Quebec
Ferry...............	Point Levis
Quebec Central R'y..	Sherbrooke
Boston & Maine R.R.	Lunenburg
Maine Central R.R...	Zealand Jc.
Prof. & F. Notch R.R.	Profile House
Prof. & F. Notch R.R.	Zealand Jc.
Maine Central R.R...	Crawford House
Maine Central R.R...	Fabyan's
Con. & Mont'l R.R...	Base Mt. Wash.
Mt. Washington R'y.	Summit
Stage...............	Glen Site
Stage...............	Glen
Maine Central R.R...	Portland
Boston & Maine R.R.	Boston

Through Rates.

Niagara Falls..$39.85	Syracuse.......$37.00
Rochester...... 38.60	Utica........... 36.85

Route 119—Boston, Mass.

Forms Ex. 399 and Ex. 417.

R., W. & O. R.R. ....to	Clayton
R. & O. Nav. Co.....	Alexandria Bay
R. & O. Nav. Co.....	Montreal
Grand Trunk R'y or R. & O. Nav. Co.	Quebec
Ferry...............	Point Levis
Quebec Central R'y..	Sherbrooke
Boston & Maine R.R.	Wells River
Con. & Mont'l R.R..	Nashua
Boston & Maine R.R.	Boston

Through Rates.

Niagara Falls..$25.50	Syracuse.......$22.65
Rochester...... 24.25	Utica........... 22.50

Route 120—Boston, Mass.

Forms Ex. 400 and Ex. 417.

R., W. & O. R.R. ....to	Clayton
R. & O. Nav. Co.....	Alexandria Bay
R. & O. Nav. Co.....	Montreal
Can. Pac. R'y or R. & O. Nav. Co.	Quebec
Ferry...............	Point Levis
Quebec Central R'y..	Sherbrooke
Boston & Maine R.R.	Wells River
Con. & Mont'l R.R...	Nashua
Boston & Maine R.R.	Boston

Through Rates.

Niagara Falls..$25.50	Syracuse.......$22.65
Rochester...... 24.25	Utica........... 22.50

Route 121—Boston, Mass.

Forms Ex. 399 and Ex. 708.

R., W. & O. R.R. ....to	Clayton
R. & O. Nav. Co.....	Alexandria Bay
R. & O. Nav. Co.....	Montreal
Grand Trunk R'y or R. & O. Nav. Co.	Quebec
Ferry...............	Point Levis
Quebec Central R'y.	Sherbrooke
Boston & Maine R.R.	Lunenburg
Maine Central R.R...	North Conway
Boston & Maine R.R.	Boston

Through Rates.

Niagara Falls..$25.50	Syracuse.......$22.65
Rochester...... 24.25	Utica........... 22.50

Route 122—Boston, Mass.

Forms Ex. 400 and Ex. 708.

R., W. & O. R.R. ....to	Clayton
R. & O. Nav. Co.....	Alexandria Bay
R. & O. Nav. Co.....	Montreal
Can. Pac. R'y or R. & O. Nav. Co.	Quebec
Ferry...............	Point Levis
Quebec Central R'y..	Sherbrooke
Boston & Maine R.R.	Lunenburg
Maine Central R.R...	North Conway
Boston & Maine R.R.	Boston

Through Rates.

Niagara Falls..$25.50	Syracuse.......$22.65
Rochester...... 24.25	Utica........... 22.50

Route 123—Boston, Mass.

Forms Ex. 399 and Ex. 710.

R., W. & O. R.R. ....to	Clayton
R. & O. Nav. Co.....	Alexandria Bay
R. & O. Nav. Co.....	Montreal
Grand Trunk R'y or R. & O. Nav. Co.	Quebec
Ferry...............	Point Levis
Quebec Central R'y..	Dudswell Jc.
Maine Central R.R...	North Conway
Boston & Maine R.R.	Boston

Through Rates.

Niagara Falls..$25.50	Syracuse.......$22.65
Rochester...... 24.25	Utica........... 22.50

Route 124—Boston, Mass.

Forms Ex. 400 and Ex. 750.

R., W. & O. R.R. ....to	Clayton
R. & O. Nav. Co.....	Alexandria Bay
R. & O. Nav. Co.....	Montreal
Can. Pac. R'y or R. & O. Nav. Co.	Quebec
Ferry...............	Point Levis
Quebec Central R'y..	Dudswell Jc.
Maine Central R.R..	North Conway
Boston & Maine R.R.	Boston

Through Rates.

Niagara Falls..$25.50	Syracuse.......$22.65
Rochester...... 24.25	Utica........... 22.50

Route 125—Boston, Mass.

Forms Ex. 399 and Ex. 709.

R., W. & O. R.R. ....to	Clayton
R. & O. Nav. Co......	Alexandria Bay
R. & O. Nav. Co......	Montreal
Grand Trunk R'y or R. & O. Nav. Co.	Quebec
Ferry...............	Point Levis
Quebec Central R'y..	Sherbrooke
Boston & Maine R.R.	Lunenburg
Maine Central R.R...	Portland
Boston & Maine R.R.	Boston

Through Rates.

Niagara Falls..$25.50	Syracuse.......$22.65
Rochester...... 24.25	Utica........... 22.50

Route 126—Boston, Mass.

Forms Ex. 400 and Ex. 709.

R., W. & O. R.R. ....to	Clayton
R. & O. Nav. Co.....	Alexandria Bay
R. & O. Nav. Co.....	Montreal
Can. Pac. R'y or R. & O. Nav. Co.	Quebec
Ferry...............	Point Levis
Quebec Central R'y..	Sherbrooke
Boston & Maine R.R.	Lunenburg
Maine Central R.R..	Portland
Boston & Maine R.R.	Boston

Through Rates.

Niagara Falls..$25.50	Syracuse.......$22.65
Rochester...... 24.25	Utica........... 22.50

Route 127—Boston, Mass.

Forms Ex. 399 and Ex. 751.

R., W. & O. R.R. ....to	Clayton
R. & O. Nav. Co.....	Alexandria Bay
R. & O. Nav. Co.....	Montreal
Grand Trunk R'y or R. & O. Nav. Co.	Quebec
Ferry...............	Point Levis
Quebec Central R'y..	Dudswell Jc.
Maine Central R.R...	Portland
Boston & Maine R.R.	Boston

Through Rates.

Niagara Falls..$25.50	Syracuse.......$22.65
Rochester...... 24.25	Utica........... 22.50

Route 128—Boston, Mass.

Forms Ex. 400 and Ex. 751.

R., W. & O. R.R. ....to	Clayton
R. & O. Nav. Co.....	Alexandria Bay
R. & O. Nav. Co.....	Montreal
Can. Pac. R'y or R. & O. Nav. Co.	Quebec
Ferry...............	Point Levis
Quebec Central R'y..	Dudswell Jc.
Maine Central R.R...	Portland
Boston & Maine R.R.	Boston

Through Rates.

Niagara Falls..$25.50	Syracuse.......$22.65
Rochester...... 24.25	Utica........... 22.50

Route 129—Boston, Mass.

Forms Ex. 399 and Ex. 710.

R., W. & O. R.R. ....to	Clayton
R. & O. Nav. Co.....	Alexandria Bay
R. & O. Nav. Co.....	Montreal
Grand Trunk R'y or R. & O. Nav. Co.	Quebec
Ferry...............	Point Levis
Quebec Central R'y.	Sherbrooke
Boston & Maine R.R.	Lunenburg
Maine Central R.R..	Portland
International S.S. Co.	Boston

Through Rates.

Niagara Falls..$24.00	Syracuse.......$21.15
Rochester...... 22.75	Utica........... 21.00

Route 130—Boston, Mass.

Forms Ex. 400 and Ex. 710.

R., W. & O. R.R. ....to	Clayton
R. & O. Nav. Co.....	Alexandria Bay
R. & O. Nav. Co.....	Montreal
Can. Pac. R'y or R. & O. Nav. Co.	Quebec
Ferry...............	Point Levis
Quebec Central R'y..	Sherbrooke
Boston & Maine R.R.	Lunenberg
Maine Central R.R..	Portland
International S.S. Co.	Boston

Through Rates.

Niagara Falls..$24.00	Syracuse.......$21.15
Rochester...... 22.75	Utica........... 21.00

Route 131—Boston, Mass.

Forms Ex. 399 and Ex. 752.

R., W. & O. R.R. ....to	Clayton
R. & O. Nav. Co.....	Alexandria Bay
R. & O. Nav. Co.....	Montreal
Grand Trunk R'y or R. & O. Nav. Co.	Quebec
Ferry...............	Point Levis
Quebec Central R'y.	Dudswell Jc.
Maine Central R.R..	Portland
International S.S. Co.	Boston

Through Rates.

Niagara Falls..$24.00	Syracuse.......$21.15
Rochester...... 22.75	Utica........... 21.00

Route 132—Boston, Mass.

Forms Ex. 400 and Ex. 752.

R., W. & O. R.R. ....to	Clayton
R. & O. Nav. Co.....	Alexandria Bay
R. & O. Nav. Co.....	Montreal
Can. Pac. R'y or R. & O. Nav. Co.	Quebec
Ferry...............	Point Levis
Quebec Central R'y..	Dudswell Jc.
Maine Central R.R..	Portland
International S.S. Co.	Boston

Through Rates.

Niagara Falls..$24.00	Syracuse.......$21.15
Rochester...... 22.75	Utica........... 21.00

SEE NOTE ON PAGE 119 REGARDING STOP-OVER AT ALEXANDRIA BAY.

Route 133—Boston, Mass.
Forms Ex. 399 and Ex. 603.

R., W. & O. R.R.....to	Clayton
R. & O. Nav. Co.....	Alexandria Bay
R. & O. Nav. Co.....	Montreal
Grand Trunk R'y or R. & O. Nav. Co.	Quebec
Ferry..................	Point Levis
Quebec Central R'y..	Sherbrooke
Boston & Maine R.R.	Lunenburg
Maine Central R.R...	Fabyan's
Con. & Mont'l R.R...	Nashua
Boston & Maine R.R.	Boston

Through Rates.

Niagara Falls	$25.50	Syracuse	$22.65
Rochester	24.25	Utica	22.50

Route 134—Boston, Mass.
Forms Ex. 400 and Ex. 603.

R., W. & O. R.R.....to	Clayton
R. & O. Nav. Co.....	Alexandria Bay
R. & O. Nav. Co.....	Montreal
Can. Pac. R'y or R. & O. Nav. Co.	Quebec
Ferry..................	Point Levis
Quebec Central R'y..	Sherbrooke
Boston & Maine R.R.	Lunenburg
Maine Central R.R..	Fabyan's
Con. & Mont'l R.R...	Nashua
Boston & Maine R.R.	Boston

Through Rates.

Niagara Falls	$25.50	Syracuse	$22.65
Rochester	24.25	Utica	22.50

Route 135—Boston, Mass.
Forms Ex. 399 and Ex. 604.

R., W. & O. R.R.....to	Clayton
R. & O. Nav. Co.....	Alexandria Bay
R. & O. Nav. Co.....	Montreal
Grand Trunk R'y or R. & O. Nav. Co.	Quebec
Ferry..................	Point Levis
Quebec Central R'y..	Sherbrooke
Boston & Maine R.R.	Lunenburg
Maine Central R.R...	North Conway
Boston & Maine R.R.	Wolfboro
L. Win. St'mb't Co...	Weir's
Con. & Mont'l R.R...	Nashua
Boston & Maine R.R.	Boston

Through Rates.

Niagara Falls	$28.00	Syracuse	$25.15
Rochester	26.75	Utica	25.00

Route 136—Boston, Mass.
Forms Ex. 400 and Ex. 604.

R., W. & O. R.R.....to	Clayton
R. & O. Nav. Co.....	Alexandria Bay
R. & O. Nav. Co.....	Montreal
Can. Pac. R'y or R. & O. Nav. Co.	Quebec
Ferry..................	Point Levis
Quebec Central R'y..	Sherbrooke
Boston & Maine R.R.	Lunenburg
Maine Central R.R...	North Conway
Boston & Maine R.R.	Wolfboro
L. Win. St'mb't Co...	Weir's
Con. & Mont'l R.R..	Nashua
Boston & Maine R.R.	Boston

Through Rates.

Niagara Falls	$28.00	Syracuse	$26.15
Rochester	26.75	Utica	25.00

Route 137—Boston, Mass.
Forms Ex. 399 and Ex. 711.

R., W. & O. R.R.....to	Clayton
R. & O. Nav. Co.....	Alexandria Bay
R. & O. Nav. Co.....	Montreal
Grand Trunk R'y or R. & O. Nav. Co.	Quebec
Ferry..................	Point Levis
Quebec Central R'y..	Sherbrooke
Boston & Maine R.R.	Lunenburg
Maine Central R.R...	Zealand Jc.
Prof. & F. Notch R.R.	Profile House
Stage..................	No. Woodstock
Con. & Mont'l R.R..	Nashua
Boston & Maine R.R.	Boston

Through Rates.

Niagara Falls	$27.80	Syracuse	$24.95
Rochester	26.55	Utica	24.80

Route 138—Boston, Mass.
Forms Ex. 400 and Ex. 711.

R., W. & O. R.R.....to	Clayton
R. & O. Nav. Co.....	Alexandria Bay
R. & O. Nav. Co.....	Montreal
Can. Pac. R'y or R. & O. Nav. Co.	Quebec
Ferry..................	Point Levis
Quebec Central R'y..	Sherbrooke
Boston & Maine R.R.	Lunenburg
Maine Central R.R..	Zealand Jc.
Prof. & F. Notch R.R.	Profile House
Stage..................	No. Woodstock
Con. & Mont'l R.R..	Nashua
Boston & Maine R.R.	Boston

Through Rates.

Niagara Falls	$27.80	Syracuse	$24.95
Rochester	26.55	Utica	24.80

Route 139—Boston, Mass.
Forms Ex. 399 and Ex. 418.

R., W. & O. R.R.....to	Clayton
R. & O. Nav. Co.....	Alexandria Bay
R. & O. Nav. Co.....	Montreal
Grand Trunk R'y or R. & O. Nav. Co.	Quebec
Ferry..................	Point Levis
Quebec Central R'y..	Sherbrooke
Boston & Maine R.R.	White River Jc.
Cent. Vermont R.R..	Windsor
Vermont Valley R.R.	Bellows Falls
Fitchburg R.R.......	Boston

Through Rates.

Niagara Falls	$25.50	Syracuse	$22.65
Rochester	24.25	Utica	22.50

Route 140—Boston, Mass.
Forms Ex. 400 and Ex. 418.

R., W. & O. R.R.....to	Clayton
R. & O. Nav. Co.....	Alexandria Bay
R. & O. Nav. Co.....	Montreal
Can. Pac. R'y or R. & O. Nav. Co.	Quebec
Ferry..................	Point Levis
Quebec Central R'y..	Sherbrooke
Boston & Maine R.R.	White River Jc.
Cent. Vermont R.R..	Windsor
Vermont Valley R.R.	Bellows Falls
Fitchburg R.R.......	Boston

Through Rates.

Niagara Falls	$25.50	Syracuse	$22.65
Rochester	24.25	Utica	22.50

Route 141—Boston, Mass.
Forms Ex. 399 and Ex. 430.

R., W. & O. R.R.....to	Clayton
R. & O. Nav. Co.....	Alexandria Bay
R. & O. Nav. Co.....	Montreal
Grand Trunk R'y or R. & O. Nav. Co.	Quebec
Ferry..................	Point Levis
Intercolonial R'y.....	Halifax
Intercolonial R'y.....	St John
Can. Pac. R'y........	Vanceboro
Maine Central R.R...	Portland
Boston & Maine R.R.	Boston

Through Rates.

Niagara Falls	$41.80	Syracuse	$38.95
Rochester	40.55	Utica	38.80

Route 142—Boston, Mass.
Forms Ex. 400 and Ex. 430.

R., W. & O. R.R.....to	Clayton
R. & O. Nav. Co.....	Alexandria Bay
R. & O. Nav. Co.....	Montreal
Can. Pac. R'y or R. & O. Nav. Co.	Quebec
Ferry..................	Point Levis
Intercolonial R'y.....	Halifax
Intercolonial R'y.....	St. John
Can. Pac. Ry	Vanceboro
Maine Central R.R..	Portland
Boston & Maine R.R.	Boston

Through Rates.

Niagara Falls	$41.80	Syracuse	$38.95
Rochester	40.55	Utica	38.80

Route 143—Boston, Mass.
Forms Ex. 399 and Ex. 432.

R., W. & O. R.R.....to	Clayton
R. & O. Nav. Co.....	Alexandria Bay
R. & O. Nav. Co.....	Montreal
Grand Trunk R'y or R. & O. Nav. Co.	Quebec
Ferry..................	Point Levis
Intercolonial R'y. ..	Halifax
Intercolonial R'y.....	St. John
International S.S. Co.	Portland
Boston & Maine R.R.	Boston

Through Rates.

Niagara Falls	$38.80	Syracuse	$35.95
Rochester	37.55	Utica	35.80

Route 144—Boston, Mass.
Forms Ex. 400 and Ex. 432.

R., W. & O. R.R.....to	Clayton
R. & O. Nav. Co.....	Alexandria Bay
R. & O. Nav. Co.....	Montreal
Can. Pac. R'y or R. & O. Nav. Co.	Quebec
Ferry..................	Point Levis
Intercolonial R'y.....	Halifax
Intercolonial R'y.....	St. John
International S.S. Co.	Portland
Boston & Maine R.R.	Boston

Through Rates.

Niagara Falls	$38.80	Syracuse	$35.95
Rochester	37.55	Utica	35.80

Route 145—Boston, Mass.
Forms Ex. 399 and Ex. 429.

R., W. & O. R.R.....to	Clayton
R. & O. Nav. Co.....	Alexandria Bay
R. & O. Nav. Co.....	Montreal
Grand Trunk R'y or R. & O. Nav. Co.	Quebec
Ferry..................	Point Levis
Intercolonial R'y.....	Pt. du Chene
Charl't'n St. Nav. Co.	Summerside
P. E. Island R'y.....	Charlottetown
Charl't'n St. Nav. Co.	Pictou
Intercolonial R'y.....	Halifax
Intercolonial R'y.....	St. John
Can. Pac. R'y........	Vanceboro
Maine Central R.R...	Portland
Boston & Maine R.R.	Boston

Through Rates.

Niagara Falls	$46.75	Syracuse	$43.90
Rochester	45.50	Utica	43.75

Route 146—Boston, Mass.
Forms Ex. 400 and Ex. 429.

R., W. & O. R.R.....to	Clayton
R. & O. Nav. Co	Alexandria Bay
R. & O. Nav. Co.....	Montreal
Can. Pac. R'y or R. & O. Nav. Co.	Quebec
Ferry..................	Point Levis
Intercolonial R'y.....	Pt. du Chene
Charl't'n St. Nav. Co.	Summerside
P. E. Island R'y.. ...	Charlottetown
Charl't'n St. Nav. Co.	Pictou
Intercolonial R'y.....	Halifax
Intercolonial R'y	St. John
Can. Pac. R'y........	Vanceboro
Maine Central R.R...	Portland
Boston & Maine R.R.	Boston

Through Rates.

Niagara Falls	$46.75	Syracuse	$43.90
Rochester	45.50	Utica	43.75

Route 147—Boston, Mass.
Forms Ex. 399 and Ex. 498.

R., W. & O. R.R.....to	Clayton
R. & O. Nav. Co.....	Alexandria Bay
R. & O. Nav. Co.....	Montreal
Can. Pac. R'y or R. & O. Nav. Co.	Quebec
Ferry..................	Point Levis
Intercolonial R'y.....	Pt. du Chene
Charl't'n St. Nav. Co.	Summerside
P. E. Island R'y......	Charlottetown
Charl't'n St. Nav. Co.	Pictou
Intercolonial R'y.....	Halifax
Intercolonial R'y.....	St. John
International S.S. Co.	Portland
Boston & Maine R.R.	Boston

Through Rates.

Niagara Falls	$43.75	Syracuse	$40.90
Rochester	42.50	Utica	40.75

SEE NOTE ON PAGE 119 REGARDING STOP-OVER AT ALEXANDRIA BAY.

Route 148—Boston, Mass.

Forms Ex. 400 and Ex. 495.

R., W. & O. R.R.	to Clayton
R. & O. Nav. Co.	Alexandria Bay
R. & O. Nav. Co.	Montreal
Can. Pac. R'y or R. & O. Nav. Co.	Quebec
Ferry	Point Levis
Intercolonial R'y	Pt. du Chene
Charl't'n St. Nav. Co.	Summerside
P. E. Island R'y	Charlottetown
Charl't'n St. Nav. Co.	Pictou
Intercolonial R'y	Halifax
Intercolonial R'y	St. John
International S.S. Co.	Portland
Boston & Maine R.R.	Boston

Through Rates.

Niagara Falls $43.75	Syracuse $40.90
Rochester 42.30	Utica 40.75

Route 149—Boston, Mass.

Forms Ex. 399 and Ex. 794.

R., W. & O. R.R.	to Clayton
R. & O. Nav. Co.	Alexandria Bay
R. & O. Nav. Co.	Montreal
Grand Trunk R'y or R. & O. Nav. Co.	Quebec
Quebec S.S. Co. (Meals included)	Summerside
Charl't'n St. Nav. Co.	Pt. du Chene
Intercolonial R'y	St. John
Can. Pac. R'y	Vanceboro
Maine Central RR.	Portland
Boston & Maine R.R.	Boston

Through Rates.

Niagara Falls $43.75	Syracuse $40.90
Rochester 42.50	Utica 40.75

Route 150—Boston, Mass.

Forms Ex. 400 and Ex. 794.

R., W. & O. R.R.	to Clayton
R. & O. Nav. Co.	Alexandria Bay
R. & O. Nav. Co.	Montreal
Can. Pac. R'y or R. & O. Nav. Co.	Quebec
Quebec S. S. Co. (Meals included)	Summerside
Charl't'n St. Nav. Co.	Pt. du Chene
Intercolonial R'y	St. John
Can. Pac. R'y	Vanceboro
Maine Central R.R.	Portland
Boston & Maine R.R.	Boston

Through Rates.

Niagara Falls $43.75	Syracuse $40.90
Rochester 42.50	Utica 40.75

Route 151—Boston, Mass.

Forms Ex. 399 and Ex. 793

R., W. & O. R.R.	to Clayton
R. & O. Nav. Co.	Alexandria Bay
R. & O. Nav. Co.	Montreal
Grand Trunk R'y or R. & O. Nav. Co.	Quebec
Quebec S.S. Co. (Meals included)	Summerside
Charl't'n St. Nav. Co.	Pt. du Chene
Intercolonial R'y	St. John
International S.S. Co.	Boston

Through Rates.

Niagara Falls $38.25	Syracuse $35.40
Rochester 37.00	Utica 35.25

Route 152—Boston, Mass.

Forms Ex. 400 and Ex. 793

R., W. & O. R.R.	to Clayton
R. & O. Nav. Co.	Alexandria Bay
R. & O. Nav. Co.	Montreal
Can. Pac. R'y or R. & O. Nav. Co.	Quebec
Quebec S. S. Co. (Meals included)	Summerside
Charl't'n St. Nav. Co.	Pt. du Chene
Intercolonial R'y	St. John
International S. S. Co.	Boston

Through Rates.

Niagara Falls $38.25	Syracuse $35.40
Rochester 37.00	Utica 35.25

Route 153—Boston, Mass.

Forms Ex. 399 and Ex. 712.

R., W. & O. R.R.	to Clayton
R. & O. Nav. Co.	Alexandria Bay
R. & O. Nav. Co.	Montreal
Grand Trunk R'y or R. & O. Nav. Co.	Quebec
Quebec S.S. Co. (Meals included)	Summerside
P. E. Island R'y	Charlottetown
Charl't'n St. Nav. Co.	Pictou
Intercolonial R'y	Mulgrave
Bras d'Or S. Nav. Co.	Sydney
Bras d'Or S. Nav. Co.	Mulgrave
Intercolonial R'y	Halifax
Dominion Atlantic R'y	Annapolis
Bay of Fundy S.S. Co.	St. John
International S.S. Co.	Boston

Through Rates.

Niagara Falls $55.40	Syracuse $52.55
Rochester 54.15	Utica 52.40

Route 154—Boston, Mass.

Forms Ex. 400 and Ex. 712.

R., W. & O. R.R.	to Clayton
R. & O. Nav. Co.	Alexandria Bay
R. & O. Nav. Co.	Montreal
Can. Pac. R'y or R. & O. Nav. Co.	Quebec
Quebec S. S. Co. (Meals included)	Summerside
P. E. Island R'y	Charlottetown
Charl't'n St. Nav. Co.	Pictou
Intercolonial R'y	Mulgrave
Bras d'Or S. Nav. Co.	Sydney
Bras d'Or S. Nav. Co.	Mulgrave
Intercolonial R'y	Halifax
Dominion Atlantic R'y	Annapolis
Bay of Fundy S.S. Co.	St. John
International S. S. Co.	Boston

Through Rates.

Niagara Falls $55.40	Syracuse $52.55
Rochester 54.15	Utica 52.40

Route 155—Boston, Mass.

Forms Ex. 399 and Ex. 862.

R., W. & O. R.R.	to Clayton
R. & O. Nav. Co.	Alexandria Bay
R. & O. Nav. Co.	Montreal
Grand Trunk R'y or R. & O. Nav. Co.	Quebec
Quebec S.S. Co. (Meals included)	Pictou
Intercolonial R'y	Halifax
Dominion Atlantic R'y	Annapolis
Bay of Fundy S.S. Co.	St. John
Can. Pac. R'y	Vanceboro
Maine Central R.R.	Portland
Boston & Maine R.R.	Boston

Through Rates.

Niagara Falls $48.40	Syracuse $45.55
Rochester 47.15	Utica 45.40

Route 156—Boston, Mass.

Forms Ex. 400 and Ex. 862.

R., W. & O. R.R.	to Clayton
R. & O. Nav. Co.	Alexandria Bay
R. & O. Nav. Co.	Montreal
Can. Pac. R'y or R. & O. Nav. Co.	Quebec
Quebec S.S. Co. (Meals included)	Pictou
Intercolonial R'y	Halifax
Dominion Atlantic R'y	Annapolis
Bay of Fundy S.S. Co.	St. John
Can. Pac. R'y	Vanceboro
Maine Central R.R.	Portland
Boston & Maine R.R.	Boston

Through Rates.

Niagara Falls $48.40	Syracuse $45.55
Rochester 47.15	Utica 45.40

Route 157—Boston, Mass.

Forms Ex. 399 and Ex. 863.

R., W. & O. R.R.	to Clayton
R. & O. Nav. Co.	Alexandria Bay
R. & O. Nav. Co.	Montreal
Grand Trunk R'y or R. & O. Nav. Co.	Quebec
Quebec S.S. Co. (Meals included)	Pictou
Intercolonial R'y	Halifax
Dominion Atlantic R'y	Annapolis
Bay of Fundy S.S. Co.	St. John
International S.S. Co.	Boston

Through Rates.

Niagara Falls $44.20	Syracuse $41.35
Rochester 42.95	Utica 41.20

Route 158—Boston, Mass.

Forms Ex. 400 and Ex. 863

R., W. & O. R.R.	to Clayton
R. & O. Nav. Co.	Alexandria Bay
R. & O. Nav. Co.	Montreal
Can. Pac. R'y or R. & O. Nav. Co.	Quebec
Quebec S.S. Co. (Meals included)	Pictou
Intercolonial R'y	Halifax
Dominion Atlantic R'y	Annapolis
Bay of Fundy S.S. Co.	St. John
International S. S. Co.	Boston

Through Rates.

Niagara Falls $44.20	Syracuse $41.35
Rochester 42.95	Utica 41.20

Route 159—Boston, Mass.

Forms Ex. 399 and Ex. 864.

R., W. & O. R.R.	to Clayton
R. & O. Nav. Co.	Alexandria Bay
R. & O. Nav. Co.	Montreal
Grand Trunk R'y or R. & O. Nav. Co.	Quebec
Quebec S.S. Co. (Meals included)	Pictou
Intercolonial R'y	Halifax
Dominion Atlantic R'y	Annapolis
Dominion Atlantic R'y	Yarmouth
Yarmouth S. S. Co., (Limited)	Boston

Through Rates.

Niagara Falls $43.40	Syracuse $40.55
Rochester 42.15	Utica 40.40

Route 160—Boston, Mass.

Forms Ex. 400 and Ex. 864.

R., W. & O. R.R.	to Clayton
R. & O. Nav. Co.	Alexandria Bay
R. & O. Nav. Co.	Montreal
Can. Pac. R'y or R. & O. Nav. Co.	Quebec
Quebec S.S. Co. (Meals included)	Pictou
Intercolonial R'y	Halifax
Dominion Atlantic R'y	Annapolis
Dominion Atlantic R'y	Yarmouth
Yarmouth S. S. Co., (Limited)	Boston

Through Rates.

Niagara Falls $43.40	Syracuse $40.55
Rochester 42.15	Utica 40.40

Route 161—Boston, Mass.

Forms Ex. 399 and Ex. 435.

R., W. & O. R.R.	to Clayton
R. & O. Nav. Co.	Alexandria Bay
R. & O. Nav. Co.	Montreal
Grand Trunk R'y or R. & O. Nav. Co.	Quebec
Quebec S.S. Co. (Meals included)	Pictou
Intercolonial R'y	Halifax
Canada Atlantic & Plant S.S. Co.	Boston

Through Rates.

Niagara Falls $39.50	Syracuse $36.65
Rochester 38.25	Utica 36.50

SEE NOTE ON PAGE 119 REGARDING STOP-OVER AT ALEXANDRIA BAY.

Route 162—Boston, Mass.

Forms Ex. 400 and Ex. 435.

R., W. & O. R.R.....to	Clayton
R. & O. Nav. Co.....	Alexandria Bay
R. & O. Nav. Co.....	Montreal
Can Pac. R'y or R. & O. Nav. Co.	Quebec
Quebec S.S Co..... (Meals included)	Pictou
Intercolonial R'y	Halifax
Canada Atlantic & Plant S.S. Co.	Boston

Through Rates.

Niagara Falls	$39.50	Syracuse	$36.65
Rochester	38.25	Utica	36.50

Route 163—Bridgton Junction, Me.

Form N 12.

R., W. & O. R.R.....to	Norwood
Cent. Vermont R.R..	Swanton
St. J. & L. C. R.R....	Lunenburg
Maine Central R.R...	Bridgton Jc

Through Rates.

	Unlim'd	Lim'd
Niagara Falls	$15.00	$13.15
Rochester	13.50	11.60
Syracuse	11.90	.....
Utica	10.90	.....

Route 164—Brockville, Canada.

Form Ex. 225.

R., W. & O. R.R.....to	Clayton
R. & O. Nav. Co.....	Alexandria Bay
R. & O. Nav. Co.....	Brockville

Through Rates.

Niagara Falls	$7.65	Syracuse	$4.90
Rochester	6.50	Utica	4.75

Route 165—Burlington, Vt.

Form Ex. 610.

R., W. & O. R.R.....to	Norwood
Cent. Vermont R.R..	Burlington

Through Rates.

Niagara Falls	$10.05	Syracuse	$7.10
Rochester	8.70	Utica	7.00

Route 166—Burlington, Vt.

Form Ex. 611.

R., W. & O. R.R.....to	Norwood
C. V. R.R. (O. & L. C. Div.)	Rouse's Point
D. & H. R.R.........	Bluff Point
Cham. Trans. Co.....	Burlington

Through Rates.

Niagara Falls	$11.10	Syracuse	$8.00
Rochester	9.60	Utica	7.90

Route 167—Cape Vincent, N. Y.

R., W. & O. R.R.....to	Cape Vincent

Through Rates.

Niagara Falls	$5.90	Syracuse	$2.95
Rochester	4.55	Utica	3.30

Route 168—Carleton Island, N. Y.

Form Ex. 612.

R., W. & O. R.R.....to	Cape Vincent
Thous. Isl St'b't Co.	Carleton Island

Through Rates.

Niagara Falls	$6.40	Syracuse	$3.45
Rochester	5.05	Utica	3.60

Route 169—Carleton Island, N. Y. and Return.

Form Ex. 613.

R., W. & O. R.R.....to	Cape Vincent
Thous. Isl. St'b't Co.	Carleton Island

RETURNING SAME ROUTE.

Through Rates.

Niagara Falls	$11.10	Syracuse	$6.25
Rochester	9.00	Utica	5.75

Route 170—Central Park, N. Y.

Form Ex 680.

R., W. & O. R.R.....to	Clayton
Steamer..............	Central Park

Through Rates.

Niagara Falls	$6.85	Syracuse	$3.90
Rochester	5.50	Utica	3.75

Route 171—Central Park, N. Y. and Return.

Form Ex. 681.

R., W. & O. R.R.....to	Clayton
Steamer..............	Central Park

RETURNING SAME ROUTE.

Through Rates.

Niagara Falls	$12.50	Syracuse	$6.75
Rochester	9.25	Utica	6.75

Route 172—Chateaugay Chasm, N. Y.

Form Ex. 682.

R., W. & O. R R.....to	Norwood
C. V. R.R. (O. & L. C. Div.)	Chateaugay
Stage.................	Chat'g'y Chasm

Through Rates.

Niagara Falls	$9.10	Syracuse	$6.15
Rochester	7.75	Utica	6.05

Route 173—Chateaugay Chasm, N. Y. and Return.

Form Ex. 683.

R., W. & O. R.R.....to	Norwood
C. V. R.R. (O. & L. C. Div.)	Chateaugay
Stage.................	Chat'g'y Chasm

RETURNING SAME ROUTE.

Through Rates.

Niagara Falls	$15.50	Syracuse	$11.45
Rochester	13.35	Utica	11.35

Route 174—Chatham, Mass.

Form N 17.

R., W. & O. R.R.....to	Norwood
Cent. Vermont R.R..	White River Jc.
Boston & Maine R.R.	Concord
Con. & Mont'l R.R...	Nashua
Boston & Maine R.R.	Boston
N.Y., N. H. & H. R.R.	Chatham

Through Rates.

	Unlim'd	Lim'd
Niagara Falls	$20.10	$11.80
Rochester	18.75	11.50
Syracuse	17.15	.....
Utica	17.05	.....

Route 175—Chatham, Mass. and Return.

Form Ex. 570.

R., W. & O. R.R.....to	Norwood
Cent. Vermont R.R..	White River Jc.
Boston & Maine R.R.	Concord
Con. & Mont'l R.R...	Nashua
Boston & Maine R.R.	Boston
N. Y., N. H. & H. R.R.	Chatham

RETURNING SAME ROUTE.

Through Rates.

	Unlim'd	Lim'd
Niagara Falls	$32.50	$22.80
Rochester	30.50	22.20
Syracuse	28.25	.....
Utica	27.00	.....

Route 176—Chatham, Mass. and Return.

Form Ex. 571.

R., W. & O. R.R.....to	Norwood
Cent. Vermont R.R..	White River Jc.
Boston & Maine R.R.	Concord
Con. & Mont'l R.R...	Nashua
Boston & Maine R.R.	Boston
N. Y., N. H. & H. R.R.	Chatham
N. Y., N. H. & H. R.R.	Boston
Boston & Maine R.R.	North Conway
Maine Central R.R...	Lunenburg
St. J. & L. C. R.R....	Swanton
Cent. Vermont R.R..	Norwood
R., W. & O. R.R....	starting point

Through Rates.

	Unlim'd	Lim'd
Niagara Falls	$38.00	$24.05
Rochester	36.00	22.20
Syracuse	33.75	.....
Utica	32.50	.....

Route 177—Chicoutimi, P. Q.

Forms Ex. 399 and Ex. 781.

R., W. & O. R.R.....to	Clayton
R. & O. Nav. Co.....	Alexandria Bay
R. & O. Nav. Co.....	Montreal
Grand Trunk R'y or R. & O. Nav. Co.	Quebec
Q. & L. St J. R'y....	Roberval
Q. & L. St. J. R'y....	Chicoutimi

Through Rates.

Niagara Falls	$20.50	Syracuse	$17.65
Rochester	19.25	Utica	17.50

Route 178—Chicoutimi, P. Q.

Forms Ex. 400 and Ex. 781.

R., W. & O. R.R.....to	Clayton
R. & O. Nav. Co.....	Alexandria Bay
R. & O. Nav. Co.....	Montreal
Can. Pac. R'y or R. & O. Nav. Co.	Quebec
Q. & L. St. J. R'y....	Roberval
Q. & L. St. J. R'y....	Chicoutimi

Through Rates.

Niagara Falls	$20.50	Syracuse	$17 65
Rochester	19.25	Utica	17.50

Route 179—Chicoutimi, P. Q. and Return.

Forms Ex. 286 and Ex. 783 R.

R., W. & O. R.R.....to	Clayton
R. & O. Nav. Co.....	Alexandria Bay
R. & O. Nav. Co.....	Montreal
R. & O. Nav. Co.....	Quebec
Q. & L. St. J. R'y....	Roberval
Q. & L. St. J. R'y....	Chicoutimi
R. & O. Nav. Co.....	Quebec
Can. Pac. R'y via Mont'l & Ottawa.	Prescott
Ferry................	Ogdensburg
R., W. & O. R.R	starting point

Through Rates.

Niagara Falls	$35.00	Syracuse	$31.35
Rochester	33.85	Utica	31.35

Route 180—Clayton, N. Y.

Form Ex. 123.

R., W. & O. R.R.....to	Clayton

Through Rates.

Niagara Falls	$6.35	Syracuse	$3.40
Rochester	5.00	Utica	3.25

Route 181—Cottage City, Mass.

Form Ex. 556.

R., W. & O. R.R.....to	Norwood
Cent. Vermont R.R..	White River Jc.
Boston & Maine R.R.	Concord
Con. & Mont'l R.R...	Nashua
Boston & Maine R.R.	Boston
N.Y., N. H. & H. R.R.	Cottage City

Through Rates.

	Unlim'd	Lim'd
Niagara Falls	$20.05	$11.75
Rochester	18.70	11.45
Syracuse	17.10	.....
Utica	17.00	.

Route 182—Cottage City, Mass. and Return.

Form Ex. 557 or Ex. 570.

R., W. & O. R.R.....to	Norwood
Cent. Vermont R.R..	White River Jc.
Boston & Maine R.R.	Concord
Con. & Mont'l R.R...	Nashua
Boston & Maine R.R.	Boston
N. Y., N. H. & H. R.R.	Cottage City

RETURNING SAME ROUTE.

Through Rates.

	Unlim'd	Lim'd
Niagara Falls	$31 50	$21.60
Rochester	29.50	21.20
Syracuse	27.25	.
Utica	26.00	.....

SEE NOTE ON PAGE 119 REGARDING STOP-OVER AT ALEXANDRIA BAY.

Route 183—Cottage City, Mass. and Return.

Form Ex. 568 or Ex 571.

R., W. & O. R.R.	to Norwood
Cent. Vermont R.R..	White River Jc.
Boston & Maine R.R.	Concord
Con. & Mont'l R.R...	Nashua
Boston & Maine R.R.	Boston
N. Y., N. H. & H. R.R.	Cottage City
N. Y., N. H. & H. R.R.	Boston
Boston & Maine R.R.	North Conway
Maine Central R.R...	Lunenburg
St. J. & L. C. R.R....	Swanton
Cent. Vermont R.R..	Norwood
R., W. & O. R.R....	starting point

Through Rates.

	Unlim'd	Lim'd
Niagara Falls	$37.00	$23.05
Rochester	35.00	21.20
Syracuse	32.75	.....
Utica	31.50	....

Route 184—Crawford's, N. H.

Form N 12.

R., W. & O. R.R.	to Norwood
Cent. Vermont R.R..	Swanton
St. J. & L. C. R.R....	Lunenburg
Maine Central R.R...	Crawford's

Through Rates.

	Unlim'd	Lim'd
Niagara Falls	$13 05	.....
Rochester	11.55	....
Syracuse	9 85	.....
Utica	8.95	.....

Route 185—Crawford's, N. H. and Return.

Form Ex. 612

R., W. & O. R.R.	to Norwood
Cent. Vermont R.R..	Swanton
St. J. & L. C. R.R....	Lunenburg
Maine Central R.R...	Crawford's

RETURNING SAME ROUTE.

Through Rates.

Niagara Falls	$23.90	Syracuse	$19.65
Rochester	21.80	Utica	18.40

Route 186—Crawford's, N. H.

Forms Ex. 254 and Ex. 613.

R., W. & O. R.R.	to Clayton
R. & O. Nav. Co.....	Alexandria Bay
R. & O. Nav. Co.....	Montreal
Can. Pac. R'y.......	Newport
Boston & Maine R.R.	Lunenburg
Maine Central R.R...	Crawford's

Through Rates.

Niagara Falls	$17.70	Syracuse	$14.85
Rochester	16.45	Utica	14.70

Route 187—Crawford's, N. H.

Forms Ex 254 and Ex. 346.

R., W. & O. R.R.	to Clayton
R. & O. Nav. Co.....	Alexandria Bay
R. & O. Nav. Co. ...	Montreal
Grand Trunk R'y....	St. John's
Cent. Vermont R.R..	Montpelier
Mont. & W. R. R.R..	Wells River
Con. & Mont'l R.R..	Fabyan's
Maine Central R.R...	Crawford's

Through Rates.

Niagara Falls	$17.70	Syracuse	$14.85
Rochester	16.45	Utica	14.70

Route 188—Crawford's, N. H.

Forms Ex 154 and Ex. 247

R., W. & O. R.R.	to Clayton
R. & O. Nav. Co.....	Alexandria Bay
R. & O. Nav. Co.....	Montreal
Grand Trunk R'y....	Alpine House (Gorham)
Stage..............	Glen Site
Stage..............	Sum't Mt. Wash.
Mt. Washington R'y.	Base
Con. & Mont'l R. R..	Fabyan's
Maine Central R.R...	Crawford's

Through Rates.

Niagara Falls	$28.55	Syracuse	$25.70
Rochester	27.30	Utica	25.55

Route 189—Crawford's, N. H.

Forms Ex. 399 and Ex. 441.

R., W. & O. R.R.	to Clayton
R. & O. Nav. Co.....	Alexandria Bay
R. & O. Nav. Co.....	Montreal
Grand Trunk R'y or R. & O. Nav. Co.	Quebec
Ferry..............	Point Levis
Grand Trunk R'y....	Alpine House (Gorham)
Stage..............	Glen Site
Stage..............	Sum't Mt. Wash.
Mt. Washington R'y.	Base
Con. & Mont'l R.R...	Fabyan's
Maine Central R.R...	Crawford's

Through Rates.

Niagara Falls	$32.65	Syracuse	$29.80
Rochester	31.40	Utica	29.65

Route 190—Crawford's, N. H.

Forms Ex. 400 and Ex. 753.

R., W. & O. R.R.	to Clayton
R. & O. Nav. Co.....	Alexandria Bay
R. & O. Nav. Co.....	Montreal
Can. Pac. R'y or R. & O. Nav. Co.	Quebec
Ferry..............	Point Levis
Quebec Central R'y..	Dudswell Jc.
Maine Central R.R...	Crawford's

Through Rates.

Niagara Falls	$22.10	Syracuse	$19.25
Rochester	20.85	Utica	19.10

Route 191—Crawford's, N. H.

Forms Ex. 399 and Ex. 614.

R., W. & O. R.R.	to Clayton
R. & O. Nav. Co.....	Alexandria Bay
R. & O. Nav. Co.....	Montreal
Grand Trunk R'y or R. & O. Nav. Co.	Quebec
Ferry..............	Point Levis
Quebec Central R'y..	Sherbrooke
Boston & Maine R.R.	Lunenburg
Maine Central R.R...	Crawford's

Through Rates.

Niagara Falls	$22.10	Syracuse	$19.25
Rochester	20.85	Utica	19.10

Route 192—Crawford's, N. H.

Forms Ex. 400 and Ex. 614.

R., W. & O. R.R.	to Clayton
R. & O. Nav. Co. ...	Alexandria Bay
R. & O. Nav. Co.....	Montreal
Can. Pac. R'y or R. & O. Nav. Co.	Quebec
Ferry..............	Point Levis
Quebec Central R'y..	Sherbrooke
Boston & Maine R.R.	Lunenburg
Maine Central R.R...	Crawford's

Through Rates.

Niagara Falls	$22.10	Syracuse	$19.25
Rochester	20.85	Utica	19 10

Route 193—Fabyan's, N. H.

Form N 12

R., W. & O. R.R.	to Norwood
Cent. Vermont R.R..	Swanton
St. J. & L. C. R.R ...	Lunenburg
Maine Central R.R...	Fabyan's

Through Rates.

	Unlim'd	Lim'd
Niagara Falls	$12.75	.....
Rochester	11.25	.....
Syracuse	9.65	.....
Utica	8.65	.....

Route 194—Fabyan's, N. H. and Return.

Form Ex. 612.

R., W. & O. R.R.	to Norwood
Central Vermont R.R.	Swanton
St. J. & L. C. R.R....	Lunenburg
Maine Central R.R...	Fabyan's

RETURNING SAME ROUTE.

Through Rates.

Niagara Falls	$23.40	Syracuse	$18.55
Rochester	21.40	Utica	16.45

Route 195—Fabyan's, N. H.

Form N 14.

R., W. & O. R.R.	to Norwood
Cent. Vermont R.R..	Montpelier
Mont. & W. R. R.R..	Wells River
Con. & Mont'l R.R..	Fabyan's

Through Rates.

Niagara Falls	$12.75	Syracuse	$9.65
Rochester	11.25	Utica	8.65

Route 196—Fabyan's, N. H. and Return.

Form Ex. 578.

R., W. & O. R.R.	to Norwood
Cent. Vermont R.R..	Montpelier
Mont. & W. R. R.R..	Wells River
Con. & Mont'l R.R...	Fabyan's

RETURNING SAME ROUTE.

Through Rates.

Niagara Falls	$23.40	Syracuse	$18.35
Rochester	21.40	Utica	16.45

Route 197—Fabyan's, N. H.

Form Ex. 615.

R., W. & O. R.R.	to Clayton
R. & O. Nav. Co.....	Alexandria Bay
R. & O. Nav. Co.....	Prescott
Ferry..............	Ogdensburg
Cent. Vermont R.R..	Swanton
St. J. & L. C. R.R..	Lunenburg
Maine Central R.R...	Fabyan's

Through Rates.

Niagara Falls	$17.40	Syracuse	$14.55
Rochester	16.15	Utica	14.40

Route 198—Fabyan's, N. H.

Forms Ex. 254 and Ex. 348

R., W. & O. R.R.	to Clayton
R. & O. Nav. Co.....	Alexandria Bay
R. & O. Nav. Co.....	Montreal
Grand Trunk R'y....	St. John's
Cent. Vermont R.R..	Montpelier
Mont. & W. R. R.R..	Wells River
Con. & Mont'l R.R...	Fabyan's

Through Rates.

Niagara Falls	$17.40	Syracuse	$14.55
Rochester	16.15	Utica	14.40

Route 199—Fabyan's, N. H. and Return.

Forms Ex. 255 and Ex. 349.

R., W. & O. R.R.	to Clayton
R. & O. Nav. Co.....	Alexandria Bay
R. & O. Nav. Co.....	Montreal
Grand Trunk R'y....	St. John's
Cent. Vermont R.R..	Montpelier
Mont. & W. R. R.R..	Wells River
Con. & Mont'l R.R ..	Fabyan's

RETURNING SAME ROUTE.

Through Rates.

Niagara Falls	$26.50	Syracuse	$24.00
Rochester	26.50	Utica	24.00

Route 200—Fabyan's, N. H.

Forms Ex. 154, Ex. 348 and Ex 198.

R., W. & O. R.R.	to Clayton
R. & O. Nav. Co.....	Alexandria Bay
R. & O. Nav. Co.....	Montreal
Grand Trunk R'y....	St. John's
Cent. Vermont R.R..	Montpelier
Mont. & W. R. R.R..	Wells River
Con. & Mont'l R.R ..	Bethlehem Jc.
Prof. & F. Notch R.R.	Profile House
Prof. & F. Notch R.R.	Bethlehem Jc.
Con. & Mont'l R.R...	Fabyan's

Through Rates.

Niagara Falls	$20.40	Syracuse	$17.55
Rochester	19.15	Utica	17.40

Route 201—Fabyan's, N. H.

Forms Ex. 254 and Ex. 616

R., W. & O. R.R.	to Clayton
R. & O. Nav. Co.....	Alexandria Bay
R. & O. Nav. Co.....	Montreal
Can. Pac. R'y.......	Newport
Boston & Maine R.R.	Lunenburg
Maine Central R.R..	Fabyan's

Through Rates.

Niagara Falls	$17.40	Syracuse	$14.55
Rochester	16.15	Utica	14.40

SEE NOTE ON PAGE 119 REGARDING STOP-OVER AT ALEXANDRIA BAY.

Route 202—Fabyan's, N. H. and Return.

Forms Ex. 255 and Ex. 617.

R., W. & O. R.R.....to Clayton
R. & O. Nav. Co...... Alexandria Bay
R. & O. Nav. Co...... Montreal
Can. Pac. R'y......... Newport
Boston & Maine R.R. Lunenburg
Maine Central R.R... Fabyan's

RETURNING SAME ROUTE.

Through Rates.

Niagara Falls	$28.50	Syracuse	$24.00
Rochester	26.50	Utica	24.00

Route 203—Fabyan's, N. H. and Return.

Form Ex. 572.

R., W. & O. R.R.....to Clayton
R. & O. Nav. Co...... Alexandria Bay
R. & O. Nav. Co...... Montreal
Can. Pac. R'y......... Newport
Boston & Maine R.R. Lunenburg
Maine Central R.R... Fabyan's
Maine Central R.R .. Lunenburg
St. J. & L. C. R.R.... Swanton
Cent. Vermont R.R.. Norwood
R., W. & O. R.R.. .. starting point

Through Rates.

Niagara Falls	$28.50	Syracuse	$24.00
Rochester	26.50	Utica	24.00

Route 204—Fabyan's, N. H.

Forms Ex. 400 and Ex. 713.

R., W. & O. R.R.....to Clayton
R. & O. Nav. Co...... Alexandria Bay
R. & O. Nav. Co...... Montreal
Can. Pac. R'y or R. & O. Nav. Co. } Quebec
Ferry..................... Point Levis
Quebec Central R'y.. Sherbrooke
Boston & Maine R.R. Lunenburg
Maine Central R.R... Fabyan's

Through Rates.

Niagara Falls	$21.80	Syracuse	$18.95
Rocheste	20.55	Utica	18.80

Route 205—Falmouth, Mass.

Form N 11.

R., W. & O. R.R.....to Norwood
Cent. Vermont R.R.. White River Jc.
Boston & Maine...... Concord
Con. & Mont'l R.R... Nashua
Boston & Maine R.R. Boston
N.Y., N. H. & H. R.R. Falmouth

Through Rates.

	Unlim'd	Lim'd
Niagara Falls	$19.35	$11.05
Rochester	18.00	10.75
Syracuse	16.40	.....
Utica	16.30	.....

Route 206—Falmouth, Mass.

Form Ex. 570.

R., W. & O. R.R.....to Norwood
Cent. Vermont R.R.. White River Jc.
Boston & Maine R.R. Concord
Con. & Mont'l R.R... Nashua
Boston & Maine R.R. Boston
N.Y., N. H. & H. R.R. Falmouth

RETURNING SAME ROUTE.

Through Rates.

	Unlim'd	Lim'd
Niagara Falls	$31.25	$21.55
Rochester	29.25	20.95
Syracuse	27.00	....
Utica	25.75	.....

Route 207—Falmouth, Mass. and Return.

Form Ex. 571.

R., W. & O. R.R.....to Norwood
Cent. Vermont R.R.. White River Jc.
Boston & Maine R.R. Concord
Con. & Mont'l R.R... Nashua
Boston & Maine R.R. Boston
N.Y., N. H. & H. R.R. Falmouth
N.Y., N. H. & H. R.R. Boston
Boston & Maine R.R. North Conway
Maine Central R.R... Lunenburg
St. J. & L. C. R.R.... Swanton
Cent. Vermont R. R.. Rouse's Point
R., W. & O. R.R..... starting point

Through Rates.

	Unlim'd	Lim'd
Niagara Falls	$36.75	$22.80
Rochester	34.75	20.95
Syracuse	32.50	....
Utica	31.25	.....

Route 208—Fisher's Island, N. Y.

Form Ex. 565.

R., W. & O. R.R.....to Norwood
Cent. Vermont R.R.. White River Jc.
Boston & Maine R.R. Concord
Con. & Mont'l R.R... Nashua
Boston & Maine R.R. Boston
N.Y., N. H. & H. R.R. Providence
N.Y., N. H. & H. R.R. New London
Steamer.............. Fisher's Island

Through Rates.

	Unlim'd	Lim'd
Niagara Falls	$20.55	$12.25
Rochester	19.20	11.25
Syracuse	17.60	.....
Utica	17.50	.....

Route 209—Fisher's Island, N. Y. and Return.

Form Ex. 566.

R., W. & O. R.R.....to Norwood
Cent. Vermont R.R.. White River Jc.
Boston & Maine R.R. Concord
Con. & Mont'l R.R... Nashua
Boston & Maine R.R. Boston
N.Y., N.H. & H. R.R. Providence
N.Y., N.H. & H. R.R. New London
Steamer.............. Fisher's Island

RETURNING SAME ROUTE.

Through Rates.

	Unlim'd	Lim'd
Niagara Falls	$34.20	$24.60
Rochester	32.20	23.90
Syracuse	29.45	.....
Utica	28.70	.....

Route 210—Fisher's Island, N. Y. and Return.

Form Ex. 567.

R., W. & O. R.R.....to Norwood
Cent. Vermont R.R.. White River Jc.
Boston & Maine R.R. Concord
Con. & Mont'l R.R.. Nashua
Boston & Maine R.R. Boston
N.Y., N.H. & H. R.R. Providence
N.Y., N. H. & H. R.R. New London
Steamer.............. Fisher's Island
Steamer.............. New London
N.Y., N.H. & H.R.R. Providence
N.Y., N. H. & H.R.R. Boston
Boston & Maine R.R. North Conway
Maine Central R.R... Lunenburg
St. J. & L. C. R.R.... Swanton
Cent. Vermont R.R.. Norwood
R., W. & O. R.R..... starting point

Through Rates.

	Unlim'd	Lim'd
Niagara Falls	$39.70	$25.75
Rochester	37.70	23.90
Syracuse	35.45	.....
Utica	34.20	.....

Route 211—Fryeburg, Me.

Form N 12.

R., W. & O. R.R.....to Norwood
Cent. Vermont R.R.. Swanton
St. J. & L. C. R.R.... Lunenburg
Maine Central R.R... Fryeburg

Through Rates.

	Unlim'd	Lim'd
Niagara Falls	$14.90	$13.15
Rochester	13.40	11.60
Syracuse	11.80	....
Utica	10.60	.....

Route 212—Fryeburg, Me. and Return.

Form Ex. 612.

R., W. & O. R.R.....to Norwood
Cent. Vermont R.R.. Swanton
St. J. & L. C. R.R.... Lunenburg
Maine Central R.R.. Fryeburg

RETURNING SAME ROUTE.

Through Rates.

	Unlim'd	Lim'd
Niagara Falls	$26.40	$24.60
Rochester	24.40	22.70
Syracuse	21.35	....
Utica	19.45	.....

Route 213—Glen House, N. H.

Form Ex. 513.

R., W. & O. R.R.....to Norwood
Cent. Vermont R.R.. Swanton
St. J. & L. C. R.R.... Lunenburg
Maine Central R.R.. Glen
Glen House Stage.... Glen House

Through Rates.

	Unlim'd	Lim'd
Niagara Falls	Off	Off
Rochester	sale.	sale.
Syracuse	"	"
Utica	"	"

Route 214—Glen House, N. H. and Return.

Form Ex. 514.

R., W. & O. R.R.....to Norwood
Cent. Vermont R.R... Swanton
St. J. & L. C. R.R.... Lunenburg
Maine Central R.R... Glen
Glen House Stage.... Glen House

RETURNING SAME ROUTE.

Through Rates.

	Unlim'd	Lim'd
Niagara Falls	Off	Off
Rochester	sale.	sale.
Syracuse	"	"
Utica	"	"

Route 215—Glen House, N. H.

Form Ex. 515.

R., W. & O. R.R.....to Norwood
Cent. Vermont R.R.. Swanton
St. J. & L. C. R.R.... Lunenburg
Maine Central R.R... Fabyan's
Con. & Mont'l R.R.. Base Mt. Wash.
Mt. Washington R'y. Sum't Mt. Wash.
Glen House Stage.... Glen House

Through Rates.

	Unlim'd	Lim'd
Niagara Falls	Off	Off
Rochester	sale.	sale.
Syracuse	"	"
Utica	"	"

Route 216—Glen House, N. H. and Return.

Form Ex. 516.

R., W. & O. R.R.....to Norwood
Cent. Vermont R.R.. Swanton
Maine Central R.R... Fabyan's
Con. & Mont'l R.R... Base Mt. Wash
Mt. Washington R'y. Sum't Mt. Wash.
Glen House Stage.... Glen House
Glen House Stage.... Glen
Maine Central R.R... Lunenburg
St. J. & L. C. R.R.... Swanton
Cent. Vermont R.R.. Norwood
R., W. & O. R.R..... starting point

Through Rates.

Niagara Falls	Off	Syracuse	Off
Rochester	sale.	Utica	sale.

Route 217—Glen House, N. H.

Form Ex. 793.

R., W. & O. R.R.....to Norwood
Cent. Vermont R.R.. Swanton
St. J. & L. C. R.R.... Lunenburg
Maine Central R.R... Scott's
Con. & Mont'l R.R... Gorham
Stage.................. Glen House

Through Rates.

Niagara Falls	Off	Syracuse	Off
Rochester	sale.	Utica	sale.

SEE NOTE ON PAGE 119 REGARDING STOP-OVER AT ALEXANDRIA BAY.

Route 218—Glen, N. H.

Form N 19.

R., W. & O. R.R.....to	Norwood
Cent. Vermont R.R...	Swanton
St. J. & L. C. R.R....	Lunenburg
Maine Central R.R...	Glen

Through Rates.

	Unlim'd	Lim'd
Niagara Falls	$14.50	$13.15
Rochester	13.00	11.60
Syracuse	11.40	.....
Utica	10.40	.....

Route 219—Glen, N. H. and Return.

Form Ex. 612.

R., W. & O. R.R.....to	Norwood
Cent. Vermont R.R..	Swanton
St. J. & L. C. R.R....	Lunenburg
Maine Central R.R...	Glen

RETURNING SAME ROUTE.

Through Rates.

	Unlim'd	Lim'd
Niagara Falls	$26.15	$24.80
Rochester	24.15	22.70
Syracuse	21.10	.....
Utica	19.20	.....

Grand View Park, N. Y.

Fare from Thousand Island Park, 10 cents one way.

Route 220—Gorham, N. H.

Form Ex. 854.

R., W. & O. R.R.....to	Norwood
Cent. Vermont R.R..	Swanton
St. J. & L. C. R.R....	Lunenburg
Maine Central R.R...	Hazen's Jc.
Con. & Mont'l R.R...	Gorham

Through Rates.

Niagara Falls	$13.45	Syracuse	$10.35
Rochester	11.95	Utica	9.35

Route 221—Groveton, N. H.

Form Ex. 853.

R., W. & O. R.R.....to	Norwood
Cent. Vermont R.R...	Swanton
St. J. & L. C. R.R....	Lunenburg
Maine Central R.R...	Hazen's Jc.
Con. & Mont'l R.R...	Groveton

Through Rates.

	Unlim'd	Lim'd
Niagara Falls	$13.20	.....
Rochester	11.70	.....
Syracuse	10.10	.....
Utica	9.10	.....

Route 222—Groveton, N. H. and Return.

Form Ex. 853 R.

R., W. & O. R.R.....to	Norwood
Cent. Vermont R.R...	Swanton
St. J. & L. C. R.R....	Lunenburg
Maine Central R.R...	Hazen's Jc.
Con. & Mont'l R.R...	Groveton

RETURNING SAME ROUTE.

Through Rates.

Niagara Falls	$24.20	Syracuse	$19.50
Rochester	22.20	Utica	17.60

Route 223—Halifax, N. S.

Form Ex. 561 or N 18.

R., W. & O. R.R.....to	Norwood
Cent. Vermont R.R..	Swanton
St. J. & L. C. R.R....	Lunenburg
Maine Central R.R...	Vanceboro
Can. Pac. R'y........	St. John
Intercolonial R'y.....	Halifax

Through Rates.

Niagara Falls	$26.50	Syracuse	$23.65
Rochester	25.00	Utica	22.65

Route 224—Halifax, N. S. and Return.

Form Ex. 562.

R., W. & O. R.R.....to	Norwood
Cent. Vermont R.R..	Swanton
St. J. & L. C. R.R....	Lunenburg
Maine Central R.R..	Vanceboro
Can. Pac. R'y........	St. John
Intercolonial R'y.....	Halifax

RETURNING SAME ROUTE.

Through Rates.

Niagara Falls	$42.25	Syracuse	$38.00
Rochester	40.50	Utica	38.00

Route 225—Halifax, N. S.

Form Ex. 114.

R., W. & O. R.R.....to	Norwood
Cent. Vermont R.R..	Swanton
St. J. & L. C. R.R....	Lunenburg
Maine Central R.R. (via Portland)	Vanceboro
Can. Pac. R'y........	St. John
Bay of Fundy S.S.Co.	Annapolis
Dominion Atlantic R'y	Halifax

Through Rates.

Niagara Falls	$30.30	Syracuse	$27.15
Rochester	28.80	Utica	26.15

Route 226—Halifax, N. S.

Form Ex. 115.

R., W. & O. R.R.....to	Norwood
Cent. Vermont R.R..	Swanton
St. J. & L. C. R.R....	Lunenburg
Maine Central R. R. (Via Portland)	Vanceboro
Can. Pac. R'y........	St. John.
Intercolonial R'y.....	Pt. du Chene
Charl't'n St. Nav. Co.	Summerside
P. E. Island R'y......	Charlottetown
Charl't'n St. Nav. Co.	Pictou
Intercolonial R'y...	Halifax

Through Rates.

Niagara Falls	$33.40	Syracuse	$30.55
Rochester	31.90	Utica	29.55

Route 227—Halifax, N. S.

Forms Ex. 254 and Ex. 867.

R., W. & O. R.R.....to	Clayton
R. & O. Nav. Co.....	Alexandria Bay
R. & O. Nav. Co.....	Montreal
Can. Pac. R'y.......	St. John
Bay of Fundy S.S. Co.	Annapolis
Dominion Atlantic R'y	Halifax

Through Rates.

Niagara Falls	$30.30	Syracuse	$27.45
Rochester	29.05	Utica	27.30

Route 228—Halifax, N. S.

Forms Ex. 254 and Ex. 718.

R., W. & O. R.R.....to	Clayton
R. & O. Nav. Co.....	Alexandria Bay
R. & O. Nav. Co.....	Montreal
Can. Pac. R'y.......	St. John
Intercolonial R'y.....	Pt. du Chene
Charl't'n St. Nav. Co..	Summerside
P. E. Island R'y......	Charlottetown
Charl't'n St. Nav. Co.	Pictou
Intercolonial R'y.....	Halifax

Through Rates.

Niagara Falls	$31.40	Syracuse	$28.55
Rochester	30.15	Utica	28.40

Route 229—Halifax, N. S.

Forms Ex. 309 and Ex. 444.

R., W. & O. R.R.....to	Clayton
R. & O. Nav. Co.....	Alexandria Bay
R. & O. Nav. Co.....	Montreal
Grand Trunk R'y or R. & O. Nav. Co.	Quebec
Ferry................	Point Levis
Intercolonial R'y.....	Halifax

Through Rates.

Niagara Falls	$26.50	Syracuse	$23.65
Rochester	25.25	Utica	23.50

Route 230—Halifax, N. S.

Forms Ex. 409 and Ex. 444.

R., W. & O. R.R.....to	Clayton
R. & O. Nav. Co.....	Alexandria Bay
R. & O. Nav. Co.....	Montreal
Can. Pac. R'y or R. & O. Nav. Co.	Quebec
Ferry................	Point Levis
Intercolonial R'y.....	Halifax

Through Rates.

Niagara Falls	$26.50	Syracuse	$23.65
Rochester	25.25	Utica	23.50

Route 231—Halifax, N. S.

Forms Ex. 399 and Ex. 448.

R., W. & O. R.R.....to	Clayton
R. & O. Nav. Co.....	Alexandria Bay
R. & O. Nav. Co.....	Montreal
Grand Trunk R'y or R. & O. Nav. Co.	Quebec
Ferry................	Point Levis
Intercolonial R'y.....	Pt du Chene
Charl't'n St. Nav. Co.	Summerside
P. E. Island R'y......	Charlottetown
Charl't'n St. Nav. Co.	Pictou
Intercolonial R'y.....	Halifax

Through Rates.

Niagara Falls	$31.40	Syracuse	$28.55
Rochester	30.15	Utica	28.40

Route 232—Halifax, N. S.

Forms Ex. 400 and Ex. 443.

R., W. & O. R.R.....to	Clayton
R. & O. Nav. Co.....	Alexandria Bay
R. & O. Nav. Co.....	Montreal
Can. Pac. R'y or R. & O. Nav. Co.	Quebec
Ferry................	Point Levis
Intercolonial R'y.....	Pt du Chene
Charl't'n St. Nav. Co.	Summerside
P. E. Island R'y......	Charlottetown
Charl't'n St. Nav. Co.	Pictou
Intercolonial R'y.....	Halifax

Through Rates.

Niagara Falls	$31.40	Syracuse	$28.55
Rochester	30.15	Utica	28.40

Route 233—Henderson Harbor, N. Y.

Form Ex. 674.

R., W. & O. R. R.....to	Sackett's Harbor
Steamer.............	Henderson Har.

Through Rates.

Niagara Falls..	Off	Syracuse	Off
Rochester	sale	Utica	sale

Route 234—Henderson Harbor, N. Y. and Return.

Form Ex. 675.

R., W. & O. R. R.....to	Sackett's Harbor
Steamer.............	Henderson Har.

RETURNING SAME ROUTE.

Through Rates.

Niagara Falls..	Off	Syracuse	Off
Rochester	sale	Utica	sale

Route 235—Highgate Springs, Vt.

Form Ex. 683.

R., W. & O. R. R.....to	Norwood
Cent. Vermont R. R.	Highgate Sp'gs.

Through Rates.

Niagara Falls	$10.45	Syracuse	$7.50
Rochester	9.10	Utica	7.40

Route 236—Highgate Springs, Vt. and Return.

Form Ex. 684.

R., W. & O. R. R..... to	Norwood
Cent. Vermont R. R..	Highgate Sp'gs.

RETURNING SAME ROUTE.

Through Rates.

Niagara Falls	$19.10	Syracuse	$14.50
Rochester	17.40	Utica	14.35

Route 237—Hyannis, Mass.

Form N 17.

R., W. & O. R.R.....to	Norwood
Cent. Vermont R.R..	White River Jc.
Boston & Maine R.R..	Concord
Con. & Mont'l R R....	Nashua
Boston & Maine R.R..	Boston
N.Y., N.H. & H. R.R.	Hyannis

Through Rates.

	Unlim'd	Lim'd
Niagara Falls	$19.60	$17.30
Rochester	18.25	11.00
Syracuse	16.65	.
Utica	15.55	.....

SEE NOTE ON PAGE 119 REGARDING STOP-OVER AT ALEXANDRIA BAY.

Route 238—Hyannis, Mass. and Return.

Form Ex. 510.

R. W., & O. R. R.R..	to Norwood
Cent. Vermont R.R...	White River Jc.
Boston & Maine R.R..	Concord
Con. & Mont'l R.R...	Nashua
Boston & Maine R.R..	Boston
N.Y., N.H. & H R.R..	Hyannis

RETURNING SAME ROUTE.

Through Rates.

	Unlim'd	Lim'd
Niagara Falls	$31.50	$21.80
Rochester	29.50	21.20
Syracuse	27.25	.....
Utica	26.00	.....

Route 239—Hyannis, Mass. and Return.

Form Ex. 571.

R., W. & O. R.R....	to Norwood
Cent. Vermont R.R...	White River Jc.
Con. & Mont'l R.R...	Nashua
Boston & Maine R.R.	Boston
N.Y., N.H. & H. R.R.	Hyannis
N.Y., N.H. & H. R.R.	Boston
Boston & Maine R.R.	North Conway
Maine Central R.R...	Lunenburg
St. J. & L. C. R.R.....	Swanton
Cent. Vermont R.R...	Norwood
R., W. & O. R.R.....	starting point

Through Rates.

	Unlim'd	Lim'd
Niagara Falls	$37.00	$23.05
Rochester	35.00	21.20
Syracuse	32.75	.....
Utica	31.50	.....

Route 240—Intervale, N. H.

Form N 12.

R., W. & O. R.R.....	to Norwood
Cent. Vermont R.R..	Swanton
St. J. & L. C. R.R....	Lunenburg
Maine Central R.R...	Intervale

Through Rates.

	Unlim'd	Lim'd
Niagara Falls	$11.65	$13.15
Rochester	13.15	11.60
Syracuse	11.55	.....
Utica	10.55	.....

Route 241—Jefferson Station, N. H.

Form N 12.

R., W. & O.R.R......	to Norwood
Cent. Vermont R.R..	Swanton
St. J. & L. C. R.R.....	Lunenburg
Maine Central R.R...	Jefferson

Through Rates.

	Unlim'd	Lim'd
Niagara Falls	$12.85	....
Rochester	11.35	.....
Syracuse	9.75	.....
Utica	8.75	.....

Route 242—Jefferson Station, N. H. and Return.

Form Ex. 612.

R. W. & O. R.R......	to Norwood
Cent. Vermont R.R...	Swanton
St. J. & L. C. R.R....	Lunenburg
Maine Central R.R..	Jefferson

RETURNING SAME ROUTE.

Through Rates.

Niagara Falls	$23.60	Syracuse	$18.85
Rochester	21.60	Utica	16.95

Route 243—Jefferson Hill, N. H.

Form N 12.

R., W. & O. R.R.....	to Norwood
Cent. Vermont R.R...	Swanton
St. J. & L. C. R.R....	Lunenburg
Maine Central R.R...	Jefferson Hill

Through Rates.

Niagara Falls	$13.00	Syracuse	$9.90
Rochester	11.50	Utica	8.90

Route 244—Kingston, Ont.

Form V. 1.

R., W. & O. R.R.....	to Cape Vincent
St. L. R. St'mb't Co..	Kingston

Through Rates.

Niagara Falls	$6.35	Syracuse	$3.95
Rochester	5.55	Utica	4.30

Route 245—Lake Bonaparte, N. Y.

Form C 1.

R., W. & O. R.R.....	to Carthage
Car. & Ad. R.R.......	Lake Bonaparte

Through Rates.

Niagara Falls	$6.60	Syracuse	$3.30
Rochester	5.20	Utica	2.60

Route 246—Lake Bonaparte, N. Y. and Return.

Form C. 1. R.

R., W. & O. R.R.....	to Carthage
Car. & Ad. R.R	Lake Bonaparte

RETURNING SAME ROUTE.

Through Rates.

Niagara Falls	$11.05	Syracuse	$5.45
Rochester	8.65	Utica	4.60

Route 247—Lake Edward, P. Q.

Forms Ex. 399 and Ex. 784.

R., W. & O. R.R....	to Clayton
R. & O. Nav. Co.....	Alexandria Bay
R. & O. Nav. Co......	Montreal
Grand Trunk R'y or R. & O. Nav. Co.	Quebec
Q. & L. St. J. R'y.....	Lake Edward

Through Rates.

Niagara Falls	$17.90	Syracuse	$15.05
Rochester	16.65	Utica	14.90

Route 248—Lake Edward, P. Q.

Forms Ex. 400 and Ex. 184.

R., W. & O. R.R.....	to Clayton
R. & O. Nav. Co	Alexandria Bay
R. & O. Nav. Co.....	Montreal
Can. Pac. R'y or R. & O. Nav. Co.	Quebec
Q. & L. St. J. R'y....	Lake Edward

Through Rates.

Niagara Falls	$17.50	Syracuse	$15.05
Rochester	16.65	Utica	14.90

Route 249—Lake Megantic, P. Q.

Forms Ex. 254 and Ex. 512.

R., W. & O. R.R.....	to Clayton
R. & O. Nav. Co.....	Alexandria Bay
R. & O. Nav. Co.....	Montreal
Can. Pac. R'y........	Lake Megantic

Through Rates.

Niagara Falls	$17.10	Syracuse	$14.25
Rochester	15.85	Utica	14.10

Route 250—Lancaster, N. H.

Form N 12.

R., W & O. R.R.....	to Norwood
Cent. Vermont RR...	Swanton
St. J. & L. C. R.R....	Lunenburg
Maine Central R.R...	Lancaster

Through Rates.

	Unlim'd	Lim'd
Niagara Falls	$12.95	.....
Rochester	11.45	.....
Syracuse	9.85	.....
Utica	8.85	.....

Route 251—Lancaster, N. H. and Return.

Form Ex. 612.

R., W. & O. R.R.....	to Norwood
Cent. Vermont R.R...	Swanton
St. J. & L. C. R.R....	Lunenburg
Maine Central R.R...	Lancaster

RETURNING SAME ROUTE.

Through Rates.

Niagara Falls	$23.85	Syracuse	$18.80
Rochester	21.85	Utica	16.90

Route 252—Lancaster, N. H.

Forms Ex. 254 and Ex. 585.

R., W. & O. R.R.....	to Clayton
R. & O. Nav. Co.....	Alexandria Bay
R. & O. Nav. Co.....	Montreal
Can. Pac. R'y.........	Newport
Boston & Maine R.R.	Lunenburg
Maine Central R.R...	Scott's
Con. & Mont'l R.R...	Lancaster

Through Rates.

Niagara Falls	$17.15	Syracuse	$14.30
Rochester	15.90	Utica	14.15

Route 253—Lancaster, N. H.

Forms Ex. 254 and Ex. 351.

R., W. & O. R.R.....	to Clayton
R. & O. Nav. Co.....	Alexandria Bay
R. & O. Nav. Co.....	Montreal
Grand Trunk R'y....	St. John's
Cent. Vermont R.R ..	Montpelier
Mont. & W. R. R.R..	Wells River
Cont. & Mont'l R.R..	Lancaster

Through Rates.

Niagara Falls	$17.15	Syracuse	$14.30
Rochester	15.90	Utica	14 15

Route 254—Lancaster, N. H. and Return.

Forms Ex. 255 and Ex. 352.

R., W. & O. R.R.....	to Clayton
R. & O. Nav. Co.....	Alexandria Bay
R. & O. Nav. Co.....	Montreal
Grand Trunk R'y....	St. John's
Cent. Vermont R.R..	Montpelier
Mont. & W. R. R.R..	Wells River
Con. & Mont'l R.R...	Lancaster

RETURNING SAME ROUTE.

Through Rates.

Niagara Falls	$28.00	Syracuse	$23.50
Rochester	26.00	Utica	23.50

Route 255—Lancaster, N. H.

Forms Ex. 399 and Ex. 446.

R., W. & O. R.R.....	to Clayton
R. & O. Nav. Co.....	Alexandria Bay
R. & O. Nav. Co......	Montreal
Grand Trunk R'y or R. & O. Nav. Co.	Quebec
Ferry.................	Point Levis
Grand Trunk R'y	Groveton
Con. & Mont'l R.R...	Lancaster

Through Rates.

Niagara Falls	$21.35	Syracuse	$18.50
Rochester	20.10	Utica	18.35

Route 256—Lancaster, N. H.

Forms Ex. 400 and Ex. 718.

R., W. & O. R.R.....	to Clayton
R. & O. Nav. Co.....	Alexandria Bay
R. & O. Nav. Co.....	Montreal
Can. Pac. R'y or R. & O. Nav. Co.	Quebec
Ferry	Point Levis
Quebec Central R'y..	Dudswell Jc.
Maine Central R.R...	Lancaster

Through Rates.

Niagara Falls	$21.35	Syracuse	$18.50
Rochester	20.10	Utica	18.35

Route 257—Lisbon, N. H.

Form N 13.

R., W. & O. R.R.....	to Norwood
Cent. Vermont R.R..	Swanton
St. J. & L. C. R. R.R.	Lunenburg
Maine Central R.R...	Scott's
Con. & Mont'l R.R...	Lisbon

Through Rates.

	Unlim'd	Lim'd
Niagara Falls	$12 50	.....
Rochester	11 00	.....
Syracuse	9 40	.....
Utica	8 40	.....

SEE NOTE ON PAGE 119 REGARDING STOP-OVER AT ALEXANDRIA BAY.

Route 258—Lisbon, N. H. and Return.

Form Ex. 577.

R., W. & O. R.R.....to	Norwood
Cent. Vermont R.R..	Swanton
St. J. & L. C. R.R....	Lunenburg
Maine Central R.R...	Scott's
Con. & Mont'l R.R..	Lisbon

RETURNING SAME ROUTE.

Through Rates.

Niagara Falls	$23.20	Syracuse	$18.15
Rochester	21.20	Utica	16.25

Route 259—Lisbon, N. H.

Form Ex. 786.

R., W. & O. R.R.....to	Norwood
Cent. Vermont R.R..	Swanton
St. J. & L. C. R.R....	St. Johnsbury
Boston & Maine R.R.	Wells River
Con. & Mont'l R.R...	Lisbon

Through Rates.

Niagara Falls	$12.50	Syracuse	$9.40
Rochester	11.00	Utica	8.40

Route 260—Lisbon, N. H. and Return.

Form Ex. 587.

R., W. & O. R.R.....to	Norwood
Cent. Vermont R.R...	Swanton
St. J. & L. C. R.R....	St. Johnsbury
Boston & Maine R.R.	Wells River
Con. & Mont'l R.R...	Lisbon

RETURNING SAME ROUTE.

Through Rates.

Niagara Falls	$23.20	Syracuse	$18.15
Rochester	21.20	Utica	16.25

Route 261—Lisbon, N. H.

Form N 14.

R., W. & O. R.R.....to	Norwood
Cent. Vermont R.R..	Montpelier
Mont. & W. R. R.R..	Wells River
Con. & Mont'l R.R...	Lisbon

Through Rates.

Niagara Falls	$12.50	Syracuse	$9.40
Rochester	11.00	Utica	8.40

Route 262—Lisbon, N. H. and Return.

Form Ex. 578.

R., W. & O. R.R.....to	Norwood
Cent. Vermont R.R...	Montpelier
Mont. & W. R. R.R..	Wells River
Con. & Mont'l R.R...	Lisbon

RETURNING SAME ROUTE.

Through Rates.

Niagara Falls	$23.20	Syracuse	$18.15
Rochester	21.20	Utica	16.25

Route 263—Littleton, N. H.

Form N 13.

R., W. & O. R.R.....to	Norwood
Cent. Vermont R.R..	Swanton
St. J. & L. C. R.R....	Lunenburg
Maine Central R.R...	Scott's
Con. & Mont'l R.R...	Littleton

Through Rates.

	Unlim'd	Lim'd
Niagara Falls	$12.50	.....
Rochester	11.00	.....
Syracuse	9.40	.....
Utica	8.40	.....

Route 264—Littleton, N. H. and Return.

Form Ex. 577.

R., W. & O. R.R.....to	Norwood
Cent. Vermont R.R..	Swanton
St. J. & L. C. R.R....	Lunenburg
Maine Central R.R...	Scott's
Con. & Mont'l R.R...	Littleton

RETURNING SAME ROUTE.

Through Rates.

Niagara Falls	$23.40	Syracuse	$18.15
Rochester	21.20	Utica	16.25

Route 265—Littleton, N. H.

Form N 14.

R., W. & O. R.R.....to	Norwood
Cent. Vermont R.R..	Montpelier
Mont. & W. R. R.R..	Wells River
Con. & Mont'l R.R...	Littleton

Through Rates.

Niagara Falls	$12.50	Syracuse	$8.40
Rochester	11.00	Utica	8.40

Route 266—Littleton, N. H. and Return.

Form Ex. 578.

R., W. & O. R.R.....to	Norwood
Cent. Vermont R.R..	Montpelier
Mont. & W. R.R. ...	Wells River
Con. & Mont'l R.R...	Littleton

RETURNING SAME ROUTE.

Through Rates.

Niagara Falls	$23.20	Syracuse	$18.15
Rochester	21.20	Utica	16.25

Route 267—Maplewood, N. H.

Form Ex. 686.

R., W. & O. R.R.....to	Norwood
Cent. Vermont R.R..	Swanton
St. J. & L. C. R.R....	Lunenburg
Maine Central R.R...	Zealand Jc.
Prof. & F. Notch R.R.	Maplewood

Through Rates.

	Unlim'd	Lim'd
Niagara Falls	$13.00	.....
Rochester	11.50	.....
Syracuse	9.90	.....
Utica	8.90	.....

Route 268—Maplewood, N. H. and Return.

Form Ex. 666 R.

R., W. O. & R.R .....to	Norwood
Cent. Vermont R.R.	Swanton
St. J. & L. C. R.R....	Lunenburg
Maine Central R.R...	Zealand Jc.
Prof. & F. Notch R.R.	Maplewood

RETURNING SAME ROUTE.

Through Rates.

Niagara Falls	$23.90	Syracuse	$18.85
Rochester	21.90	Utica	16.95

Route 269—Maplewood, N. H.

Forms N 13 and Ex. 217.

R., W. & O. R.R.....to	Norwood
Cent. Vermont R.R..	Swanton
St. J. & L. C. R.R....	Lunenburg
Maine Central R.R...	Scott's
Con. & Mont'l R.R...	Bethlehem Jc.
Prof. & F. Notch R.R.	Maplewood

Through Rates.

Niagara Falls	$13.00	Syracuse	$9.90
Rochester	11.50	Utica	8.90

Route 270—Maplewood, N. H. and Return.

Form Ex. 69\

R., W. & O. R.R.....to	Norwood
Cent. Vermont R.R..	Swanton
St. J. & L. C. R.R....	Lunenburg
Maine Central R.R...	Scott's
Con. & Mont'l R.R...	Bethlehem Jc.
Prof. & F. Notch R.R.	Maplewood

RETURNING SAME ROUTE.

Through Rates.

Niagara Falls	$23.90	Syracuse	$18.85
Rochester	21.90	Utica	16.95

Route 271—Maplewood, N. H.

Forms N 14 and Ex. 217.

R., W. & O. R.R.....to	Norwood
Cent. Vermont R.R..	Montpelier
Mont. & W. R. R.R..	Wells River
Con. & Mont'l R.R...	Bethlehem Jc.
Prof. & F. Notch R.R.	Maplewood

Through Rates.

Niagara Falls	$13.00	Syracuse	$9.90
Rochester	11.50	Utica	8.90

Route 272—Maplewood, N. H. and Return.

Form Ex. 580.

R., W. & O. R.R.....to	Norwood
Cent. Vermont R.R..	Montpelier
Mont. & W. R. R.R..	Wells River
Con. & Mont'l R.R...	Bethlehem Jc.
Prof. & F. Notch R.R.	Maplewood

RETURNING SAME ROUTE.

Through Rates.

Niagara Falls	$23.90	Syracuse	$18.85
Rochester	21.90	Utica	16.95

Route 273—Maplewood, N. H.

Forms Ex. 254 and Ex. 754.

R., W. & O. R.R.....to	Clayton
R. & O. Nav. Co.....	Alexandria Bay
R. & O. Nav. Co.....	Montreal
Grand Trunk R'y....	St. John's
Cent. Vermont R.R..	Montpelier
Mont. & W. R. R.R..	Wells River
Con. & Mont'l R.R...	Bethlehem Jc.
Prof. & F. Notch R.R.	Maplewood

Through Rates.

Niagara Falls	$17.65	Syracuse	$14.80
Rochester	16.40	Utica	14.65

Route 274—Massena Springs, N. Y.

R., W. & O. R.R.....to	Massena Sp'gs

Through Rates.

Niagara Falls	$7.80	Syracuse	$4.85
Rochester	6.45	Utica	4.75

Route 275—Massena Springs, N. Y. and Return.

Form Ex. 691.

R., W. & O. R.R.....to	Massena Sp'gs

RETURNING SAME ROUTE.

Through Rates.

Niagara Falls	$13.30	Syracuse	$8.75
Rochester	11.60	Utica	8.55

Route 276—Montreal, P. Q.

Form Ex. 254.

R., W. & O. R.R.....to	Clayton
R. & O. Nav. Co.....	Alexandria Bay
R. & O. Nav. Co.....	Montreal

Through Rates.

Niagara Falls	$11.50	Syracuse	$8.65
Rochester	10.25	Utica	8.50

Route 277—Montreal, P. Q. and Return.

Form Ex. 255.

R., W. & O. R.R.....to	Clayton
R. & O. Nav. Co.....	Alexandria Bay
R. & O. Nav. Co.....	Montreal

RETURNING SAME ROUTE.

Through Rates.

Niagara Falls	$19.00	Syracuse	$11.50
Rochester	17.00	Utica	14.50

Route 278—Montreal, P. Q. and Return.

Form Ex. 592.

R., W. & O. R.R.....to	Clayton
R. & O. Nav. Co.....	Alexandria Bay
R. & O. Nav. Co.....	Montreal
Grand Trunk R'y....	Rouse's Point
C. V. R.R. (O. & L. C. Div.)	Norwood
R., W. & O. R.R.....	starting point.

Through Rates.

Niagara Falls	$20.75	Syracuse	$16.50
Rochester	19.00	Utica	16.50

Route 279—Montreal, P. Q. and Return.

Form Ex. 259.

R., W. & O. R.R.....to	Clayton
R. & O. Nav. Co.....	Alexandria Bay
R. & O. Nav. Co.....	Montreal
Grand Trunk R'y....	Brockville
Ferry................	Morristown
R., W. & O. R.R.....	starting point

Through Rates.

Niagara Falls	$19.75	Syracuse	$15.35
Rochester	17.95	Utica	15.35

SEE NOTE ON PAGE 119 REGARDING STOP-OVER AT ALEXANDRIA BAY.

Route 280—Montreal, P. Q. and Return.

Form Ex. 270.

R., W. & O. R.R.....to	Clayton
R. & O. Nav. Co.....	Alexandria Bay
R. & O. Nav. Co.....	Montreal
Grand Trunk R'y....	Prescott
Ferry	Ogdensburg
R., W. & O. R.R.....	starting point

Through Rates.

Niagara Falls $19 75	Syracuse $15 35
Rochester...... 17.85	Utica........... 15.35

Route 281—Montreal, P. Q. and Return.

Form Ex. 273.

R., W. & O. R.R.....to	Clayton
R. & O. Nav. Co.....	Alexandria Bay
R. & O. Nav. Co.....	Montreal
Can. Pac. R'y (via Ottawa)	Prescott
Ferry................	Ogdensburg
R., W. & O. R.R.....	starting point

Through Rates.

Niagara Falls $21.00	Syracuse.......$16.35
Rochester 18.85	Utica.... .... 16.35

Route 282—Montreal, P. Q. and Return.

Form Ex. 513.

R., W. & O. R.R.....to	Clayton
R. & O. Nav. Co.....	Alexandria Bay
R. & O. Nav. Co.....	Montreal
Grand Trunk R'y....	Massena Sp'gs
R., W. & O. R.R.....	starting point

Through Rates.

Niagara Falls $19.85	Syracuse.......$14.95
Rochester...... 17.85	Utica........... 14.95

Route 283—Montreal, P. Q.

Form Ex 514.

R., W. & O. R.R.....to	Clayton
R. & O. Nav. Co.....	Alexandria Bay
R. & O. Nav. Co.....	Prescott
Ferry	Ogdensburg
C. V. R.R. (O. & L. C. Div.)	Norwood
R., W. & O. R.R.....	Massena Sp'gs
Grand Trunk R'y....	Montreal

Through Rates.

Niagara Falls $11.30	Syracuse.........$8.35
Rochester 9.95	Utica...... ...... 8.20

Route 284—Montreal, P. Q.

Form Ex. 259.

R., W. & O. R.R. .. to	Clayton
R. & O. Nav. Co.....	Alexandria Bay
R. & O. Nav. Co.....	Prescott
Can. Pac. R'y........	Ottawa
Ottawa River N. Co..	Montreal

Through Rates.

Niagara Falls $12.45	Syracuse $9.50
Rochester...... 11.10	Utica............ 9.35

Route 285—Montreal, P. Q. and Return.

Form Ex. 272.

R., W. & O. R.R.....to	Clayton
R. & O. Nav. Co.....	Alexandria Bay
R. & O. Nav. Co.....	Prescott
Can. Pac. R'y........	Ottawa
Ottawa River N. Co..	Montreal
Grand Trunk R'y....	Prescott
Ferry..................	Ogdensburg
R., W. & O. R.R.....	starting point

Through Rates.

Niagara Falls $21.30	Syracuse $16.70
Rochester...... 19.55	Utica 16.70

Route 286—Montreal, P. Q.

Form Ex. 264.

R., W. & O. R.R.....to	Clayton
R. & O. Nav. Co.....	Alexandria Bay
R. & O. Nav. Co.....	Prescott
Can. Pac. R'y (via Ottawa)	Montreal

Through Rates.

Niagara Falls $12.45	Syracuse $9.50
Rochester...... 11.10	Utica............. 9.35

Route 287—Montreal, P. Q.

Form Ex. 258.

R., W. & O. R.R.....to	Clayton
R. & O. Nav. Co.....	Alexandria Bay
R. & O. Nav. Co.....	Brockville
Can. Pac. R'y........	Ottawa
Ottawa River N. Co..	Montreal

Through Rates.

Niagara Falls $12.45	Syracuse........$9.50
Rochester 11.10	Utica 9.35

Route 288—Montreal, P. Q.

Form Ex. 265.

R., W. & O. R.R.....to	Clayton
R. & O. Nav. Co	Alexandria Bay
R. & O. Nav. Co.....	Brockville
Can. Pac. R'y (via Ottawa)	Montreal

Through Rates.

Niagara Falls $12.45	Syracuse $9.50
Rochester...... 11.10	Utica.............. 9.35

Route 289—Montreal, P. Q.

Form Ex. 268.

R., W. & O. R.R.....to	Clayton
R. & O. Nav. Co.....	Alexandria Bay
R. & O. Nav. Co.....	Montreal
R. & O. Nav. Co......	Quebec
Can. Pac. R'y	Montreal

Through Rates.

Niagara Falls $16.50	Syracuse.......$13.65
Rochester........ 15.25	Utica............ 13.50

Route 290—Montreal, P. Q.

Form Ex. 256.

R., W. & O. R.R..... to	Morristown
Ferry.................	Brockville
R. & O. Nav. Co......	Montreal

Through Rates.

Niagara Falls $10.60	Syracuse $7.60
Rochester....... 9.20	Utica............ 7.50

Route 291—Montreal, P. Q.

Form Ex. 262.

R., W. & O. R.R.....to	Morristown
Ferry.................	Brockville
Grand Trunk R'y....	Montreal

Through Rates.

Niagara Falls $10.85	Syracuse........$7.85
Rochester....... 9.45	Utica............ 7.75

Route 292—Montreal, P. Q. and Return.

Form Ex. 271.

R., W. & O. R.R.....to	Morristown
Ferry	Brockville
Grand Trunk R'y....	Montreal

RETURNING SAME ROUTE.

Through Rates.

Niagara Falls $19.00	Syracuse... ...$13.70
Rochester...... 17.00	Utica.......... 13.45

Route 293—Montreal, P. Q.

Form Ex. 267.

R., W. & O. R.R.....to	Morristown
Ferry	Brockville
Can. Pac. R'y (via Ottawa)	Montreal

Through Rates.

Niagara Falls $11.70	Syracuse........$8.70
Rochester...... 10.30	Utica............ 8.60

Route 294—Montreal, P. Q.

Form Ex. 261.

R., W. & O. R.R.....to	Morristown
Ferry....................	Brockville
Can. Pac. R'y........	Ottawa
Ottawa River N. Co.	Montreal

Through Rates.

Niagara Falls $11.70	Syracuse.........$8.70
Rochester...... 10.30	Utica............ 8.60

Route 295—Montreal, P. Q.

Form Ex. 257.

R., W. & O. R.R.....to	Ogdensburg
Ferry	Prescott
R. & O. Nav. Co.....	Montreal

Through Rates.

Niagara Falls $10.60	Syracuse $7.65
Rochester....... 9.25	Utica............. 7.50

Route 296—Montreal, P. Q.

Form Ex. 263.

R., W. & O. R.R.....to	Ogdensburg
Ferry	Prescott
Grand Trunk R'y....	Montreal

Through Rates.

Niagara Falls $10.70	Syracuse $7.75
Rochester....... 9.35	Utica 7.60

Route 297—Montreal, P. Q.

Form Ex. 266.

R., W. & O. R.R.....to	Ogdensburg
Ferry................	Prescott
Can. Pac. R'y (via Ottawa)	Montreal

Through Rates.

Niagara Falls $11.95	Syracuse.... ...$9.00
Rochester...... 10.60	Utica....... .... 8.85

Route 298—Montreal, P. Q.

Form Ex. 260.

R., W. & O. R.R.....to	Ogdensburg
Ferry	Prescott
Can. Pac. R'y........	Ottawa
Ottawa River N. Co.	Montreal

Through Rates.

Niagara Falls $11.95	Syracuse....... $9.00
Rochester.... .. 10.60	Utica......... ...8.85

Route 299—Montreal, P. Q.

Form Z 1.

R., W. & O. R.R.....to	Massena Sp'gs
Grand Trunk R'y....	Montreal

Through Rates.

Niagara Falls $10.50	Syracuse $7.55
Rochester....... 9.15	Utica............. 7.45

Route 300—Montreal, P. Q. and Return.

Form Ex. 173 R.

R., W. & O. R.R.....to	Massena Sp'gs
Grand Trunk R'y....	Montreal

RETURNING SAME ROUTE.

Through Rates.

Niagara Falls $17.80	Syracuse $13.25
Rochester...... 16.10	Utica 13.05

Route 301—Montreal, P. Q.

Form Ex. 855.

R., W. & O. R.R.....to	Norwood
Cen. Vermont R.R ..	Malone Junc.
N.Y. C. & H. R. R.R.	Montreal

Through Rates.

Niagara Falls $10.50	Syracuse $7.55
Rochester...... 9.15	Utica......... .. 7.45

Route 302—Montreal, P. Q. and Return.

Form Ex. 855 R.

R., W. & O. R.R.....to	Norwood
Cen. Vermont R.R....	Malone Junc.
N. Y. C. & H. R. R.R.	Montreal

RETURNING SAME ROUTE.

Through Rates.

Niagara Falls $17.80	Syracuse.......$13 25
Rochester...... 16.10	Utica........... 13.05

SEE NOTE ON PAGE 119 REGARDING STOP-OVER AT ALEXANDRIA BAY

Route 303—Nantasket, Mass.

Form N 11.

R., W. & O. R.R.....to	Norwood
Cent. Vermont R.R..	White River Jc.
Boston & Maine R.R.	Concord
Con. & Mont'l R.R ..	Nashua
Boston & Maine R.R.	Boston
N.Y., N.H & H. R.R.	Nantasket

Through Rates.

	Unlim'd	Lim'd
Niagara Falls	$18.10	$10.65
Rochester	16.75	9.50
Syracuse	15.15	.....
Utica	15.05	.....

Route 304—Nantasket, Mass. and Return.

Form Ex. 510.

R., W. & O. R.R.....to	Norwood
Cent. Vermont R.R..	White River Jc.
Boston & Maine R.R.	Concord
Con. & Mont'l R.R..	Nashua
Boston & Maine R.R.	Boston
N.Y., N. H. & H. R.R.	Nantasket

RETURNING SAME ROUTE.

Through Rates.

	Unlim'd	Lim'd
Niagara Falls	$29.25	$20.05
Rochester	27.25	18.95
Syracuse	25.00	.....
Utica	23.75	.....

Route 305—Nantasket, Mass. and Return.

Form Ex. 571.

R. W., & O. R.R.....to	Norwood
Cent. Vermont R.R..	White River Jc.
Boston & Maine R.R.	Concord
Con. & Mont'l R.R ..	Nashua
Boston & Maine R.R.	Boston
N.Y., N. H. & H. R.R.	Nantasket
N.Y., N. H. & H. R.R.	Boston
Boston & Maine R.R.	North Conway
Maine Central R.R...	Lunenburg
St. J. & L. C. R.R....	Swanton
Cent. Vermont R.R..	Norwood
R., W. & O. R.R.....	starting point

Through Rates.

	Unlim'd	Lim'd
Niagara Falls	$34.75	$20.80
Rochester	32.75	18.85
Syracuse	30.50	.....
Utica	29.25	.....

Route 306—Nantucket, Mass.

Form Ex. 553.

R., W. & O. R.R.....to	Norwood
Cent. Vermont R.R..	White River Jc.
Boston & Maine R.R.	Concord
Con. & Mont'l R.R..	Nashua
Boston & Maine R.R.	Boston
N.Y., N. H. & H. R.R.	Nantucket

Through Rates.

	Unlim'd	Lim'd
Niagara Falls	$21.05	$12.75
Rochester	19.70	12.45
Syracuse	18.10	.....
Utica	18.00	.....

Route 307—Nantucket, Mass. and Return.

Form Ex. 554.

R., W. & O. R.R.....to	Norwood
Cent. Vermont R.R..	White River Jc.
Boston & Maine R.R.	Concord
Con. & Mont'l R.R...	Nashua
Boston & Maine R.R.	Boston
N.Y., N. H. & H. R.R.	Nantucket

RETURNING SAME ROUTE.

Through Rates.

	Unlim'd	Lim'd
Niagara Falls	$32.50	$22.80
Rochester	30.50	22.20
Syracuse	26.25	....
Utica	27.00	....

Route 308—Nantucket, Mass. and Return.

Form Ex. 555.

R., W. & O. R.R.....to	Norwood
Cent. Vermont R.R..	White River Jc.
Boston & Maine R.R.	Concord
Con. & Mont'l R.R..	Nashua
Boston & Maine R.R.	Boston
N.Y., N.H. & H. R.R.	Nantucket
N.Y., N.H. & H. R.R.	Boston
Boston & Maine R.R.	North Conway
Maine Central R.R...	Lunenburg
St. J. & L. C. R.R.....	Swanton
Cent. Vermont R.R...	Norwood
R., W. & O. R.R.....	starting point

Through Rates.

	Unlim'd	Lim'd
Niagara Falls	$38.00	$24.05
Rochester	36.00	22.20
Syracuse	33.75	.....
Utica	32.50	.....

Route 309—Narragansett Pier, R. I.

Form Ex. 559.

R., W. & O. R.R.....to	Norwood
Cent. Vermont R.R..	White River Jc.
Boston & Maine R.R.	Concord
Con. & Mont'l R.R..	Nashua
Boston & Maine R.R.	Boston
N.Y., N. H. & H. R.R.	Providence
N.Y., N.H. & H. R.R.	Kingston
Narragans't P'r R.R.	Narragans't P'r

Through Rates.

	Unlim'd	Lim'd
Niagara Falls	$19.88	11.56
Rochester	18.53	11.28
Syracuse	16.93	.....
Utica	16.83	.....

Route 310—Narragansett Pier, R. I. and Return.

Form Ex. 560.

R., W. & O. R.R.....to	Norwood
Cent. Vermont R.R..	White River Jc.
Boston & Maine......	Concord
Con. & Mont'l R.R...	Nashua
Boston & Maine R.R.	Boston
N.Y., N. H. & H. R.R.	Providence
N.Y., N.H. & H. R.R.	Kingston
Narragans't P'r R.R.	Narragans't P'r

RETURNING SAME ROUTE.

Through Rates.

	Unlim'd	Lim'd
Niagara Falls	$31.75	$22.05
Rochester	29.75	21.45
Syracuse	27.50	....
Utica	26.25	.....

Route 311—Narragansett Pier, R. I. and Return.

Form Ex. 561.

R., W. & O. R.R.....to	Norwood
Cent. Vermont R.R..	White River Jc.
Boston & Maine R.R.	Concord
Con. & Mont'l R.R..	Nashua
Boston & Maine R.R.	Boston
N.Y., N.H. & H. R.R.	Providence
N.Y., N. H. & H.R.R.	Kingston
Narragans't P'r R.R.	Narragans't P'r
Narragans't P'r R.R.	Kingston
N.Y., N.H. & H. R.R.	Providence
N.Y., N. H. & H. R.R.	Boston
Boston & Maine R.R.	North Conway
Maine Central R.R...	Lunenburg
St. J. & L. C. R.R....	Swanton
Cent. Vermont R.R..	Norwood
R., W. & O. R.R.....	starting point

Through Rates.

	Unlim'd	Lim'd
Niagara Falls	$37.25	$23.30
Rochester	35.25	21.45
Syracuse	33.00	...
Utica	31.75	.....

Route 312—Narragansett Pier, R. I.

Form Ex. 557.

R., W. & O. R.R.....to	Norwood
Cent. Vermont R.R..	White River Jc.
Boston & Maine R.R.	Concord
Con. & Mont'l R.R...	Nashua
Boston & Maine R.R.	Worcester
N.Y., N. H. & H. R.R.	Kingston
Narragans't P'r R.R.	Narragans't P'r

Through Rates.

	Unlim'd	Lim'd
Niagara Falls	$20.38	$12.08
Rochester	19.03	11.78
Syracuse	17.43	....
Utica	17.33	.....

Route 313—Newport, R. I.

Form N 11.

R., W. & O. R.R.....to	Norwood
Cent. Vermont R.R..	White River Jc.
Boston & Maine R.R.	Concord
Con. & Mont'l R.R..	Nashua
Boston & Maine R.R.	Boston
N.Y., N. H. & H. R.R.	Newport

Through Rates.

	Unlim'd	Lim'd
Niagara Falls	$19.40	$11.10
Rochester	18.05	10.80
Syracuse	16.45	....
Utica	16.35	....

Route 314—Newport, R. I. and Return.

Form Ex. 570.

R., W. & O. R.R.....to	Norwood
Cent. Vermont R.R..	White River Jc.
Boston & Maine R.R.	Concord
Con. & Mont'l R.R...	Nashua
Boston & Maine R.R.	Boston
N.Y., N.H. & H. R.R.	Newport

RETURNING SAME ROUTE.

Through Rates.

	Unlim'd	Lim'd
Niagara Falls	$31.00	$21.30
Rochester	29.00	20.70
Syracuse	26.75	.
Utica	25.50	.....

Route 315—Newport, R. I. and Return.

Form Ex. 511.

R., W. & O. R.R.....to	Norwood
Cent. Vermont R.R..	White River Jc.
Boston & Maine R.R.	Concord
Con. & Mont'l R.R..	Nashua
Boston & Maine R.R.	Boston
N. Y., N. H. & H. R.R.	Newport
N. Y., N. H. & H. R.R.	Boston
Boston & Maine R.R.	North Conway
Maine Central R.R...	Lunenburg
St. J. & L. C. R.R....	Swanton
Cent. Vermont R.R..	Norwood
R., W. & O. R.R.....	starting point

Through Rates

	Unlim'd	Lim'd
Niagara Falls	$36.50	22.55
Rochester	34.50	20.70
Syracuse	32.25	....
Utica	31.00	....

Route 316—New York, N.Y.

Form Ex. 237.

R., W. & O. R.R.....to	Norwood
C. V. R.R. (O. & L. C. Div.)	Rouse's Point
D. & H. R. R. (via Saratoga)	Troy.
N.Y. C. & H. R R. R.	New York.

Through Rates.

Niagara Falls	$18.45	Syracuse	$15.35
Rochester	16.95	Utica	15.25

SEE NOTE ON PAGE 119 REGARDING STOP-OVER AT ALEXANDRIA BAY.

Route 317—New York, N. Y.

Form Ex. 935.

R., W. & O. R.R.....to	Norwood
C. V. R.R. (O. & L. C. Div.)	Rouse's Point
D. & H. R.R.........	Plattsburg
D. & H. R.R. or Cham. Trans. Co.	Ft. Ticonderoga
D. & H. R.R.........	Baldwin
L. Geo. St'mb't Co...	Caldwell
D. & H. R.R. (via Saratoga)	Troy
N. Y. C. & H. R. R.R.	New York

Through Rates.

Niagara Falls	$19.95	Syracuse	$16.85
Rochester	18.45	Utica	16.75

Route 318—New York, N. Y.

Form Ex. 593.

R., W. & O. R.R.....to	Norwood
Cent. Vermont R.R..	Swanton
St. J. & L. C. R.R...	Lunenburg
Maine Central R.R..	Scott's
Con. & Mont'l R.R...	Nashua
Boston & Maine R.R.	Boston
Armstrong Trans. Co.	N. Y., N. H. & H. R.R Dep.
Fall River Line......	New York

Through Rates.

Niagara Falls	$20.30	Syracuse	$17.05
Rochester	18.80	Utica	16.05

Route 319—New York, N. Y.

Form Ex. 719.

R., W. & O. R.R.....to	Norwood
Cent. Vermont R.R..	Swanton
St. J. & L. C. R.R....	Lunenburg
Maine Central R.R...	Portland
Boston & Maine R.R.	Boston
Armstrong Trans. Co.	N. Y., N. H & H. R.R. Dep.
Fall River Line......	New York

Through Rates.

Niagara Falls	$21.50	Syracuse	$18.40
Rochester	20.00	Utica	17.40

Route 320—New York, N. Y.

Form Ex. 120.

R., W. & O. R.R.....to	Norwood
Cent. Vermont R.R..	Swanton
St. J. & L. C. R.R....	Lunenburg
Maine Central R.R...	North Conway
Boston & Maine R.R.	Boston
Armstrong Trans. Co.	N. Y., N. H. & H R.R. Dep.
Fall River Line	New York

Through Rates.

Niagara Falls	$21.50	Syracuse	$18.40
Rochester	20.00	Utica	17.40

Route 321—New York, N. Y.

Forms Ex. 254 and Ex. 851.

R., W. & O. R.R.....to	Clayton
R. & O. Nav. Co.....	Alexandria Bay
R. & O. Nav. Co.....	Montreal
N.Y. C. & H. R. R.R.	New York

Through Rates.

Niagara Falls	$21.50	Syracuse	$18.65
Rochester	20.25	Utica	18.50

Route 322—New York, N. Y.

Form Ex. 253.

R., W. & O. R.R.....to	Clayton
R. & O. Nav. Co.....	Alexandria Bay
R. & O. Nav. Co.....	Prescott
Ferry	Ogdensburg
C. V. R.R. (O. & L. C. Div.)	Rouse's Point
D. & H. R.R.........	Plattsburg
D. & H. R. R. or Cham. Trans. Co.	Ft. Ticonderoga
D. & H. R.R. (via Saratoga)	Troy
N. Y. C. & H. R. R.R.	New York

Through Rates.

Niagara Falls	$19.77	Syracuse	$16 82
Rochester	19.42	Utica	16.67

Route 323—New York, N. Y.

Form Ex. 252.

R., W. & O. R.R.....to	Clayton
R. & O. Nav. Co.....	Alexandria Bay
R. & O. Nav. Co.....	Prescott
Ferry	Ogdensburg
C. V. R.R. (O. & L. C Div.)	Rouse's Point
D. & H. R.R.........	Plattsburg
D. & H. R.R. or Cham. Trans. Co.	Ft. Ticonderoga
D. & H. R.R	Baldwin
L. Geo. St'mb't Co...	Caldwell
D. & H. R.R. (via Saratoga)	Troy
N. Y. C. & H. R. R.R.	New York

Through Rates.

Niagara Falls	$21 27	Syracuse	$18.32
Rochester	19.92	Utica	18.17

Route 324—New York, N. Y.

Form Ex. 236.

R., W. & O. R.R.....to	Clayton
R. & O. Nav. Co.....	Alexandria Bay
R. & O. Nav. Co.....	Montreal
Grand Trunk R'y....	Rouse's Point
D. & H. R.R. (via Saratoga)	Troy
N. Y. C. & H. R. R.R.	New York

Through Rates.

Niagara Falls	$21.50	Syracuse	$18.65
Rochester	20.25	Utica	18.50

Route 325—New York, N. Y.

Forms Ex. 254 and Ex. 190.

R., W. & O. R.R.....to	Clayton
R. & O. Nav. Co.....	Alexandria Bay
R. & O. Nav. Co.....	Montreal
Grand Trunk R'y....	St. John's
Cent. Vermont R.R..	Rutland
Benn. & Rut. R'y....	White Creek
Fitchburg R.R.......	Troy
N. Y. C. & H. R. R.R.	New York

Through Rates.

Niagara Falls	$21.50	Syracuse	$18.65
Rochester	20.25	Utica	18.50

Route 326—New York, N. Y.

Forms Ex. 254 and Ex. 356.

R., W. & O. R.R.....to	Clayton
R. & O. Nav. Co......	Alexandria Bay
R. & O. Nav. Co......	Montreal
Grand Trunk R'y....	Rouse's Point
D. & H. R.R.........	Plattsburg
D. & H. R.R. or Cham. Trans. Co.	Ft. Ticonderoga
D. & H. R.R.	Albany
N. Y. C. & H. R. R.R.	New York

Through Rates.

Niagara Falls	$21.50	Syracuse	$18.65
Rochester	20.25	Utica	18.50

Route 327—New York, N. Y.

Forms Ex. 254 and Ex. 354.

R., W. & O. R.R.....to	Clayton
R. & O. Nav. Co.....	Alexandria Bay
R. & O. Nav. Co.....	Montreal
Grand Trunk R'y....	Rouse's Point
D. & H. R.R.........	Plattsburg
D. & H. R.R. or Cham. Trans. Co.	Ft. Ticonderoga
D. & H. R.R.........	Baldwin
L. Geo. St'mb't Co...	Caldwell
D. & H. R.R.........	Albany
N. Y. C. & H. R. R.R.	New York

Through Rates.

Niagara Falls	$23.00	Syracuse	$20.15
Rochester	21.75	Utica	20.00

Route 328—New York, N. Y.

Forms Ex. 254 and Ex. 358.

R., W. & O. R.R.....to	Clayton
R. & O. Nav. Co.....	Alexandria Bay
R. & O. Nav. Co....	Montreal
Grand Trunk R'y....	Rouse's Point
D. & H. R.R.......	Plattsburg
D. & H. R.R. or Cham. Trans. Co.	Ft. Ticonderoga
D. & H. R.R.........	Albany
People's Line St'rs...	New York

Through Rates.

Niagara Falls	$20.45	Syracuse	$17.60
Rochester	19.20	Utica	17.45

Route 329—New York, N. Y.

Forms Ex. 254 and Ex. 355.

R., W. & O. R.R.....to	Clayton
R. & O. Nav. Co.....	Alexandria Bay
R. & O. Nav. Co......	Montreal
Grand Trunk R'y....	Rouse's Point
D. & H. R.R.........	Plattsburg
D. & H. R.R. or Cham. Trans. Co.	Ft. Ticonderoga
D. & H. R.R.........	Baldwin
L. Geo. St'mb't Co...	Caldwell
D. & H. R.R.........	Albany
People's Line St'rs ...	New York

Through Rates.

Niagara Falls	$21.95	Syracuse	$19.10
Rochester	20.70	Utica	18.95

Route 330—New York, N. Y.

Forms Ex. 254 and Ex. 359.

R., W. & O. R.R.....to	Clayton
R. & O. Nav. Co......	Alexandria Bay
R. & O. Nav. Co......	Montreal
Grand Trunk R'y....	Rouse's Point
D. & H. R.R.........	Plattsburg
D. & H. R.R. or Cham. Trans. Co.	Ft. Ticonderoga
D. & H. R.R.........	Albany
Day Line Steamers...	New York

Through Rates.

Niagara Falls	$21.10	Syracuse	$18 25
Rochester	19.85	Utica	18.10

Route 331—New York, N. Y.

Forms Ex. 254 and Ex. 360.

R., W. & O. R.R.....to	Clayton
R. & O. Nav. Co.....	Alexandria Bay
R. & O. Nav. Co.....	Montreal
Grand Trunk R'y....	Rouse's Point
D. & H. R.R.........	Plattsburg
D. & H. R.R. or Cham. Trans. Co.	Ft. Ticonderoga
D. & H. R.R.........	Baldwin
L. Geo. St'mb't Co...	Caldwell
D. & H. R.R.........	Albany
N. Y. & Albany Day Line Steamers	New York

Through Rates.

Niagara Falls	$22.60	Syracuse	$19.75
Rochester	21.35	Utica	19.60

Route 332—New York, N. Y.

Forms Ex. 254 and Ex. 373.

R., W. & O. R.R.....to	Clayton
R. & O. Nav. Co.....	Alexandria Bay
R. & O. Nav. Co.....	Montreal
Grand Trunk R'y....	St. John's
Cent. Vermont R.R..	Burlington
Cham. Trans. Co....	Ft. Ticonderoga
D. & H. R.R.........	Albany
N. Y. C. & H. R. R.R.	New York

Through Rates.

Niagara Falls	$21.50	Syracuse	$18.65
Rochester	20.25	Utica	18.50

SEE NOTE ON PAGE 119 REGARDING STOP-OVER AT ALEXANDRIA BAY

Route 333—New York, N. Y.

Forms Ex. 254 and Ex. 374.

R., W. & O. R.R.....to	Clayton
R. & O. Nav. Co.....	Alexandria Bay
R. & O. Nav. Co.....	Montreal
Grand Trunk R'y....	St. John's
Cent. Vermont R.R..	Burlington
Cham. Trans. Co.....	Ft. Ticonderoga
D. & H. R.R.........	Baldwin
L. Geo. St'mb't Co...	Caldwell
D. & H. R.R.........	Albany
N. Y. C. & H. R. R.R.	New York

Through Rates.

Niagara Falls..$23.00	Syracuse.......$20.15
Rochester...... 21.75	Utica........... 20.00

Route 334—New York, N. Y.

Forms Ex. 254 and Ex. 372.

R., W. & O. R.R.....to	Clayton
R. & O. Nav. Co.....	Alexandria Bay
R. & O. Nav. Co.....	Montreal
Grand Trunk R'y....	St. John's
Cent. Vermont R.R..	Burlington
Cham. Trans. Co.....	Ft. Ticonderoga
D. & H. R.R.........	Albany
People's Line St'rs....	New York

Through Rates.

Niagara Falls.$20.45	Syracuse.......$17.60
Rochester...... 19.20	Utica 17.45

Route 335—New York, N. Y.

Forms Ex. 254 and Ex. 376.

R., W. & O. R.R.....to	Clayton
R. & O. Nav. Co.....	Alexandria Bay
R. & O. Nav. Co.....	Montreal
Grand Trunk R'y....	St. John's
Cent. Vermont R.R..	Burlington
Cham. Trans. Co.....	Ft. Ticonderoga
D. & H. R.R.........	Baldwin
L. Geo. St'mb't Co...	Caldwell
D. & H. R.R.	Albany
People's Line St'rs...	New York

Through Rates.

Niagara Falls $21.95	Syracuse.......$19.10
Rochester...... 20.70	Utica...... ..... 13.95

Route 336—New York, N. Y.

Forms Ex. 254 and Ex. 371.

R., W. & O. R.R.....to	Clayton
R. & O. Nav. Co.....	Alexandria Bay
R. & O. Nav. Co.....	Montreal
Grand Trunk R'y....	St. John's
Cent. Vermont R.R..	Burlington
Cham. Trans. Co.....	Ft. Ticonderoga
D. & H. R.R.........	Albany
Day Line Steamers...	New York

Through Rates.

Niagara Falls.$21.10	Syracuse.. .....$18.25
Rochester...... 19.85	Utica........ .... 18.10

Route 337—New York, N. Y.

Forms Ex. 254 and Ex. 375.

R., W. & O. R.R.....to	Clayton
R. & O. Nav. Co.....	Alexandria Bay
R. & O. Nav. Co.....	Montreal
Grand Trunk R'y....	St. John's
Cent. Vermont R.R..	Burlington
Cham. Trans. Co.....	Ft. Ticonderoga
D. & H. R.R.........	Baldwin
L. Geo. St'mb't Co...	Caldwell
D. & H. R.R.........	Albany
N.Y. & Albany Day Line Steamers	New York

Through Rates.

Niagara Falls.$22.60	Syracuse.......$19.75
Rochester 21.35	Utica.......... 19.60

Route 338—New York, N. Y.

Forms Ex. 254 and Ex. 378.

R., W. & O. R.R.....to	Clayton
R. & O. Nav. Co.....	Alexandria Bay
R. & O. Nav. Co.....	Montreal
Grand Trunk R'y....	St. John's
Cent. Vermont R.R..	Burlington
Cham. Trans. Co	Ft. Ticonderoga
D. & H. R.R.........	Troy
Citizens' Line St'rs..	New York

Through Rates.

Niagara Falls.$20.45	Syracuse........$17.60
Rochester 19.20	Utica 17.45

Route 339—New York, N. Y.

Forms Ex. 254 and Ex. 377.

R., W. & O. R.R.....to	Clayton
R. & O. Nav. Co.....	Alexandria Bay
R. & O. Nav. Co.....	Montreal
Grand Trunk R'y....	St. John's
Cent. Vermont R.R..	Burlington
Cham. Trans. Co.....	Ft. Ticonderoga
D. & H. R.R.........	Baldwin
L. Geo. St'mb't Co...	Caldwell
D. & H. R.R.........	Troy
Citizens' Line St'rs...	New York

Through Rates.

Niagara Falls.$21.95	Syracuse $19.10
Rochester...... 20.70	Utica........... 18.95

Route 340—New York, N. Y.

Forms Ex. 254 and Ex. 365.

R., W. & O. R.R. ...to	Clayton
R. & O. Nav. Co.....	Alexandria Bay
R. & O. Nav. Co.....	Montreal
Grand Trunk R'y....	Rouse's Point
D. & H. R.R.........	Plattsburg
Cham. Trans. Co.....	Burlington
Cent. Vermont R.R .	Bellows Falls
Vermont Valley R.R.	Brattleboro
Cent. Vermont R.R..	South Vernon
Conn. River R.R	Springfield
N.Y., N. H. & H. R.R.	New Haven
N.Y., N. H. & H. R.R.	New York

Through Rates.

Niagara Falls.$22.35	Syracuse $19.50
Rochester...... 21.10	Utica....... ... 19.35

Route 341—New York, N. Y.

Forms Ex. 254 and Ex. 381.

R., W. & O. R.R.....to	Clayton
R. & O. Nav. Co.....	Alexandria Bay
R. & O. Nav. Co.....	Montreal
Grand Trunk R'y....	St. John's
Cent. Vermont R.R..	Bellows Falls
Vermont Valley R.R.	Brattleboro
Cent. Vermont R.R..	South Vernon
Conn. River R.R.....	Springfield
N.Y., N. H. & H. R.R.	New Haven
N.Y., N. H. & H. R.R.	New York

Through Rates.

Niagara Falls.$21.50	Syracuse........$13.65
Rochester...... 20.25	Utica... .... 18.63

Route 342—New York, N. Y.

Forms Ex. 254 and Ex. 370.

R., W. & O. R.R.....to	Clayton
R. & O. Nav. Co.....	Alexandria Bay
R. & O. Nav. Co.....	Montreal
Grand Trunk R'y....	Rouse's Point
D. & H. R.R.........	Plattsburg
Cham. Trans. Co.....	Burlington
Cent. Vermont R.R..	Montpelier
Mont. & W. R. R.R..	Wells River
Con. & Mont'l R.R...	Base Mt. Wash.
Mt. Washington R'y.	Summit
Mt. Washington R'y.	Base
Con. & Mont'l R.R...	Fabyan's
Maine Central R.R...	North Conway
Boston & Maine R.R.	Boston
Fall River Line.......	New York

Through Rates.

Niagara Falls.$32.95	Syracuse...... $30.10
Rochester...... 31.70	Utica 29.95

Route 343—New York, N. Y.

Forms Ex. 254, Ex. 368, Ex. 129 and Ex. 137.

R., W. & O. R.R.....to	Clayton
R. & O. Nav. Co.....	Alexandria Bay
R. & O. Nav. Co.....	Montreal
Grand Trunk R'y....	Rouse's Point
D. & H. R.R.........	Plattsburg
Cham. Trans. Co.....	Burlington
Cent. Vermont R.R..	Montpelier
Mont. & W. R. R.R..	Wells River
Con. & Mont'l R.R...	Bethlehem Jc.
Prof. & F. Notch R.R.	Profile House
Prof. & F. Notch R.R.	Bethlehem Jc.
Con. & Mont'l R.R...	Fabyan's
Maine Central R.R...	Crawford's
Maine Central R.R...	Fabyan's
Con. & Mont'l R.R..	Base Mt. Wash.
Mt. Washington R'y.	Summit
Stage..................	Glen Site
Stage..................	Glen
Maine Central R.R...	Portland
Boston & Maine R.R.	Boston
Fall River Line	New York

Through Rates.

Niagara Falls.$39.95	Syracuse $37.10
Rochester...... 38.70	Utica 36.95

Route 344—New York, N. Y.

Forms Ex. 254, Ex. 383 and Ex. 129.

R., W. & O. R.R.....to	Clayton
R. & O. Nav. Co	Alexandria Bay
R. & O. Nav. Co	Montreal
Grand Trunk R'y....	St. John's
Cent. Vermont R.R ..	Montpelier
Mont. & W. R. R.R..	Wells River
Con. & Mont'l R.R...	Bethlehem Jc.
Prof. & F. Notch R.R.	Profile House
Prof. & F. Notch R.R.	Bethlehem Jc.
Con. & Mont'l R.R...	Fabyan's
Maine Central R.R...	Portland
Boston & Maine R.R.	Boston
Fall River Line......	New York

Through Rates.

Niagara Falls.$27.50	Syracuse.......$24.65
Rochester...... 26.25	Utica........... 24 50

Route 345—New York, N. Y.

Forms Ex. 254, Ex. 758, Ex. 129 and Ex. 229.

R., W. & O. R.R.....to	Clayton
R. & O. Nav. Co.....	Alexandria Bay
R. & O. Nav. Co.....	Montreal
Grand Trunk R'y....	St. John's
Cent. Vermont R.R..	Montpelier
Mont. & W. R. R.R..	Wells River
Con. & Mont'l R.R...	Bethlehem Jc.
Prof. & F. Notch R.R.	Profile House
Prof. & F. Notch R.R.	Bethlehem Jc.
Con. & Mont'l R.R..	Fabyan's
Maine Central R.R...	Portland
Boston & Maine R.R.	Boston
N. Y., N. H. & H. R.R.	Providence
Providence Line.....	New York

Through Rates.

Niagara Falls.$27.50	Syracuse $24.65
Rochester...... 26.25	Utica....... .. 24.50

Route 346—New York, N. Y.

Forms Ex. 254, Ex. 385. Ex. 129 and Ex. 137.

R., W. & O. R.R.....to	Clayton
R. & O. Nav. Co.....	Alexandria Bay
R. & O. Nav. Co.....	Montreal
Grand Trunk R'y....	St. John's
Cent. Vermont R.R..	Montpelier
Mont. & W. R. R.R..	Wells River
Con. & Mont'l R.R...	Bethlehem Jc.
Prof. & F. Notch R.R.	Profile House
Prof. & F. Notch R.R.	Bethlehem Jc.
Con. & Mont'l R.R...	Fabyan's
Maine Central R.R...	Crawford's
Maine Central R.R ..	Fabyan's
Con. & Mont'l R.R...	Base Mt. Wash.
Mt. Washington R'y.	Summit
Stage............	Glen Site
Stage.....	Glen
Maine Central R.R ..	North Conway
Boston & Maine R.R.	Boston
Fall River Line......	New York

Through Rates.

Niagara Falls.$39.75	Syracuse $35.90
Rochester...... 37.50	Utica...............35.75

SEE NOTE ON PAGE 119 REGARDING STOP-OVER AT ALEXANDRIA BAY.

Route 347—New York, N. Y.

Forms Ex. 254, Ex. 759, Ex. 129 and Ex. 131.

R., W. & O. R.R.	to Clayton
R. & O. Nav. Co.	Alexandria Bay
R. & O. Nav. Co.	Montreal
Grand Trunk R'y	St. John's
Cent. Vermont R.R.	Montpelier
Mont. & W. R. R.R.	Wells River
Con. & Mont'l R.R.	Bethlehem Jc.
Prof. & F. Notch R.R.	Profile House
Prof. & F. Notch R.R.	Bethlehem Jc.
Con. & Mont'l R.R.	Fabyan's
Maine Central R.R.	Crawford's
Maine Central R.R.	Fabyan's
Con. & Mont'l R.R.	Base Mt. Wash.
Mt. Washington R'y.	Summit
Stage	Glen Site
Stage	Glen
Maine Central R.R.	North Conway
Boston & Maine R.R.	Worcester
N.Y., N. H. & H. R.R.	Providence
Providence Line	New York

Through Rates.

Niagara Falls $38.10	**Syracuse** $35.25
Rochester 36.85	**Utica** 35.10

Route 348—New York, N. Y.

Forms Ex. 254, Ex. 364, Ex. 129 and Ex. 131.

R., W. & O. R.R.	to Clayton
R. & O. Nav. Co.	Alexandria Bay
R. & O. Nav. Co.	Montreal
Grand Trunk R'y	St. John's
Cent. Vermont R.R.	Montpelier
Mont. & W. R. R.R.	Wells River
Con. & Mont'l R.R.	Bethlehem Jc.
Prof. & F. Notch R.R.	Profile House
Prof. & F. Notch R.R.	Bethlehem Jc.
Con. & Mont'l R.R.	Fabyan's
Maine Central R.R.	Crawford's
Maine Central R.R.	Fabyan's
Con. & Mont'l R.R.	Wells River
Boston & Maine R.R.	White River Jc.
Cent. Vermont R.R.	Windsor
Vermont Valley R.R.	Brattleboro
Cent. Vermont R.R.	Miller's Falls
New Lon. Nor. R.R.	New London
N. & N. Y. T. Co.	New York

Through Rates.

Niagara Falls $29.25	**Syracuse** $26.40
Rochester 28.00	**Utica** 26.25

Route 349—New York, N. Y.

Forms Ex. 254 and Ex 379.

R., W. & O. R.R.	to Clayton
R. & O. Nav. Co.	Alexandria Bay
R. & O. Nav. Co.	Montreal
Grand Trunk R'y	St. John's
Cent. Vermont R.R.	Bellows Falls
Vermont Valley R.R.	Brattleboro
Cent. Vermont R.R.	Miller's Falls
New Lon. Nor. R.R.	New London
N. & N. Y. T. Co	New York

Through Rates.

Niagara Falls $21.00	**Syracuse** $18.15
Rochester 19.75	**Utica** 18.00

Route 350—New York, N. Y.

Forms Ex. 254 and Ex. 357.

R., W. & O. R.R.	to Clayton
R. & O. Nav. Co.	Alexandria Bay
R. & O. Nav. Co.	Montreal
Grand Trunk R'y	Portland
Boston & Maine R.R.	Boston
Fall River Line	New York

Through Rates.

Niagara Falls $24.50	**Syracuse** $21.65
Rochester 23.25	**Utica** 21.50

Route 351—New York, N. Y.

Forms Ex. 254 and Ex. 616.

R., W. & O. R.R.	to Clayton
R. & O. Nav. Co.	Alexandria Bay
R. & O. Nav. Co.	Montreal
Grand Trunk R'y	Groveton
Con. & Mont'l R.R.	Nashua
Boston & Maine R.R.	Lowell
N.Y., N. H. & H. R.R.	Fall River
Fall River Line	New York

Through Rates.

Niagara Falls $24.50	**Syracuse** $21.65
Rochester 23.25	**Utica** 21.50

Route 352—New York, N. Y.

Forms Ex. 254 and Ex. 780.

R., W. & O. R.R.	to Clayton
R. & O. Nav. Co.	Alexandria Bay
R. & O. Nav. Co.	Montreal
Grand Trunk R'y	Groveton
Con. & Mont'l R.R.	Nashua
Boston & Maine R.R.	Worcester
N.Y., N. H. & H. R.R.	Providence
Providence Line	New York

Through Rates.

Niagara Falls $23.35	**Syracuse** $20.50
Rochester 22.10	**Utica** 20.35

Route 353—New York, N. Y.

Forms Ex. 254 and Ex. 369.

R., W. & O. R.R.	to Clayton
R. & O. Nav. Co.	Alexandria Bay
R. & O. Nav. Co.	Montreal
Grand Trunk R'y	Groveton
Con. & Mont'l R.R.	Base Mt. Wash.
Mt. Washington R'y.	Summit
Stage	Glen Site
Stage	Glen
Maine Central R.R.	North Conway
Boston & Maine R.R.	Boston
Fall River Line	New York

Through Rates.

Niagara Falls $35.25	**Syracuse** $32.40
Rochester 34.00	**Utica** 32.25

Route 354—New York, N. Y.

Forms Ex. 254 and Ex. 791.

R., W. & O. R.R.	to Clayton
R. & O. Nav. Co.	Alexandria Bay
R. & O. Nav. Co.	Montreal
Grand Trunk R'y	Sherbrooke
Boston & Maine R.R.	Concord
Con. & Mont'l R.R.	Nashua
Boston & Maine R.R.	Boston
Armstrong Trans Co.	N.Y., N. H. & H. R.R. Dep.
Fall River Line	New York

Through Rates.

Niagara Falls $25.00	**Syracuse** $22.15
Rochester 23.75	**Utica** 22.00

Route 355—New York, N. Y.

Forms Ex. 254, Ex. 362 and Ex. 129.

R., W. & O. R.R.	to Clayton
R. & O. Nav. Co.	Alexandria Bay
R. & O. Nav. Co.	Montreal
Grand Trunk R'y	Gorham
Stage	Glen Site
Stage	Sum't Mt. Wash.
Mt. Washington R'y.	Base
Con. & Mont'l R.R.	Bethlehem Jc.
Prof. & F. Notch R.R.	Profile House
Prof. & F. Notch R.R.	Bethlehem Jc.
Con. & Mont'l R.R.	Nashua
Boston & Maine R.R.	Boston
Fall River Line	New York

Through Rates.

Niagara Falls $38.60	**Syracuse** $35.75
Rochester 38.35	**Utica** 35.60

Route 356—New York, N. Y.

Forms Ex. 254 and Ex. 380.

R., W. & O. R.R.	to Clayton
R. & O. Nav. Co.	Alexandria Bay
R. & O. Nav. Co.	Montreal
Grand Trunk R'y	Alpine House (Gorham)
Stage	Glen Site
Stage	Sum't Mt. Wash.
Mt. Washington R'y.	Base
Con. & Mont'l R.R.	Bethlehem Jc.
Prof. & F. Notch R.R.	Profile House
Stage	No. Woodstock
Con. & Mont'l R.R.	Nashua
Boston & Maine R.R.	Boston
Fall River Line	New York

Through Rates.

Niagara Falls $38.25	**Syracuse** $35.40
Rochester 37.00	**Utica** 35.25

Route 357—New York, N. Y.

Forms Ex. 254 and Ex. 366.

R., W. & O. R.R.	to Clayton
R. & O. Nav. Co.	Alexandria Bay
R. & O. Nav. Co.	Montreal
Can. Pac. R'y	Newport
Boston & Maine R.R.	White River Jc.
Cent. Vermont R.R.	Windsor
Vermont Valley R.R.	Brattleboro
Cent. Vermont R.R.	South Vernon
Conn. River R.R.	Springfield
N.Y., N. H. & H. R.R.	New Haven
N.Y., N. H. & H. R.R.	New York

Through Rates.

Niagara Falls $21.50	**Syracuse** $18.65
Rochester 20.25	**Utica** 18.50

Route 358—New York, N. Y.

Forms Ex. 254 and Ex. 619.

R., W. & O. R.R.	to Clayton
R. & O. Nav. Co.	Alexandria Bay
R. & O. Nav. Co.	Montreal
Can. Pac. R'y	Newport
Boston & Maine R.R.	Wells River
Con. & Mont'l R.R.	Nashua
Boston & Maine R.R.	Boston
Armstrong Trans. Co.	N. Y., N. H. & H. R.R. Dep.
Fall River Line	New York

Through Rates.

Niagara Falls $25.00	**Syracuse** $22.15
Rochester 23.75	**Utica** 22.00

Route 359—New York, N. Y.

Forms Ex. 254 and Ex. 690.

R., W. & O. R.R.	to Clayton
R. & O. Nav. Co.	Alexandria Bay
R. & O. Nav. Co.	Montreal
Can. Pac. R'y	Newport
Boston & Maine R.R.	Wells River
Con. & Mont'l R.R.	Nashua
Boston & Maine R.R.	Worcester
N. Y. & N. E. R.R.	New London
N. & N. Y. T. Co	New York

Through Rates.

Niagara Falls $23.35	**Syracuse** $20.50
Rochester 22.10	**Utica** 20.35

Route 360—New York, N. Y.

Forms Ex. 254 and Ex. 621.

R., W. & O. R.R.	to Clayton
R. & O. Nav. Co.	Alexandria Bay
R. & O. Nav. Co.	Montreal
Can. Pac. R'y	Newport
Boston & Maine R.R.	Lunenburg
Maine Central R.R.	Fabyan's
Con. & Mont'l R.R.	Nashua
Boston & Maine R.R.	Boston
Armstrong Trans. Co.	N. Y., N. H. & H. R.R. Dep.
Fall River Line	New York

Through Rates.

Niagara Falls $25.00	**Syracuse** $22.15
Rochester 23.75	**Utica** 22.00

Route 361—New York, N. Y.

Forms Ex. 254 and Ex. 622.

R., W. & O. R.R.	to Clayton
R. & O. Nav. Co.	Alexandria Bay
R. & O. Nav. Co.	Montreal
Can. Pac. R'y	Newport
Boston & Maine R.R.	Lunenburg
Maine Central R.R.	Portland
Boston & Maine R.R.	Boston
Armstrong Trans. Co.	N. Y., N. H. & H. R.R. Dep.
N.Y., N. H. & H. R.R.	Fall River
Fall River Line	New York

Through Rates.

Niagara Falls $25.00	**Syracuse** $22.15
Rochester 23.75	**Utica** 22.00

SEE NOTE ON PAGE 119 REGARDING STOP-OVER AT ALEXANDRIA BAY.

Route 362—New York, N. Y.

Forms Ex. 254 and Ex. 653.

R., W. & O. R.R.....to	Clayton
R. & O. Nav. Co.....	Alexandria Bay
R. & O. Nav. Co.....	Montreal
Can. Pac. R'y........	Newport
Boston & Maine R.R.	Lunenburg
Maine Central R.R...	North Conway
Boston & Maine R.R.	Boston
Armstrong Trans. Co.	N. Y., N. H. & H. R.R. Dep.
Fall River Line......	New York

Through Rates.

Niagara Falls	$25.00	Syracuse	$22.15
Rochester	23.75	Utica	22.00

Route 363—New York, N. Y.

Forms Ex. 254 and Ex. 722.

R., W. & O. R R.....to	Clayton
R. & O. Nav. Co.....	Alexandria Bay
R. & O. Nav. Co.....	Montreal
Can. Pac. R'y........	Newport
Boston & Maine R.R.	Lunenburg
Maine Central R.R...	Zealand Jc.
Prof. & F. Notch R.R.	Profile House
Prof. & F. Notch R.R.	Bethlehem Jc.
Con. & Mont'l R.R..	Fabyan's
Maine Central R.R..	North Conway
Boston & Maine R.R.	Boston
Armstrong Trans. Co.	N. Y., N. H. & H. R.R. Dep.
Fall River Line......	New York

Through Rates.

Niagara Falls	$28.00	Syracuse	$25.15
Rochester	26.75	Utica	25.00

Route 364—New York, N. Y.

Forms Ex. 254 and Ex. 723.

R., W. & O. R.R.....to	Clayton
R. & O. Nav. Co.....	Alexandria Bay
R. & O. Nav. Co.....	Montreal
Can. Pac. R'y........	Newport
Boston & Maine R.R.	Lunenburg
Maine Central R.R...	Zealand Jc.
Prof. & F. Notch R.R.	Profile House
Stage................	No. Woodstock
Con. & Mont'l R.R...	Nashua
Boston & Maine R.R.	Worcester
N. Y. & N. E. R.R....	New London
N. & N. Y. T. Co.....	New York

Through Rates.

Niagara Falls	$27.95	Syracuse	$25.10
Rochester	26.70	Utica	24.95

Route 365—New York, N. Y.

Forms Ex. 254 and Ex. 724.

R., W. & O. R.R.....to	Clayton
R. & O. Nav. Co.....	Alexandria Bay
R. & O. Nav. Co.....	Montreal
Can. Pac. R'y........	Newport
Boston & Maine R.R.	Lunenburg
Maine Central R.R..	Zealand Jc.
Prof. & F. Notch R.R.	Profile House
Prof. & F. Notch R.R.	Bethlehem Jc.
Con. & Mont'l R.R...	Base Mt. Wash.
Mt. Washington R'y.	Summit
Stage................	Glen Site
Stage................	Alpine House (Gorham)
Grand Trunk R'y....	Portland
Boston & Maine R.R.	Boston
Armstrong Trans. Co.	N. Y., N. H. & H. R.R. Dep.
Fall River Line......	New York

Through Rates.

Niagara Falls	38.40	Syracuse	35.55
Rochester	37.15	Utica	35.40

Route 366—New York, N. Y.

Forms Ex. 399 and Ex. 447.

R., W. & O. R.R.....to	Clayton
R. & O. Nav. Co.....	Alexandria Bay
R. & O. Nav. Co.....	Montreal
GrandTrunk R'y or R. & O. Nav. Co.	Quebec
Ferry................	Point Levis
Grand Trunk R'y....	Portland
Boston & Maine R.R.	Boston
Fall River Line......	New York

Through Rates.

Niagara Falls	$29.50	Syracuse	$26.65
Rochester	28.25	Utica	26.50

Route 367—New York, N. Y.

Forms Ex. 400 and Ex. 762.

R., W. & O. R.R.....to	Clayton
R. & O. Nav. Co.....	Alexandria Bay
R. & O. Nav. Co.....	Montreal
Can. Pac. R'y or R. & O. Nav. Co.	Quebec
Ferry................	Point Levis
Quebec Central R'y.	Dudswell Jc.
Maine Central R.R..	Portland
Boston & Maine R.R.	Boston
Armstrong Trans. Co.	N. Y., N. H. & H. R.R. Dep.
Fall River Line......	New York

Through Rates.

Niagara Falls	$30.00	Syracuse	$27.15
Rochester	28.75	Utica	27.00

Route 368—New York, N. Y.

Forms Ex. 399, Ex. 706 and Ex. 215.

R., W. & O. R.R.....to	Clayton
R. & O. Nav. Co.....	Alexandria Bay
R. & O. Nav. Co.....	Montreal
Grand Trunk R'y or R. & O. Nav. Co.	Quebec
Ferry................	Point Levis
Grand Trunk R'y....	Sherbrooke
Boston & Maine R.R.	Concord
Con. & Mont'l R.R..	Nashua
Boston & Maine R.R.	Boston
Fall River Line......	New York

Through Rates.

Niagara Falls	$29.50	Syracuse	$26.65
Rochester	28.25	Utica	26.50

Route 369—New York, N. Y.

Forms Ex. 399, Ex. 706 and Ex. 222.

R., W. & O. R.R.....to	Clayton
R. & O. Nav. Co.....	Alexandria Bay
R. & O. Nav. Co.....	Montreal
Grand Trunk R'y or R. & O. Nav. Co.	Quebec
Ferry................	Point Levis
Grand Trunk R'y....	Sherbrooke
Boston & Maine R.R.	Concord
Con. & Mont'l R.R..	Nashua
Boston & Maine R.R.	Boston
N.Y., N. H. & H. R.R.	Providence
Providence Line.....	New York

Through Rates.

Niagara Falls	$29.50	Syracuse	$26.65
Rochester	28.25	Utica	26.50

Route 370—New York, N. Y.

Forms Ex. 400, Ex. 707 and Ex. 215.

R., W. & O. R.R.....to	Clayton
R. & O. Nav. Co.....	Alexandria Bay
R. & O. Nav. Co.....	Montreal
Can. Pac. R'y or R. & O. Nav. Co.	Quebec
Ferry................	Point Levis
Quebec Central R'y..	Sherbrooke
Boston & Maine R.R.	Concord
Con. & Mont'l R.R...	Nashua
Boston & Maine R.R.	Boston
Fall River Line......	New York

Through Rates.

Niagara Falls	$29.50	Syracuse	$26.65
Rochester	28.25	Utica	26.50

Route 371—New York, N. Y.

Forms Ex. 400, Ex. 707 and Ex. 222.

R., W. & O. R.R.....to	Clayton
R. & O. Nav. Co.....	Alexandria Bay
R. & O. Nav. Co.....	Montreal
Can. Pac. R'y or R. & O. Nav. Co.	Quebec
Ferry................	Point Levis
Quebec Central R'y..	Sherbrooke
Boston & Maine R.R.	Concord
Con. & Mont'l R.R..	Nashua
Boston & Maine R.R.	Boston
N.Y., N. H. & H. R.R.	Providence
Providence Line.....	New York

Through Rates.

Niagara Falls	$29.50	Syracuse	$26.65
Rochester	28.25	Utica	26.50

Route 372—New York, N. Y.

Forms Ex. 399 and Ex. 448.

R., W. & O. R.R.....to	Clayton
R. & O. Nav. Co.....	Alexandria Bay
R. & O. Nav. Co.....	Montreal
Grand Trunk R'y or R. & O. Nav. Co.	Quebec
Ferry................	Point Levis
Grand Trunk R'y....	Sherbrooke
Boston & Maine R.R.	White River Jc.
Cent. Vermont R.R..	Windsor
Vermont Valley R.R.	Brattleboro
Cent. Vermont R.R..	South Vernon
Conn. River R.R.....	Springfield
N.Y., N. H. & H. R.R.	New Haven
N.Y., N. H. & H. R.R.	New York

Through Rates.

Niagara Falls	$26.50	Syracuse	$23.65
Rochester	25.25	Utica	23.50

Route 373—New York, N. Y.

Forms Ex. 400 and Ex. 725.

R., W. & O. R.R.....to	Clayton
R. & O. Nav. Co.....	Alexandria Bay
R. & O. Nav. Co.....	Montreal
Can. Pac. R'y or R. & O. Nav. Co.	Quebec
Ferry................	Point Levis
Quebec Central R'y..	Sherbrooke
Boston & Maine R.R.	White River Jc.
Cent. Vermont R.R..	Windsor
Vermont Valley R.R.	Brattleboro
Cent. Vermont R.R..	South Vernon
Conn. River R.R.....	Springfield
N.Y., N. H. & H. R.R.	New Haven
N.Y., N. H. & H. R.R.	New York

Through Rates.

Niagara Falls	$26.50	Syracuse	$23.65
Rochester	25.25	Utica	23.50

Route 374—New York, N. Y.

Forms Ex. 399, Ex. 726 and Ex. 137.

R., W. & O. R.R.....to	Clayton
R. & O. Nav. Co.....	Alexandria Bay
R. & O. Nav. Co.....	Montreal
Grand Trunk R'y or R. & O. Nav. Co.	Quebec
Ferry................	Point Levis
Grand Trunk R'y....	Sherbrooke
Boston & Maine R.R.	Lunenburg
Maine Central R.R...	Zealand Jc.
Prof. & F. Notch R.R.	Profile House
Prof. & F. Notch R.R.	Bethlehem Jc.
Con. & Mont'l R.R..	Fabyan's
Maine Central R.R...	Crawford's
Maine Central R.R..	Fabyan's
Con. & Mont'l R.R...	Wells River
Boston & Maine R.R.	White River Jc.
Cent. Vermont R.R..	Windsor
Vermont Valley R.R.	Brattleboro
Cent. Vermont R.R..	South Vernon
Conn. River R.R.....	Springfield
N.Y., N. H. & H. R.R.	New Haven
N.Y., N. H. & H. R.R.	New York

Through Rates.

Niagara Falls	$32.50	Syracuse	$29.65
Rochester	31.25	Utica	29.50

Route 375—New York, N. Y.

Forms Ex. 399 and Ex. 763.

R., W. & O. R.R.....to	Clayton
R. & O. Nav. Co.....	Alexandria Bay
R. & O. Nav. Co.....	Montreal
Grand Trunk R'y or R. & O. Nav. Co.	Quebec
Ferry................	Point Levis
Quebec Central R'y.	Dudswell Jc.
Maine Central R.R..	Zealand Jc.
Prof. & F. Notch R.R.	Profile House
Prof. & F. Notch R.R.	Zealand Jc.
Maine Central R.R..	Crawford's
Maine Central R.R...	Fabyan's
Con. & Mont'l R.R...	Wells River
Boston & Maine R.R.	White River Jc.
Cent. Vermont R.R..	Windsor
Vermont Valley R.R.	Brattleboro
Cent. Vermont R.R..	South Vernon
Conn. River R.R.....	Springfield
N.Y., N. H. & H. R.R.	New Haven
N.Y., N. H. & H. R.R.	New York

Through Rates.

Niagara Falls	$32.50	Syracuse	$29.65
Rochester	31.25	Utica	29.50

SEE NOTE ON PAGE 119 REGARDING STOP-OVER AT ALEXANDRIA BAY.

Route 376—New York, N. Y.

Forms 400, Ex. 721 and Ex. 137.

R., W. & O. R.R.....to	Clayton
R. & O. Nav. Co.....	Alexandria Bay
R. & O. Nav. Co.....	Montreal
Can. Pac. R'y or R. & O. Nav. Co.	Quebec
Ferry..................	Point Levis
Quebec Central R'y..	Sherbrooke
Boston & Maine R.R.	Lunenburg
Maine Central R.R...	Zealand Jc.
Prof. & F. Notch R.R.	Profile House
Prof. & F. Notch R.R.	Bethlehem Jc.
Con. & Mont'l R.R...	Fabyan's
Maine Central R.R...	Crawford's
Maine Central R.R...	Fabyan's
Con. & Mont'l R.R...	Wells River
Boston & Maine R.R.	White River Jc.
Cent. Vermont R.R..	Windsor
Vermont Valley R.R.	Brattleboro
Cent. Vermont R.R..	South Vernon
Conn. River R.R.....	Springfield
N.Y., N. H. & H. R.R.	New Haven
N.Y., N. H. & H. R.R.	New York

Through Rates.

Niagara Falls..$32.50	Syracuse $29.65
Rochester...... 31.25	Utica........... 29.50

Route 377—New York, N. Y.

Forms Ex. 399 and Ex. 728.

R., W. & O. R.R.....to	Clayton
R. & O. Nav. Co.....	Alexandria Bay
R. & O. Nav. Co.....	Montreal
Grand Trunk R'y or R. & O. Nav. Co.	Quebec
Ferry	Point Levis
Grand Trunk R'y....	Sherbrooke
Boston & Maine R.R.	Lunenburg
Maine Central R.R...	Zealand Jc.
Prof. & F. Notch R.R.	Profile House
Prof. & F. Notch R.R.	Bethlehem Jc.
Con. & Mont'l R.R...	Fabyan's
Maine Central R.R...	North Conway
Boston & Maine R.R.	Boston
Armstrong Trans. Co.	N. Y., N. H. & H. R.R. Dep.
Fall River Line......	New York

Through Rates.

Niagara Falls $33.00	Syracuse $30.15
Rochester...... 31.75	Utica........... 30.00

Route 378—New York, N. Y.

Forms Ex. 400 and Ex. 729.

R., W. & O. R.R.....to	Clayton
R. & O. Nav. Co......	Alexandria Bay
R. & O. Nav. Co.....	Montreal
Can. Pac. R'y or R. & O. Nav. Co.	Quebec
Ferry	Point Levis
Quebec Central R'y..	Sherbrooke
Boston & Maine R.R.	Lunenburg
Maine Central R.R...	Zealand Jc.
Prof. & F. Notch R.R.	Profile House
Prof. & F. Notch R.R.	Bethlehem Jc.
Con. & Mont'l R.R...	Fabyan's
Maine Central R.R...	North Conway
Boston & Maine R.R.	Boston
Armstrong Trans. Co.	N. Y., N. H. & H. R.R. Dep.
Fall River Line......	New York

Through Rates.

Niagara Falls..$33.00	Syracuse $30.15
Rochester...... 31.75	Utica........... 30.00

Route 379—New York, N. Y.

Forms Ex. 400 and Ex. 764.

R., W. & O. R.R.....to	Clayton
R. & O. Nav. Co.....	Alexandria Bay
R. & O. Nav. Co.....	Montreal
Can. Pac. R'y or R. & O. Nav. Co.	Quebec
Ferry................	Point Levis
Quebec Central R'y..	Dudswell Jc.
Maine Central R.R...	Zealand Jc.
Prof. & F. Notch R.R.	Profile House
Prof. & F. Notch R.R.	Zealand Jc.
Maine Central R.R...	North Conway
Boston & Maine R.R.	Boston
Armstrong Trans. Co.	N. Y., N. H. & H. R.R. Dep.
Fall River Line	New York

Through Rates.

Niagara Falls..$33.00	Syracuse.......$30.15
Rochester...... 31.75	Utica........... 30.00

Route 380—New York, N. Y.

Forms Ex. 399, Ex. 730 and Ex. 137.

R., W. & O. R.R.....to	Clayton
R. & O. Nav. Co.....	Alexandria Bay
R. & O. Nav. Co.....	Montreal
Grand Trunk R'y or R. & O. Nav. Co.	Quebec
Ferry................	Point Levis
Grand Trunk R'y	Sherbrooke
Boston & Maine R.R.	Lunenburg
Maine Central R.R .	Zealand Jc.
Prof. & F. Notch R.R.	Profile House
Prof. & F. Notch R.R.	Bethlehem Jc.
Con. & Mont'l R.R ..	Fabyan's
Maine Central R.R..	Crawford's
Maine Central R.R...	Fabyan's
Con. & Mont'l R.R...	Nashua
Boston & Maine R.R.	Boston
Armstrong Trans. Co.	N. Y., N. H. & H. R.R. Dep.
Fall River Line......	New York

Through Rates.

Niagara Falls..$33.50	Syracuse $30.65
Rochester...... 32.25	Utica........... 30.50

Route 381—New York, N. Y.

Forms Ex. 400, Ex. 731 and Ex. 137.

R., W. & O. R.R.....to	Clayton
R. & O. Nav. Co.....	Alexandria Bay
R. & O. Nav. Co.....	Montreal
Can. Pac. R'y or R. & O. Nav. Co.	Quebec
Ferry................	Point Levis
Quebec Central R'y..	Sherbrooke
Boston & Maine R.R.	Lunenburg
Maine Central R.R...	Zealand Jc.
Prof. & F. Notch R.R.	Profile House
Prof. & F. Notch R.R.	Bethlehem Jc.
Con. & Mont'l R.R...	Fabyan's
Maine Central R.R...	Crawford's
Maine Central R.R...	Fabyan's
Con. & Mont'l R.R..	Nashua
Boston & Maine R.R.	Boston
Armstrong Trans. Co.	N. Y., N. H. & H. R.R. Dep.
Fall River Line	New York

Through Rates.

Niagara Falls..$33.50	Syracuse $30.65
Rochester...... 32.25	Utica 30.50

Route 382—New York, N. Y.

Forms Ex. 399 and Ex. 732

R., W. & O. R.R.....to	Clayton
R. & O. Nav. Co.....	Alexandria Bay
R. & O. Nav. Co.....	Montreal
Grand Trunk R'y or R. & O. Nav. Co.	Quebec
Ferry	Point Levis
Grand Trunk R'y....	Sherbrooke
Boston & Maine R.R.	Lunenburg
Maine Central R.R ..	Zealand Jc.
Prof. & F. Notch R.R.	Profile House
Prof. & F. Notch R.R.	Bethlehem Jc.
Con. & Mont'l R.R...	Base Mt. Wash.
Mt. Washington R'y.	Summit
Mt. Washington R'y.	Base
Con. & Mont'l R.R ..	Fabyan's
Maine Central R.R..	North Conway
Boston & Maine R.R.	Wolfboro
Steamer	Weir's
Con. & Mont'l R.R ..	Nashua
Boston & Maine R.R.	Boston
Armstrong Trans. Co.	N. Y., N. H. & H. R.R. Dep.
Fall River Line......	New York

Through Rates.

Niagara Falls..$40.90	Syracuse... ...$38.05
Rochester..... 39.65	Utica........... 37.30

Route 383—New York, N. Y.

Forms Ex. 400 and Ex. 733.

R., W. & O. R.R.....to	Clayton
R. & O. Nav. Co.....	Alexandria Bay
R. & O. Nav. Co.....	Montreal
Can. Pac. R'y or R. & O. Nav. Co.	Quebec
Ferry................	Point Levis
Quebec Central R'y.	Sherbrooke
Boston & Maine R.R.	Lunenburg
Maine Central R.R..	Zealand Jc.
Prof. & F. Notch R.R.	Profile House
Prof. & F. Notch R.R.	Bethlehem Jc.
Con. & Mont'l R.R...	Base Mt. Wash.
Mt. Washington R'y.	Summit
Mt. Washington R'y.	Base
Con. & Mont'l R.R...	Fabyan's
Maine Central R.R...	North Conway
Boston & Maine R.R.	Wolfboro
Steamer	Weir's
Con. & Mont'l R.R...	Nashua
Boston & Maine R.R.	Boston
Armstrong Trans. Co.	N. Y., N. H. & H. R.R. Dep.
Fall River Line......	New York

Through Rates.

Niagara Falls..$40.90	Syracuse.......$38.05
Rochester...... 39.65	Utica........... 37.90

Route 334—New York, N. Y.

Forms Ex. 400 and Ex. 765.

R., W. & O. R.R.....to	Clayton
R. & O. Nav. Co...	Alexandria Bay
R. & O. Nav. Co.....	Montreal
Can. Pac. R'y or R. & O. Nav. Co.	Quebec
Ferry................	Point Levis
Quebec Central R'y..	Dudswell Jc.
Maine Central R.R...	Zealand Jc.
Prof. & F. Notch R.R.	Profile House
Prof. & F. Notch R.R.	Bethlehem Jc.
Con. & Mont'l R.R...	Base Mt. Wash.
Mt. Washington R'y.	Summit
Mt. Washington R'y.	Base
Con. & Mont'l R.R...	Fabyan's
Maine Central R.R...	North Conway
Boston & Maine R.R.	Wolfboro
Steamer..............	Weir's
Con. & Mont'l R.R ..	Nashua
Boston & Maine R.R.	Worcester
N.Y., N. H. & H. R.R.	Providence
Providence Line.....	New York

Through Rates.

Niagara Falls..$40.90	Syracuse.......$38.05
Rochester...... 39.65	Utica........... 37.90

Route 385—New York, N. Y.

Forms Ex. 399 and Ex. 734.

R., W. & O. R.R.....to	Clayton
R. & O. Nav. Co.....	Alexandria Bay
R. & O. Nav. Co.....	Montreal
Grand Trunk R'y or R. & O. Nav. Co.	Quebec
Ferry................	Point Levis
Grand Trunk R'y....	Sherbrooke
Boston & Maine R.R.	Lunenburg
Maine Central R.R..	Zealand Jc.
Prof. & F. Notch R.R.	Profile House
Prof. & F. Notch R.R.	Bethlehem Jc.
Con. & Mont'l R.R..	Fabyan's
Maine Central R.R..	Portland
Boston & Maine R.R.	Boston
Armstrong Trans. Co.	N. Y., N. H. & H. R.R. Dep.
Fall River Line......	New York

Through Rates.

Niagara Falls..$33.00	Syracuse...... $30.15
Rochester 31.75	Utica 30.00

Route 386—New York, N. Y.

Forms Ex. 400 and Ex. 735.

R., W. & O. R.R.....to	Clayton
R. & O. Nav. Co.....	Alexandria Bay
R. & O. Nav. Co.....	Montreal
Can. Pac. R'y or R. & O. Nav. Co.	Quebec
Ferry	Point Levis
Quebec Central R'y..	Sherbrooke
Boston & Maine R.R.	Lunenburg
Maine Central R.R...	Zealand Jc.
Prof. & F. Notch R.R.	Profile House
Prof. & F. Notch R.R.	Bethlehem Jc.
Con. & Mont'l R.R...	Fabyan's
Maine Central R.R...	Portland
Boston & Maine R.R.	Boston
Armstrong Trans. Co.	N. Y., N. H. & H. R.R. Dep.
Fall River Line......	New York

Through Rates.

Niagara Falls..$33.00	Syracuse $30.15
Rochester. 31.75	Utica........... 30.00

SEE NOTE ON PAGE 119 REGARDING STOP-OVER AT ALEXANDRIA BAY.

Route 387—New York, N. Y.

Forms Ex. 400 and Ex. 766.

R., W. & O. R.R.....to	Clayton
R. & O. Nav. Co.....	Alexandria Bay
R. & O. Nav. Co.....	Montreal
Can. Pac. R'y or R. & O. Nav. Co.	Quebec
Ferry..................	Point Levis
Quebec Central R'y..	Dudswell Jc.
Maine Central R.R..	Zealand Jc.
Prof. & F. Notch R.R.	Profile House
Prof. & F. Notch R.R.	Zealand Jc.
Maine Central R R...	Portland
Boston & Maine R.R.	Boston
Armstrong Trans. Co.	N. Y., N. H. & H. R.R. Dep.
Fall River Line	New York

Through Rates.

Niagara Falls.	$33.00	Syracuse	$30.15
Rochester......	31.75	Utica	30.00

Route 388—New York, N. Y.

Forms Ex. 399, Ex. 730 and Ex. 137.

R., W. & O. R.R.....to	Clayton
R. & O. Nav. Co.....	Alexandria Bay
R. & O. Nav. Co.....	Montreal
Grand Trunk R'y or R. & O. Nav. Co.	Quebec
Ferry..................	Point Levis
Grand Trunk R'y....	Sherbrooke
Boston & Maine R.R.	Lunenburg
Maine Central R.R...	Zealand Jc.
Prof. & F. Notch R.R.	Profile House
Prof. & F. Notch R.R.	Bethlehem Jc.
Con. & Mont'l R.R..	Fabyan's
Maine Central R.R ..	Crawford's
Maine Central R.R...	Fabyan's
Con. & Mont'l R.R...	Base Mt. Wash.
Mt. Washington R'y.	Summit
Stage..................	Glen Site
Stage..................	Alpine House (Gorham)
Grand Trunk R'y....	Portland
Boston & Maine R.R.	Boston
Armstrong Trans. Co.	N. Y., N. H. & H. R.R. Dep.
Fall River Line......	New York

Through Rates.

Niagara Falls.	$43.30	Syracuse	$40.45
Rochester......	42.05	Utica..........	40.30

Route 389—New York, N. Y.

Forms Ex. 399 and Ex. 462.

R., W. & O. R.R.....to	Clayton
R. & O. Nav. Co.....	Alexandria Bay
R. & O. Nav. Co.....	Montreal
Grand Trunk R'y or R. & O. Nav. Co.	Quebec
Ferry	Point Levis
Grand Trunk R'y....	Alpine House (Gorham)
Stage..................	Glen Site
Stage..................	Sum't Mt. Wash.
Stage..................	Glen Site
Stage..................	Glen
Maine Central R.R...	Portland
Boston & Maine R.R.	Boston
Fall River Line	New York

Through Rates.

Niagara Falls.	$39.20	Syracuse	$36.35
Rochester	37.95	Utica..........	36 20

Route 390—New York, N. Y.

Forms Ex. 399 and Ex. 463.

R., W. & O. R.R.....to	Clayton
R. & O. Nav. Co.....	Alexandria Bay
R. & O. Nav. Co.....	Montreal
Grand Trunk R'y or R. & O. Nav. Co.	Quebec
Ferry..................	Point Levis
Grand Trunk R'y....	Alpine House (Gorham)
Stage..................	Glen Site
Stage..................	Glen
Maine Central R.R ..	North Conway
Boston & Maine R.R.	Boston
Fall River Line......	New York

Through Rates.

Niagara Falls.	$33.80	Syracuse.......	$30.95
Rochester......	32.55	Utica	30.80

Route 391—New York, N. Y.

Forms Ex. 399, Ex. 632, Ex. 129 and Ex. 137.

R., W. & O. R.R.....to	Clayton
R. & O. Nav. Co.....	Alexandria Bay
R. & O. Nav. Co. ...	Montreal
Grand Trunk R'y or R. & O. Nav. Co.	Quebec
Ferry..................	Point Levis
Grand Trunk R y....	Alpine House (Gorham)
Stage..................	Glen Site
Stage..................	Sum't Mt. Wash.
Mt. Washington R'y.	Base
Con. & Mont'l R.R...	Fabyan's
Maine Central R.R...	Crawford's
Maine Central R.R...	Fabyan's
Con. & Mont'l R.R...	Bethlehem Jc.
Prof. & F. Notch R.R.	Profile House
Prof. & F. Notch R.R.	Bethlehem Jc.
Con. & Mont'l R.R...	Nashua
Boston & Maine R.R.	Boston
Armstrong Trans. Co	N. Y., N. H. & H. R.R. Dep.
Fall River Line......	New York

Through Rates.

Niagara Falls.	$44.70	Syracuse	$41.85
Rochester......	43.45	Utica.	41.70

Route 392—New York, N. Y.

Forms Ex 399, Ex. 633 and Ex. 131.

R., W. & O. R.R.....to	Clayton
R. & O. Nav. Co.....	Alexandria Bay
R. & O. Nav. Co.....	Montreal
Grand Trunk R'y or R. & O. Nav. Co.	Quebec
Ferry	Point Levis
Grand Trunk R'y....	Alpine House (Gorham)
Stage	Glen Site
Stage	Sum't Mt. Wash.
Mt. Washington R'y.	Base
Con. & Mont'l R.R...	Fabyan's
Maine Central R.R...	Crawford's
Maine Central R.R...	Fabyan's
Con. & Mont'l R.R...	Bethlehem Jc.
Prof. & F. Notch R.R.	Profile House
Stage..................	No. Woodstock
Con. & Mont'l R.R...	Nashua
Boston & Maine R.R.	Boston
Armstrong Trans. Co.	N. Y., N. H. & H. R.R. Dep.
Fall River Line.......	New York

Through Rates.

Niagara Falls.	$43.35	Syracuse	$40.50
Rochester......	42.10	Utica	40.35

Route 393—New York, N. Y.

Forms Ex. 399 and Ex. 453.

R., W. & O. R.R.....to	Clayton
R. & O. Nav. Co.....	Alexandria Bay
R. & O. Nav. Co.....	Montreal
Grand Trunk R'y or R. & O. Nav. Co.	Quebec
Ferry..................	Point Levis
Grand Trunk R'y....	Gorham
Stage	Glen Site
Stage..................	Sum't Mt. Wash.
Stage..................	Glen Site
Stage..................	Glen
Maine Central R.R ..	Fabyan's
Con. & Mont'l R.R...	Wells River
Boston & Maine R.R.	White River Jc.
Cent. Vermont R.R..	Windsor
Vermont Valley R.R.	Brattleboro
Cent. Vermont R.R..	South Vernon
Conn. River R.R.....	Springfield
N.Y., N. H. & H. R.R.	New Haven
N.Y., N. H. & H. R.R.	New York

Through Rates.

Niagara Falls.	$41.45	Syracuse......	$38.60
Rochester......	40.20	Utica..........	38.45

Route 394—New York, N. Y.

Forms Ex. 399, Ex. 631 and Ex. 137.

R., W. & O. R.R.....to	Clayton
R. & O. Nav. Co.....	Alexandria Bay
R. & O. Nav. Co.....	Montreal
Grand Trunk R'y or R. & O. Nav. Co.	Quebec
Ferry..................	Point Levis
Grand Trunk R'y....	Alpine House (Gorham)
Stage..................	Glen Site
Stage..................	Sum't Mt. Wash.
Mt. Washington R'y.	Base
Con. & Mont'l R.R...	Fabyan's
Maine Central R.R...	Crawford's
Maine Central R.R..	Fabyan's
Con. & Mont'l R.R...	Wells River
Boston & Maine R.R.	White River Jc.
Cent. Vermont R.R..	Windsor
Vermont Valley R.R.	Brattleboro
Cent. Vermont R.R..	Miller's Falls
New Lon. Nor. R.R..	New London
N. & N. Y. T. Co.....	New York

Through Rates.

Niagara Falls.	$41.20	Syracuse	$38.35
Rochester.. ...	39.95	Utica..........	38.20

Route 395—New York, N. Y.

Forms Ex. 399, Ex. 466, Ex. 129 and Ex. 137.

R., W. & O. R.R.....to	Clayton
R. & O. Nav. Co.....	Alexandria Bay
R. & O. Nav. Co.....	Montreal
Grand Trunk R'y or R. & O. Nav. Co.	Quebec
Ferry..................	Point Levis
Grand Trunk R'y....	Gorham
Stage..................	Glen Site
Stage..................	Sum't Mt. Wash.
Mt. Washington R'y.	Base
Con. & Mont'l R.R..	Fabyan's
Maine Central R.R...	Crawford's
Maine Central R.R...	Fabyan's
Con. & Mont'l R.R...	Bethlehem Jc.
Prof. & F. Notch R.R.	Profile House
Prof. & F. Notch R.R.	Bethlehem Jc.
Con. & Mont'l R.R...	Wells River
Mont. & W. R. R.R..	Montpelier
Cent. Vermont R.R..	Burlington
Cham. Trans. Co.....	Ft. Ticonderoga
D. & H. R.R.........	Baldwin
L. Geo. St'mb't Co..	Caldwell
D. & H. R.R.........	Albany
N. Y. & Albany Day Line Steamers	New York

Through Rates.

Niagara Falls.	$47.89	Syracuse	$15.04
Rochester......	45.64	Utica..........	44.89

Route 396—New York, N. Y.

Forms Ex. 393, Ex. 467, Ex. 129 and Ex. 137.

R., W. & O. R.R.....to	Clayton
R. & O. Nav. Co.....	Alexandria Bay
R. & O. Nav. Co.....	Montreal
Grand Trunk R'y or R. & O. Nav. Co.	Quebec
Ferry	Point Levis
Grand Trunk R'y....	Gorham
Stage..................	Glen Site
Stage	Sum't Mt. Wash.
Mt. Washington R'y.	Base
Con. & Mont'l R.R...	Fabyan's
Maine Central R.R...	Crawford's
Maine Central R.R...	Fabyan's
Con. & Mont'l R.R..	Bethlehem Jc.
Prof. & F. Notch R.R.	Profile House
Prof. & F. Notch R.R.	Bethlehem Jc.
Con. & Mont'l R.R...	Wells River
Mont. & W. R. R.R..	Montpelier
Cent. Vermont R.R..	Burlington
Cham. Trans. Co.....	Ft. Ticonderoga
D. & H. R.R.........	Baldwin
L. Geo. St'mb't Co...	Caldwell
D. & H. R.R..........	Albany
People's Line St'rs...	New York

Through Rates.

Niagara Falls.	$17.39	Syracuse.......	$41.54
Rochester......	46.14	Utica..........	44.39

Route 397—New York, N. Y.

Forms Ex. 399 and Ex. 469.

R., W. & O. R.R.....to	Clayton
R. & O. Nav. Co.....	Alexandria Bay
R. & O. Nav. Co.....	Montreal
Grand Trunk R'y or R. & O. Nav. Co.	Quebec
Ferry..................	Point Levis
Quebec Central R'y..	Sherbrooke
Boston & Maine R.R.	Wells River
Con. & Mont'l R.R...	Nashua
Boston & Maine R.R.	Boston
Fall River Line......	New York

Through Rates.

Niagara Falls.	$29.50	Syracuse.......	$26.65
Rochester......	28.25	Utica	26.50

SEE NOTE ON PAGE 119 REGARDING STOP-OVER AT ALEXANDRIA BAY.

Route 398—New York, N. Y.

Forms Ex. 400 and Ex. 469.

R., W. & O. R.R.....to	Clayton
R. & O. Nav. Co......	Alexandria Bay
R. & O. Nav. Co......	Montreal
Can. Pac. R'y or R. & O. Nav. Co.	Quebec
Ferry................	Point Levis
Quebec Central R'y..	Sherbrooke
Boston & Maine R.R.	Wells River
Con. & Mont'l R.R...	Nashua
Boston & Maine R.R.	Boston
Fall River Line......	New York

Through Rates.

Niagara Falls..$29.50 | Syracuse...... $26.65
Rochester...... 28.25 | Utica........... 26.50

Route 399—New York, N. Y.

Forms Ex. 399 and Ex. 471.

R., W. & O. R.R.....to	Clayton
R. & O. Nav. Co......	Alexandria Bay
R. & O. Nav. Co......	Montreal
Grand Trunk R'y or R. & O. Nav. Co.	Quebec
Ferry................	Point Levis
Quebec Central R'y..	Sherbrooke
Boston & Maine R.R.	Wells River
Con. & Mont'l R.R..	Nashua
Boston & Maine R.R.	Worcester
N. Y. & N. E. R.R...	Norwich
New Lon. Nor. R.R..	New London
N. & N. Y. T. Co......	New York

Through Rates.

Niagara Falls..$28.35 | Syracuse.......$25.50
Rochester...... 27.10 | Utica........... 25.35

Route 400—New York, N. Y.

Forms Ex. 400 and Ex. 471.

R., W. & O. R.R......to	Clayton
R. & O. Nav. Co......	Alexandria Bay
R. & O. Nav. Co......	Montreal
Can. Pac. R'y or R. & O. Nav. Co.	Quebec
Ferry................	Point Levis
Quebec Central R'y..	Sherbrooke
Boston & Maine R.R.	Wells River
Con. & Mont'l R.R..	Nashua
Boston & Maine R.R.	Worcester
N. Y. & N. E. R.R...	Norwich
New Lon. Nor. R.R..	New London
N. & N. Y. T. Co......	New York

Through Rates.

Niagara Falls..$28.35 | Syracuse.......$25.50
Rochester...... 27.10 | Utica........... 25.35

Route 401—New York, N. Y.

Forms Ex. 399 and Ex. 468.

R., W. & O. R.R.....to	Clayton
R. & O. Nav. Co......	Alexandria Bay
R. & O. Nav. Co......	Montreal
Grand Trunk R'y or R. & O. Nav. Co.	Quebec
Ferry................	Point Levis
Quebec Central R'y..	Sherbrooke
Boston & Maine R.R.	Wells River
Con. & Mont'l R.R...	Nashua
Boston & Maine R.R.	Worcester
Boston & Alb. R.R..	Springfield
N.Y., N.H. & H. R.R.	New Haven
N Y., N.H. & H. R.R.	New York

Through Rates.

Niagara Falls..$26.50 | Syracuse...... $23.65
Rochester...... 25.25 | Utica........... 23.50

Route 402—New York, N. Y.

Forms Ex. 400 and Ex. 468.

R., W. & O. R.R.....to	Clayton
R. & O. Nav. Co......	Alexandria Bay
R. & O. Nav. Co......	Montreal
Can. Pac. R'y or R. & O. Nav. Co.	Quebec
Ferry................	Point Levis
Quebec Central R'y..	Sherbrooke
Boston & Maine R.R.	Wells River
Con. & Mont'l R.R...	Nashua
Boston & Maine R.R	Worcester
Boston & Alb. R.R...	Springfield
N.Y., N. H. & H. R.R.	New Haven
N.Y., N. H. & H. R.R.	New York

Through Rates.

Niagara Falls..$26.50 | Syracuse.......$23.65
Rochester...... 25.25 | Utica........... 23.50

Route 403—New York, N. Y.

Forms Ex. 399 and Ex. 635.

R., W. & O. R.R.....to	Clayton
R. & O. Nav. Co......	Alexandria Bay
R. & O. Nav. Co......	Montreal
Grand Trunk R'y or R. & O. Nav. Co.	Quebec
Ferry................	Point Levis
Quebec Central R'y..	Sherbrooke
Boston & Maine R.R.	Lunenburg
Maine Central R.R...	Fabyan's
Con. & Mont'l R.R...	Wells River
Boston & Maine R.R.	White River Jc.
Cent. Vermont R.R..	Windsor
Vermont Valley R.R.	Brattleboro
Cent. Vermont R.R.	South Vernon
Conn. River R.R.....	Springfield
N.Y., N. H. & H. R.R.	New Haven
N.Y., N. H. & H. R.R.	New York

Through Rates.

Niagara Falls..$29.45 | Syracuse.......$26.60
Rochester...... 28.20 | Utica........... 26.45

Route 404—New York, N. Y.

Forms Ex. 400 and Ex. 635.

R. W. & O. R.R.....to	Clayton
R. & O. Nav. Co......	Alexandria Bay
R. & O. Nav. Co......	Montreal
Can. Pac. R'y or R. & O. Nav. Co.	Quebec
Ferry................	Point Levis
Quebec Central R'y..	Sherbrooke
Boston & Maine R.R.	Lunenburg
Maine Central R.R..	Fabyan's
Con. & Mont'l R.R..	Wells River
Boston & Maine R.R.	White River Jc.
Cent. Vermont R.R..	Windsor
Vermont Valley R.R.	Brattleboro
Cent. Vermont R.R..	South Vernon
Conn. River R.R......	Springfield
N.Y., N. H. & H. R.R.	New Haven
N.Y., N. H. & H. R.R.	New York

Through Rates.

Niagara Falls..$29.45 | Syracuse.......$26.60
Rochester...... 28.20 | Utica........... 26.45

Route 405—New York, N. Y.

Forms Ex. 399 and Ex. 636.

R., W. & O. R.R.....to	Clayton
R. & O. Nav. Co......	Alexandria Bay
R. & O. Nav. Co......	Montreal
Grand Trunk R'y or R. & O. Nav. Co.	Quebec
Ferry................	Point Levis
Quebec Central R'y.	Sherbrooke
Boston & Maine R.R.	Lunenburg
Maine Central R.R..	Fabyan's
Con. & Mont'l R.R...	Nashua
Boston & Maine R.R.	Boston
Armstrong Trans. Co.	N. Y., N. H. & H. R.R. Dep.
Fall River Line......	New York

Through Rates.

Niagara Falls..$30.00 | Syracuse...... $27.15
Rochester...... 28.75 | Utica........... 27.00

Route 406—New York, N. Y.

Forms Ex. 400 and Ex. 636.

R., W. & O. R.R.....to	Clayton
R. & O. Nav. Co......	Alexandria Bay
R. & O. Nav. Co......	Montreal
Can. Pac. R'y or R. & O. Nav. Co.	Quebec
Ferry................	Point Levis
Quebec Central R'y..	Sherbrooke
Boston & Maine R.R.	Lunenburg
Maine Central R.R..	Fabyan's
Con. & Mont'l R.R...	Nashua
Boston & Maine R.R.	Boston
Armstrong Trans. Co.	N. Y., N. H. & H.R.R. Dep.
Fall River Line......	New York

Through Rates.

Niagara Falls..$30.00 | Syracuse.......$27.15
Rochester...... 28.75 | Utica........... 27.00

Route 407—New York, N. Y.

Forms Ex. 399 and Ex. 637.

R., W. & O. R.R.....to	Clayton
R. & O. Nav. Co......	Alexandria Bay
R. & O. Nav. Co......	Montreal
Grand Trunk R'y or R. & O. Nav. Co.	Quebec
Ferry................	Point Levis
Quebec Central R'y..	Sherbrooke
Boston & Maine R.R.	Lunenburg
Maine Central R.R...	North Conway
Boston & Maine R.R.	Boston
Armstrong Trans. Co.	N. Y., N. H. & H. R.R. Dep.
Fall River Line......	New York

Through Rates.

Niagara Falls..$30.00 | Syracuse...... $27.15
Rochester...... 28.75 | Utica........... 27.00

Route 408—New York, N. Y.

Forms Ex. 400 and Ex. 637.

R., W. & O. R.R.....to	Clayton
R. & O. Nav. Co......	Alexandria Bay
R. & O. Nav. Co......	Montreal
Can. Pac. R'y or R. & O. Nav. Co.	Quebec
Ferry................	Point Levis
Quebec Central R'y..	Sherbrooke
Boston & Maine R.R.	Lunenburg
Maine Central R.R...	North Conway
Boston & Maine R.R.	Boston
Armstrong Trans. Co.	N. Y., N. H. & H. R.R. Dep.
Fall River Line	New York

Through Rates.

Niagara Falls..$30.00 | Syracuse.......$27.15
Rochester...... 28.75 | Utica........... 27.00

Route 409—New York, N. Y.

Forms Ex. 400 and Ex. 767.

R., W. & O. R.R.....to	Clayton
R. & O. Nav. Co......	Alexandria Bay
R. & O. Nav. Co......	Montreal
Can. Pac. R'y or R. & O. Nav. Co.	Quebec
Ferry................	Point Levis
Quebec Central R'y..	Dudswell Jc.
Maine Central R.R...	North Conway
Boston & Maine R.R.	Boston
Armstrong Trans. Co.	N. Y., N. H. & H. R.R. Dep.
Fall River Line......	New York

Through Rates.

Niagara Falls..$30.00 | Syracuse.... ..$27.15
Rochester...... 28.75 | Utica........... 27.00

Route 410—New York, N. Y.

Forms Ex. 399 and Ex. 451.

R., W. & O. R.R.....to	Clayton
R. & O. Nav. Co......	Alexandria Bay
R. & O. Nav. Co......	Montreal
Grand Trunk R'y or R. & O. Nav. Co.	Quebec
Ferry................	Point Levis
Intercolonial R'y......	Halifax
Intercolonial R'y......	St. John
International S.S. Co.	Portland
Boston & Maine R.R.	Boston
Fall River Line......	New York

Through Rates.

Niagara Falls..$41.50 | Syracuse...... $38.65
Rochester...... 40.25 | Utica........... 38.50

Route 411—New York, N. Y.

Forms Ex. 400 and Ex. 451.

R., W. & O. R.R.....to	Clayton
R. & O. Nav. Co......	Alexandria Bay
R. & O. Nav. Co. ..	Montreal
Can. Pac. R'y or R. & O. Nav. Co.	Quebec
Ferry................	Point Levis
Intercolonial R'y......	Halifax
Intercolonial R'y......	St. John
International S.S. Co.	Portland
Boston & Maine R.R.	Boston
Fall River Line......	New York

Through Rates.

Niagara Falls..$41.50 | Syracuse.......$38.65
Rochester...... 40.25 | Utica........... 38.50

SEE NOTE ON PAGE 119 REGARDING STOP-OVER AT ALEXANDRIA BAY.

Route 412—New York, N. Y.

Forms Ex. 399 and Ex. 464.

R., W. & O. R.R.....	to Clayton
R. & O. Nav. Co.....	Alexandria Bay
R. & O. Nav. Co.....	Montreal
Grand Trunk R'y or R. & O. Nav. Co.	Quebec
Ferry..............	Point Levis
Intercolonial R'y.....	Halifax
Intercolonial R'y.....	St. John
Can. Pac. R'y........	Vanceboro
Maine Central R.R...	Portland
Boston & Maine R.R.	Boston
Fall River Line......	New York

Through Rates.

Niagara Falls.$45.80	Syracuse.......$42.95
Rochester...... 44.55	Utica........... 42.80

Route 413—New York, N. Y.

Forms Ex. 400 and Ex. 464.

R., W. & O. R.R.....	to Clayton
R. & O. Nav. Co.....	Alexandria Bay
R. & O. Nav. Co.....	Montreal
Can. Pac. R'y or R. & O. Nav. Co.	Quebec
Ferry..............	Point Levis
Intercolonial R'y.....	Halifax
Intercolonial R'y.....	St. John
Can. Pac. Ry	Vanceboro
Maine Central R.R.,	Portland
Boston & Maine R.R.	Boston
Fall River Line	New York

Through Rates.

Niagara Falls.$45.80	Syracuse.......$42.95
Rochester...... 44.55	Utica........... 47.80

Route 414—New York, N. Y.

Forms Ex. 399 and Ex. 452.

R., W. & O. R.R.....	to Clayton
R. & O. Nav. Co.....	Alexandria Bay
R. & O. Nav. Co.....	Montreal
Grand Trunk R'y or R. & O. Nav. Co.	Quebec
Ferry..............	Point Levis
Intercolonial R'y.....	Pt. du Chene
Charl't'n St. Nav. Co.	Summerside
P. E. Island R'y......	Charlottetown
Charl't'n St. Nav. Co.	Pictou
Intercolonial R'y.....	Halifax
Intercolonial R'y.....	St. John
International S.S. Co.	Portland
Boston & Maine R.R.	Boston
Fall River Line......	New York

Through Rates.

Niagara Falls.$46.40	Syracuse.......$43.55
Rochester...... 45.15	Utica........... 43.40

Route 415—New York, N. Y.

Forms Ex. 400 and Ex. 452.

R., W. & O. R.R.....	to Clayton
R. & O. Nav. Co.....	Alexandria Bay
R. & O. Nav. Co.....	Montreal
Can. Pac. R'y or R. & O. Nav. Co.	Quebec
Ferry	Point Levis
Intercolonial R'y.....	Pt. du Chene
Charl't'n St. Nav. Co.	Summerside
P. E. Island R'y......	Charlottetown
Charl't'n St. Nav. Co.	Pictou
Intercolonial R'y.....	Halifax
Intercolonial R'y....	St. John
International S.S. Co.	Portland
Boston & Maine R.R.	Boston
Fall River Line......	New York

Through Rates.

Niagara Falls.$46.40	Syracuse.......$43.55
Rochester...... 45.15	Utica........... 43.40

Route 416—New York, N. Y.

Forms Ex. 399 and Ex. 465.

R., W. & O. R.R.....	to Clayton
R. & O. Nav. Co.....	Alexandria Bay
R. & O. Nav. Co.....	Montreal
Grand Trunk R'y or R. & O. Nav. Co.	Quebec
Ferry..............	Point Levis
Intercolonial R'y.....	Pt. du Chene
Charl't'n St. Nav. Co.	Summerside
P. E. Island R'y......	Charlottetown
Charl't'n St. Nav. Co.	Pictou
Intercolonial R'y.....	Halifax
Intercolonial R'y	St. John
Can. Pac. R'y........	Vanceboro
Maine Central RR...	Portland
Boston & Maine R.R.	Boston
Fall River Line......	New York

Through Rates.

Niagara Falls.$50.40	Syracuse.......$47.55
Rochester...... 49.15	Utica........... 47.40

Route 417—New York, N. Y.

Forms Ex. 400 and Ex. 465.

R., W. & O. R.R.....	to Clayton
R. & O. Nav. Co.....	Alexandria Bay
R. & O. Nav. Co.....	Montreal
Can. Pac. R'y or R. & O. Nav. Co.	Quebec
Ferry..............	Point Levis
Intercolonial R'y.....	Pt. du Chene
Charl't'n St. Nav. Co.	Summerside
P. E. Island R'y......	Charlottetown
Charl't'n St. Nav. Co.	Pictou
Intercolonial R'y.....	Halifax
Intercolonial R'y	St. John
Can. Pac. R'y........	Vanceboro
Maine Central R.R...	Portland
Boston & Maine R.R.	Boston
Fall River Line......	New York

Through Rates.

Niagara Falls.$50.40	Syracuse.......$47.55
Rochester...... 49.15	Utica........... 47.40

Route 418—New York, N. Y.

Forms Ex. 399 and Ex. 737.

R., W. & O. R.R.....	to Clayton
R. & O. Nav. Co.....	Alexandria Bay
R. & O. Nav. Co.....	Montreal
Grand Trunk R'y or R. & O. Nav. Co.	Quebec
Quebec S.S. Co..... (Meals included)	Summerside
Charl't'n St. Nav. Co.	Pt. du Chene
Intercolonial R'y.....	St. John
International S.S. Co.	Boston
Armstrong Trans. Co.	N. Y., N. H. & H. R.R. Dep.
Fall River Line......	New York

Through Rates.

Niagara Falls.$42.75	Syracuse.......$39.80
Rochester...... 41.50	Utica........... 39.75

Route 419—New York, N. Y.

Forms Ex. 400 and Ex. 137.

R., W. & O. R.R.....	to Clayton
R. & O. Nav. Co.....	Alexandria Bay
R. & O. Nav. Co.....	Montreal
Can. Pac. R'y or R. & O. Nav. Co.	Quebec
Quebec S. S. Co..... (Meals included)	Summerside
Charl't'n St. Nav. Co.	Pt. du Chene
Intercolonial R'y.....	St. John
International S.S. Co.	Boston
Armstrong Trans. Co.	N. Y., N. H. & H. R.R. Dep.
Fall River Line......	New York

Through Rates.

Niagara Falls.$42.75	Syracuse.......$39.50
Rochester...... 41.50	Utica........... 33.75

Route 420—New York, N. Y.

Forms Ex. 399 and Ex. 414.

R., W. & O. R.R.....	to Clayton
R. & O. Nav. Co.....	Alexandria Bay
R. & O. Nav. Co.....	Montreal
Grand Trunk R'y or R. & O. Nav. Co.	Quebec
Quebec S.S. Co.... (Meals included)	Pictou
Intercolonial R'y.....	Halifax
Canada Atlantic & Plant S.S. Co.	Boston
Fall River Line......	New York

Through Rates.

Niagara Falls.$43.50	Syracuse.......$40.65
Rochester...... 42.25	Utica........... 40.50

Route 421—New York, N. Y.

Forms Ex. 400 and Ex. 474.

R., W. & O. R.R.....	to Clayton
R. & O. Nav. Co.....	Alexandria Bay
R. & O. Nav. Co.....	Montreal
Can. Pac. R'y or R. & O. Nav. Co.	Quebec
Quebec S.S Co..... (Meals included)	Pictou
Intercolonial R'y	Halifax
Canada Atlantic & Plant S.S. Co.	Boston
Fall River Line......	New York

Through Rates.

Niagara Falls.$43.50	Syracuse.......$40.65
Rochester...... 42.25	Utica........... 40.50

Route 422—New York, N. Y.

Forms Ex. 399, Ex. 863 and Ex. 915.

R., W. & O. R.R.....	to Clayton
R. & O. Nav. Co.....	Alexandria Bay
R. & O. Nav. Co.....	Montreal
Grand Trunk R'y or R. & O. Nav. Co.	Quebec
Quebec S.S. Co.... (Meals included)	Pictou
Intercolonial R'y.....	Halifax
Dominion Atlantic R'y	Annapolis
Bay of Fundy S.S. Co.	St. John
International S.S. Co.	Boston
Fall River Line......	New York

Through Rates.

Niagara Falls.$47.20	Syracuse.......$44.35
Rochester...... 45.95	Utica........... 44.20

Route 423—New York, N. Y.

Forms Ex. 400, Ex. 863 and Ex. 215.

R., W. & O. R.R.....	to Clayton
R. & O. Nav. Co.....	Alexandria Bay
R. & O. Nav. Co.....	Montreal
Can. Pac. R'y or R. & O. Nav. Co.	Quebec
Quebec S.S. Co.... (Meals included)	Pictou
Intercolonial R'y.....	Halifax
Dominion Atlantic R'y	Annapolis
Bay of Fundy S.S.Co.	St. John
International S. S. Co.	Boston
Fall River Line......	New York

Through Rates.

Niagara Falls.$47.20	Syracuse.......$44.35
Rochester...... 45.95	Utica........... 44.20

Route 424—New York, N. Y.

Forms Ex. 399, Ex. 862 and Ex. 216.

R., W. & O. R.R.....	to Clayton
R. & O. Nav. Co.....	Alexandria Bay
R. & O. Nav. Co.....	Montreal
Grand Trunk R'y or R. & O. Nav. Co.	Quebec
Quebec S.S. Co..... (Meals included)	Pictou
Intercolonial R'y.....	Halifax
Dominion Atlantic R'y	Annapolis
Bay of Fundy S.S. Co.	St. John
Can. Pac. R'y........	Vanceboro
Maine Central R.R...	Portland
Boston & Maine R.R.	Boston
Fall River Line......	New York

Through Rates.

Niagara Falls.$52.40	Syracuse.......$49.55
Rochester...... 51.15	Utica........... 49.40

Route 425—New York, N. Y.

Forms Ex. 400, Ex. 862 and Ex. 215.

R., W. & O. R.R.....	to Clayton
R. & O. Nav. Co.....	Alexandria Bay
R. & O. Nav. Co.....	Montreal
Can. Pac. R'y or R. & O. Nav. Co.	Quebec
Quebec S.S. Co.... (Meals included)	Pictou
Intercolonial R'y	Halifax
Dominion Atlantic R'y	Annapolis
Bay of Fundy S.S. Co.	St. John
Can. Pac. R'y........	Vanceboro
Maine Central R.R...	Portland
Boston & Maine R.R.	Boston
Fall River Line	New York

Through Rates.

Niagara Falls.$52.40	Syracuse.......$49.55
Rochester...... 51.15	Utica........... 49.40

SEE NOTE ON PAGE 119 REGARDING STOP-OVER AT ALEXANDRIA BAY.

Route 426—North Conway, N. H.

Form N 12.

R., W. & O. R.R.....to	Norwood
Cent. Vermont R.R...	Swanton
St. J. & L. C. R.R....	Lunenburg
Maine Central R.R...	North Conway

Through Rates.

	Unlim'd	Lim'd
Niagara Falls	$14.75	$13.15
Rochester	13.25	11.60
Syracuse	11.65	.....
Utica	10.65	.....

Route 427—North Conway, N. H. and Return.

Form Ex. 612.

R., W. & O. R.R.....to	Norwood
Cent. Vermont R.R..	Swanton
St. J. & L. C. R.R....	Lunenburg
Maine Central R.R..	North Conway

RETURNING SAME ROUTE.

Through Rates.

	Unlim'd	Lim'd
Niagara Falls	$25.40	$24.80
Rochester	24.10	22.70
Syracuse	21.35	.....
Utica	19.45	.....

Route 428—North Conway, N. H.

Forms Ex. 899 and Ex. 638.

R., W. & O. R.R.....to	Clayton
R. & O. Nav. Co.....	Alexandria Bay
R. & O. Nav. Co.....	Montreal
Grand Trunk R'y or R. & O. Nav. Co.	Quebec
Ferry..................	Point Levis
Quebec Central R'y..	Sherbrooke
Boston & Maine R.R..	Lunenburg
Maine Central R.R...	North Conway

Through Rates.

Niagara Falls	$23.00	Syracuse	$20.15
Rochester	21.75	Utica	20.00

Route 429—North Conway, N. H.

Forms Ex. 400 and Ex. 638.

R., W. & O. R.R.... to	Clayton
R. & O. Nav. Co.....	Alexandria Bay
R. & O. Nav. Co......	Montreal
Can. Pac. R'y or R. & O. Nav. Co.	Quebec
Ferry..................	Point Levis
Quebec Central R'y..	Sherbrooke
Boston & Maine R.R.	Lunenburg
Maine Central R.R...	North Conway

Through Rates.

Niagara Falls	$23.00	Syracuse	$20.15
Rochester	21.75	Utica	20.00

Route 430—North Conway, N. H.

Forms Ex. 400 and Ex. 768.

R., W. & O. R.R.....to	Clayton
R. & O. Nav. Co.....	Alexandria Bay
R. & O. Nav. Co.....	Montreal
Can. Pac. R'y or R. & O. Nav. Co.	Quebec
Ferry..................	Point Levis
Quebec Central R'y..	Dudswell Jc.
Maine Central R.R...	North Conway

Through Rates.

Niagara Falls	$23.00	Syracuse	$20.15
Rochester	21.75	Utica	20.00

Route 431—Ogdensburg, N. Y.

Form Ex. 268.

R., W. & O. R.R.....to	Clayton
R. & O. Nav. Co.....	Alexandria Bay
R. & O. Nav. Co.....	Prescott
Ferry..................	Ogdensburg

Through Rates.

Niagara Falls	$7.85	Syracuse	$4.90
Rochester	6.50	Utica	4.75

Route 432—Ogdensburg, N. Y. and Return.

Form Ex. 248.

R., W. & O. R.R.....to	Clayton
R. & O. Nav. Co.....	Alexandria Bay
R. & O. Nav. Co.....	Prescott
Ferry..................	Ogdensburg
R., W. & O. R.R.....	starting point

Through Rates.

Niagara Falls	$13.35	Syracuse	$8.50
Rochester	11.00	Utica	6.55

Route 433—Old Orchard Beach, Me.

Form Ex. 666.

R., W. & O. R.R.....to	Norwood
Cent. Vermont R.R..	Swanton
St. J. & L. C. R.R...	Lunenburg
Maine Central R.R...	Portland
Boston & Maine R.R.	Old Orch'd B'ch

Through Rates.

	Unlim'd	Lim'd
Niagara Falls	$16.55	$13.50
Rochester	15.05	11.95
Syracuse	13.45	.....
Utica	12.45	.....

Route 434—Ottawa, Canada.

Form Ex. 276.

R., W. & O. R.R.....to	Clayton
R. & O. Nav. Co. ...	Alexandria Bay
R. & O. Nav. Co.....	Brockville
Can. Pac. R'y........	Ottawa

Through Rates.

Niagara Falls	$10.35	Syracuse	$7.40
Rochester	9.00	Utica	7.25

Route 435—Ottawa, Canada, and Return.

From Ex. 281.

R., W. & O. R.R.....to	Clayton
R. & O. Nav. Co.....	Alexandria Bay
R. & O. Nav. Co.	Brockville
Can. Pac. R'y........	Ottawa
Can. Pac. R'y........	Brockville
Ferry..................	Morristown
R., W. & O. R.R.....	starting point

Through Rates.

Niagara Falls	$16.85	Syracuse	$12.00
Rochester	14.75	Utica	12.00

Route 436—Ottawa, Canada.

Form Ex 278.

R., W. & O. R.R.....to	Clayton
R. & O. Nav. Co.....	Alexandria Bay
R. & O. Nav. Co.....	Prescott
Can. Pac. R'y........	Ottawa

Through Rates.

Niagara Falls	$8.95	Syracuse	$7.00
Rochester	8.60	Utica	6.85

Route 437—Ottawa, Canada, and Return.

Form Ex. 282

R., W. & O. R.R.....to	Clayton
R. & O. Nav. Co.....	Alexandria Bay
R. & O. Nav. Co.....	Prescott
Can. Pac. R'y........	Ottawa
Can. Pac. R'y........	Prescott
Ferry..................	Ogdensburg
R., W. & O. R.R.....	starting point

Through Rates.

Niagara Falls	$16.85	Syracuse	$12.00
Rochester	14.50	Utica	12.00

Route 438—Ottawa, Canada.

Form Ex 274.

R., W. & O. R.R.....to	Morristown
Ferry..................	Brockville
Can. Pac. R'y........	Ottawa

Through Rates.

Niagara Falls	$9.60	Syracuse	$6.60
Rochester	8.20	Utica	6.50

Route 439—Ottawa, Canada, and Return.

Form Ex 279.

R., W. & O. R.R.....to	Morristown
Ferry..................	Brockville
Can. Pac. R'y........	Ottawa

RETURNING SAME ROUTE.

Through Rates.

Niagara Falls	$15.50	Syracuse	$10.95
Rochester	13.40	Utica	10.70

Route 440—Ottawa, Canada.

Form Ex. 517.

R., W. & O. R.R.....to	Ogdensburg
Ferry..................	Prescott
Can. Pac. R'y........	Ottawa

Through Rates.

Niagara Falls	$9.45	Syracuse	$6.50
Rochester	8.15	Utica	6.35

Route 441—Ottawa, Canada, and Return.

Form Ex. 280.

R., W. & O. R.R.....to	Ogdensburg
Ferry..................	Prescott
Can. Pac. R'y........	Ottawa

RETURNING SAME ROUTE.

Through Rates.

Niagara Falls	$15.50	Syracuse	$11.50
Rochester	13.45	Utica	11.25

Route 442—Plymouth, Mass.

Form N 17.

R., W. & O. R.R.....to	Norwood
Cent. Vermont R.R..	White River Jc.
Boston & Maine R.R.	Concord
Con. & Mont'l R.R..	Nashua
Boston & Maine R.R.	Boston
N.Y., N. H. & H. R.R.	Plymouth

Through Rates.

	Unlim'd	Lim'd
Niagara Falls	$18.60	$10.65
Rochester	17.25	10.00
Syracuse	15.65	.....
Utica	15.55	.....

Route 443—Plymouth, Mass. and Return.

Form Ex. 510.

R., W. & O. R.R.....to	Norwood
Cent. Vermont R.R..	White River Jc.
Boston & Maine R.R.	Concord
Con. & Mont'l R.R...	Nashua
Boston & Maine R.R.	Boston
N.Y., N. H. & H. R.R.	Plymouth

RETURNING SAME ROUTE.

Through Rates.

	Unlim'd	Lim'd
Niagara Falls	$30.00	$21.55
Rochester	28.00	19.70
Syracuse	25.75	.....
Utica	24.50	.....

Route 444—Plymouth, Mass. and Return.

Form Ex. 511.

R., W. & O. R.R.....to	Norwood
Cent. Vermont R.R..	White River Jc.
Boston & Maine R.R.	Concord
Con. & Mont'l R.R...	Nashua
Boston & Maine R.R.	Boston
N.Y., N. H. & H. R.R.	Plymouth
N. Y., N. H. & H. R.R.	Boston
Boston & Maine R.R.	North Conway
Maine Central R.R ..	Lunenburg
St. J. & L. C. R.R....	Swanton
Cent. Vermont R.R..	Norwood
R., W. & O. R.R.....	starting point

Through Rates.

	Unlim'd	Lim'd
Niagara Falls	$35.50	$21.55
Rochester	33.50	19.70
Syracuse	31.25	.....
Utica	30.00	.....

Route 445—Poland Springs, Me.

Forms N 12 and Ex. 818.

R., W. & O. R.R.....to	Norwood
Cent. Vermont R.R..	Swanton
St. J. & L. C. R.R....	Lunenburg
Maine Central R.R..	Danv'e, or Poland Sp'gs Jc.
Portland and Rumford Falls R'y and Stage or H. Ricker & Son's Stage...	Poland Springs.

Through Rates.

	Unlim'd	Lim'd
Niagara Falls		
Rochester		
Syracuse		
Utica		

SEE NOTE ON PAGE 119 REGARDING STOP-OVER AT ALEXANDRIA BAY.

Route 446—Poland Springs and Return.

Forms Ex. 612 and Ex. 618 R.

R., W. & O. R.R.	to Norwood
Cent. Vermont R.R. ..	Swanton
St. J. & L. C. R.R. ...	Lunenburg
Maine Central R.R. ..	Danv'e, or Poland Sp'gs Jc.
Portland and Rumford Falls R'y and Stage or H. Ricker and Son's Stage ..	Poland Springs.

RETURNING SAME ROUTE.

Through Rates.

	Unlim'd	Lim'd
Niagara Falls		
Rochester		
Syracuse		
Utica		

Route 447—Portland, Me.

Form N 12.

R., W. & O. R.R.	to Norwood
Cent. Vermont R.R. ..	Swanton
St. J. & L. C. R.R. ...	Lunenburg
Maine Central R.R. ..	Portland

Through Rates.

	Unlim'd	Lim'd
Niagara Falls	$16.20	$13.15
Rochester	14.70	11.60
Syracuse	13.10	.....
Utica	12.10	.....

Route 448—Portland, Me. and Return.

Form Ex. 612.

R., W. & O. R.R.	to Norwood
Cent. Vermont R.R. ..	Swanton
St. J. & L. C. R.R. ...	Lunenburg
Maine Central R.R. ..	Portland

RETURNING SAME ROUTE.

Through Rates.

	Unlim'd	Lim'd
Niagara Falls	$27.00	$24.80
Rochester	24.75	22.70
Syracuse	22.15	.....
Utica	21.00	.....

Route 449—Portland, Me.

Form Ex. 380.

R., W. & O. R.R.	to Clayton
R. & O. Nav. Co.	Alexandria Bay
R. & O. Nav. Co.	Montreal
Grand Trunk R'y ...	Portland

Through Rates.

Niagara Falls	$19.00	Syracuse	$16.15
Rochester	17.75	Utica	16.00

Route 450—Portland, Me. and Return.

Form Ex. 641.

R., W. & O. R.R.	to Clayton
R. & O. Nav. Co.	Alexandria Bay
R. & O. Nav. Co.	Montreal
Grand Trunk R'y ...	Portland
Maine Central R.R. ..	Lunenburg
St. J. & L. C. R.R. ...	Swanton
Cent. Vermont R.R. ..	Norwood
R., W. & O. R.R.	starting point

Through Rates.

Niagara Falls	$32.65	Syracuse	$28.65
Rochester	30.25	Utica	26.50

Route 451—Portland, Me.

Forms Ex. 254 and Ex. 639

R., W. & O. R.R.	to Clayton
R. & O. Nav. Co.	Alexandria Bay
R. & O. Nav. Co.	Montreal
Can. Pac. R'y	Newport
Boston & Maine R.R.	Lunenburg
Maine Central R.R. .	Portland

Through Rates.

Niagara Falls	$19.00	Syracuse	$16.15
Rochester	17.75	Utica	16.00

Route 452—Portland, Me. and Return.

Forms Ex. 256 and Ex. 640.

R., W. & O. R.R.	to Clayton
R. & O. Nav. Co.	Alexandria Bay
R. & O. Nav. Co.	Montreal
Can. Pac. R'y	Newport
Boston & Maine R.R.	Lunenburg
Maine Central R.R. ..	Portland

RETURNING SAME ROUTE.

Through Rates.

Niagara Falls	$29.50	Syracuse	$25.00
Rochester	27.50	Utica	25.00

Route 453—Portland, Me. and Return.

Form Ex. 642.

R., W. & O. R.R.	to Clayton
R. & O. Nav. Co.	Alexandria Bay
R. & O. Nav. Co.	Montreal
Can. Pac. R'y	Newport
Boston & Maine R.R.	Lunenburg
Maine Central R.R. .	Portland
Maine Central R.R. ..	Lunenburg
St. J. & L. C. R.R. ...	Swanton
Cent. Vermont R.R. .	Norwood
R., W. & O. R.R. ...	starting point

Through Rates.

Niagara Falls	$32.65	Syracuse	$28.65
Rochester	30.25	Utica	28.50

Route 454—Portland, Me.

Forms Ex. 399 and Ex. 487.

R., W. & O. R.R.	to Clayton
R. & O. Nav. Co.	Alexandria Bay
R. & O. Nav. Co.	Montreal
Grand Trunk R'y or R. & O. Nav. Co.	Quebec
Ferry	Point Levis
Grand Trunk R'y ...	Portland

Through Rates.

Niagara Falls	$23.00	Syracuse	$20.15
Rochester	21.75	Utica	20.00

Route 455—Portland, Me. and Return.

Form Ex. 738 R.

R., W. & O. R.R.	to Clayton
R. & O. Nav. Co.	Alexandria Bay
R. & O. Nav. Co.	Montreal
R. & O. Nav. Co.	Quebec
Ferry	Point Levis
Grand Trunk R'y ...	Portland
Maine Central R.R. .	Lunenburg
St. J. & L. C. R.R. ...	Swanton
Cent. Vermont R.R. .	Norwood
R., W. & O. R.R. ...	starting point

Through Rates.

Niagara Falls	$36.65	Syracuse	$32.65
Rochester	34.25	Utica	32.50

Route 456—Portland, Me.

Forms Ex. 399 and Ex. 645.

R., W. & O. R.R.	to Clayton
R. & O. Nav. Co.	Alexandria Bay
R. & O. Nav. Co.	Montreal
Grand Trunk R'y or R. & O. Nav. Co.	Quebec
Ferry	Point Levis
Quebec Central R'y ..	Sherbrooke
Boston & Maine R.R.	Lunenburg
Maine Central R.R. ..	Portland

Through Rates.

Niagara Falls	$23.00	Syracuse	$20.15
Rochester	21.75	Utica	20.00

Route 457—Portland, Me.

Forms Ex. 400 and Ex 645.

R., W. & O. R.R.	to Clayton
R. & O. Nav. Co.	Alexandria Bay
R. & O. Nav. Co.	Montreal
Can. Pac. R'y or R. & O. Nav. Co.	Quebec
Ferry	Point Levis
Quebec Central R'y ..	Sherbrooke
Boston & Maine R.R.	Lunenburg
Maine Central R.R. ..	Portland

Through Rates.

Niagara Falls	$23.00	Syracuse	$20.15
Rochester	21.75	Utica	20.00

Route 458—Portland, Me.

Forms Ex. 400 and Ex. 769.

R., W. & O. R.R.	to Clayton
R. & O. Nav. Co.	Alexandria Bay
R. & O. Nav. Co.	Montreal
Can. Pac. R'y or R. & O. Nav. Co.	Quebec
Ferry	Point Levis
Quebec Central R'y ..	Dudswell Jc.
Maine Central R.R. ..	Portland

Through Rates.

Niagara Falls	$23.00	Syracuse	$20.15
Rochester	21.75	Utica	20.00

Route 459—Portland, Me.

Forms Ex. 399 and Ex. 485.

R., W. & O. R.R.	to Clayton
R. & O. Nav. Co.	Alexandria Bay
R. & O. Nav. Co.	Montreal
Grand Trunk R'y or R. & O. Nav. Co	Quebec
Ferry	Point Levis
Intercolonial R'y	Pt. du Chene
Charl't'n St. Nav. Co.	Summerside
P. E. Island R'y	Charlottetown
Charl't'n St. Nav. Co.	Pictou
Intercolonial R'y	Halifax
Intercolonial R'y	St. John
International S. S. Co.	Portland

Through Rates.

Niagara Falls	$40.40	Syracuse	$37.55
Rochester	39.15	Utica	37.40

Route 460—Portland, Me.

Forms Ex. 400 and Ex. 485.

R., W. & O. R.R.	to Clayton
R. & O. Nav. Co.	Alexandria Bay
R. & O. Nav. Co.	Montreal
Can. Pac. R'y or R. & O. Nav. Co.	Quebec
Ferry	Point Levis
Intercolonial R'y	Pt. du Chene
Charl't'n St. Nav. Co.	Summerside
P. E. Island R'y	Charlottetown
Charl't'n St. Nav. Co.	Pictou
Intercolonial R'y ...	Halifax
Intercolonial R'y ...	St. John
International S. S. Co.	Portland

Through Rates.

Niagara Falls	$40.40	Syracuse	$37.55
Rochester	39.15	Utica	37.40

Route 461—Portland, Me.

Forms Ex. 399 and Ex. 739.

R., W. & O. R.R.	to Clayton
R. & O. Nav. Co.	Alexandria Bay
R. & O. Nav. Co.	Montreal
Grand Trunk R'y or R. & O. Nav. Co.	Quebec
Quebec S.S. Co. .... (Meals included)	Summerside
Charl't'n St. Nav. Co.	Pt. du Chene
Intercolonial R'y	St. John
Can. Pac. R'y	Vanceboro
Maine Central R.R. ..	Portland

Through Rates.

Niagara Falls	$41.25	Syracuse	$38.40
Rochester	40.00	Utica	38.25

Route 462—Portland, Me.

Forms Ex 400 and Ex. 739.

R., W. & O. R.R.	to Clayton
R. & O. Nav. Co.	Alexandria Bay
R. & O. Nav. Co.	Montreal
Can. Pac. R'y or R. & O. Nav. Co.	Quebec
Quebec S. S. Co. .... (Meals included)	Summerside
Charl't'n St. Nav. Co.	Pt. du Chene
Intercolonial R'y	St. John
Can. Pac. R'y	Vanceboro
Maine Central R.R ..	Portland

Through Rates.

Niagara Falls	$41.25	Syracuse	$38.40
Rochester	40.00	Utica	38.25

SEE NOTE ON PAGE 119 REGARDING STOP-OVER AT ALEXANDRIA BAY.

Route 463—Portland, Me.

Forms Ex. 399 and Ex 740.

R., W. & O. R.R.....to	Clayton
R. & O. Nav. Co.....	Alexandria Bay
R. & O. Nav. Co.....	Montreal
Grand Trunk R'y or R. & O. Nav. Co.	Quebec
Quebec S. S. Co... (Meals included)	Summerside
Charl't'n St. Nav. Co.	Pt. du Chene
Intercolonial R'y.....	St. John
International S.S. Co.	Portland

Through Rates.

Niagara Falls	$37.75	Syracuse	$34.90
Rochester	36.50	Utica	34.75

Route 464—Portland, Me.

Forms Ex. 400 and Ex. 740.

R., W. & O. R.R.....to	Clayton
R. & O. Nav. Co.....	Alexandria Bay
R. & O. Nav. Co.....	Montreal
Can. Pac. R'y or R. & O. Nav. Co.	Quebec
Quebec S.S. Co.... (Meals included)	Summerside
Charl't'n St. Nav. Co.	Pt. du Chene
Intercolonial R'y.....	St. John
International S.S. Co.	Portland

Through Rates.

Niagara Falls	$37.75	Syracuse	$34.90
Rochester	36.50	Utica	34.75

Rout: 465—Portland, Me.

Forms Ex. 399 and Ex. 865.

R., W. & O. R.R.....to	Clayton
R. & O. Nav. Co.....	Alexandria Bay
R. & O. Nav. Co.....	Montreal
Grand Trunk R'y or R. & O. Nav. Co.	Quebec
Quebec S.S. Co.... (Meals included)	Pictou
Intercolonial R'y.....	Halifax
Dominion Atlantic R'y	Annapolis
Bay of Fundy S.S. Co.	St. John
Can. Pac. R'y........	Vanceboro
Maine Central R.R...	Portland

Through Rates.

Niagara Falls	$47.20	Syracuse	$44.35
Rochester	45.95	Utica	44.20

Route 466—Portland, Me.

Forms Ex. 400 and Ex. 865.

R., W. & O. R.R.....to	Clayton
R. & O. Nav. Co.....	Alexandria Bay
R. & O. Nav. Co.....	Montreal
Can. Pac. R'y or R. & O. Nav. Co.	Quebec
Quebec S.S. Co.... (Meals included)	Pictou
Intercolonial R'y.....	Halifax
Dominion Atlantic R'y	Annapolis
Bay of Fundy S.S. Co.	St. John
Can. Pac. R'y........	Vanceboro
Maine Central R.R...	Portland

Through Rates.

Niagara Falls	$47.20	Syracuse	$44.35
Rochester	45.95	Utica	44.20

Route 467—Portland, Me.

Forms Ex. 399 and Ex. 866.

R., W. & O. R.R.....to	Clayton
R. & O. Nav. Co.....	Alexandria Bay
R. & O. Nav. Co.....	Montreal
Grand Trunk R'y or R. & O. Nav. Co.	Quebec
Quebec S.S. Co.... (Meals included)	Pictou
Intercolonial R'y....	Halifax
Dominion Atlantic R'y	Annapolis
Bay of Fundy S.S. Co.	St. John
International S.S. Co.	Portland

Through Rates.

Niagara Falls	$43.70	Syracuse	$40.85
Rochester	42.45	Utica	40.70

Route 468—Portland, Me.

Forms Ex. 400 and Ex. 866.

R., W. & O. R.R.....to	Clayton
R. & O. Nav. Co.....	Alexandria Bay
R. & O. Nav. Co.....	Montreal
Can. Pac. R'y or R. & O. Nav. Co..	Quebec
Quebec S.S. Co..... (Meals included)	Pictou
Intercolonial R'y.....	Halifax
Dominion Atlantic R'y	Annapolis
Bay of Fundy S.S. Co.	St. John
International S.S. Co.	Portland

Through Rates.

Niagara Falls	$43.70	Syracuse	$40.85
Rochester	42.45	Utica	40.70

Route 469—Prescott, Ont.

Form Ex. 938.

R., W. & O. R.R.....to	Clayton
R. & O. Nav. Co.....	Alexandria Bay
R. & O. Nav. Co.....	Prescott

Through Rates.

Niagara Falls	$7.85	Syracuse	$4.90
Rochester	6.50	Utica	4.75

Route 470—Prescott, Ont. and Return.

Form Ex. 939.

R., W. & O. R.R.....to	Clayton
R. & O. Nav. Co.....	Alexandria Bay
R. & O. Nav. Co.....	Prescott
Ferry................	Ogdensburg
R., W. & O. R.R	starting point

Through Rates.

Niagara Falls	$13.35	Syracuse	$8.50
Rochester	11.00	Utica	8.50

Route 471—Profile House, N. H.

Form Ex. 666.

R., W. & O. R.R.....to	Norwood
Cent. Vermont R.R..	Swanton
St. J. & L. C. R.R....	Lunenburg
Maine Central R.R...	Zealand Jc.
Prof. & F. Notch R.R.	Profile House

Through Rates.

	Cullm'd	Lim'd
Niagara Falls	$14.15	. ..
Rochester	12.65	.
Syracuse	11.05	.....
Utica	10.05	.....

Route 472—Profile House, N. H. and Return.

Form Ex. 686 R.

R., W. & O. R.R.....to	Norwood
Cent. Vermont R.R..	Swanton
St. J. & L. C. R.R....	Lunenburg
Maine Central R.R...	Zealand Jc.
Prof. & F. Notch R.R.	Profile House

RETURNING SAME ROUTE.

Through Rates.

Niagara Falls	$26.20	Syracuse	$21.15
Rochester	24.20	Utica	19.25

Route 473—Profile House, N. H.

Forms N 14 and Ex. 217.

R., W. & O. R.R.....to	Norwood
Cent. Vermont R.R..	Swanton
St. J. & L. C. R.R....	Lunenburg
Maine Central R.R...	Scott's
Con. & Mont'l R.R..	Bethlehem Jc.
Prof. & F. Notch R.R.	Profile House

Through Rates.

Niagara Falls	$14.15	Syracuse	$11.05
Rochester	12.65	Utica	10.05

Route 474—Profile House, N. H. and Return.

Form Ex 590.

R., W. & O. R.R. ...to	Norwood
Cent. Vermont R.R..	Swanton
St. J. & L. C. R.R....	Lunenburg
Maine Central R.R...	Scott's
Con. & Mont'l R.R...	Bethlehem Jc.
Prof. & F. Notch R.R.	Profile House

RETURNING SAME ROUTE.

Through Rates.

Niagara Falls	$26.20	Syracuse	$21.15
Rochester	24.20	Utica	19.25

Route 475—Profile House, N. H.

Forms N 14 and Ex. 217.

R., W. & O. R.R.....to	Norwood
Cent. Vermont R.R..	Montpelier
Mont. & W. R. R.R..	Wells River
Con. & Mont'l R.R. .	Bethlehem Jc.
Prof. & F. Notch R.R.	Profile House

Through Rates.

Niagara Falls	$14.15	Syracuse	$11.05
Rochester	12.65	Utica	10.05

Route 476—Profile House, N. H. and Return.

Form Ex. 583.

R. W. & O. R.R.....to	Norwood
Cent. Vermont R.R..	Montpelier
Mont. & W. R. R.R..	Wells River
Con. & Mont'l R.R...	Bethlehem Jc.
Prof. & F. Notch R.R.	Profile House

RETURNING SAME ROUTE.

Through Rates.

Niagara Falls	$26.20	Syracuse	$21.15
Rochester	24.20	Utica	19.25

Route 477—Profile House, N. H.

Forms Ex 254 and Ex. 395

R., W. & O. R.R.....to	Clayton
R. & O. Nav. Co......	Alexandria Bay
R. & O. Nav. Co......	Montreal
Grand Trunk R'y....	St. John's
Cent. Vermont R.R..	Montpelier
Mont. & W. R. R.R..	Wells River
Con. & Mont'l R.R...	Bethlehem Jc.
Prof. & F. Notch R.R.	Profile House

Through Rates.

Niagara Falls	$18.80	Syracuse	$15.95
Rochester	17.55	Utica	15.80

Route 478—Profile House, N. H. and Return.

Forms Ex 255 and Ex. 396.

R., W. & O. R.R. .. to	Clayton
R. & O. Nav. Co.....	Alexandria Bay
R. & O. Nav. Co.....	Montreal
Grand Trunk R'y....	St. John's
Cent. Vermont R.R..	Montpelier
Mont. & W. R. R.R..	Wells River
Con. & Mont'l R.R..	Bethlehem Jc.
Prof. & F. Notch R.R.	Profile House

RETURNING SAME ROUTE.

Through Rates.

Niagara Falls	$31.50	Syracuse	$27.00
Rochester	29.50	Utica	27.00

Route 479—Profile House, N. H.

Forms Ex. 254, Ex. 396 and Ex. 157.

R., W. & O. R.R.....to	Clayton
R. & O. Nav. Co.....	Alexandria Bay
R. & O. Nav. Co.....	Montreal
Grand Trunk R'y....	Alpine House (Gorham)
Stage................	Glen Site
Stage................	Sum't Mt. Wash.
Mt. Washington R'y.	Base
Con. & Mont'l R. R..	Fabyan's
Maine Central R.R...	Crawford's
Maine Central R.R...	Fabyan's
Con. & Mont'l R.R...	Bethlehem Jc.
Prof. & F. Notch R.R.	Profile House

Through Rates.

Niagara Falls	$30.56	Syracuse	$27.71
Rochester	29.31	Utica	27.56

Route 480—Profile House, N. H.

Forms Ex. 251 and Ex. 741.

R., W. & O. R.R.....to	Clayton
R. & O. Nav. Co.....	Alexandria Bay
R. & O. Nav. Co.....	Montreal
Can. Pac. R'y........	Newport
Boston & Maine R.R.	Lunenberg
Maine Central R.R...	Zealand Jc.
Prof. & F. Notch R.R.	Profile House

Through Rates.

Niagara Falls	$18.80	Syracuse	$15.95
Rochester	17.55	Utica	15.80

SEE NOTE ON PAGE 119 REGARDING STOP-OVER AT ALEXANDRIA BAY.

Route 481—Profile House, N. H.

Forms Ex. 399, Ex. 478 and Ex. 137.

R., W. & O. R.R.....to	Clayton
R. & O. Nav. Co.....	Alexandria Bay
R. & O. Nav. Co.....	Montreal
Grand Trunk R'y or R. & O. Nav. Co.	Quebec
Ferry................	Point Levis
Grand Trunk R'y....	Alpine House (Gorham)
Stage................	Glen Site
Stage................	Sum't Mt. Wash.
Mt. Washington R'y..	Base
Con. & Mont'l R.R..	Fabyan's
Maine Central R.R...	Crawford's
Maine Central R.R...	Fabyan's
Con. & Mont'l R.R...	Bethlehem Jc.
Prof. & F. Notch R.R.	Profile House

Through Rates.

Niagara Falls	$34.66	Syracuse	$31.81
Rochester	33.41	Utica	31.66

Route 482—Profile House, N. H.

Forms Ex. 399 and Ex. 142.

R., W. & O. R.R.....to	Clayton
R. & O. Nav. Co.....	Alexandria Bay
R. & O. Nav. Co.....	Montreal
Grand Trunk R'y or R. & O. Nav. Co.	Quebec
Ferry................	Point Levis
Quebec Central R'y..	Sherbrooke
Boston & Maine R.R.	Lunenburg
Maine Central R.R...	Zealand Jc.
Prof. & F. Notch R.R.	Profile House

Through Rates.

Niagara Falls	$23.20	Syracuse	$20.35
Rochester	21.95	Utica	20.20

Route 483—Profile House, N. H.

Forms Ex. 400 and Ex. 142.

R., W. & O. R.R.....to	Clayton
R. & O. Nav. Co.....	Alexandria Bay
R. & O. Nav. Co.....	Montreal
Can. Pac. R'y or R. & O. Nav. Co.	Quebec
Ferry................	Point Levis
Quebec Central R'y..	Sherbrooke
Boston & Maine R.R.	Lunenburg
Maine Central R.R..	Zealand Jc.
Prof. & F. Notch R.R.	Profile House

Through Rates.

Niagara Falls	$23.20	Syracuse	$20.35
Rochester	21.95	Utica	20.20

Route 484—Profile House, N. H.

Forms Ex. 400 and Ex. 717.

R., W. & O. R.R.....to	Clayton
R. & O. Nav. Co.....	Alexandria Bay
R. & O. Nav. Co.....	Montreal
Can. Pac. R'y or R. & O. Nav. Co.	Quebec
Ferry................	Point Levis
Quebec Central R'y..	Dudswell Jc.
Maine Central R.R..	Zealand Jc.
Prof. & F. Notch R.R.	Profile House

Through Rates.

Niagara Falls	$23.20	Syracuse	$20.35
Rochester	21.95	Utica	20.20

Route 485—Provincetown, Mass.

Form N 17.

R., W. & O. R.R.....to	Norwood
Cent. Vermont R.R..	White River Jc.
Boston & Maine R.R..	Concord
Con. & Mont'l R R....	Nashua
Boston & Maine R.R..	Boston
N.Y., N. H. & H. R.R.	Provincetown

Through Rates.

	Unlim'd	Lim'd
Niagara Falls	$20.65	$12.35
Rochester	19.30	12.05
Syracuse	17.70	.....
Utica	17.60	.....

Route 486—Provincetown, Mass. and Return.

Form Ex. 570.

R. W., & O. R. R.R..to	Norwood
Cent. Vermont R.R..	White River Jc.
Boston & Maine R.R..	Concord
Con. & Mont'l R.R...	Nashua
Boston & Maine R.R..	Boston
N.Y., N. H. & H. R.R.	Provincetown

RETURNING SAME ROUTE.

Through Rates.

	Unlim'd	Lim'd
Niagara Falls	$33.30	$23.60
Rochester	31.30	23.00
Syracuse	29.05	.....
Utica	27.80	.....

Route 487—Provincetown, Mass. and Return.

Form Ex. 571.

R., W. & O. R.R.....to	Norwood
Cent. Vermont R.R..	White River Jc.
Boston & Maine R.R.	Concord
Con. & Mont'l R.R..	Nashua
Boston & Maine R.R.	Boston
N. Y., N. H. & H. R.R.	Provincetown
N. Y., N. H. & H. R.R.	Boston
Boston & Maine R.R.	North Conway
Maine Central R.R. .	Lunenburg
St. J. & L. C. R.R....	Swanton
Cent. Vermont R.R..	Norwood
R., W. & O. R.R.....	starting point

Through Rates.

	Unlim'd	Lim'd
Niagara Falls	$38.80	$24.85
Rochester	36.60	23.00
Syracuse	34.55	.....
Utica	33.30	.....

Route 488—Quebec, P. Q.

Form Ex. 399.

R., W. & O. R.R.....to	Clayton
R. & O. Nav. Co.....	Alexandria Bay
R. & O. Nav. Co.....	Montreal
Grand Trunk R'y or R. & O. Nav. Co.	Quebec

Through Rates.

Niagara Falls	$14.50	Syracuse	$11.65
Rochester	13.25	Utica	11.50

Route 489—Quebec, P. Q.

Form Ex. 400.

R., W. & O. R.R.....to	Clayton
R. & O. Nav. Co.....	Alexandria Bay
R. & O. Nav. Co.....	Montreal
Can. Pac. R'y or R. & O. Nav. Co.	Quebec

Through Rates.

Niagara Falls	$14.50	Syracuse	$11.65
Rochester	13.25	Utica	11.50

Route 490—Quebec, P. Q.

Form Ex. 265.

R., W. & O. R.R.....to	Clayton
R. & O. Nav. Co.....	Alexandria Bay
R. & O. Nav. Co......	Prescott
Can. Pac. R'y (via Ottawa & Mont'l)	Quebec

Through Rates

Niagara Falls	$15.45	Syracuse	$12.50
Rochester	14.10	Utica	12.35

Route 491—Quebec, P. Q. and Return.

Form Ex. 288.

R., W. & O. R.R.....to	Clayton
R. & O. Nav. Co.....	Alexandria Bay
R. & O. Nav. Co.....	Montreal
R. & O. Nav. Co.....	Quebec
Can. Pac. R'y (via Mont'l & Ottawa)	Prescott
Ferry................	Ogdensburg
R., W. & O. R.R.....	starting point

Through Rates.

Niagara Falls	$26.00	Syracuse	$21.35
Rochester	23.85	Utica	21.35

Route 492—Roberval, P. Q.

Forms Ex. 399 and Ex. 648.

R., W. & O. R.R.....to	Clayton
R. & O. Nav. Co.....	Alexandria Bay
Grand Trunk R'y or R. & O. Nav. Co.	Quebec
Que. & L. St. J. R'y...	Roberval

Through Rates.

Niagara Falls	$20.20	Syracuse	$17.35
Rochester	10.95	Utica	17.20

Route 493—Roberval, P. Q.

Forms Ex. 400 and Ex. 648.

R., W. & O. R.R.....to	Clayton
R. & O. Nav. Co.....	Alexandria Bay
R. & O. Nav. Co.....	Montreal
Can. Pac. R'y or R. & O. Nav. Co.	Quebec
Que. & L. St. J. R'y..	Roberval

Through Rates.

Niagara Falls	$20.20	Syracuse	$17.35
Rochester	18.95	Utica	17.20

Route 494—Roberval, P. Q. and Return.

Forms Ex. 265, Ex. 194 and Ex. 649.

R., W. & O. R.R.....to	Clayton
R. & O. Nav. Co.....	Alexandria Bay
R. & O. Nav. Co.....	Montreal
Grand Trunk R'y or R. & O. Nav. Co.	Quebec
Que. & L. St. J. R'y...	Roberval

RETURNING SAME ROUTE.

Through Rates.

Niagara Falls	$31.50	Syracuse	$27.00
Rochester	29.50	Utica	27.00

Route 495—Roberval, P. Q. and Return.

Forms Ex. 265, Ex. 191 and Ex. 649.

R., W. & O. R. R....to	Clayton
R. & O. Nav. Co.....	Alexandria Bay
R. & O. Nav. Co.....	Montreal
Can. Pac. R'y or R. & O. Nav. Co.	Quebec
Que. & L. St. J. R'y...	Roberval

RETURNING SAME ROUTE.

Through Rates.

Niagara Falls	$31.50	Syracuse	$27.00
Rochester	29.50	Utica	27.00

Route 496—Roberval, P. Q. and Return.

Forms Ex. 286 and Ex. 649

R., W. & O. RR......to	Clayton
R. & O. Nav. Co.....	Alexandria Bay
R. & O. Nav. Co.....	Montreal
R. & O. Nav. Co.....	Quebec
Que. & L. St. J. R'y...	Roberval
Que. & L. St. J. R'y..	Quebec
Can. Pac. R'y (via Mont'l & Ottawa)	Prescott
Ferry................	Ogdensburg
R., W. & O. R.R.....	starting point

Through Rates.

Niagara Falls	$33.50	Syracuse	$28.85
Rochester	31.35	Utica	28.85

Route 497—Round Island, N. Y.

Form Ex. 650.

R., W. & O. R.R.....to	Clayton
Thous. Isl. St'b't Co.	Round Island

Through Rates.

Niagara Falls	$6.60	Syracuse	$3.65
Rochester	5.25	Utica	3.50

Route 498—Round Island, N. Y. and Return.

Form Ex. 651.

R., W. & O. R.R.....to	Clayton
Thous. Isl. St'b't Co.	Round Island

RETURNING SAME ROUTE.

Rates may be obtained of all R., W. & O. R.R. Ticket Agents.

SEE NOTE ON PAGE 119 REGARDING STOP-OVER AT ALEXANDRIA BAY.

Route 499—Rouse's Point, N Y.

Form Ex. 240.

R., W. & O. R.R.....to Clayton
R. & O. Nav. Co..... Alexandria Bay
R. & O. Nav. Co..... Prescott
Ferry.................. Ogdensburg
Cent. Vermont R.R.. Rouse's Point

Through Rates.

Niagara Falls	$11.40	Syracuse	$8.45
Rochester	10.05	Utica	8.30

Route 500—Rouse's Point, N. Y.

Form Ex. 315.

R., W. & O. R.R.....to Clayton
R. & O. Nav. Co..... Alexandria Bay
R. & O. Nav. Co..... Montreal
Grand Trunk R'y.... Rouse's Point

Through Rates.

Niagara Falls	$13.40	Syracuse	$10.55
Rochester	12.15	Utica	10.40

Route 501—Rouse's Point, N. Y.

Form N 1.

R., W. & O. R. R.....to Norwood
Cent. Vermont R.R.. Rouse's Point

Through Rates.

Niagara Falls	$10.05	Syracuse	$7.10
Rochester	8.70	Utica	7.00

Route 502—Saratoga, N. Y.

Form Ex. 245.

R., W. & O. R.R.....to Norwood
Cent. Vermont R.R.. Rutland
D. & H. R.R......... Saratoga

Through Rates.

Niagara Falls	$13.94	Syracuse	$10.99
Rochester	12.59	Utica	10.89

Route 503—Saratoga, N. Y.

Form Ex. 246.

R., W. & O. R.R.....to Norwood
Cent. Vermont R.R.. Burlington
Cham. Trans. Co..... Ft. Ticonderoga
D. & H. R.R......... Baldwin
L. Geo. St'mb't Co... Caldwell
D. & H. R.R......... Saratoga

Through Rates.

Niagara Falls	$15.44	Syracuse	$12.49
Rochester	14.09	Utica	12.39

Route 504—Saratoga, N. Y.

Form Ex. 244.

R., W. & O. R.R.....to Norwood
Cent. Vermont R.R... Rouse's Point
D. & H. R.R......... Plattsburg
D. & H. R. R. or Cham. Trans. Co. } Ft. Ticonderoga
D. & H. R.R......... Baldwin
L. Geo. St'mb't Co... Caldwell
D. & H. R.R......... Saratoga

Through Rates.

Niagara Falls	$15.44	Syracuse	$12.49
Rochester	14.09	Utica	12 39

Route 505—Saratoga, N. Y. and Return.

Form Ex. 241.

R., W. & O. R.R.....to Norwood
Cent. Vermont R.R.. Rouse's Point
D. & H. R.R......... Plattsburg
D. & H. R.R. or Cham. Trans. Co. } Ft. Ticonderoga
D. & H. R.R......... Baldwin
L. Geo. St'mb't Co... Caldwell
D. & H. R.R......... Saratoga
D. & H. R.R......... Rouse's Point
C. V. R.R. (O. & L. C. Div.) } Norwood
R., W. & O. R.R..... starting point.

Through Rates.

Niagara Falls	$29.05	Syracuse	$23.25
Rochester	26.25	Utica	23.25

Route 506—Saratoga, N. Y.

Form Ex. 243.

R., W. & O. R.R.....to Clayton
R. & O. Nav. Co..... Alexandria Bay
R. & O. Nav. Co..... Prescott
Ferry.................. Ogdensburg
Cent. Vermont R.R.. Rouse's Point
D. & H. R.R......... Plattsburg
D. & H. R.R. or Cham. Trans. Co. } Ft. Ticonderoga
D. & H. R.R......... Baldwin
L. Geo. St'mb't Co... Caldwell
D. & H. R.R......... Saratoga

Through Rates.

Niagara Falls	$17 50	Syracuse	$14.55
Rochester	16.15	Utica	14.40

Route 507—Saratoga, N. Y.

Form Ex. 241.

R., W. & O. R.R.....to Clayton
R. & O. Nav. Co..... Alexandria Bay
R. & O. Nav. Co..... Montreal
Grand Trunk R'y.... Rouse's Point
D. & H. R.R......... Saratoga

Through Rates.

Niagara Falls	$18.00	Syracuse	$15.15
Rochester	16.75	Utica	15 00

Route 508—Saratoga. N. Y.

Forms Ex. 254 and Ex. 404.

R., W. & O. R.R.....to Clayton
R. & O. Nav. Co..... Alexandria Bay
R. & O. Nav. Co..... Montreal
Grand Trunk R'y.... Rouse's Point
D. & H. R.R. .... Plattsburg
D. & H. R.R. or Cham. Trans. Co. } Ft. Ticonderoga
D. & H. R.R......... Saratoga

Through Rates.

Niagara Falls	$18.00	Syracuse	$15.15
Rochester	16.75	Utica	15.00

Route 509—Saratoga. N. Y.

Form Ex. 242.

R., W. & O. R.R.....to Clayton
R. & O. Nav. Co..... Alexandria Bay
R. & O. Nav. Co..... Montreal
Grand Trunk R'y.... Rouse's Point
D. & H. R.R......... Plattsburg
D. & H. R.R. or Cham. Trans. Co. } Ft. Ticonderoga
D. & H. R.R......... Baldwin
L. Geo. St'mb't Co... Caldwell
D. & H. R.R....... Saratoga

Through Rates.

Niagara Falls	$19.50	Syracuse	$16.65
Rochester	18.25	Utica	16.50

Route 510—Saratoga, N. Y.

Forms Ex. 254 and Ex. 402.

R., W. & O. R.R.....to Clayton
R. & O. Nav. Co..... Alexandria Bay
R. & O. Nav. Co..... Montreal
Grand Trunk R'y.... St. John's
Cent. Vermont R.R.. Rutland
D. & H. R.R......... Saratoga

Through Rates.

Niagara Falls	$18 00	Syracuse	$15.15
Rochester	16.75	Utica	15.00

Route 511—Saratoga, N. Y.

Forms Ex. 254 and Ex. 403.

R., W. & O. R.R.....to Clayton
R. & O. Nav. Co..... Alexandria Bay
R. & O. Nav. Co..... Montreal
Grand Trunk R'y.... St. John's
Cent. Vermont R.R.. Burlington
Cham. Trans. Co.. .. Ft. Ticonderoga
D. & H. R.R......... Saratoga

Through Rates.

Niagara Falls	$18.00	Syracuse	$15.15
Rochester	16.75	Utica	15.00

Route 512—Saratoga, N. Y.

Forms Ex. 254 and Ex. 407.

R., W. & O. R.R.....to Clayton
R. & O. Nav. Co..... Alexandria Bay
R. & O. Nav. Co..... Montreal
Grand Trunk R'y.... St. John's
Cent. Vermont R.R.. Burlington
Cham. Trans. Co.. .. Ft. Ticonderoga
D. & H. R.R......... Baldwin
L. Geo. St'mb't Co... Caldwell
D. & H. R.R......... Saratoga

Through Rates.

Niagara Falls	$15.50	Syracuse	$16.65
Rochester	13.25	Utica	16.50

Route 513—Saratoga, N. Y.

Forms Ex. 254 and Ex. 405.

R., W. & O. R. R.....to Clayton
R. & O. Nav. Co..... Alexandria Bay
R. & O. Nav. Co..... Montreal
Grand Trunk R'y.... Gorham
Stage .... Glen Site
Stage .... Sum't Mt. Wash.
Mt. Washington R'y. Base
Con. & Mont'l R.R.. Bethlehem Jc.
Prof. & F. Notch R.R. Profile House
Stage .... No. Woodstock
Con. & Mont'l R.R.. Wells River
Mont. & W. R. R.R.. Montpelier
Cent. Vermont R.R.. Burlington
Cham. Trans. Co..... Ft. Ticonderoga
D. & H. R.R......... Baldwin
L. Geo. St'mb't Co... Caldwell
D. & H. R.R......... Saratoga

Through Rates.

Niagara Falls	$42.07	Syracuse	$39.22
Rochester	43.82	Utica	39.07

Route 514—Saratoga. N. Y.

Forms Ex. 254 and Ex. 654.

R., W. & O. R.R.. ..to Clayton
R. & O. Nav. Co..... Alexandria Bay
R. & O. Nav. Co..... Montreal
Can. Pac. R'y........ Newport
St. J. & L. C. R.R... Lunenburg
Maine Central R.R... Fabyan's
Con. & Mont'l R.R.. Base Mt. Wash.
Mt. Washington R'y. Summit
Mt. Washington R'y. Base
Con. & Mont'l R.R... Bethlehem Jc.
Prof. & F. Notch R.R. Profile House
Stage.................. No. Woodstock
Con. & Mont'l R.R... Wells River
Mont. & W. R. R.R.. Montpelier
Cent. Vermont R.R.. Burlington
Cham. Trans. Co..... Ft. Ticonderoga
D. & H. R.R......... Baldwin
L. Geo. St'mb't Co... Caldwell
D. & H. R.R....... Saratoga

Through Rates.

Niagara Falls	$37.22	Syracuse	$34.37
Rochester	35.97	Utica	34.22

Route 515—Sebago Lake, Me.

Form N 12.

R., W. & O. R.R....to Norwood
Cent. Vermont R.R.. Swanton
St. J. & L. C. R.R.... Lunenburg
Maine Central R.R.. Sebago Lake

Through Rates.

	Unlim'd	Lim'd
Niagara Falls	$15.70	$13.15
Rochester	14.20	11.60
Syracuse	12.60	.....
Utica	11.60	.....

Route 516—Sebago Lake, Me. and Return.

Form Ex. 612.

R., W. & O. R.R.....to Norwood
Cent. Vermont R.R.. Swanton
St. J. & L. C. R.R ... Lunenburg
Maine Central R.R .. Sebago Lake

RETURNING SAME ROUTE.

Through Rates.

	Unlim'd	Lim'd
Niagara Falls	$27.00	$24.[illegible]
Rochester	24.75	22.70
Syracuse	22.15	.....
Utica	21.00	.....

Route 517—St. Andrews, N. B.

Form Ex. 143.

R., W. & O. R.R.....to	Norwood
Cent. Vermont R.R..	Swanton
St. J. & L. C. R.R....	Lunenburg
Maine Central R. R. (via Portland)	Vanceboro
Can. Pac. R'y........	St. Andrews

Through Rates.

	Unlim'd	Lim'd
Niagara Falls	$24.50	$19.15
Rochester	23.00	19.60
Syracuse	21.40	....
Utica	23.40	.....

Route 518—St. Andrews, N. B. and Return.

Form Ex. 144 R.

R., W. & O. R.R.....to	Norwood
Cent. Vermont R.R..	Swanton
St. J. & L. C. R.R....	Lunenburg
Maine Central R.R (via Portland)	Vanceboro
Can. Pac. R'y........	St. Andrews

RETURNING SAME ROUTE.

Through Rates.

	Unlim'd	Lim'd
Niagara Falls	$35.70	$33.95
Rochester	33.95	31.95
Syracuse	31.45	.....
Utica	30.45	.....

Route 519—St. Andrews, N. B. and Return.

Form Ex. 145 R.

R., W. & O. R.R.....to	Clayton
R. & O. Nav. Co.....	Alexandria Bay
R. & O. Nav. Co......	Montreal
Can. Pac. R'y........	St. Andrews
Can. Pac. R'y........	Vanceboro
Maine Central R.R...	Lunenburg
St. J. & L. C. R.R....	Swanton
Cent. Vermont R.R..	Norwood
R., W. & O. R.R.....	starting point

Through Rates.

Niagara Falls	$41.55	Syracuse	$33.77
Rochester	40.30	Utica	33.55

Route 520—St. John, N. B.

Form Ex. 746.

R., W. & O. R.R.....to	Norwood
Cent. Vermont R.R..	Swanton
St. J. & L. C. R.R...	Lunenburg
Maine Central R.R. (via Portland)	Vanceboro
Can. Pac. R'y.......	St. John

Through Rates.

	Unlim'd	Lim'd
Niagara Falls	$24.90	$19.15
Rochester	23.00	17.60
Syracuse	21.40	.....
Utica	20.40	.....

Route 521—St. Johnsbury, Vt.

Form N 20.

R., W. & O. R.R.....to	Norwood
Cent. Vermont R.R...	Swanton
St. J. & L. C. R.R....	St. Johnsbury

Through Rates.

Niagara Falls	$12.45	Syracuse	$9.35
Rochester	10.95	Utica	8.35

Route 522—St. Johnsbury, Vt. and Return.

Form Ex. 636 R.

R., W. & O. R.R.....to	Norwood
Cent. Vermont R.R..	Swanton
St J. & L. C. R.R....	St. Johnsbury

RETURNING SAME ROUTE.

Through Rates.

Niagara Falls	$21.50	Syracuse	$16.45
Rochester	19.50	Utica	14.55

Route 523—Star Lake, N. Y. (Oswegatchie) and Return.

Form Ex. 670.

R., W. & O. R.R.....to	Carthage
Car. & Ad. R.R......	Oswegatchie

RETURNING SAME ROUTE.

Through Rates.

Niagara Falls	$12.30	Syracuse	$6.70
Rochester	9.60	Utica	5.80

Route 524—Summit Mt. Washington, N. H.

Form Ex. 657.

R., W. & O. R.R.....to	Norwood
Cent. Vermont R.R..	Swanton
St. J. & L. C. R.R....	Lunenburg
Maine Central R.R...	Fabyan's
Con. & Mont'l R.R..	Base Mt. Wash.
Mt. Washington R'y.	Sum't Mt. Wash.

Through Rates.

	Unlim'd	Lim'd
Niagara Falls	$16.75	.....
Rochester	15.25	.....
Syracuse	13.65	. ..
Utica	12.65	.....

Route 525—Summit Mt. Washington, N. H. and Return.

Form Ex. 658.

R., W. & O. R.R.....to	Norwood
Cent. Vermont R.R..	Swanton
St. J. & L. C. R.R....	Lunenburg
Maine Central R.R...	Fabyan's
Con. & Mont'l R.R..	Base Mt. Wash.
Mt. Washington R'y.	Sum't Mt. Wash.

RETURNING SAME ROUTE.

Through Rates.

Niagara Falls	$29 40	Syracuse	$24 35
Rochester	27 40	Utica	22 45

Route 526—Summit Mt. Washington, N. H.

Form Ex. 655.

R., W. & O. R.R.....to	Norwood
Cent. Vermont R.R..	Montpelier
Mont. & W. R. R.R..	Wells River
Con. & Mont'l R.R...	Base Mt. Wash.
Mt. Washington R'y.	Sum't Mt. Wash.

Through Rates.

Niagara Falls	$16.75	Syracuse	$13.65
Rochester	15.25	Utica	12.65

Route 527—Summit Mt. Washington, N. H. and Return.

Form Ex. 656.

R., W. & O. R.R.....to	Norwood
Cent. Vermont R.R..	Montpelier
Mont. & W. R. R.R..	Wells River
Con. & Mont'l R.R...	Base Mt. Wash.
Mt. Washington R'y.	Sum't Mt. Wash.

RETURNING SAME ROUTE.

Through Rates.

Niagara Falls	$29.40	Syracuse	$24.35
Rochester	27.40	Utica	22.45

Route 528—Thousand Island Park, N. Y.

Form Ex. 652.

R., W. & O. R.R.....to	Clayton
Thous. Isl. St'b't Co.	Thous. Isl. Park

Through Rates.

Niagara Falls	$6.70	Syracuse	$3.75
Rochester	5.35	Utica	3.60

Route 529—Thousand Island Park, N. Y. and Return.

Form Ex. 653.

R., W. & O. R.R.....to	Clayton
Thous. Isl. St'b't Co.	Thous. Isl. Park

RETURNING SAME ROUTE.

Through Rates.

Rates may be obtained of all R., W. & O. R.R. Ticket Agents.

Route 530—Thousand Islands and Adirondack Tour.

Forms Ex. 254 and Ex. 851.

R., W. & O. R.R......to	Clayton
R. & O. Nav. Co......	Alexandria Bay
R. & O. Nav. Co.....	Montreal
N. Y. C. & H. R. R.R.	starting point

Through Rates.

Niagara Falls	$19.85	Rome	$14 95
Rochester	17.85	Utica	14.95
Syracuse	14.95		

Above Tour from Watertown, same route, to Montreal.

Forms Ex. 254 and Ex. 860.

N. Y. C. & H. R. R.R.to	Utica
R., W. & O. R.R.....	Watertown

Through Rate.

Watertown.............. $15.30

Above Tour from Oswego, same route, to Montreal.

Forms Ex. 251 and Ex. 861.

N. Y. C. & H. R. R.R.to	Syracuse
R., W. & O. R.R......	Oswego

Through Rate.

Oswego.......... ....$15.45

Route 531—Twin Mountain House, N. H.

Form N 12.

R., W. & O. R.R.....to	Norwood
Cent. Vermont R.R..	Swanton
St. J. & L. C. R.R....	Lunenburg
Maine Central R.R...	Twin Mt. House

Through Rates.

	Unlim'd	Lim'd
Niagara Falls	$12.65	.
Rochester	11.75	....
Syracuse	9.55	.....
Utica	8.55	.....

Route 532—Twin Mountain House, N. H. and Return.

Form Ex. 612.

R., W. & O. R.R.....to	Norwood
Cent. Vermont R.R..	Swanton
St. J. & L. C. R.R....	Lunenburg
Maine Central R.R...	Twin Mt. House

RETURNING SAME ROUTE.

Through Rates.

Niagara Falls	$23.20	Syracuse	$18.15
Rochester	21.20	Utica	16.25

Route 533—Twin Mountain House, N. H.

Forms Ex. 660 or N 14.

R., W. & O. R.R. .. to	Norwood
Cent. Vermont R.R..	Montpelier
Mont. & W. R. R.R..	Wells River
Con. & Mont'l R.R...	Twin Mt. House

Through Rates.

Niagara Falls	$12.65	Syracuse	$9.55
Rochester	11.15	Utica	8.55

Route 534—Twin Mountain House, N. H. and Return.

Forms Ex. 661 or Ex. 578.

R., W. & O. R.R.....to	Norwood
Cent. Vermont R.R..	Montpelier
Mont. & W. R. R.R..	Wells River
Con. & Mont'l R.R...	Twin Mt. House

RETURNING SAME ROUTE.

Through Rates.

Niagara Falls	$23.20	Syracuse	$18.15
Rochester	21.20	Utica	16.25

SEE NOTE ON PAGE 119 REGARDING STOP-OVER AT ALEXANDRIA BAY.

Route 535—Twin Mountain House, N. H.

Forms Ex. 254 and Ex. 408

R., W. & O. R.R.....to	Clayton
R. & O. Nav. Co......	Alexandria Bay
R. & O. Nav. Co......	Montreal
Grand Trunk R'y....	St. John's
Cent. Vermont R.R..	Montpelier
Mont. & W. R. R.R..	Wells River
Con. & Mont'l R.R..	Twin Mt. House

Through Rates.

Niagara Falls	$17.30	**Syracuse**	$14.45
Rochester	16.05	**Utica**	14.30

Route 536—Twin Mountain House, N. H.

Forms Ex. 254 and Ex. 659.

R., W. & O. R.R.....to	Clayton
R. & O. Nav. Co......	Alexandria Bay
R. & O. Nav. Co......	Montreal
Can. Pac. R'y........	Newport
Boston & Maine R.R.	Lunenburg
Maine Central R.R...	Twin Mt. House

Through Rates.

Niagara Falls	$17.30	**Syracuse**	$14.45
Rochester	16.05	**Utica**	14.30

Route 537—Watch Hill, R. I.

Form Ex. 562.

R., W. & O. R.R.....to	Norwood
Cent. Vermont R.R..	White River Jc.
Boston & Maine R.R.	Concord
Con. & Mont'l R.R...	Nashua
Boston & Maine R.R.	Boston
N.Y., N. H. & H. R.R.	Providence
N.Y., N.H. & H. R.R.	Stonington
Ferry..................	Watch Hill

Through Rates.

	Unlim'd	Lim'd
Niagara Falls	$20.15	$11.85
Rochester	18.80	11.55
Syracuse	17.20	.....
Utica	17.10	.....

Route 538—Watch Hill, R. I. and Return.

Form Ex. 563.

R., W. & O. R.R.....to	Norwood
Cent. Vermont R.R..	White River Jc.
Boston & Maine R.R.	Concord
Con. & Mont'l R.R...	Nashua
Boston & Maine R.R.	Boston
N.Y., N. H. & H. R.R.	Providence
N.Y., N.H. & H. R.R.	Stonington
Ferry..................	Watch Hill

RETURNING SAME ROUTE.

Through Rates.

	Unlim'd	Lim'd
Niagara Falls	$32.35	$22.65
Rochester	30.35	22.35
Syracuse	28.10	.....
Utica	26.65	.....

Route 539—Watch Hill, R. I and Return.

Form Ex. 564.

R., W. & O. R.R.....to	Norwood
Cent. Vermont R.R..	White River Jc.
Boston & Maine R.R.	Concord
Con. & Mont'l R.R...	Nashua
Boston & Maine R.R.	Boston
N.Y., N. H. & H. R.R.	Providence
N.Y., N. H. & H. R.R.	Stonington
Ferry..................	Watch Hill
Ferry..................	Stonington
N.Y., N. H. & H. R.R.	Providence
N.Y., N. H. & H. R.R.	Boston
Boston & Maine R.R.	North Conway
St. J. & L. C. R.R....	Lunenburg
Cent. Vermont R.R..	Rouse's Point
R., W. & O. R.R.....	starting point

Through Rates.

	Unlim'd	Lim'd
Niagara Falls	$37.85	$23.90
Rochester	35.85	22.05
Syracuse	33.60	.....
Utica	32.35	.....

Route 540—Whitefield, N. H.

Form N 12.

R., W. & O. R.R.....to	Norwood
Cent. Vermont R.R..	Swanton
St. J. & L. C. R.R....	Lunenburg
Maine Central R.R...	Whitefield

Through Rates.

	Unlim'd	Lim'd
Niagara Falls	$12.65	.....
Rochester	11.15	.....
Syracuse	9.55	.....
Utica	8.55	.....

Route 541—Whitefield, N. H. and Return.

Form Ex. 612.

R., W. & O. R.R.....to	Norwood
Cent. Vermont R.R...	Swanton
St. J. & L. C. R.R....	Lunenburg
Maine Central R.R...	Whitefield

RETURNING SAME ROUTE.

Through Rates.

Niagara Falls	$23.20	**Syracuse**	$18.15
Rochester	21.20	**Utica**	16.25

Route 542—Whitefield, N. H.

Forms Ex. 254 and Ex. 410.

R., W. & O. R.R.....to	Clayton
R. & O. Nav. Co.....	Alexandria Bay
R. & O. Nav. Co.....	Montreal
Grand Trunk R'y....	St. John's
Cent. Vermont R.R..	Montpelier
Mont. & W. R. R.R..	Wells River
Con. & Mont'l R.R..	Whitefield

Through Rates.

Niagara Falls	$17.15	**Syracuse**	$14.30
Rochester	15.90	**Utica**	14.15

Route 543—Whitefield, N. H.

Forms Ex. 254 and Ex. 660.

R., W. & O. R.R.....to	Clayton
R. & O. Nav. Co.....	Alexandria Bay
R. & O. Nav. Co.....	Montreal
Can. Pac. R'y........	Newport
Boston & Maine R.R.	Lunenburg
Maine Central R.R...	Whitefield

Through Rates.

Niagara Falls	$17.15	**Syracuse**	$14.30
Rochester	15.90	**Utica**	14.15

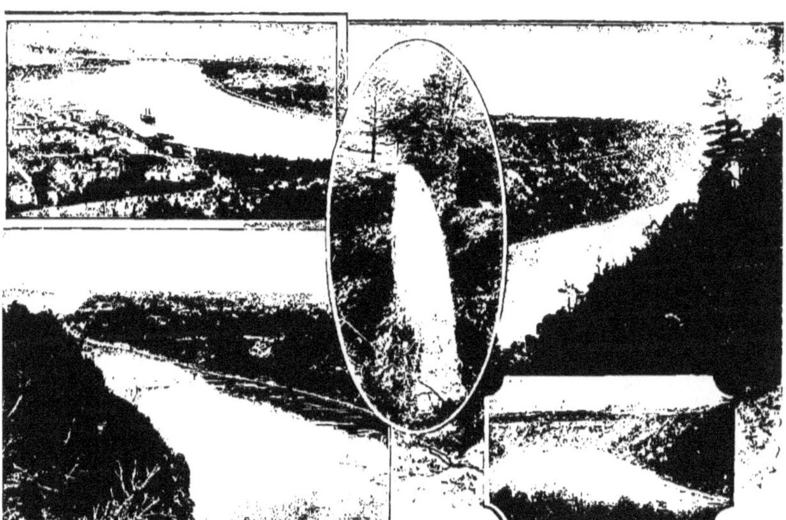

R., W. & O. R.R.—VIEWS ALONG THE NIAGARA RIVER.

SIDE TRIPS.

Ausable Chasm (Adirondacks) and Return. Ex. 195.

From Port Kent.

K., Ausable Ch. & L. Ch. R.R....... to Ausable Chasm

RETURNING SAME ROUTE.

Rate............50c.

Baldwin (Lake George) and Return. Ex. 126.

From Albany.

D. & H. R.R.........to Caldwell
L. George St'mb't Co. Baldwin

RETURNING SAME ROUTE.

Rate............$7.85

Bar Harbor (Mt. Desert Island) and Return.—Ex. 159.

From Portland.

Maine Central R.R.. to Bar Harbor

RETURNING SAME ROUTE.

Rate............$11.00

Limited to continuous passage in each direction.

Rate............$8.50

Bar Harbor (Mt. Desert Island) and Return.—Ex. 160.

From Portland.

Maine Central R.R...to Bath
Penob. Sh. Line R.R.. Rockland
Steamer.............. Bar Harbor

RETURNING SAME ROUTE.

Rate............$7.00

Bethlehem (White Mountains) and Return. Form Ex. 801 R.

From Zealand Junction.

Prof. & F. Notch R.R. to Bethlehem

RETURNING SAME ROUTE.

Rate............$1.00

Bethlehem (White Mountains).—Ex. 181.

From Bethlehem Junction.

Prof. & F. Notch R.R. to Bethlehem

Rate............50c.

Bethlehem (White Mountains) and Return.—Ex. 128.

From Bethlehem Junction.

Prof. & F. Notch R.R. to Bethlehem

RETURNING SAME ROUTE.

Rate............$1.00

Block Island, R. I. Form Ex. 196.

From Boston.

N.Y., N. H. & H. R.R. to Newport
Steamer.............. Block Island

Rate............$2.20

Block Island, R. I. and Return. Form Ex. 197.

From Boston.

N.Y., N. H. & H. R. .to Newport
Steamer.............. Block Island

RETURNING SAME ROUTE.

Rate............$3.50

Block Island, R. I. Form Ex. 803.

From New York.

Stonington Line......to Stonington
Ferry.................. Watch Hill
Steamer.............. Block Island

Rate............$2.40

Block Island, R. I. and Return. Form Ex. 804 R.

From New York.

Stonington Line......to Stonington
Ferry.................. Watch Hill
Steamer.............. Block Island

RETURNING SAME ROUTE.

Rate............$4.30

Boston, Mass.—Ex. 161.

From Portland.

International S.S. Co. to Boston

Rate............$1.00

Boston, Mass. and Return.—Ex. 162.

From Portland.

International S.S. Co. to Boston

RETURNING SAME ROUTE.

Rate............$2.00

Boston, Mass. and Return.—Ex. 163.

From Portland.

International S.S. Co. to Boston
Boston & Maine R.R. Portland

Rate............$4.00

Boston, Mass.—Ex. 214.

From New York.

Old Col. St'mb't Co. .to Fall River
N.Y., N. H. & H. R.R. Boston

Rate............$4.00

Boston, Mass. and Return.—Ex. 155.

From New York.

Old Col. St'mb't Co. .to Fall River
N.Y., N. H. & H. R.R. Boston

RETURNING SAME ROUTE.

Rate............$8.00

Boston, Mass. Form Ex. 219.

From New York.

Stonington Line......to Stonington
N.Y., N. H. & H. R.R. Providence
N.Y., N. H. & H. R.R. Boston

Rate............$4.00

Boston, Mass. and Return.—Ex. 156.

From New York.

Stonington Line......to Stonington
N.Y., N. H. & H. R.R. Providence
N.Y., N. H. & H. R.R. Boston

RETURNING SAME ROUTE.

Rate............$8.00

Boston, Mass. Form Ex. 221.

From New York.

Providence Line......to Providence
N.Y., N. H. & H. R.R. Boston

Rate............$4.00

Boston, Mass. and Return. Form Ex. 220 R.

From New York.

Providence Line......to Providence
N.Y., N. H. & H. R.R. Boston

RETURNING SAME ROUTE.

Rate............$8.00

Caldwell (Lake George) and Return. Ex. 125.

From Albany.

D. & H. R.R........ to Caldwell

RETURNING SAME ROUTE.

Rate............$4.85

Caldwell (Lake George) and Return. Ex. 173.

From Saratoga.

D. & H. R.R..........to Caldwell

RETURNING SAME ROUTE.

Rate............$2.88

Chatham, Mass. Form Ex. 198.

From Boston.

N.Y., N. H. & H. R.R. to Chatham

Rate............$2.40

Chatham, Mass. and Return. Form Ex. 199.

From Boston.

N.Y., N. H. & H. R.R. to Chatham

RETURNING SAME ROUTE.

Rate............$4.00

Chateaugay Chasm, N. Y. and Return. Ex. 136.

From Chateaugay.

Stage.................. to Ch't'gay Chasm

RETURNING SAME ROUTE.

Rate............50c.

Chicoutimi, P. Q., and Return. Form Ex. 782 R.

From Quebec.

Que. & L. St. J. R'y.. to Roberval
Que. & L. St. J. R'y.. Chicoutimi

RETURNING SAME ROUTE.

Rate............$9.00

Chicoutimi, P. Q., and Return. Form Ex. 783 R.

From Quebec.

Que. & L. St. J. R'y.. to Roberval
Que. & L. St. J. R'y.. Chicoutimi
R. & O. Nav. Co...... Quebec

Rate............$10.00

Cooperstown, N. Y. and Return.—Ex. 172.

From Richfield Springs.

Stage Line & St'mer.. to Cooperstown

RETURNING SAME ROUTE.

Rate............$2.00

Cottage City, Mass. Form Ex. 200.

From Boston.

N.Y., N. H. & H. R.R. to Cottage City

Rate............$2.35

Cottage City, Mass. and Return. Form Ex. 201.

From Boston.

N.Y., N. H. & H. R.R. to Cottage City

RETURNING SAME ROUTE.

Rate............$3.60

Crawford's (White Mountains).—Ex. 182.

From Fabyan's.

Maine Central R.R... to Crawford's

Rate............30c.

SEE NOTE ON PAGE 119 REGARDING STOP-OVER AT ALEXANDRIA BAY.

...wford's (White Mountains) and Return. Ex. 137.
From Fabyan's.
...ine Central R.R...to Crawford's
RETURNING SAME ROUTE.
Rate..........50c.

...abyan's (White Mountains).—Ex. 183.
From Glen Site.
...ge..................to Glen
...ine Central R.R... Fabyan's
Rate..........Off Sale.

...abyan's (White Mountains).—Ex. 184.
From Glen.
...ge..................to Glen Site
...ge.................. Sum't Mt.Wash.
..., Washington R'y.. Base
...1. & Mont'l R.R... Fabyan's
Rate..........$11.50

Falmouth, Mass.
Form Ex. 198.
From Boston.
...Y., N. H. & H. R.R...to Falmouth
Rate..........$1.65

Falmouth, Mass. and Return.
Form Ex. 199.
From Boston.
..., N. H. & H. R.R.to Falmouth
RETURNING SAME ROUTE.
Rate..........$2.75

Fisher's Island, N. Y.
Form Ex. 204.
From Boston.
..., N. H. & H. R.R.to Providence
..., N. H. & H. R.R. New London
...amer.............. Fisher's Island
Rate..........$2.85

Fisher's Island, N. Y. and Return.
Form Ex 205.
From Boston.
..., N. H. & H. R.R.to Providence
..., N. H. & H. R.R. New London
...mer.............. Fisher's Island
RETURNING SAME ROUTE.
Rate..........$5.70

Glen Site (White Mountains) and Return.—Ex. 143.
From Gorham.
...ge..................to Glen Site
RETURNING SAME ROUTE.
Rate..........Off Sale.

...n Site (White Mountains).—Ex. 185.
From Fabyan's.
...ne Central R.R...to Glen
...ge..................Glen Site
Rate..........Off Sale.

Glen Site (White Mountains) and Return.—Ex. 142.
From Glen.
...ge..................to Glen Site
RETURNING SAME ROUTE.
Rate..........Off Sale.

Glen Site (White Mountains) and Return.—Ex. 186.
From Fabyan's.
..., & Mont'l R.R...to Base Mt. Wash.
... Washington R'y.. Summit
...ge.................. Glen Site
...ge.................. Glen
...ne Central R.R... Fabyan's
Rate..........Off Sale.

Glen (White Mountains). Ex. 187.
From Fabyan's.
...ne Central R.R...to Glen
Rate..........$1.75

Ha-Ha Bay (Saguenay River) and Return. Ex. 193.
From Quebec.
R. & O. Nav. Co.....to Ha-Ha Bay
RETURNING SAME ROUTE.
Rate..........$8.00

Hyannis, Mass.
Form Ex. 198.
From Boston.
N.Y., N. H. & H. R.R.to Hyannis
Rate..........$1.90

Hyannis, Mass. and Return.
Form Ex. 199.
From Boston.
N.Y., N. H. & H. R.R.to Hyannis
RETURNING SAME ROUTE.
Rate..........$3.00

Lake Edward, P. Q., and Return.
Form Ex. 785 R.
From Quebec.
Que. & L. St. J. R'y..to Lake Edward
RETURNING SAME ROUTE.
Rate..........$4.50

Lake Placid (Adirondacks) and Return.
Form Ex. 817 R.
From Malone Junc.
N. Y. C. & H. R. R.R.to Saranac Lake
S. & L. P. R.R........ Lake Placid
RETURNING SAME ROUTE.
Rate..........$4 63

Loon Lake House (Adirondacks) and Return.
Form Ex. 814 R.
From Malone Junc.
N. Y. C. & H. R. R.R.to Loon Lake Sta.
Stage.................. Loon Lake H'se
RETURNING SAME ROUTE.
Rate..........$2.75

Magog (Lake Memphremagog) and Return. Ex. 154.
From Newport.
St'mr "Lady of Lake" to Magog
RETURNING SAME ROUTE.
Rate..........$1.00

Nantasket, Mass.
Form Ex. 198.
From Boston.
N.Y., N. H. & H. R.R.to Nantasket
Rate..........40c.

Nantasket, Mass. and Return.
Form Ex. 199.
From Boston.
N.Y., N. H. & H. R.R.to Nantasket
RETURNING SAME ROUTE.
Rate..........75c.

Nantucket, Mass.
Form Ex. 202.
From Boston.
N.Y., N. H. & H. R.R.to Nantucket
Rate..........$3.35

Nantucket, Mass. and Return.
Form Ex. 203.
From Boston.
N.Y., N. H. & H. R.R.to Nantucket
RETURNING SAME ROUTE.
Rate..........$4.00

Narragansett Pier, R. I.
Form Ex 206.
From Boston.
N.Y., N. H. & H. R.R.to Providence
N.Y., N. H. & H. R.R. Kingston
Narrag'sett Pier R.R. Narrag'sett Pier
Rate..........$2.18

Narragansett Pier, R. I. and Return.
Form Ex 207.
From Boston.
N.Y., N. H. & H. R.R.to Providence
N.Y., N. H. & H. R.R. Kingston
Narrag'sett Pier R.R. Narrag'sett Pier
RETURNING SAME ROUTE.
Rate..........$3.25

Narragansett Pier, R. I.
Form Ex. 805.
From New York.
Stonington Line......to Stonington
N.Y., N. H. & H. R.R. Kingston
Narrag'sett Pier R.R.. Narrag'sett Pier
Rate..........$2.81

Narragansett Pier, R. I. and Return.
Form Ex. 806 R.
From New York.
Stonington Line......to Stonington
N.Y., N. H. & H. R.R. Kingston
Narrag'sett Pier R.R. Narrag'sett Pier
RETURNING SAME ROUTE.
Rate..........$5.00

Newport, R. I.
Form Ex. 198.
From Boston.
N.Y., N. H. & H. R.R.to Newport
Rate..........$1.70

Newport, R. I. and Return.—Ex. 131.
From Boston.
N. Y., N. H. & H. R.R.to Newport
RETURNING SAME ROUTE.
Rate..........$2.50

New York, N. Y.—Ex. 215.
From Boston.
N.Y., N. H. & H. R.R.to Fall River
Old Col. St'mbt Co... New York
Rate..........$4.00

New York, N. Y. and Return.—Ex. 216.
From Boston.
N. Y., N. H. & H. R.R.to Fall River
Old Col. St'mbt Co... New York
RETURNING SAME ROUTE.
Rate..........$8.00

New York.
Form Ex. 222.
From Boston.
N. Y., N.H. & H. R.R.to Providence
Providence Line...... New York
Rate..........$4.00

New York and Return.
Form Ex. 224 R.
From Boston.
N.Y., N. H. & H. R.R.to Providence
Providence Line...... New York
RETURNING SAME ROUTE.
Rate..........$8.00

New York and Return.
Form Ex. 800 R.
From Boston.
N.Y., N. H. & H. R.R.to Providence
N.Y., N. H. & H. R.R. Stonington
Stonington Line...... New York
Rate..........$8.00

New York, N. Y.—Ex. 179.
From Albany.
Day Line Steamers...to New York
Rate.......... $2.00

New York, N. Y.—Ex. 180.
From Albany.
People's Line St'rs...to New York
Rate..........$1.50

SEE NOTE ON PAGE 119 REGARDING STOP-OVER AT ALEXANDRIA BAY.

North Conway (White Mountains) and Return.—Ex. 138.
From Fabyan's.
Maine Central R.R...to North Conway
RETURNING SAME ROUTE.
Rate............$3.00

North Creek (Adirondacks) and Return. Ex. 174.
From Saratoga.
Adirondack R'y......to North Creek
RETURNING SAME ROUTE.
Rate............$3.50

Old Orchard Beach, Me. and Return, Ex. 164.
From Portland.
Boston & Maine R.R. to Old Orchard B'h
RETURNING SAME ROUTE.
Rate............50c.

Ottawa, Canada, and Return.—Ex. 132.
From Brockville.
Can. Pac. R'y..........to Ottawa
RETURNING SAME ROUTE.
Rate............$3.50

Ottawa, Canada, and Return.—Ex. 165.
From Prescott.
Can. Pac. R'y.........to Ottawa
RETURNING SAME ROUTE.
Rate............$3.50

Ottawa, Canada, and Return.—Ex. 150.
From Montreal.
Can. Pac. R'y.........to Ottawa
RETURNING SAME ROUTE.
Rate............$5.00

Ottawa, Canada, and Return.—Ex. 151.
From Montreal.
Can. Pac. R'y.........to Ottawa
Ottawa River N. Co.. Montreal
Rate............$5.00

Paul Smith's (Adirondacks) and Return
Form Ex. 813 R.
From Malone Junc.
N. Y. C. & H. R. R.R.to Paul Smith's Sta
Stage................. Paul Smith's
RETURNING SAME ROUTE.
Rate $3.47

Plymouth, Mass.
Form Ex. 198.
From Boston.
N.Y., N. H. & H. R.R.to Plymouth
Rate............90c.

Plymouth, Mass. and Return.
Form Ex. 199.
From Boston.
N.Y., N. H. & H. R.R.to Plymouth
RETURNING SAME ROUTE.
Rate............$1.50

Poland Springs, Me.
Form Ex. 818.
From Portland.
Maine Central R.R. { to Danville or Poland Springs Jc.
Portland and Rumford Falls R'y and Stage or H. Ricker & Son's Stage } Poland Springs
Rate............$2.00

Poland Springs, Me. and Return.
Form Ex. 818 R.
From Portland.
Maine Central R.R. { to Danville or Poland Springs Jc.
Portland and Rumford Falls R'y and Stage or H. Ricker & Son's Stage } Poland Springs
RETURNING SAME ROUTE.
Rate...........$3.00

Portland, Me.—Ex. 130.
From Boston.
International S.S. Co.to Portland
Rate.............$1.00

Profile House (White Mountains) and Return.—Ex. 129.
From Bethlehem Junction.
P. & F. Notch R.R...to Profile House
RETURNING SAME ROUTE.
Rate............$3.00

Profile House (White Mountains) and Return.
Form Ex. 602 R.
From Zealand Junction.
Prof. & F. Notch R.R.to Profile House
RETURNING SAME ROUTE.
Rate............$3.00

Provincetown, Mass.
Form Ex. 196.
From Boston.
N.Y., N. H. & H. R.R.to Provincetown
Rate............$2.85

Provincetown, Mass. and Return.
Form Ex. 199.
From Boston.
N.Y., N. H. & H. R.R.to Provincetown
RETURNING SAME ROUTE.
Rate............$4.80

Quebec, P. Q.—Ex. 191.
From Montreal.
Grand Trunk R'y or R. & O. Nav. Co. } to Quebec
Rate............$3.00

Quebec, P. Q.—Ex. 189.
From Montreal.
Can. Pac. R'y or R. & O. Nav. Co. } to Quebec
Rate............$3.00

Quebec, P. Q. and Return.—Ex. 194.
From Montreal.
Grand Trunk R'y or R. & O. Nav. Co. } to Quebec
RETURNING SAME ROUTE.
Rate............$5.00

Quebec, P. Q. and Return.—Ex. 190.
From Montreal.
Can. Pac. R'y or R. & O. Nav. Co. } to Quebec
RETURNING SAME ROUTE.
Rate............$5.00

Roberval, P. Q.—Ex. 648.
From Quebec.
Que. & L. St. J. R'y..to Roberval
Rate............$5.70

Roberval, P. Q. and Return.—Ex. 649.
From Quebec.
Que. & L. St. J. R'y..to Roberval
RETURNING SAME ROUTE.
Rate............$7.50

Saranac Inn Hotel (Adirondacks) and Return.
Form Ex. 816 R.
From Malone Junc.
N. Y. C. & H. R. R.R.to Saranac Inn Sta.
Stage................. Saranac Inn H'l
RETURNING SAME ROUTE.
Rate...........$3.70

Saranac Lake and Return.
Form Ex. 815 R.
From Malone Junc.
N. Y. C. & H. R. R.R.to Saranac Lake
RETURNING SAME ROUTE.
Rate...........$2.88

Saratoga, N. Y. and Return.—Ex. 127.
From Albany.
D. & H. R.R.........to Saratoga
RETURNING SAME ROUTE.
Rate...........$2.34

Saratoga, N. Y. and Return.—Ex. 176.
From South Schenectady.
D. & H. R.R..........to Saratoga
RETURNING SAME ROUTE.
Rate............$1.84

Ste. Anne de Beaupre and Return.
Form Ex. 186 R.
From Quebec.
Q., M. & Char. R'y { to Ste. Anne de Beaupré
RETURNING SAME ROUTE.
Rate............1.20

Summit Mt. Washington (White Mountains) and Return.—Ex. 139.
From Fabyan's.
Con. & Mont'l R.R...to Base
Mt. Washington R'y. Summit
RETURNING SAME ROUTE.
Rate...........$6.00

Summit Mt. Washington (White Mountains) and Return.—Ex. 140.
From Fabyan's.
Con. & Mont'l R.R...to Base
Mt. Washington R'y. Summit
Stage................ Glen Site
Stage................ Glen
Maine Central R.R... Fabyan's
Rate............$11.25

Tadousac (Saguenay River) and Return. Ex. 192.
From Quebec.
R. & O. Nav. Co.....to Tadousac
RETURNING SAME ROUTE.
Rate............$5.00

Toronto, Canada, and Return.—Ex. 157.
From Niagara Falls.
N. Y. C. & H. R. R.R.to Lewiston
Niag'a Nav. Co's Str. Toronto
RETURNING SAME ROUTE.
Rate............$2.25

Watch Hill, R. I.
Form Ex. 208
From Boston.
N.Y., N. H. & H. R.R.to Providence
N.Y., N. H. & H. R.R. Stonington
Ferry.................. Watch Hill
Rate............$2.45

Watch Hill, R. I. and Return.
Form Ex. 209.
From Boston.
N.Y., N. H. & H. R.R.to Providence
N.Y., N. H. & H. R.R. Stonington
Ferry.................. Watch Hill
RETURNING SAME ROUTE.
Rate............$3.85

Watch Hill, R. I.
Form Ex. 807.
From New York.
Stonington Line......to Stonington
Ferry.................. Watch Hill
Rate............$1.75

Watch Hill, R. I. and Return.
Form Ex. 808 R.
From New York.
Stonington Line......to Stonington
Ferry.................. Watch Hill
RETURNING SAME ROUTE.
Rate............$3.40

Waterbury, Vt. and Return.—Ex. 171.
From Rouse's Point.
Cent. Vermont R.R..to Waterbury
RETURNING SAME ROUTE.
Rate............$3.50

SEE NOTE ON PAGE 119 REGARDING STOP-OVER AT ALEXANDRIA BAY.

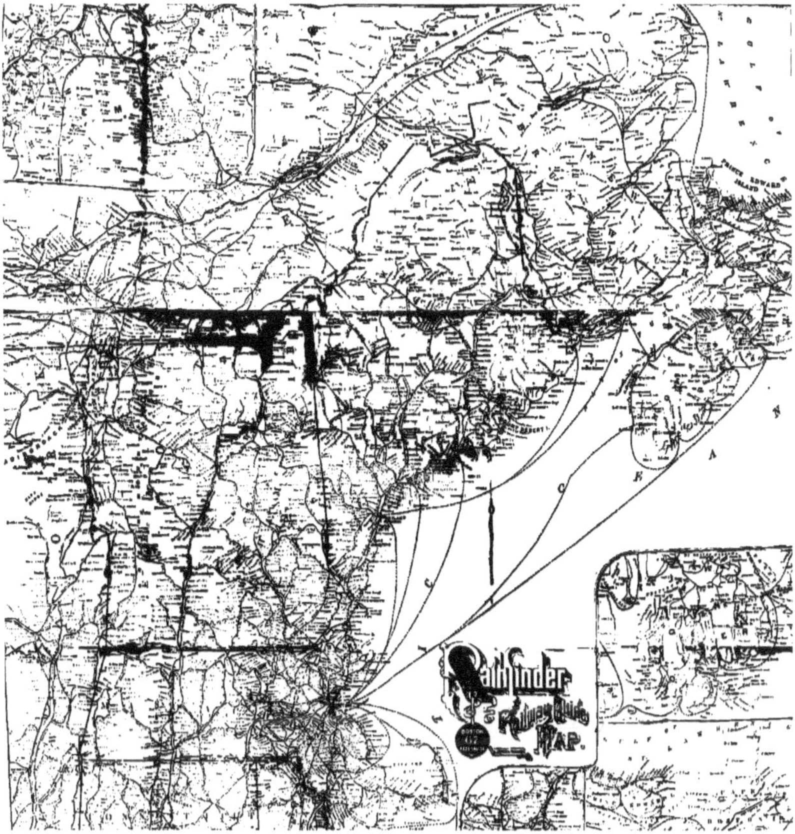
Pathfinder
Railway Guide
MAP.

DEWEY ISLAND—SUMMER HOME OF E. H. DEWEY, NEW YORK.

ROME, WATERTOWN & OGDENSBURG RAILROAD

N. Y. C. & H. R. R.R. CO. LESSEE

List of Summer Hotels and Boarding Houses

SEASON OF 1895.

NOTE—Under the heading of Region, localities designated are as follows:
NORTHERN NEW YORK—This section of the country is noted for its pure air, and the places described in this region are within a few miles of the great North Woods.
NORTH WOODS—This region is celebrated for its pure air and water, and is unrivaled in health-restoring properties. Persons sojourning in these woods, which have the characteristics of the primeval forest, can enjoy excellent trout fishing, and by a journey of a few miles in almost any direction find numerous lakes of the Adirondack region and good deer shooting.
ADIRONDACK REGION—This region embraces the western slope of the mountains, and the primeval forest noted for its pure, balsamic air, and numerous streams and lakes, and from the great abundance of trout and deer found within its limits it is aptly termed the sportsman's paradise. The hunting and fishing grounds of the Adirondack region are reached only via the ROME, WATERTOWN & OGDENSBURG RAILROAD.
THOUSAND ISLANDS—Places named in this section are in the midst of the Thousand Islands and fishing grounds of the River St. Lawrence.
ST. LAWRENCE RIVER—Designates places on the St. Lawrence River in the vicinity of, but not among, the Thousand Islands.
LAKE ONTARIO—Resorts named in this region are noted for good fishing, and are pleasant places to spend the summer.
LAKE CHAMPLAIN—Resorts named in this section are on or near Lake Champlain.
WHITE MOUNTAINS—Designates the well-known resorts in the White Mountain region.
MAINE HILLS—Resorts named in this section are in the Lake and Hill regions of Maine.
ATLANTIC COAST—Designates the much frequented sea-coast resorts of Maine, New Hampshire and Massachusetts.

REGION.	Name of Hotel.	Proprietor.	Post-Office Address.	Room Capacity.	Rate per Day.	Rate per Week.	Nearest Railroad Station.	Dist. from R. R. Sta. in miles.	How Reached from Railroad Station.
Niagara Falls	Cataract House	J. E. Devereux, M'ger	Niagara Falls, N. Y.	600	$4 00	*	Niagara Falls	near	Omnibus
do	International Hotel	H. C. Fox, M'ger	Niagara Falls, N. Y.	600	4 00	*	Niagara Falls	near	Omnibus
do	Hotel Kaltenbach	A. Kaltenbach	Niagara Falls, N. Y.	50	3 00	*	Niagara Falls	near	Omnibus
do	Hotel Atlantique	D. Detrick	Niagara Falls, N. Y.	75	2 00	*	Niagara Falls	near	Omnibus
do	Prospect House	D. Isaacs	Niagara Falls, N. Y.	150	3 to 4	*	Niagara Falls	near	Omnibus
do	Hotel Porter	R. P. Murphy	Niagara Falls, N. Y.	75	3 50-5	*	Niagara Falls	near	Walk
do	Niagara House	John Hayes	Niagara Falls, N. Y.	75	2 00	*	Niagara Falls	near	Omnibus
do	Salt's New Hotel	F. H. Salt	Niagara Falls, N. Y.	150	2 00	$10 00	Niagara Falls	near	Walk
do	Imperial Hotel	C. N. Owen	Niagara Falls, N. Y.	175	2 00	*	Niagara Falls	near	Walk
do	Temperance Hotel	C. R. Phelps	Niagara Falls, N. Y.	60	1 50	*	Niagara Falls	near	Omnibus
do	United States Hotel	M. McMahon	Niagara Falls, N. Y.	60	2 00	*	Niagara Falls	near	Walk
do	Niagara Falls House	R. A. Ferguson	Niagara Falls, N. Y.	75	2 00	*	Niagara Falls	near	Omnibus
do	Falls Hotel	W. H. Whiting	Niagara Falls, N. Y.	30	1 50	*	Niagara Falls	near	Omnibus
	On Canadian Side.								
do	Clifton House	G. M. Colburn	Niagara Falls, N. Y.	400	4 00	*	Niagara Falls	½m	Omnibus
do	Hotel Dolphin	S. K. Wilder	Station A, Niagara Falls, N. Y.	135	2 00	10 00	Susp. Bridge	near	Walk
do	Columbian House	J. V. Carr	Niagara Falls, N. Y.	60	2 00	*	Niagara Falls	near	Walk
do	European Hotel	Frank Nosway	Niagara Falls, N. Y.	60	2 00	*	Niagara Falls	near	Walk

Niagara Falls	Atwood's W. Hotel	Walter P. Horne	Station A, Niagara Falls, N.Y.	60	$2 00	$10 00	Susp. Bridge	near	Walk
do	New Spencer House	J. J. & C. H. Mahoney	Station A, Niagara Falls, N.Y.	20	2 00	10 00	Susp. Bridge	near	Walk
do	N. Y. Central Hotel	J. Felix Nassoiy	Station A, Niagara Falls, N.Y.	60	2 00	10 50	Susp. Bridge	near	Walk
do	Exchange Hotel	Jos. Shickaluna	Station A, Niagara Falls, N.Y.	20	2 00	10 50	Susp. Bridge	near	Walk
do	Pitze Hotel	P. Pitze	Lewiston, N.Y.	30	2 00	8 00	Lewiston	1½m	Omnibus; fare, 25 cents
do	Frontier House	M. Raymond	Lewiston, N.Y.	50	2 00	7 00	Lewiston	1½m	Omnibus; fare, 25 cents
do	American Hotel	H. Cornell	Lewiston, N.Y.	40	2 00	8 00	Lewiston	1½m	Omnibus; fare, 25 cents
Lake Ontario	Hotel Sutherland	Secord & Bigger	Wilson, Niagara Co., N.Y.	80	2 00	6 00 to 12 00	Wilson	¾m	Free omnibus
do	Temperance House	T. U. Parsons	Wilson, Niagara Co., N.Y.	20	1 00	5 00	Wilson	⅓m	Omnibus; fare, 10 cents
do	Grove House	W. H. Tenbrook	Olcott, Niagara Co., N.Y.	17	2 00	7 50	Newfane	1⅓m	Stage; fare, 10 cents
do	Lake Shore House	W. J. Blackley	Olcott, Niagara Co., N.Y.	14	2 00	7 50	Newfane	1¼m	Stage; fare, 10 cents
do	Boarding House	P. M. Humphrey	Olcott, Niagara Co., N.Y.	7	1 00	5 00	Newfane	1½m	Stage; fare, 10 cents
do	Cottage Boarding H'se.	O. W. Baker	Olcott, Niagara Co., N.Y.	12	1 00	5 00	Newfane	1m	Carriage
do	Barker's House	W. McAdams	Barker's, Niagara Co., N.Y.	15	1 50	3 50 to 7 00	Somerset	near	Walk
do	Lyndonville Hotel	Mrs. Warren	Lyndonville, Orleans Co., N.Y.	20	1 50	....	Lyndonville	near	Omnibus
do	Johnson's Hotel	A. Johnson	Waterport, Orleans Co., N.Y.	15	1 00	4 50	Waterport	½m	Stage; fare, 10 cents
do	Lakeside Hotel	B. S. Hoag	Lakeside Park, Orleans Co., N.Y.	100	1-2 00	7 00 to 14 00	Waterport	4m	Stage daily, 4 p.m.; fare, 25 cents
do	Ontario House	M. J. Storer, Troutb'g.	Morton, Orleans Co., N.Y.	25	2 00	8 00	Morton	2½m	Livery, 75 cents
do	Bush House	Van R. Cady, Troutb'g	Morton, Orleans Co., N.Y.	50	1 00	5 00	Morton	2½m	Free omnibus
do	Hamlin House	D. R. Singleton	Hamlin, Monroe Co., N.Y.	20	1 50	5 00	Hamlin	½m	Carriage, if notified
do	Park House	A. M. La Barron	East Hamlin, Monroe Co., N.Y.	50	1 00	3 50	East Hamlin	¼m	Livery
do	Lake House	W. Barrend	East Hamlin, Monroe Co., N.Y.	50	1 00	3 50	East Hamlin	3m	Livery
do	North Parma House	John Piggott	North Parma, Monroe Co., N.Y.	12	1 50	4 00	Parma	near	Walk
do	Commercial House	A. D. Clint	North Parma, Monroe Co., N.Y.	12	1 50	4 00	Parma	near	Walk
do	Hotel Ontario	W. Sweency	Charlotte, Monroe Co., N.Y.	100	3 to 4	15 00	Charlotte	¼m	
do	Cottage Hotel	E. P. Olmstead, M'ger.	Charlotte, Monroe Co., N.Y.	150	3 to 4	15 00	Charlotte	¼m	
do	Wurtz Cottage	Mrs. Wurtz	Charlotte, Monroe Co., N.Y.	20	2 00	10 00	Charlotte	¼m	
do	Lotta House	F. Beattey	Charlotte, Monroe Co., N.Y.	25	2 00	10 00	Charlotte	¼m	
do	Hotel Kensington	H. Cole	Charlotte, Monroe Co., N.Y.	50	2 00	10 00	Charlotte	¼m	
do	Powers Hotel	Buck & Sanger	Rochester, N.Y.	200	4 00	*	Rochester	....	Street car
do	Whitcomb House	Whitcomb & Downs	Rochester, N.Y.	141	2 00	*	Rochester	....	Street car
do	New Osborne	Elmer E. Almy	Rochester, N.Y.	175	2 00	*	Rochester	....	Street car
do	Hotel Brunswick	Ernst Brucher	Rochester, N.Y.	65	Eur.	*	Rochester	....	Street car
do	Congress Hall	J. A. Maxwell	Rochester, N.Y.	80	2 00	*	Rochester	....	Street car
do	National Hotel	J. W. Hannan	Rochester, N.Y.	60	2 00	*	Rochester	....	Street car
do	Hotel Livingston	H. Gallagher	Rochester, N.Y.	125	2 to 3	*	Rochester	....	Street car
do	Palmer Place	Mrs. O. C. Palmer	Union Hill, Monroe Co., N.Y.	6	1 50	7 00	Union Hill	2½m	Private conveyance
do	Private Residence	H. Deyo	Union Hill, Monroe Co., N.Y.	5	1 50	5 00	Union Hill	3m	Private conveyance
do	Williamson Hotel	John Olmsted	Williamson, Wayne Co., N.Y.	40	2 00	7 00	Williamson	⅞m	Omnibus; fare, 10 cents
do	Railroad House	F. E. Derrin	Williamson, Wayne Co., N.Y.	10	1 50	5 00	Williamson	near	Walk
do	Lake View House	V. B. Shaw	Pultneyville, Wayne Co., N.Y.	....	1 50	5 00	Williamson	3m	Omnibus; fare, 25 cents
do	Whitney House	E. N. Snyder	Sodus, Wayne Co., N.Y.	50	2 00	8 00	Sodus	½m	Omnibus; fare, 10 cents
do	Van Tassell House	J. Van Tassell	Sodus, Wayne Co., N.Y.	25	1 50	5 00	Sodus	½m	Omnibus; fare, 10 cents
do	Wallington Hotel	C. D. Lent	Wallington, Wayne Co., N.Y.	20	1 50	4 50	Wallington	near	Walk
do	Spencer House	G. B. Ackerman	Wallington, Wayne Co., N.Y.	20	1 00	4 20	Wallington	near	Walk
do	Shaver Hotel	A. Shaver	Wallington, Wayne Co., N.Y.	10	1 25	3 50	Wallington	near	Walk
do	Lake Bluff Hotel	E. B. Fuller	Sodus Point, N.Y.	200	2 00	8 00	Rose	8m	Livery
do	Bay View Hotel	C. Kelly	Port Glasgow, N.Y.	100	2 00	....	Rose	2½m	Livery to Port Glasgow
do	North Rose Hotel	H. Countermarsh	North Rose, N.Y.	15	1 50	....	Rose	near	Walk
do	Rose Valley	M. Brant	Rose, N.Y.	12	1 50	....	Rose	2½m	Stage
do	Resort Bay Hotel	A. Sherman	Rose, N.Y.	10	1 50	5 00	Rose	2m	Stage
do	Wolcott House	S. A. Williams	Wolcott, Wayne Co., N.Y.	150	2 00	6 00 to 10 00	Wolcott	½m	Omnibus; fare, 10 cents
do	Railroad House	M. P. Connor	Wolcott, Wayne Co., N.Y.	50	1 00	4 00	Wolcott	near	
do	Boarding House	Mrs. Wm. Colburn	Wolcott, Wayne Co., N.Y.	50	1 00	4 00	Wolcott	½m	
do	Red Creek House	H. C. Van Alstine	Red Creek, N.Y.	....	1 50	....	Red Creek	near	Free omnibus
do	Taylor House	Mrs. E. Taylor	Red Creek, N.Y.	....	1 50	....	Red Creek	near	Free omnibus
do	Cayuga House	K. Shaw	Sterling, Cayuga Co., N.Y.	20	1 00	....	Sterling Valley	1m	Private conveyance
do	Hotel Dietel	W. I. Allen	Fair Haven, N.Y.	....	2 00	8 00 to 12 00	Fair Haven	near	Walk
do	Russell House	J. N. Russell	Fair Haven, N.Y.	30	1 50	5 00	Fair Haven	¼m	Carriage
do	American Hotel	Mrs. E. C. Van Auken	Hannibal, Oswego Co., N.Y.	30	2 00	....	Hannibal	½m	Omnibus; fare, 10 cents

LIST OF SUMMER HOTELS AND BOARDING HOUSES.

REGION.	Name of Hotel.	Proprietor.	Post-Office Address.	Room Capacity.	Rate per Day.	Rate per Week.	Nearest Rail-road Station.	Dist. from R. R. Sta. in miles.	How Reached from Railroad Station.
Lake Ontario	Doolittle House	J. G. Bennett	Oswego, Oswego Co., N.Y	130	$2 to 3	$12 00 to 21 00	Oswego	near	Omnibus
do	Lake Shore Hotel	C. E. Keyes	Oswego, Oswego Co., N.Y	75	2 00	7 00 to 14 00	Oswego	near	
do	Hamilton House	Burch & Ott	Oswego, Oswego Co., N.Y	70	1 50	7 00	Oswego	near	Omnibus
do	Ringland House	Mrs. Joseph Ringland	Oswego, Oswego Co., N.Y	50	1 00	5 00 to 7 00	Oswego	near	Omnibus
do	Rathbun Place	Daniel Perry	Oswego, Oswego Co., N.Y., P.O. Box 1266	15	1 25	5 00 to 7 00	Oswego	3m	Carriage will meet guests
do	Private Residence	Mrs. E. Corning Lamb	Fruit Valley, Oswego Co., N.Y	6	1 00	6 00	Oswego	1½m	Free carriage, if notified
do	Oak Spring	Mrs. F. T. Payne	Fulton, Oswego Co., N.Y., P.O. Box 924	....	......	6 00 to 7 00	Fulton	2m	Free carriage, if notified
do	Pleasant Point Hotel	Capt. S. Nichols	Demster, Oswego Co., N.Y	75	2 00	7 00 to 10 00	New Haven	2m	Livery
do	Demster Beach Hotel	Jerome Fones	Demster, Oswego Co., N.Y	60	2 00	7 00 to 10 00	New Haven	1m	Free omnibus
do	Mexico House	Noble & Dawley	Mexico, Oswego Co., N.Y	20	2 00	10 00	Mexico	1m	Free omnibus
do	Boyd House	Capt. D. Boyd	Mexico, Oswego Co., N.Y	35	2 00	10 00	Mexico	¾m	Free omnibus
do	Maplewood Lawn	G. H. Utter	Mexico, Oswego Co., N.Y	....	1 25	7 00	Mexico	¾m	Free omnibus
do	Wright's Hotel	Geo. Hinds, Mex. Pt.	Texas, Oswego Co., N.Y	30	2 00	4 00 to 5 00	Mexico	4m	Stage
do	Lake Grove House	F. M. Earle, Mex. Pt.	Texas, Oswego Co., N.Y	100	2 00	10 00	Mexico	4m	Stage
do	Mexico Point Inn	L. M. Hayes	Mexico Point, Oswego Co., N. Y	30	2 00	800 to 10 00	Mexico	4m	Carriage or Stage
Central N. Y.	The Yates	Averill & Gregory	Syracuse, N.Y	400	4 00	*	Syracuse	near	Omnibus
do	Globe Hotel	Spaulding & Nealy	Syracuse, N.Y	150	2 50–3	*	Syracuse	near	Omnibus
do	Vanderbilt	Jas. A. Barry	Syracuse, N.Y	150	2 50–3	*	Syracuse	near	Omnibus
do	Empire House	E. T. Talbot	Syracuse, N.Y	160	2 00	*	Syracuse	near	Omnibus
do	Congress Hall	R. S. Town	Syracuse, N.Y	65	2–2 50	*	Syracuse	near	Walk
do	Hotel Burns	Townsend Bros.	Syracuse, N.Y	116	2 00	*	Syracuse	near	Walk
do	Dixon Hotel	Leland & Hickok	Syracuse, N.Y	75	1 70	*	Syracuse	near	Walk
do	Candee House	C. E. Candee	Syracuse, N.Y	140	2 00	*	Syracuse	near	Omnibus
do	Kingsley House		Syracuse, N.Y	40	1 50	*	Syracuse	near	Omnibus
do	Onondaga House	J. E. Dockery	Syracuse, N.Y	56	1 50	*	Syracuse	near	Walk
do	Mansion Hotel	Hand & Gang	Syracuse, N.Y	60	1 00	*	Syracuse	near	Walk
do	Seneca House	J. W. Shipman	Syracuse, N.Y	52	1–1 50	*	Syracuse	near	Walk
do	Amos Hotel	N. Lattimer	Syracuse, N.Y	30	1 50	*	Syracuse	near	Walk
do	Clarendon Hotel	M. A. Clapp	Syracuse, N.Y	40	2 00	*	Syracuse	near	Walk
do	Syracuse House	Geo. Wollner	Syracuse, N.Y	38	1 00	*	Syracuse	near	Walk
do	Hart House	Charles Hart	Syracuse, N.Y	30	1 00	*	Syracuse	near	Walk
do	Windsor House	T. A. Rockfellow	Syracuse, N.Y	25	1 00	*	Syracuse	near	Walk
do	Ft. Brewerton House	H. Emmons	Brewerton, Onondaga Co., N.Y	20	1 00	6 00	Brewerton	near	Walk
do	Washburn House	C. E. Washburn	Brewerton, Onondaga Co., N.Y	40	1 25	6 00	Brewerton	near	Walk
do	Miller House	Wm. Miller	Brewerton, Onondaga Co., N.Y	20	1 00	5 00	Brewerton	near	Walk
do	Private House	Burnet Wood	Brewerton, Onondaga Co., N.Y	5	1 00	5 00	Brewerton	near	Walk
do	Private House	Jas. Sweeney	Brewerton, Onondaga Co., N.Y	7	1 00	5 00	Brewerton	near	Walk
do	Johnson House	W. H. Johnson	Central Square, Oswego Co., N.Y	20	1 20	8 00	Central Square	½m	Stage; fare, 10 cents
do	Fancher House	Lewis Fancher	Central Square, Oswego Co., N.Y	20	1 00	6 00	Central Square	½m	Stage; fare, 10 cents
do	Revoir House	P. Revoir	Mallory, Oswego Co., N.Y	10	1 00	4 00	Mallory	1¼m	Stage; fare, 10 cents
do	Hewitt House	Geo. J. Loren	Hastings, Oswego Co., N.Y	12	1 50	6 00	Hastings	1m	Stage; fare, 10 cents
Northern N. Y.	Commercial Hotel	Ackley Bros.	Parish, Oswego Co., N.Y	25	2 00	5 00	Parish	½m	Stage; fare, 10 cents
do	Snell House	L. D. Snell	Parish, Oswego Co., N.Y	25	1 50	4 00	Parish	½m	Stage; fare, 10 cents
do	Empire House	C. H. Heller	Parish, Oswego Co., N.Y	25	1 50	4 00	Parish	near	Walk
do	Hotel Randall	Benj. D. Randall	Pulaski, Oswego Co., N.Y	31	2 00	7 00 upwards	Pulaski	¼m	Omnibus
do	Salmon River House	Hubbard & Bishop	Pulaski, Oswego Co., N.Y	20	2 00	6 00	Pulaski	¼m	Omnibus
do	Kelly House	Kelly Bros.	Pulaski, Oswego Co., N.Y	15	2 00	....	Pulaski	¼m	Omnibus
do	Bliss House	Mrs. C. J. Powers	Pulaski, Oswego Co., N.Y	11	1 50	4 00 to 5 00	Pulaski	¼m	Omnibus
do	Pulaski House	A. H. Springsteen	Pulaski, Oswego Co., N.Y	20	1 50	3 50 to 6 00	Pulaski	¼m	Omnibus
do	Railroad Boarding H'se	H. E. Macomber	Pulaski, Oswego Co., N.Y	10	1 00	5 00	Pulaski	near	Walk

Northern N.Y.	Boarding House	Mrs. A. S. Richards	Pulaski, Oswego Co., N.Y.	15	$1 00	$4 00	Pulaski	¼m	Omnibus
do	Port Ontario Hotel	Wm. Place	Port Ontario, Oswego Co., N.Y.	40	1 00	5 00	Pulaski	3m	Will meet guests
Central N. Y.	Stanwix Hall	Levis & Warner	Rome, N.Y.	80	2 50	10 00	Rome	near	Free omnibus
do	Arlington Hotel	S. Hodge	Rome, N.Y.	100	2 00	10 00	Rome	near	Free omnibus
do	Commercial Hotel	J. Cackett	Rome, N.Y.	56	1 50	6 00	Rome	near	Free omnibus
do	Willett House	Daniel Tully	Rome, N.Y.	30	1 00	5 00	Rome	near	Walk
dc	Mansion House	R. Brown	Rome, N.Y.	30	1 00	5 00	Rome	near	Walk
do	Temperance House	Sam. Tallman	Rome, N.Y.	60	1 00	5 00	Rome	near	Walk
do	United States Hotel	O. L. Peck	Taberg, Oneida Co., N.Y.	30	1 00	4 50	Taberg	2½m	Stage; fare, 15 cents
do	O'Connor's Hotel	J. J. O'Connor	Taberg, Oneida Co., N.Y.	10	1 00	4 50	Taberg	2¼m	Stage; fare, 15 cents
do	Mitchell House	John Mitchell	Taberg, Oneida Co., N.Y.	6	1 00	4 50	Taberg	2½m	Stage; fare, 15 cents
do	Union House	A. B. Chrestien	McConnellsville, Oneida Co., N.Y.	15	1 00	4 00	McConnellsville	½m	Stage; fare, 10 cents
do	Boarding House	R. Tuttle	McConnellsville, Oneida Co., N.Y.	8	1 00	4 00	McConnellsville	½m	Stage; fare, 10 cents
do	Whitney House	D. J. Crimmins	Camden, Oneida Co., N.Y.	50	2 00	5 00	Camden	near	Omnibus
do	Commercial House	C. L. Roberts	Camden, Oneida Co., N.Y.	30	2 00	3 50 to 5 00	Camden	near	Omnibus
do	Irwin House	M. G. Ronan	Camden, Oneida Co., N.Y.	16	2 00	5 00	Camden	near	Walk
do	Empire House	P. B. Malone	Camden, Oneida Co., N.Y.	22	1 50	4 00	Camden	near	Walk
do	American	W. H. McDaniels	Camden, N.Y.	30	....	3 50 to 4 00	Camden	near	Walk
do	Van de Waker House	J. L. Stormes	Osceola, Lewis Co., N.Y.	40	1 50	5 00	Camden	18m	Daily stage
do	Sage House	J. J. Burlingame	Williamstown, Oswego Co., N.Y.	...	2 00	....	Williamstown	near	Walk
do	Kasoag Hotel	M. McDermott	Kasoag, N.Y.	8	1 00	6 00	Kasoag	near	Walk
do	Fortune House	W. O. Elmer	Sand Bank, Oswego Co., N.Y.	15	1 50	5 00	Sand Bank	near	Walk
do	Cottage Hotel	R. Burke, Manager	Sand Bank, Oswego Co., N.Y.	25	2 00	4 00 to 7 00	Sand Bank	near	Walk
do	Richland House	A. Wright	Richland, Oswego Co., N.Y.	....	2 00	5 00	Richland	near	Walk
do	Ripsom House	Mrs. S. B. Ripsom	Richland, Oswego Co., N.Y.	....	1 00	4 00	Richland	near	Walk
do	Frost House	I. Frost	Richland, Oswego Co., N.Y.	....	1 00	3 00	Richland	near	Walk
do	Averill House	J. Doneburg	Richland, Oswego Co., N.Y.	....	1 00	4 00	Richland	near	Walk
do	Spring Brook House	M. C. Hammond	Richland, Oswego Co., N.Y.	....	1 00	4 00	Richland	near	Walk
do	Shady Nook Cottage	Mrs. May Thompson	Orwell, Oswego Co., N.Y.	15	1 25	7 00	Richland	2½m	Stage
Lake Ontario	Watkins House	H. Tavernick	Sandy Creek, Oswego Co., N.Y.	15	1 50	5 00	Sandy Creek	1m	Free omnibus
do	Sandy Creek House	M. F. Thomas	Sandy Creek, Oswego Co., N.Y.	10	2 00	4 00 to 8 00	Sandy Creek	1m	Free omnibus
do	Wigwam Cove	C. M. Groat	Sandy Creek, Oswego Co., N.Y.	40	2 00	7 00 to 12 00	Sandy Creek	3m	Carriage
do	Central Hotel	C. E. Meyers	Lacona, Oswego Co., N.Y.	20	2 00	4 00 to 7 00	Sandy Creek	near	
do	Lacona House	F. C. Plummer	Lacona, Oswego Co., N.Y.	10	2 00	4 00 to 7 00	Sandy Creek	near	
do	Jefferson House	C. S. Gibean	Mannsville, Jefferson Co., N.Y.	35	1 50	6 00 to 10 00	Mannsville	near	Free omnibus
do	Mannsville House	E. L. Matthews	Mannsville, Jefferson Co., N.Y.	6	1 00	5 00 to 8 00	Mannsville	near	
do	Pierrepont Manor H'se	S. J. Andrus	Pierrepont Manor, Jefferson Co., N.Y.	15	1 60	4 00	Pierrepont Man'r	½m	Free omnibus
do	Exchange Hotel	E. J. Tenney	Pierrepont Manor, Jefferson Co., N.Y.	12	1 00	4 00	Pierrepont Man'r	near	Walk
do	Lake View House	G. M. Wood	Woodville, Jefferson Co., N.Y.	21	1 50	7 00	Pierrepont Man'r	7m	Stage, $1; in parties, 75c. each
do	Hotel Gardner	G. L. Gardner	Adams, Jefferson Co., N.Y.	40	2 00	4 00 to 6 00	Adams	near	Free omnibus
do	Archer House	F. M. Blasier	Adams, Jefferson Co., N.Y.	10	1 00	3 50 to 5 00	Adams	near	Walk
do	Boarding House	Mrs. H. Morgan	Adams, Jefferson Co., N.Y.	10	1 00	4 00	Adams	near	Walk
do	Railroad Exchange	H. Buell	Adams Centre, Jefferson Co., N.Y.	12	1 50	4 00	Adams Centre	near	Walk
do	Centre House	G. W. Carpenter	Adams Centre, Jefferson Co., N.Y.	10	1 50	4 00	Adams Centre	near	Walk
do	Brownville Hotel	O. D. Grennell	Brownville, Jefferson Co., N.Y.	25	1 50	5 00	Brownville	near	Walk
do	Underwood Hotel	H. D. Reed	Dexter, Jefferson Co., N.Y.	30	2 00	7 00	Limerick	2m	Stage; fare, 25 cents
do	Manigold House	J. Manigold	Dexter, Jefferson Co., N.Y.	20	1 50	4 00 to 10 00	Limerick	2m	Stage; fare, 25 cents
do	Booth Hotel	C. O. F. Booth	Limerick, Jefferson Co., N.Y.	20	1 50	7 00	Limerick	near	Walk
do	Warner House	Bushnell & Main	Chaumont, Jefferson Co., N.Y.	30	1 50	7 00	Chaumont	2m	Free omnibus
do	Peck House	L. Crouse	Chaumont, Jefferson Co., N.Y.	20	1 50	5 00	Chaumont	near	Walk
do	National Hotel	B. J. Saxe	Chaumont, Jefferson Co., N.Y.	25	2 00	5 00	Chaumont	near	Walk
do	Central Hotel	W. E. Hall	Three-Mile Bay, Jefferson Co., N.Y.	12	1 50	7 00	Three-Mile Bay	1m	Stage; fare, 15 cents
do	Rosiere Hotel	J. B. Donaldson	Rosiere, Jefferson Co., N.Y.	8	1 00	4 00	Rosiere	near	Walk
Northern N. Y.	Brick Hotel	Peter Farmer	Evan's Mills, Jefferson Co., N.Y.	10	1 00	4 00 to 6 00	Evan's Mills	near	Walk
do	Central House	G. H. Reamer	Evan's Mills, Jefferson Co., N.Y.	10	1 00	4 00 to 6 00	Evan's Mills	near	Walk
do	Whitney House	W. M. Whitney	Evan's Mills, Jefferson Co., N.Y.	12	1 50	4 00 to 6 00	Evan's Mills	near	Walk
do	Eagle Hotel	F. Wilson	Philadelphia, Jefferson Co., N.Y.	75	2 00	3 50	Philadelphia	¾m	Omnibus
do	Fisher's Hotel	Geo. Fisher	Philadelphia, Jefferson Co., N.Y.	25	2 00	3 50	Philadelphia	near	Walk
do	Proctor House	J. R. Richner	Antwerp, Jefferson Co., N.Y.	75	2 00	4 00	Antwerp	near	Free omnibus
do	Foster House	N. J. Ryder	Antwerp, Jefferson Co., N.Y.	75	1 50	4 00	Antwerp	near	Free omnibus

LIST OF SUMMER HOTELS AND BOARDING HOUSES.

REGION.	Name of Hotel.	Proprietor.	Post-Office Address.	Room Capacity.	Rate per Day.	Rate per Week.	Nearest Railroad Station.	Dist. from R. R. Sta. in miles.	How Reached from Railroad Station.
Northern N.Y.	Simonet House	Eugene Simonet	Spragueville, St. Lawrence Co., N.Y.	25	$2 00	$10 00	Keene's	near	Walk
Adirondack	St. Lawrence Inn	R. P. Murphy	Gouverneur, St. Lawrence Co., N.Y.	62	2 to 3	5 00 to 20 00	Gouverneur	near	Walk
do	Peck House	D. Peck	Gouverneur, St. Lawrence Co., N.Y.	60	2 00	4 00 to 14 00	Gouverneur	near	Free omnibus
do	Kinney's Hotel	Mrs. C. M. Kinney	Gouverneur, St. Lawrence Co., N.Y.	20	1 to 2	3 00 to 5 00	Gouverneur	near	Walk
do	Brooklyn Hotel	Mrs. S. L. Nash	Gouverneur, St. Lawrence Co., N.Y.	20	1 to 2	3 00 to 5 00	Gouverneur	½m	Walk
do	Grove House	John Wainwright	Gouverneur, St. Lawrence Co., N.Y.	35	1 to 2	3 00 to 8 00	Gouverneur	½m	Walk
do	Hotel Lynde	Mrs. Olive Storrin	Richville, St. Lawrence Co., N.Y.	75	1 50	5 00	Richville	1½m	Stage; fare, 20 cents
do	Sylvan Lake House	Henry Soper	Fowler, St. Lawrence Co., N.Y.	12	2 00	10 00	Hailesboro	6m	Will meet guests
do	Hailesboro House	S. D. Rich	Hailesboro, St. Lawrence Co., N.Y.	20	1 00	4 00	Hailesboro	near	Walk
do	Riverside House	W. O. Garrison	Hailesboro, St. Lawrence Co., N.Y.	12	1 00	4 00	Hailesboro	near	Walk
do	Pettys House	Geo. Pettys	Taleville, St. Lawrence Co., N.Y.	20	2 00	10 00 to 15 00	Dodgeville	near	Walk
do	Trout Lake House	O. Ackerman	Edwards, St. Lawrence Co., N.Y.	50	2 00	8 00	Edwards	2½m	Stage; fare, 50 cents or livery
do	Thomas House	G. M. Thomas	Edwards, St. Lawrence Co., N.Y.	100	2 00	4 00 to 6 00	Edwards	......	Free omnibus
do	Haven House	J. M. Haven	Canton, St. Lawrence Co., N.Y.	100	2 00	7 00 to 10 00	Canton	near	Free omnibus
do	American House	Getman Bros	Canton, St. Lawrence Co., N.Y.	28	2 00	4 00 to 8 00	Canton	near	Free omnibus
do	Wellington Place	Mrs. L. W. Wellington	Canton, St. Lawrence Co., N.Y.	75	1 00	6 00	Canton	near	Carriage
do	The International	Jno. Tyo	Dundee, Que.	......	......	......	Ft. Covington	½m	Omnibus
do	Lake View House	Jno. Tyo	Hopkins Point, Que.	100	1 50–2	......	Ft. Covington	......	Steamer from Dundee
do	Curtis House	G. W. Curtis	Canton, St. Lawrence Co., N.Y.	26	1 00	3 00 to 5 00	Canton	near	Free omnibus
do	Albion House	A. J. Holmes	Potsdam, St. Lawrence Co., N.Y.	125	2 00	......	Potsdam	near	Omnibus
do	Windsor Hotel	Sheridan & Cameron	Potsdam, St. Lawrence Co., N.Y.	75	1 75	......	Potsdam	near	Omnibus
do	Frontier House	F. LaDuke	Potsdam, St. Lawrence Co., N.Y.	25	1 00	......	Potsdam	near	Omnibus
do	Gale's Hotel	E. P. Gale	Gale's, St. Lawrence Co., N.Y.	20	1 00	......	Potsdam	45m	Stage; fare, $3.00
do	Seavy House	J. Seavy	Stark, St. Lawrence Co., N.Y.	20	1 00	......	Potsdam	30m	Stage; fare, $3.00
do	Forest House	Jno. Roach	Stark, St. Lawrence Co., N.Y.	40	1 00	......	Potsdam	20m	Stage; fare, $2.00
do	Sylvan Falls House	Lewis & Dyke	Parishville, St. Lawrence Co., N.Y.	60	2 00	8 00 to 10 00	Potsdam	17m	Livery or carriage on order
do	American Hotel	Bailey & Welch	Norwood, St. Lawrence Co., N.Y.	32	2 00	7 00	Norwood	near	Walk
do	Whitney Hotel	S. R. Phelps	Norwood, St. Lawrence Co., N.Y.	30	2 00	......	Norwood	near	Free omnibus
do	Atwater House	J. S. Kellogg	Norfolk, St. Lawrence Co., N.Y.	12	1 50	7 00 to 10 00	Norwood	3m	Carriage
do	Riverside Farm	Mrs. J. H. Bixby	Stark, St. Lawrence Co., N.Y.	8	......	3 50 to 4 00	Potsdam	2½m	Stage; fare, $2.00
Oswegatchie	Hatfield House	Hatfield Brothers	Hatfield, St. Lawrence Co., N.Y.	200	2 50	10 00 to 14 00	Massena Springs	near	Free omnibus
do	White's Hotel	Caroline White	Massena, St. Lawrence Co., N.Y.	75	2 00	7 00 to 10 50	Massena Springs	1m	Free omnibus
do	Allen House	J. W. Reed	Massena, St. Lawrence Co., N.Y.	20	1 50	7 00	Massena Springs	1m	Free omnibus
do	Harrowgate House	Shedden & Stearns / W. R. Stearns, M'r.	Hatfield, St. Lawrence Co., N.Y.	50	2 00	7 00 to 10 00	Massena Springs	near	Free omnibus
do	Boarding House	E. M. Smith	Hatfield, St. Lawrence Co., N.Y.	25	1 50	7 00 to 10 00	Massena Springs	near	
do	American House	S. T. Bero	Hogansburg, Franklin Co., N.Y.	25	......	......	Bombay		
do	Clark House	Robt. Thompson	Waddington, N.Y.	60	1 50–2	5 00 to 9 00	Madrid	9m	Stage
do	Goulding House	Hurley Bros	De Kalb Junc., St. Lawrence Co., N.Y.	20	2 00	4 00 to 10 00	DeKalb Junction	near	Walk
do	Thomas House	J. B. Wainwright	De Kalb Junc., St. Lawrence Co., N.Y.	15	2 00	4 00 to 10 00	DeKalb Junction	near	Walk
do	Cranberry Lake House	R. Bishop	Clarksboro, St. Lawrence Co., N.Y.	20	2 00	4 00 to 10 00	DeKalb Junction	38m	Livery, $10.00
do	Clifton House	H. M. Gordon	Clarksboro, St. Lawrence Co., N.Y.	15	2 00	4 00 to 10 00	DeKalb Junction	24m	Livery, $6.00
do	Russell House	O. C. Richardson	Russell, St. Lawrence Co., N.Y.	25	2 00	4 00 to 10 00	DeKalb Junction	12m	Livery, $4.00
do	Hermon House	S. H. Ladd	Hermon, St. Lawrence Co., N.Y.	30	2 00	4 00 to 10 00	DeKalb Junction	4m	Livery, $2.00
do	Snyder House	Wood & Co.	Heuvelton, St. Lawrence Co., N.Y.	15	1 50	5 00	Heuvelton	near	Omnibus
do	Van Heuvel Hotel	J. W. Miller	Heuvelton, St. Lawrence Co., N.Y.	9	1 50	5 00	Heuvelton	near	Walk
do	Mason House	J. G. Thornton	DePeyster, St. Lawrence Co., N.Y.	10	1 50	5 00	Heuvelton	5m	Daily mail wagon
do	Fish Creek Hotel	E. H. Perry	Pope's Mills, St. Lawrence Co., N.Y.	8	1 00	4 00	Heuvelton	14m	Daily mail wagon
do	Hastings House	F. Hastings	Pope's Mills, St. Lawrence Co., N.Y.	10	1 00	4 00	Heuvelton	14m	Daily mail wagon
St. Lawrence River	Seymour House	F. J. Tallman	Ogdensburg, N.Y.	80	2 to 3	10 00	Ogdensburg	½m	Street car

St. Lawrence River	Hotel Lovejoy	Charles Harris	Ogdensburg, N. Y.	25	$2 00	$7 00 to 9 00	Ogdensburg	1¼m	Carriage
do	Hotel Windsor	J. B. Jillson	Ogdensburg, N. Y.	40	2 00	7 00 to 9 00	Ogdensburg	1¼m	Carriage
do	Sterling House	W. F. White	Ogdensburg, N.Y.	30	1 50	8 00	Ogdensburg	¼m	
do	Franklin House	Thos. Drake	Ogdensburg, N.Y.	30	1 50	8 00	Ogdensburg	1m	Street car
do	National	J. H. Normand	Ogdensburg, N.Y.	20	1 50	8 00	Ogdensburg	¼m	Street car
do	Oswegatchie	E. B. Capron	Ogdensburg, N.Y.	32	1 50	7 00	Ogdensburg	⅛m	
do	Summer Home	Wm. C. Brooks	Oak Point, St. Lawrence Co., N.Y.	25	1 50	8 00 to 10 00	Ogdensburg	20m	Steamer "Massena" to dock
do	Daniels' Hotel	L. H. Daniels	Prescott, Ont	60	2 to 3	7 00 to 20 00	Ogdensburg	¼m	Ferry and omnibus
do	Mansion House	D. Higgins	Prescott, Ont.	25	2 00	7 00	Ogdensburg	1¼m	Ferry
do	Revere House	Mrs. J. S. Huntington	Prescott, Ont	30	1 50	5 00	Ogdensburg	1¼m	Ferry and omnibus
do	Bradley House	Mrs. J. Bradley	Prescott, Ont	30	1 00	3 50	Ogdensburg	1¼m	Ferry and omnibus
do	Queen's Hotel	J. F. Graham	Prescott, Ont	30	1 00	3 00	Ogdensburg	1¼m	Ferry
Central N. Y.	Bagg's Hotel	Kelly & Johnson	Utica, N.Y.	300	4 00	*	Utica	near	Walk
do	Butterfield House	C. A. Nott & Co.	Utica, N.Y.	150	3 00	*	Utica	1¼m	Omnibus
do	Clarendon (family)	Mrs. G. W. Griffith	Utica, N.Y.	100	2 00	*	Utica	¼m	Street car; fare, 5 cents
do	Metropolitan Hotel	Mrs. A. Noyes	Utica, N.Y.	210	2 00	*	Utica	near	Omnibus
do	St. James Hotel	Smith & White	Utica, N.Y.	200	2-2 50	*	Utica	near	Walk
do	Dudley House	J. P. Keegan	Utica, N.Y.	75	1 50	*	Utica	near	Walk
do	The Kenmore	Mrs. J. A. Hall	Utica, N. Y.	40	1 50	7 00 to 10 00	Utica	near	Street car; fare, 5 cents
Northern N. Y.	Clarendon Hotel	I. D. Thomson	Holland Patent, N.Y.	26	2 00	6 00 to 12 00	Holland Patent	near	Walk
do	Dawson House	G. W. Dawson	Trenton, N.Y.	15	1 50	5 00 to 7 00	Trenton	½m	Stage; fare, 10 cents
do	Brooklyn House	A. G. Griffiths	Trenton, N.Y.	10	1 00	5 00	Trenton	¾m	Stage; fare, 10 cents
do	Moore's Hotel	Mrs. M. Moore	Trenton Falls, N.Y.	100	3-3 50	14 00 to 21 00	Trenton Falls	½m	Stage; fare, 25 cents
do	Kauyahoora House	C. E. Moore	Trenton Falls, N.Y.	30	2 to 3	7 00 to 10 00	Trenton Falls	½m	Stage; fare, 25 cents
do	Bagg's Hotel	J. J. Bannon	Prospect, N.Y.	50	1 50	6 00	Prospect	1½m	Stage; fare, 15 cents
do	Dodge House	W. S. Hodge	Prospect, N.Y.	40	1 50	6 00	Prospect	1½m	Stage; fare, 15 cents
do	Goshen Hall	Fred. Hubbard	Prospect, N.Y.	25	1 00	6 00	Prospect	1½m	Stage; fare, 15 cents
do	Private Residence	G. Hinckley, Jr.	Hinckley, Herkimer Co., N. Y.	...	.....	6 00 to 7 00	Prospect	4m	Stage
do	Empire House	M. J. Ryan	Hinckley, Herkimer Co., N.Y.	100	1 50	6 00	Prospect	4m	Stage; fare, 30 cents
North Woods	Hunter's Home	Ed. Wilkinson	Wilmurt, Herkimer Co., N.Y.	30	1 50	5 00	Prospect	17½m	Carriage
do	Private Residence	A. Odit	Northwood, Herkimer Co., N.Y.	12	1 00	5 00	Prospect	12m	Stage; fare, 45 cents
do	Honanday Lodge	E. Flansburg, Mgr.	Prospect, N. Y.	100	2 00	*	Prospect	17½m	Stage and buckboard
do	Forest Lodge	A. D. Barber, Jr.	Wilmurt, Herkimer Co., N.Y.	100	2 00	....	Prospect	17½m	Stage and 12m buckboard
do	Noblesboro House	Fred Reymonda	Wilmurt, Herkimer Co., N.Y.	50	1 00	6 00	Prospect	20m	Carriage on notice
do	Wagner Hotel	A. Hoffmeister	Wilmurt, Herkimer Co., N. Y.	12	2 00	12 00	Prospect	20m	Carriage
do	Hubbard House	P. Bouban	Wilmurt, Herkimer Co., N. Y.	10	2 00	12 00	Prospect	20m	Carriage
do	Boarding House	Fred. Beecraft	Morehouseville, N.Y.	20	1 00	4 50	Prospect	25m	Carriage; $2.00
do	Garlock House	A. H. Legg	Grant, Herkimer Co., N.Y.	10	1 to 2	5 00 to 7 00	Prospect	7m	Stage; fare, 45 cents
do	Hart Hotel	W. Hart	Grant, Herkimer Co., N.Y.	10	1 00	6 00	Prospect	7m	Stage; fare, 45 cents
do	Mountain Home	A. Wheeler	Morehouseville, N.Y.	25	1 25	7 00	Prospect	24m	Stage } $2.00 stage
do	Kreitzer Hotel	A. Hoffmeister	Morehouseville, N.Y.	15	2 00	12 00	Prospect	24m	Carriage } $2.00 stage
do	Private Residence	Mrs. Hoffmeister	Morehouseville, N.Y.	15	1 00	7 00	Prospect	24m	Carriage } $2.00 stage
do	Private Residence	Mr. Kassing	Morehouseville, N.Y.	15	1 00	7 00	Prospect	24m	Carriage } $2.00 stage
do	Private Residence	Mr. Hagadorn	Morehouseville, N.Y.	10	1 00	7 00	Prospect	24m	Carriage } $2.00 stage
do	Private Residence	Joe Lane	Morehouseville, N.Y.	12	1 00	7 00	Prospect	24m	Carriage } $2.00 stage
Northern N. Y.	Hotel Bristol	Friend Bristol	Remsen, N.Y.	16	1 50	7 00	Remsen	near	Walk
North Woods	Boarding House	H. R. Roberts	Remsen, N.Y.	10	1 00	7 00	Remsen	9m	Carriage
do	Read's House	J. Read	Remsen, N.Y.	12	1 00	5 00 to 7 00	Remsen	19m	Carriage
do	Williams House	J. H. Williams	Remsen, N.Y.	15	1 00	5 00	Remsen	near	Walk
do	Spinning House	J. H. Van Dyke	White Lake Corners, N. Y.	35	1 00	7 00	White Lake	10m	Stage
Northern N. Y.	Thurston's Hotel	G. L. Thurston	Alder Creek, N.Y.	25	1 50	6 00 to 8 00	Alder Creek	¾m	Stage or private carriage
do	Private House	Mrs. Calen	Alder Creek, N.Y.	8	.....	5 00	Alder Creek	¾m	Stage or private carriage
do	Getman House	Chas. Getman	Forestport, Oneida Co., N.Y.	40	1 50	5 50	Alder Creek	3m	Stage
do	Hulburt House	Geo. H. Beck	Boonville, N.Y.	100	2 00	10 00	Boonville	¼m	Free omnibus
do	American Hotel	Geo. M. Youngs	Boonville, N.Y.	45	1 50	4 00 to 6 00	Boonville	near	Walk
do	Central Hotel	Jerry Buckley	Boonville, N.Y.	40	1 50	4 00 to 6 00	Boonville	.....	Free omnibus
do	Windsor	W. Commerford	Boonville, N.Y.	21	2 00	5 00 to 8 00	Boonville	near	Walk
do	Private Residence	Miss K. Griffith	Boonville, N.Y.	15	1 00	3 50 to 4 00	Boonville	near	Walk
do	Private Residence	Mrs. M. E. Esler	Boonville, N. Y.	10	1 25	7 00	Boonville	near	Walk
do	Private Residence	Mrs. D. E. Sanborn	Boonville, N. Y.	6	.....	5 00	Boonville	1m	Carriage

LIST OF SUMMER HOTELS AND BOARDING HOUSES.

REGION.	Name of Hotel.	Proprietor.	Post-Office Address.	Room Capacity.	Rate per Day.	Rate per Week.	Nearest Railroad Station.	Dist. from R. R. Sta. in miles.	How Reached from Railroad Station.
Northern N.Y.	Riverside Farm	J. A. Fiske	Boonville, N. Y.	10	......	$5 00	Boonville	near	Walk
do	Powers House	M. Powers	Port Leyden, Lewis Co., N.Y.	25	$2 00	5 00 to 10 00	Port Leyden	near	Walk
do	Hotel Brunswick	A. Secoy	Port Leyden, Lewis Co., N.Y.	25	2 00	6 00 to 12 00	Port Leyden	......	Walk
do	Walton House	M. H. Grace	Lyons Falls, Lewis Co., N.Y.	20	1 50	5 00 to 7 00	Lyons Falls	near	Walk
do	Gaffney House	Jno. Gaffney	Lyons Falls, Lewis Co., N.Y.	20	1–1 50	3 50 to 7 00	Lyons Falls	near	Walk
do	Private Residence	H. J. Hubbard	Constableville, Lewis Co., N.Y.		1 00	5 00	Lyons Falls	near	Walk
do	Higby House	E. D. Burdick	Glendale, Lewis Co., N.Y.	75	1 50	4 00	Glendale	near	Walk
do	Phillips House	Ossant & Burton	Glendale, Lewis Co., N.Y.	30	1 50	4 00	Glendale	near	Walk
do	Central House	Jas. Calhoun	Greig, Lewis Co., N.Y.	20	1 00	3 50 to 4 00	Glendale	3m	Carriage
do	Riverside Hotel	Geo. W. Dekin	Greig, Lewis Co., N.Y.	20	1 50	4 00	Glendale	1m	Carriage
do	The Glastonbury	Mrs. J. P. Halstead	Houseville, Lewis Co., N.Y.	25	1 00	7 00 to 10 00	Glendale	3½m	Carriage
North Woods	Grove Hotel	Truman Hess	Brantingham, Lewis Co., N.Y.	25	1 50	4 00	Glendale	5m	Carriage; price, $1.50 to $2 00
do	Branting'm Lake H'se	Leon S. Graves	Brantingham, Lewis Co., N. Y.	35	2 00	7 00 to 10 00	Glendale	7m	Carriage or stage
do	Chase's Lake House	John Gleason	Chase's Lake, Lewis Co., N.Y.	50	......	6 00 upwards	Glendale	7m	Carriage on notice
do	Otter Lake Hotel	F. G. Burdick	Glendale, Lewis Co., N.Y.	100	1 50	8 00	Glendale	......	Livery
do	Stony Lake House	George V. Norton	Chase's Lake, Lewis Co., N.Y.	25	1 to 2	7 00 to 10 00	Glendale	13m	Stage
Northern N. Y.	Summit House	E. J. Brady	Martinsburg, Lewis Co., N.Y.	20	1 00	6 00	Martinsburg	3m	Stage
do	Kellogg House	C. H. Bateman	Lowville, N.Y.	200	2 00	*	Lowville	¼m	Free omnibus
do	Windsor Hotel	Jno. Gleason	Lowville, N.Y.	150	2 00	5 00 to 7 00	Lowville	¼m	
do	Strife House	Jacob Strife	Lowville, N.Y.	50	2 00	*	Lowville	near	Walk
do	Railroad Hotel	Samuel Raine	Lowville, N.Y.	10	2 00	*	Lowville	near	Walk
do	Private Residence	Chas. House	Lowville, N.Y.	4	1 50	4 00 to 5 00	Lowville	near	Walk
do	Brook House	John Kieb	Lowville, N.Y.	25	1 50	5 00	Lowville	¼m	Walk
Adirondack	Fenton's Hotel	Chas. Fenton	Watson, Lewis Co., N.Y. (No. 4)	150	2 00	*	Lowville	18m	Carriages; $5 single, or about $2 each if in parties; or will meet parties at depot.
do	......	Monroe Young	Watson, Lewis Co., N.Y. (No. 4)	10	1 50	4 00 to 5 00	Lowville	18m	Carriage
Northern N. Y.	Castor Land Hotel	Glenn & Wetmore	Castor Land, N.Y.	20	1 50	6 00	Castor Land	near	Walk
do	Union Hotel	G. N. Goutermont	Castor Land, N.Y.	20	2 00	9 00	Castor Land	near	Walk
do	Miller House	C. N. Wright	Croghan, N.Y.	50	2 00	*	Castor Land	8m	Stage (or 10 miles from Lowville)
do	Bald Mountain House	E. W. Putnam	Belfort, Lewis Co., N.Y.	75	2 00	10 00	Castor Land	18m	Stage to Croghan, team to house
Adirondack	Grant House	A. E. Prentice	Belfort, N.Y. (Long Pond)	25	2 00	*	Castor Land	19m	Stage (or 22 miles from Lowville)
do	Bald Mountain House	Bald Mt. Fsh & GmeClb	Belfort, N.Y. (Long Pond)	30	2 00	9 00	Castor Land	19m	Stage
do	Nortz House	Geo. Nortz	Belfort, N.Y.	30	2 00	*	Castor Land	11m	Stage
do	Wire House	John Wernly	Naumburg, N.Y.	25	1 50	6 00	Castor Land	1m	Stage
Northern N. Y.	Davenport House	Davenport Bros.	Copenhagen, Lewis Co., N. Y.	25	1 50	5 00 to 7 00	Deer River	5½m	Carriage if notified
do	Deer River Hotel	M. L. Dunham	Deer River, Lewis Co., N.Y.	16	1 00	3 50	Deer River	¾m	Stage
do	Grand Union	M. Gleason	Carthage, N.Y.	40	2 00	5 00	Carthage	⅛m	Free omnibus
do	Kenmore	P. H. Brown	Carthage, N.Y.	40	2 00	4 00	Carthage	near	Walk
do	Hotel Elmhurst	Mrs. S. E. Hatch	Carthage, N.Y.	50	1 50	4 50	Carthage	⅛m	Free omnibus
do	Levis House	J. Carney	Carthage, N.Y.	40	1 50	4 50	Carthage	¼m	Free omnibus
do	Gill House	R. Gill	Carthage, N.Y.	35	1 50	4 50	Carthage	near	Walk
do	Central House	Jas. A. Walsh	Carthage, N.Y.	30	1 00	3 50	Carthage	near	Walk
do	Park House	John Hines	Carthage, N.Y.	35	1 00	4 00	Carthage	½m	Carriage
do	Brunswick Hotel	Mrs. W. Austin	Carthage, N.Y.	25	1 00	4 00	Carthage	near	Walk
do	Hatch House	Mrs. Murray	Carthage, N.Y.	25	1 00	4 00	Carthage	near	Walk
do	Kimball B'rding Hous:	John Donlan	Carthage, N.Y.	10	1 00	5 00	Carthage	near	Walk
North Woods	King Jos's Hermitage	J. Pahud	Harrisville, Lewis Co., N.Y.	50	2 00	10 00 to 15 00	King's Crossing	½m	Carriage
do	Kenwood Hall	E. P. Lake & Co.	Harrisville, Lewis Co., N.Y.	25	2 00	5 00 to 10 00	Harrisville	½m	Carriage
do	Riverside House	T. Whalen	Harrisville, Lewis Co., N.Y.	25	1 50	4 00 to 6 00	Harrisville	½m	Carriage
do	Forest Home	Warren Humes	Harrisville, Lewis Co., N.Y.	100	2 00	10 50	Harrisville	5m	Carriage

Northern N. Y.	Harrisville Hotel	Lake & Blood	Harrisville, Lewis Co., N.Y.	30	$1 50	$4 00	Harrisville	20m	Carriage
do	Central House	M. Fargo	Natural Bridge, Jefferson Co., N.Y.	30	1 50	3 50 to 5 00	Natural Bridge	¼m	Carriage
do	Union House	L. L. Bowen	Natural Bridge, Jefferson Co., N.Y.	30	1 00	4 00	Natural Bridge	½m	Carriage
Oswegatchie	Hotel	Geo. Freeman	Star Lake, St. Lawrence Co., N.Y.	100	1 50	4 50	Oswegatchie	1¼m	Omnibus
do	Cottage Hotel	F. J. Redway	Oswegatchie, St. Lawrence Co., N.Y.	60	1 50	7 00 to 10 00	Oswegatchie	2½m	Carriage
do	Star Lake Hotel	Foley & Lyman	Oswegatchie, St. Lawrence Co., N.Y.	75	2 00	7 00 to 18 00	Oswegatchie	2m	Omnibus
do	Oswegatchie House	Wm. Wilcox	Oswegatchie, St. Lawrence Co., N.Y.	30	1 50	4 50	Oswegatchie	near	Walk
do	Edgewood	J. C. Lee	Oswegatchie, St. Lawrence Co., N.Y.	180	3 00	8 00 to 18 00	Oswegatchie	2m	Omnibus
do	Forest House	C. H. Kimball	Oswegatchie, St. Lawrence Co., N.Y.	50	1 00	7 00	Oswegatchie	near	Walk
do	Forest Union House	J. B. Hurlburt	Oswegatchie, St. Lawrence Co., N.Y.	30	1 00	7 00	Oswegatchie	near	Walk
do	Cranberry Lake House	W. R. Bishop	Harewood, St. Lawrence Co., N.Y.	75	2 00	8 00 to 14 00	Benson Mines	8m	Stage tri-weekly
Northern N.Y.	Woodruff House	C. A. Hungerford	Watertown, N.Y.	150	2 50-3	14 00 to 20 00	Watertown	near	Walk
do	Crowner House	Wilder Bros.	Watertown, N.Y.	30	1 50	7 00 to 10 00	Watertown	near	Free omnibus
do	Otis House	A. D. Williams & Co.	Watertown, N.Y.	100	2 to 3	10 00 to 20 00	Watertown	near	Free omnibus
do	American Hotel	Joseph Marrian	Watertown, N.Y.	25	1 00	4 00 to 7 00	Watertown	near	Walk
do	Harris House	W. J. Wylie	Watertown, N.Y.	35	1 00	4 00 to 5 00	Watertown	near	Walk
do	City Hotel	Romang & Myers	Watertown, N.Y.	44	1 00	4 00 to 5 00	Watertown	near	Walk
Lake Ontario	Earl House	Jas. Galloway	Sackett's Harbor, N.Y.	100	2 00	6 00 to 10 00	Sackett's Harbor	near	Walk
do	Graham House	John Graham	Sackett's Harbor, N.Y.	100	2 00	6 00 to 10 00	Sackett's Harbor	near	Walk
do	Edge Water Cottage	G. H. Warner	Henderson Harbor, Jefferson Co., N.Y.	50	1 50	8 00	Sackett's Harbor	8m	Steamer
do	Tyler's Cottage	E. Tyler	Henderson Harbor, Jefferson Co., N.Y.	30	1 50	8 00	Sackett's Harbor	8m	Steamer
do	Frontier Hotel	J. H. Lovelee	Henderson Harbor, Jefferson Co., N.Y.	30	1 50	8 00	Sackett's Harbor	8m	Steamer
do	The Windsor	Wheeler Bros.	Henderson Harbor, Jefferson Co., N.Y.	30	1 50	8 00	Sackett's Harbor	8m	Steamer
do	New York House	H. B. Phelps	Henderson Harbor, Jefferson Co., N.Y.	30	1 50	6 00	Sackett's Harbor	8m	Steamer
do	Gill House	H. H. Gill	Henderson Harbor, Jefferson Co., N.Y.	50	2 00	8 00 to 12 00	Sackett's Harbor	8m	Steamer
do	Almont House	A. J. Sprague	Henderson Harbor, Jefferson Co., N.Y.	20	1 50	7 00	Sackett's Harbor	9m	Steamer
do	Campbell's Point Hotel	J. B. Roseboom	Sackett's Harbor, N. Y.	30	1 00		Sackett's Harbor	3m	Steamer
do	Stony Island House	H. H. Gill	Sackett's Harbor, N. Y.		1 50	7 00	Sackett's Harbor	10m	Steamer
Thousand Islands	The Arlington	C. E. Reed	Cape Vincent, Jefferson Co., N.Y.	50	2-2 50	10 00 to 15 00	Cape Vincent	near	Walk
do	Jerome's New Hotel	C. A. Jerome	Cape Vincent, Jefferson Co., N.Y.	50	2 00		Cape Vincent	near	Omnibus
do	Union House	H. T. Frisbee	Cape Vincent, Jefferson Co., N.Y.	40	1 50	5 00 to 8 00	Cape Vincent	near	Walk
do	Riverside House	Capt. S. Griffin	Millen's Bay, P.O. Cape Vincent, N.Y.	51	2 00	8 00 to 10 00	Cape Vincent	6m	Steamer, direct line
do	Channel Grove House	Geo. Briggs	Simcoe Island, P.O. Cape Vincent, N.Y.	40	2 00	7 00 to 10 00	Cape Vincent	4m	Steamer to Kingston
do	Hubbard House	Mrs. E. M. Hubbard	Clayton, N.Y.	200	2½ up	14 00 to 17 50	Clayton	near	Free omnibus
do	Walton House	T. M. Esselstyn, M'g'r.	Clayton, N.Y.	150	2 50	14 00 to 17 50	Clayton	near	Free omnibus
do	New Windsor Hotel	W. P. Hawes	Clayton, N.Y.	80	2 50	14 00 to 17 50	Clayton	near	Free omnibus
do	Hayes House	P. K. Hayes	Clayton, N.Y.	20	1 50	10 00	Clayton	near	Walk
do	Dewey House	B. J. Bettinger	Clayton, N.Y.	40	1 50	10 00	Clayton	near	Walk
do	Boarding House	Mrs. D. E. Smith	Clayton, N. Y.	20	1 25	7 00 to 9 00	Clayton	near	Walk
do	Boarding House	Mrs. H. B. Dewey	Clayton, N. Y.	20	1 25	7 00 to 9 00	Clayton	near	Walk
do	Th. Isl'ds B'd'g House	Mrs. Thos. Rees	Clayton, N.Y.	16	1 50	7 00 to 9 00	Clayton	near	Walk
do	The Frontenac	E. D. Dickenson	Clayton, N.Y.	350	3-4 00	16 00 to 28 00	Clayton	2m	Steamer, direct line, fare 25 cents
do	Kendall's Cottage	F. Kendall	Clayton, N.Y.	15	1 50		Clayton		Ferry
do	Boarding House	Mrs. M. W. Atwood	Clayton, N.Y.	20	1 00		Clayton	near	Walk
do	Point Pleasant	Mrs. A. S. Kendall	Clayton, N. Y.	20	1 50	10 00	Clayton	1½m	Boat
do	Grand View House	E. M. Child	Grand View Park, N.Y.	125	2-2 50	8 00 to 14 00	Clayton	6m	Steamer, ferry from T. I. Park
do	No. 9 Island House	Mrs. Zera Coy	Alexandria Bay, N.Y.	20	1 25	7 00	Clayton		Steamer
do	New Eng. Dining Hall	W. R. Rogers	Thousand Island Park, N.Y.			8 00 to 15 00	Clayton		Steamer, direct line
do	The New England	W. H. Prine, M'g'r	Thousand Island Park, N.Y.	300	1 50	8 00 to 10 00	Clayton		Steamer, direct line
do	Rochester Cottage	Mrs. A. Hebbard	Thousand Island Park, N.Y.	10	1 50	8 00 to 9 00	Clayton		Steamer
do	Wiley Cottage	H. W. Millard	Thousand Island Park, N. Y.	14	1 00	4 75 to 6 00	Clayton	6m	Steamer
do	New York Cottage	D. L. Bronk	Thousand Island Park, N.Y.	15		7 00 to 10 00	Clayton	6m	Steamer
do	FernCot'ge, Th. Isl. Pk.	J. P. Billings	Rodman, Jefferson Co., N. Y.	100	1 50	7 00 to 10 00	Clayton	5m	Steamer
do	Hough Cottage	D. L. Bronk	Thousand Island Park, N. Y.	15	2 00		Clayton		Steamer
do	Fine View House	Geo. W. Bretsch	Fine View, via T. I. Park, N.Y.	100	2 00	10 00 to 14 00	Clayton	5m	Steamer
do	Pullman House	W. P. Rogers	Pullman, N.Y.	60	2 00	10 00 to 14 00	Clayton	4m	Steamer, direct line, fare 25 cents
do	The Columbian	Inglehart & Son	Thousand Island Park, N.Y.	350	3 00	14 00 to 17 50	Clayton		Steamer, direct line
do	Central Park	E. E. Spangenberg	St. Lawrence Park, Jefferson Co., N. Y.	100	2 3 00	12 00 to 17 00	Clayton	9m	Steamer, direct line, fare 50 cents
do	Thousand Isl'd House	J. B. Wistar	Alexandria Bay, N.Y.	700	4 00	21 00 to 28 00	Clayton	12m	St'r to dock near hotel, fare 50c.
do	The Crossmon	C. W. Crossmon	Alexandria Bay, N.Y.	400	4 00	21 00 to 28 00	Clayton	12m	St'r to dock near hotel, fare 50c.

LIST OF SUMMER HOTELS AND BOARDING HOUSES.

REGION.	Name of Hotel.	Proprietor.	Post-Office Address.	Room Capacity.	Rate per Day.	Rate per Week.	Nearest Railroad Station.	Dist. from R. R. Sta. in miles.	How Reached from Railroad Station.
Thousand Islands..	Boarding House	W. J. Woodworth	Alexandria Bay, N.Y	30	$1 50	$10 00	Clayton	12m	St'r to dock near hotel, fare 50c.
do	Walton Cottage	W. B. Walton	Alexandria Bay, N.Y	40	2 00	12 00 to 14 00	Clayton	12m	St'r to dock near hotel, fare 50c.
do	Bay View House	Weston Fall	Alexandria Bay, N.Y	40	2 00	*	Clayton	12m	St'r to dock near hotel, fare 50c.
do	Jefferson House	J. A. Bigness	Alexandria Bay, N.Y	100	2 00	10 00 to 14 00	Clayton	12m	St'r to dock near hotel, fare 50c.
do	Marsden House	G. A. Marsden	Alexandria Bay, N.Y	40	2 00	10 00 to 12 00	Clayton	12m	St'r to dock near hotel, fare 50c.
do	St. James	H. Zollor	Alexandria Bay, N.Y	40	2 00	....	Clayton	12m	St'r to dock near hotel, fare 50c.
do	Edgewood Park Hotel	J. P. Lamson	Alexandria Bay, N.Y	.....	4 00	17 50 to 21 00	Clayton	12m	St'r to dock near hotel, fare 50c.
do	Boarding House	L. C. Watson	Alexandria Bay, N.Y	10	2 00	*	Clayton	12m	St'r to dock near hotel, fare 50c.
do	Boarding House	S. B. Miller	Alexandria Bay, N.Y	20	1 50	*	Clayton	12m	St'r to dock near hotel, fare 50c.
do	Woodworth Cottage	W. J. Woodworth	Alexandria Bay, N.Y	30	1 50	10 00	Clayton	12m	Steamer to Alex. Bay
do	Boarding House	Mrs E. A. Barker	Alexandria Bay, N.Y	.....	1 50	10 00	Clayton	12m	Steamer to Alex. Bay
do	Witherstine Cottage	Mrs. Witherstine	Thousand Island Park, N. Y	.....	1 25	....	Clayton	......	Steamer
do	Hotel Westminster	H. F. Inglehart	Alexandria Bay, N.Y	250	2 50	12 00 to 17 50	Clayton	13m	Steamer Alex. Bay and ferry
do	Grenadier Island	Joseph Senecal	Alexandria Bay, N.Y	25	1 50	*	Clayton	17m	Steamer Alex. Bay and row boat
do	Boarding House	Robert Poole	Poole's Resort, Ont	20	1 50	....	Clayton	18m	Steamer Alex. Bay and row boat
do	Island View House	Theo. Lear	Rockport, Ont	25	1 50	....	Clayton	16m	St'r Alex. Bay, row boat or ferry
do	Echo Lodge	O. L. Potter	Ivy Lea, Ont	.....	2 00	7 00 to 10 00	Clayton	......	Steamer Alex. Bay and boat
do	Mountain View	Wm. Carpenter	Ivy Lea, Ont	8	1 00	5 00	Clayton	......	Steamer Alex. Bay and boat
do	Provincial Hotel	Neil McCarney	Gananoque, Ont	50	2 00	7 00 to 9 00	Clayton	6m	Ferry
do	Tremont Park	C. A. See	Gananoque, Ont	.....	1 50	9 00 to 10 50	Clayton	6m	Ferry
do	Boarding House	J. Turcotte, B'twick Is	Gananoque, Ont. (P. O. Box 35.)	30	1 00	5 00	Clayton	......	Steamer
Steamboats make	immediate connections	at Clayton depot dock	and run to Cornwall dock, Alexandria	Bay	very	near all	hotels, etc.		
Indian River	Getman House	Getman Bros	Theresa, N. Y	40	2 00	5 00 to 14 00	Theresa	¼m	Omnibus
do	Doolittle House	Doolittle & Co	Theresa, N. Y	35	1 50	4 50 to 7 00	Theresa	4½m	Boat or Livery
Redwood Lakes	Farley House	M. W. Farley	Redwood, N.Y	27	2 00	10 00	Redwood	near	Omnibus
do	Dollinger House	J. B. Wistar	Redwood, N.Y	50	2-3 00	12 00 to 15 00	Redwood	near	Omnibus
St. Lawrence River	Boarding House	M. Forrester	North Hammond, N.Y	20	1 50	7 00	Hammond	6m	Carriage or st'r from Morristown
do	Cedar Island House	M. P. Phillips	Chippewa Bay, N.Y	60	1 50-3	7 00 to 15 00	Hammond	4m	St'r from Morrist'n or Alex. Bay
do	Franklin House	F. Franklin	Hammond, N.Y	10	1 50	7 00	Hammond	near	
do	Rossie House	L. G. Garand	Rossie, N.Y	50	1 50	7 00	Hammond	6m	Stage or Livery
do	Lake View Hotel	K. E. Capron	Edwardsville, N. Y	15	1 50	7 00	Hammond	7m	Livery
do	Black Lake House	H. Perry	Edwardsville, N. Y	15	1 50	7 00	Hammond	7m	Livery
do	Maple Farm	L. G. Miller	Cedars, St. Lawrence Co., N. Y	20	1 25	7 00	Brier Hill	2m	Carriage
do	Frontier House	J. F. Culligan	Morristown, N.Y	20	2 00	*	Morristown	near	Walk
do	Revere House	John C. Bann	Brockville, Ont	80	2 50	....	Morristown	1¼m	Ferry and omnibus
do	St. Lawrence Hall	A. Robinson	Brockville, Ont	100	2 50	....	Morristown	1¼m	Ferry and omnibus
do	Central Hotel	S. Connors	Brockville, Ont	60	2 00	9 00	Morristown	1¼m	Ferry and omnibus
do	Boarding House	Miss Moore	Brockville, Ont	10	1 00	6 00	Morristown	1¼m	Ferry and walk
do	Cedar Park Hotel	Fred Drewry	Charleston Lake, Ont	75	1 50-2	....	Athens, Ont	4m	Stage
do	Armstrong House	Mrs. E. Armstrong	Athens, Ont	60	1 50	9 00	Athens, Ont	5m	Stage
do	Duffield House	A. Foster	Charleston Lake, Ont	40	1 50	9 00	Athens, Ont	5m	Stage
do	Wells Hotel	R. Wells	Delta, Ont	20	1 50	9 00	Delta, Ont	......	
do	Hotel DeBrown	Alex. Van Alstine	Delta, Ont	30	1 50	7 00	Delta, Ont	......	
do	Wyte House	W. Wyte	Newboro, Ont	15	1 50	9 00	Newboro, Ont	......	Omnibus
do	Hart's Hotel	John Hart	Newboro, Ont	15	1 50	9 00	Newboro, Ont	......	Omnibus
do	Wardrobe House	D. Wardrobe	Westport, Ont	21	1 50	9 00	Westport, Ont	......	Omnibus
do	Curtis's Hotel	Platt Curtis	Westport, Ont	20	1 50	9 00	Westport, Ont	......	Omnibus
Lake Ontario	Sand B'ch Sum'r Res'rt	McDonald & McDonald	West Lake, Prince Edward Co., Ont	.....	1 00	6 00	Bloomfield, Ont	4m	Omnibus
St. Lawrence River	Black Lake House	Henry J. Perry	Edwardsville, St. Lawrence Co., N.Y	.....	.....	....	Morristown	5m	Livery
do	Terrace House	Henry Easton	Morristown, N.Y	60	2 to 3	Special	Morristown Park	near	Trains stop in front of hotel

Adirondack Mt'ns.	Meacham Lake House	A. R. Fuller	Meacham, Franklin Co., N.Y.	75	$2½-3	$10 00 to 17 50	Meacham	5m	Meacham Lake Stage
do	McCollum's House	C. A. McArthur	Paul Smith's, Franklin Co., N.Y.	60	2 00	10 00 to 14 00	Paul Smith's	7m	Stage
do	Paul Smith's	A. A. Smith	Paul Smith's, Franklin Co., N.Y.	500	4 00	17 50 to 35 00	Paul Smith's	near	Walk
do	Kushaqua Lodge	A. S. Dominick & Co.	Lake Kushaqua, Franklin Co., N. Y.	60	2 50	10 00 to 15 00	Lake Kushaqua	¼m	Carriage
do	Rainbow Lake Hotel	J. M. Wardner	Rainbow, Franklin Co., N.Y.	50	2 50	10 00 to 15 00	Rainbow Lake	2m	Walk
do	Saranac Inn	D. W. Riddle, Manager	Saranac Inn, Franklin Co., N.Y.	150	3 50	17 50 to 40 00	Saranac Inn	1½m	Saranac Inn Carriage
do	Blue Mountain House	Henry Phelps	Santa Clara, Franklin Co., N.Y.	50	1 50	6 00 to 8 00	Spring Cove	4½m	Stage
do	Santa Clara House	A. T. Kingsley	Santa Clara, Franklin Co., N.Y.	30	2 00	6 00 to 10 00	Santa Clara	near	Walk
do	Kingsley's Hotel	J. Kingsley	Santa Clara, Franklin Co., N.Y.	50	1 50	4 00 to 9 00	Santa Clara	near	Spring wagon
do	Dimmick House	E. T. Dimmick	Santa Clara, Franklin Co., N.Y.	20	1 50	4 00 to 9 00	Santa Clara	1m	Spring wagon
do	Waverly House	L. C. Goodrich	St. Regis Falls, Franklin Co., N.Y.	70	1 50	6 00 to 8 00	St. Regis Falls	near	
do	Fernwood Hall	Frederic M. Heath	St. Regis Falls, Franklin Co., N. Y.	40	2-3 00	10 00 to 16 00	St. Regis Falls	7m	Livery or Stage
do	Bay Pond House	H. G. Baker	Brandon, Franklin Co., N.Y.	150	2 00	10 00 to 12 00	Paul Smith's Sta.	¼m	Spring wagon
do	Buck Mountain House	J. & A. McKillip	Brandon, Franklin Co., N.Y.	50	2 00	10 00 to 12 00	Paul Smith's Sta.	near	Walk
do	Brandon House	N. F. Lee	Brandon, Franklin Co., N.Y.	50	1 50	6 00 to 10 00	Paul Smith's Sta.	¼m	Spring wagon
do	Wawbeek Lodge	F. W. Foster, Manager	Wawbeek, Franklin Co., N.Y.	100	3 50-4	15 00 to 30 00	Tupper L. Sta. Saranac Inn	8m 7m	Stage Steamer "Saranac"
do	Hiawatha House		Wawbeek, Franklin Co., N.Y.	30	2 50	10 00 to 14 00	Tupper Lake Sta.	11m	Stage, boat and carry
do	Rustic Lodge	E. B. McCoy	Wawbeek, Franklin Co., N.Y.	40	2 00	10 00 to 12 00	Tupper Lake Sta.	15m	Stage and boat
do	Saranac Club	F. W. Foster	Wawbeek, Franklin Co., N.Y.	50	2 50	12 00 to 25 00	Tupper Lake Sta.	15m	Stage and boat
do	Hotel Childwold	Wm. F. Ingold	Massawepie, St. Lawrence Co., N.Y.	300	3-4 00	17 50 to 35 00	Childwold Sta.	6m	Ingold's Stage
do	Pond View House	E. P. Gale	Childwold, St. Lawrence Co., N.Y.	40	1 00	7 00 to 14 00	Childwold Sta.	6m	Stage
do	Ruisseaumont House	T. Edward Krumbholz	Lake Placid, Essex Co., N.Y.	125	3 50-4	21 00 to 50 00	Saranac Lake	9m	Stage
do	Algonquin	John Harding	Algonquin, Franklin Co., N.Y.	125	3 00-4	15 00 to 25 00	Saranac Lake	2m	Concord Coach
do	Tupper Lake House	Wm. J. Burke, Mgr.	Moody, Franklin Co., N.Y.	100	3 00	14 00 to 21 00	Tupper Lake Sta.	7m	Boat
do	Grand View House	Henry Allen	Lake Placid, Essex Co., N.Y.	125	3 00	14 00 to 17 50	Saranac Lake	9m	Stage
do	Castle Rustico	W. B. Leggett	Lake Placid, Essex Co., N.Y.	50	2 50	*	Saranac Lake	9m	Stage
do	Mirror Lake Hotel	C. E. Martin, Manager	Lake Placid, Essex Co., N.Y.		3 00	17 50 to	Saranac Lake	9m	Stage
do	Mountain View House	Chas. H. Green	Bloomingdale, Essex Co., N.Y.		2 00	8 00 to 12 00	Bloomingdale	near	
do	Ridgewood Farm	J. J. Fitzgerald	Harrietstown, Franklin Co., N. Y.	10	1 50	7 00 to 10 00	Bloomingdale	2½m	Stage or private conveyance
• do	Camp Crag	H. H. Covey	Big Moose, N. Y.	25	3 00	14 00	Big Moose	3½m	Stage and boat
do	Higby Camp	J. H. Higby	Big Moose, Herkimer Co., N.Y.	40	2 00	10 50 to 12 00	Big Moose	4m	Stage and boat
do	Hotel Ampersand	Eaton & Young	Saranac Lake, N. Y.	200	......	21 00 and up	Saranac Lake	1m	
do	Baker Cottage	A. J. Baker	Saranac Lake, N.Y.	12	......	9 00 to 10 00	Saranac Lake	½m	
do	Villa Dorsey	W. C. Rice	Saranac Lake, N.Y.	25	......	12 00 to 20 00	Saranac Lake	......	
do	Moody's	Martin Moody	Moody, Franklin Co., N.Y.	25	2 00	10 00 to 12 00	Tupper Lake Sta.	4m	Boat
do	Mt. Morris House	J. F. Hatch	Moody, Franklin Co., N.Y.	50	2 00	6 00 to 12 00	Tupper Lake Sta.	3m	Boat
do	Hamilton House	P. A. Robbins	Moody, Franklin Co., N.Y.	85	3 00	12 00	Tupper Lake Sta.	13m	Boat and carry
do	Freeman Cottage	P. M. Freeman	Moody, Franklin Co., N.Y.		1 50	8 00 to 10 00	Tupper Lake Sta.	3m	Boat
do	Tromblee's	O. Tromblee	Wawbeek, Franklin Co., N.Y.	20	2 00	10 00	Tupper Lake Sta.	7m	Boat
do	Raquette Falls House	— McClellan	Wawbeek, Franklin Co., N.Y.	40	2 00	10 00 to 12 00	Tupper Lake Sta.	18m	Boat
do	Cranberry Lake House	Mrs. E. J. Bishop	Russell, St. Lawrence Co., N.Y.	75	2 00	10 50	Tupper Lake Sta.	22m	Boat and carry
do	Windfall House	J. Sevey	Sevey, St. Lawrence Co., N.Y.	25	1 00	7 00	Childwold Sta.	14m	Stage
do	Mountain View House	W. P. Southworth	Tupper Lake, Franklin Co., N. Y.		1 00	5 00	Tupper Lake Sta.	⅛m	
do	Raquette Pond House	N. M. Parks	Tupper Lake, Franklin Co., N.Y.	75	1-2 50	3 00 to 6 00	Tupper Lake Sta.	near	
do	Altamont Hotel	J. H. & T. L. Weir	Tupper Lake, Franklin Co., N.Y.	80	2 50-5	8 00 to 12 00	Tupper Lake Sta.	near	
Adirondacks	Brushton House	E. W. & F. D. Woods	Brushton, St. Lawrence Co., N. Y.	30	2 00	4 00 to 7 00	Brushton	near	
do	Adirondack Hotel	J. A. McNeil	Moira, Franklin Co., N.Y.	20	1 50	5 00	Moira	near	
do	Hotel Flanagan	W. R. & S. J. Flanagan	Malone, Franklin Co., N. Y.	75	2 to 3	10 50 to 17 50	Malone	near	
do	Mountain View House	R. G. Lowe	Malone, Franklin Co., N. Y.	40	2 00	10 00 to 17 00	Malone	12m	
do	Hotel Ayers	W. J. Ayers & Son	Duane, Franklin Co., N. Y.	100	2-3 00	12 00 to 21 00	Malone	11m	Livery
do	Chasm House	Chateaugay Chasm Co	Chateaugay, Franklin Co., N. Y.	100	2 25	10 00 to 14 00	Chateaugay	1½m	Stage
do	Banner House	Bennett & Kirby	Chateaugay Lake, Franklin Co., N. Y.	75	2-2 50	10 00 to 15 00	Chateaugay	7m	Stage
do	Ralph's	J. W. Hutton	Lyon Mountain, Clinton Co., N. Y.	100	2 50	14 00 to 17 50	Chateaugay	15m	Stage
do	Merrill's	O. Young	Merrill, Clinton Co., N. Y.	50	2 50	10 00 to 14 00	Chateaugay	13m	
Lake Champlain	Hotel Windsor	Chas. F. Beck	Rouse's Point, N. Y.	100	3 00	14 00	Rouse's Point	¾m	
do	Holland House	A. E. Barnett	Rouse's Point, N. Y.	50	2 00	5 00 to 10 00	Rouse's Point	near	
do	Massachusetts House	J. Cogan	Rouse's Point, N. Y.	50	2 00	5 00 to 10 00	Rouse's Point	near	
do	Mansion House	W. A. Stone	Alburgh Springs, Vt.	100	2 00	5 00 to 15 00	Alburgh Springs	1½m	
do	Van Ness	H. N. Clark, Manager	Burlington, Vt.	500	3 00	20 00 and up	Burlington	¼m	Omnibus

LIST OF SUMMER HOTELS AND BOARDING HOUSES.

REGION.	Name of Hotel.	Proprietor.	Post-Office Address.	Room Capacity.	Rate per Day.	Rate per Week.	Nearest Railroad Station.	Dist. from R. R. Sta. in miles.	How Reached from Railroad Station.
Lake Champlain	Boarding House	Mrs. F. L. Lee	Burlington, Vt., No. 2 Colchester Ave.	12	$ 100	$5 00 to 8 00	Burlington	1m	Electric cars or hack
do	Private Residence	Mrs. C. C. Reed	Burlington, Vt., No. 128 Colchester Ave.	12	1 & up	5 00 and up	Burlington	1m	Electric cars
do	Private Residence	Miss Laura C. Durfey	Burlington, Vt., No. 210 No. Willard St.	7	1 50	....	Burlington	1m	Electric cars
do	Private Residence	Mrs. B. A. Muir	Burlington, Vt., No. 500 So. Willard St.	6	1 00	5 00	Burlington	1½m	Electric cars
do	Lake House	Mrs. A. C. Farr	Larabee's Point, Vt.	75	2 00	8 00 to 12 00	Orwell	2m	Carriage
do	Eagle Inn	F. B. Kimball	Orwell, Vt.	50	2 00	Apply	Orwell	......	Carriage
do	Queen City Park	L. Webb	Burlington, Vt.	100	1 50	8 00 to 10 00	Burlington	2m	On Shelburne Bay
do	Hotel Champlain	O. D. Seavey	Hotel Champlain, N. Y.	350	.....	Apply	Bluff Point	......	
do	Iodine Spring House	G. W. Squires	So. Hero, Vt.	60	.....	7 00 to 10 00	Milton	3m	Or steamer from Burlington
do	Hotel Champlain	C. F. Smith	Maquam, Vt.	90	2 50	9 00 to 14 00	Maquam	near	
do	Brigham House	J. V. Spooner	Bakersfield, Vt.	50	2 00	7 00 to 12 00	East Fairfield	3m	Coach from house
do	Quincy House	H. H. Best	Enosburgh Falls, Vt.	20	2 00	4 00 to 8 00	Enosburgh Falls		
do	Boarding House	Mrs. Geo. Vincent	East Berkshire, Vt.	10	.....	6 00	East Berkshire	½m	
do	Boarding House	Mrs. G. C. Manuel	Richford, Vt.	4	.....	4 00	Richford	½m	Private conveyance
do	Pleasant View House	John P. Garland	Newbury, Vt.	10	1 00	5 00	Newbury	near	Walk
do	Franklin House	J. L. Scott	Highgate Springs, Vt.	125	3 00	15 00 to 18 00	Highgate Spr'gs.	near	
do	Elmwood House	H. Phelps	Highgate Springs, Vt.	150	2 00	7 00 to 10 00	Highgate Spr'gs.	near	
do	Pavilion	J. S. Viles	Montpelier, Vt.	160	2 to 3	8 00 to 15 00	Montpelier	near	
do	Breezy Hill	H. H. Moore	Warren, Vt.	5	1 50	6 00	Roxbury, Vt.	7m	Stage
do	Welden House	Wm. Landon	St. Albans, Vt.	400	2 50	12 00 to 20 00	St. Albans	near	
do	American House	J. J. Thompson	St. Albans, Vt.	150	2 00	7 00 to 14 00	St. Albans	near	
do	Park View House	J. LeBeau	St. Albans, Vt.	50	1 50	Special	St. Albans	near	
do	Samson's Lake View	W. J. Samson, Mgr.	St. Albans, Vt.	60	2 00	9 00 to 17 00	St. Albans	6m	Carriage, if notified
do	Rocky Point Hotel	C. T. Knapton	St. Albans, Vt.	50	2 00	10 00 to 12 00	St. Albans	6m	Coach
do	Camp Rich	David R. Bean	Miltonboro, Vt.	25	.....	5 00 to 7 00	Milton	7m	Carriage
do	Sunnyside	Obed Whipple	North Pomfret, Vt.	12	.....	4 00	West Hartford	4½m	Stage
do	Congress Hall	Mrs. E. W. Fitch	Sheldon Springs, Vt.	125	2 50	10 00 to 15 00	Sheldon Springs	near	
do	Portland Hotel	Geo. H. Thomas	Sheldon, Franklin Co., Vt.	30	.....	4 00 to 6 00	Sheldon	near	Walk
do	The Randall	C. F. Randall	Morrisville, Vt.	50	2 00	7 00 to 10 00	Morrisville	near	Walk
do	St. Johnsbury House	S. B. Krogman, Jr.	St. Johnsbury, Vt.	100	2 00	10 00 to 14 00	St. Johnsbury	near	
do	Avenue House	B. G. Howe	St. Johnsbury, Vt.	80	2 00	5 00 to 10 00	St. Johnsbury	near	
do	Winooski Hotel	R. J. O'Neil	Cabot, Vt.	20	1 50	6 00 to 9 00	Walden	4m	Stage
do	Willoughby Lake H'se	Mrs. N. R. Richardson	Willoughby, Vt.	75	2 00	8 00 to 14 00	West Burke	6m	Coach
White Mountains	Crawford House	Barron & Merrill	Crawford House, N. H.	400	4 50	21 00 to 28 00	Crawford House	......	
do	Codman House	F. B. Morse	Enfield Centre, N. H.	50	.....	7 00 to 10 00	Enfield	5m	Free Carriage
do	Forest Hills Hotel	Priest & Dudley	Franconia, N. H.	175	3 50	15 00 to 24 00	Bethlehem	4m	
do	Goodnow House	E. H. Goodnow & Co.	Franconia, N. H.	275	2 50	8 00 to 12 00	Bethlehem	4m	
do	Lafayette House	Richardson Brothers	Franconia, N. H.	75	.....	7 00 to 10 00	Bethlehem	4m	
do	Phillips House	W. B. Phillips	Franconia, N. H.	75	2 00	7 00 to 10 00	Bethlehem	4m	
do	Profile House	Taft & Greenleaf	Profile House, N. H.	600	4 50	21 00 to 28 00	Profile House	......	
do	Flume House	Elliot Bros., Managers		150	3 50	14 00 to 17 50	Profile House	......	
do	Maplewood Hotel	Ainslie & Webster	Maplewood, N. H.	400	4 50	....	Maplewood	......	
do	Maplewood Cottage		Maplewood, N. H.	100	3 00	10 00 to 18 00	Maplewood	......	
do	Sinclair House	Durgin & Co.	Bethlehem, N. H.	350	3 50	17 50 to 24 50	Bethlehem	......	
do	Alpine House	C. H. Clark	Bethlehem, N. H.	65	.....	9 00 to 17 00	Bethlehem	......	
do	Highland House	J. H. Clark	Bethlehem, N. H.	100	2 50-3	18 00 to 30 00	Bethlehem	......	
do	Bellevue House	David S. Phillips	Bethlehem, N. H.	90	1 50-2	7 00 to 10 00	Bethlehem	......	
do	Prospect House	Mrs. Geo. W. Phillips	Bethlehem, N. H.	85	2 00	7 00 to 10 00	Bethlehem	......	
do	Strawberry Hill House	J. K. Barrett	Bethlehem, N. H.	100	2 50	10 00 to 16 00	Bethlehem	......	
do	Howard House	C. E. Bunker	Bethlehem, N. H.	60	2 00	10 00 to 12 00	Bethlehem	......	

White Mountains..	Ranlet House	D. W. Ranlet	Bethlehem, N. H	100			Bethlehem		
do	Mt. Washington House	C. L. Bartlett	Bethlehem, N. H	60	$2 50	$10 00 to 14 00	Bethlehem		
do	Bethlehem House	E. A. Cook	Bethlehem, N. H	80		8 00 to 14 00	Bethlehem	¼m	
do	Mount Agassiz House	Horatio Nye	Bethlehem, N. H	65	2 00	8 00 to 12 00	Bethlehem		
do	Avenue House	C. M. Bean	Bethlehem, N. H	60	2 50	8 00 to 15 00	Bethlehem		
do	Turner House	James N. Turner	Bethlehem, N. H	75	2 00	8 00 to 15 00	Bethlehem		
do	Elm House	R. M. Hodgdon	Bethlehem, N. H	25	1 50		Bethlehem	3m	
do	Farm Cottage	A. S. Phillips	Bethlehem, N. H	30	1 00	6 00	Bethlehem	1½m	
do	Fabyan House	Barron & Merrill	Fabyan House, N. H	400	4 50	17 50 to 28 00	Fabyan's		
do	Kelsey Cottage	Benj. Kelsey	Gorham, N. H	16		5 00 to 6 00	Gorham	5m	Carriage
do	Willis Cottage	Mrs. F. H. Evans	Gorham, N. H	40	1 50	7 00 to 10 00	Gorham	near	Free Carriage
do	Randolph Hill House	Irving R. Leighton	Gorham, N. H. (P. O. Box 43)	60	2 00	8 50 to 14 00	Randolph	3m	Stage
do	Intervale House	S. Mudgett & Sons	Intervale, N. H	300	3 00	8 00 to 24 00	Intervale		
do	Bellevue House	J. A. Barnes' Sons	Intervale, N. H	80	2 00	10 00 to 25 00	Intervale		
do	Pendexter Mansion	Parkman Drown	Intervale, N. H	50	150-2	14 00 to 18 00	Intervale		
do	The Waumbek	Porter & Judd	Jefferson, N. H	300	2 to 4	17 50 to 25 00	Jefferson		
do	Plaisted House	P. C. Plaisted	Jefferson, N. H	125	2 50	8 00 to 12 00	Jefferson		
do	Jefferson Hill House	E. E. Bedell	Jefferson, N. H	100	2 50	10 00 to 15 00	Jefferson		
do	Mount Adams House	J. W. Crawshaw	Jefferson Highlands, N. H	60		7 00 to 12 00	Jefferson		
do	Pliny Range House	G. W. Crawford & Son	Jefferson Highlands, N. H	85		6 00 to 9 00	Jefferson		
do	Highland House	G. A. & G. L. Pottle	Jefferson Highlands, N. H	60		7 00 to 10 00	Jefferson		
do	Glen Ellis House	S. N. Thompson	Jackson, N. H	125	2 50	8 00 to 15 00	Glen Station		Tally-ho coach
do	Arden House }								
do	Wentworth Hall }	M. C. Wentworth	Jackson, N. H	200	4 to 5	12 00 to 28 00	Glen Station		Tally-ho coach
do	Thorn Mt. House }								
do	Jackson Falls House	Trickey Bros	Jackson, N. H	75	2 50-3	12 00 to 21 00	Glen Station		Tally-ho coach
do	Eagle Mountain	C. E. Gale	Jackson, N. H	70	2 00	8 00 to 12 00	Glen Station		Tally-ho coach
do	Iron Mt. House	Meserve Bros	Jackson, N. H	75					
do	Gray's Inn	C. W. Gray	Jackson, N. H	75	2 00	7 00 to 12 00	Glen Station		Tally-ho coach
do	Lancaster House	W. H. Whipp	Lancaster, N. H	150	2 50	10 00 to 17 50	Lancaster		
do	Williams House	John N. Hopkins	Lancaster, N. H	50	1 50	7 00 to 10 00	Lancaster		
do	Breezy Hill House	Wells & Woolson	Lisbon, N. H	100	2 50-3	10 00 to 17 00	Lisbon	3½m	Carriages and coaches from hotel
do	Lake View Cottage	F. M. Aldrich	Lisbon, N. H. (P. O. Box 191)	17	1 25	5 50 to 8 00	Lisbon	10m	Carriage on notice
do	Thayer's Hotel	H. L. Thayer & Son	Littleton, N. H	100	3 00	10 00 to 17 50	Littleton		
do	Oak Hill House	Farr & Jarvis	Littleton, N. H	150	3 00	9 00 to 15 00	Littleton		
do	Chiswick Inn	G. W. Smith	Littleton, N. H	100	3 00	12 00 to 15 00	Littleton		
do	Ivanhoe House	Scott W. Powers	Littleton, N. H. (P. O. Box 384)	50	2 00	8 00 to 10 00	Littleton	near	Hotel coach
do	Cottage Farm	John M. Pulsifer	Plymouth, Grafton Co., N. H	10		5 00	Livermore Falls	1m	Carriage
do	Farm Home	Mrs. E. G. Sargent	Plymouth, Grafton Co., N. H	12		5 00 to 7 00	Plymouth	1m	Carriage
do	Lamphere House	N. S. Lamphere	Lyme, N. H			4 50	East Hetford	1m	
do	Mt. Pleasant House	Anderson & Price	Fabyan House, N. H	450	4 50		Mt. Pleasa't H'se		
do	Kearsarge House	L. J. Ricker	North Conway, N. H	300	3-3 50	10 50 to 21 00	North Conway		
do	Sunset Pavilion	M. L. Mason	North Conway, N. H	150	3 00	10 00 to 21 00	North Conway		
do	McMillan House	F. S. Plummer	North Conway, N. H	75	3 00	8 00 to 14 00	North Conway		
do	Eastman House	A. Eastman	North Conway, N. H	75	2 00	7 00 to 12 00	North Conway		
do	The Ridge	H. H. Dow	North Conway, N. H	100	3 00	10 50 to 21 00	North Conway		
do	North Conway House	L. J. Ricker	North Conway, N. H	60	2 00	8 00 to 14 00	North Conway		
do	Mt. Lookoff House	B. L. Peaslee	Woodstock, N. H	10	1 25	5 00	Woodstock	¼m	Carriage from house
do	Mt. Liberty House	C. A. Hunt	North Woodstock, N. H	30	2 00	7 00 to 12 00	North Woodstock	4m	Carriage
do	Carroll	G. W. Huse	Ossipee, N. H	75	1 50-2	7 00 to 10 00	Ossipee		
do	Summit House	Barron & Merrill	Fabyan House, N. H	200	5 00		Sum't Mt. Wash.		
do	Shelburne Spring H'se	S. J. Morse	Shelburne, N. H	60	1 50	5 00 to 8 00	Shelburne	⅓m	
do	Twin Mountain House	W. A. Barron, M'g'r	Twin Mountain, N. H	300	4 00	17 50 to 28 00	Twin Mt. House		
do	Gilman's Hotel	G. E. Gilman	West Ossipee, N. H	30	1 25-2	5 00 to 8 00	West Ossipee		
do	Chocorua House	D. Knowles	West Ossipee, N. H	50	1 50-2	7 00 to 10 00	West Ossipee		
do	Maplewood Farm H'se	Henry L. Kimball, Goffstown, N. H	Manchester, N. H		1 00	5 00 to 7 00	Manchester	3m	Carriage on notice
do	Ascutney View House	A. R. Campbell	Claremont, N. H	20	1 50	7 00	Claremont	¼m	Coach
do	Grafton House	Edward Fitzgerald	Grafton, N. H	20	2 00	7 00 to 12 00	Grafton	near	Walk
do	Glen Cottage	Levi Horne	Wolfeborough, N. H	40	1 00-2	6 00 to 8 00	Wolfeborough	near	

LIST OF SUMMER HOTELS AND BOARDING HOUSES.

REGION.	Name of Hotel.	Proprietor.	Post-Office Address.	Room Capacity.	Rate Per Day.	Rate per week.	Nearest Railroad Station.	Dist. from R. R. Sta. in miles.	How Reached from Railroad Station.
White Mountains..	Mountain View House	Wm. F. Dodge & Sons.	Whitefield, N. H	150	$2 00	$7 00 to 12 00	Whitefield		
do	White Mountain House	R. D. Rounsevel	Fabyan House, N. H	150	2 00	10 50	White Mt. House		
Atlantic Coast	New Boar's Head	S. H. Dumas	Hampton, N. H	150	2 to 3	7 00 to 20 00	Hampton		
do	Eagle	Lewis P. Nudd	Hampton, N. H	60	1 to 2	6 00 to 12 00	Hampton		
do	Hotel Whittier	O. H. Whittier	Hampton, N. H	75	1 to 2	7 00 to 14 00	Hampton		
do	Farragut	F. A. Chilbrick	North Hampton, N. H	175	3 50-4	21 00 to 25 00	North Hampton		
do	Seaview	George G. Lougee	North Hampton, N. H	120	3 50	15 00 to 25 00	North Hampton		
do	Wentworth Hotel	W. R. Hill, Manager	New Castle, N. H	500	4 50	21 00 to 28 00	New Castle		
do	Rockingham Hotel	W. R. Hill, Manager	Portsmouth, N. H	300	4 00	20 00 to 25 00	Portsmouth		
do	Appledore Hotel	Laighton Bros	Portsmouth, N. H. (Isle of Shoals)	500	3 50	17 50 to 21 00	Portsmouth		
do	Oceanic Hotel	Laighton Bros	Portsmouth, N. H. (Isle of Shoals)	400	3 50	17 50 to 21 00	Portsmouth		
do	West End	O. M. Shaw & Son	Bar Harbor, Me	400	3-3 50	14 00 to 21 00	Bar Harbor		
do	St. Sauveur	Alley Brothers	Bar Harbor, Me	175	2 50-4	18 00 to 25 00	Bar Harbor		
do	Malvern	E. C. Berdzon	Bar Harbor, Me	150	......	23 00 to 30 00	Bar Harbor		
do	Newport House	William M. Roberts	Bar Harbor, Me	150	2 to 3	14 00 to 21 00	Bar Harbor		
do	Louisburg	J. A. Butler	Bar Harbor, Me	300	5 00	......	Bar Harbor		
do	Hotel des Isles	A. Higgins	Bar Harbor, Me	120	2 00	10 00 to 14 00	Bar Harbor		
do	Rockaway House	F. L. Roberts	Bar Harbor, Me	100	2-2 50	12 00 to 18 00	Bar Harbor		
do	Belmont	J. C. Manchester	Bar Harbor, Me	130	2 50	12 00 to 18 00	Bar Harbor		
do	Lynam House	J. S. Lynam	Bar Harbor, Me	125	2 25	12 00 to 18 00	Bar Harbor		
do	Marlborough House	Herbert P. Higgins	Bar Harbor, Me	100	2 to 3	10 00 to 18 00	Bar Harbor		
do	Menawarmet House	C. Tryon	Boothbay, Me	100	2 to 3	15 00 to 20 00			
do	Boothbay House	Fred. Harris	Boothbay, Me	75	1 to 2	7 00 to 10 00			
do	Sea View Cottage	B. B. Rodick	Pond Cove, Cape Elizabeth, Me	20	2 00	10 00	Cape Eliz'h Dep.		
do	Arcadian Hotel	W. A. Walker	Castine, Me	200	2 00	9 00 to 14 00	Portland		Steamer
do	Glen Mountain House	John M. Tobin	Bryant's Pond, Oxford Co., Me	30	2 00	7 00	Bryant's Pond	near	Carriage
do	Lake View House	O. S. Keene	West Poland, Me	22	1 50	7 00	Poland		Carriage on notice
do	National House	E. G. Reynolds	Dixfield, Me	30	1 50-2	6 00 to 8 00	Dixfield	½m	Coach
do	North Turner House	Elias Keene	North Turner, Me	40	1 00	3 50 to 5 00	North Leeds	7m	Stage
do	Ottawa House (Cushing's Island).	C. R. Costello	Portland, Me	400	3 to 4	14 00 to 30 00	Portland		Steamer
do	Hotel Park Field	J. E. Frisbee	Kittery Point, Me	75	2 to 3	10 00 to 18 00	Kittery Point		
do	Pepperell House	E. F. Safford	Kittery Point, Me	75	2 to 3	10 00 to 18 00	Kittery Point		
do	Hotel Pocahontas	H. A. Cobb	Kittery Point, Me	125	3 00	12 00 to 20 00	Kittery Point		
do	Champernowne	H. Mitchell, Jr	Kittery Point, Me	100	2 to 3	10 00 to 20 00	Kittery Point		
do	Willow Lane Farm	E. Day & Son	Kennebunk, Me. (P. O. Box 223)	15	......	7 00 to 9 00	Kennebunk	4m	
do	Ocean Bluff	Stimpson & Devnell	Kennebunkport, Me	450	3 to 4	15 00 to 28 00	Kennebunkport		
do	Parker House	S. D. Thompson	Kennebunkport, Me	150	2 50-4	15 00 to 25 00	Kennebunkport		
do	Beach House	Owen Wentworth	Kennebunkport, Me	70	1 50-2	8 00 to 12 00	Kennebunk B'ch		
do	Granite State House	A. Stuart	Kennebunkport, Me	80	2 00	10 00 to 13 00	Grove Station		
do	Cliff House }	B. F. Eldridge	Kennebunkport, Me	150	......	7 00 to 15 00	Kennebunkport		
do	Glen Cottage }								
do	Riverside House	Geo. Gooch	Kennebunkport, Me	75	2 00	8 00 to 15 00	Kennebunkport		
do	Beckford House	J. W. Beckford	Kennebunkport, Me	75	2 00	9 00 to 15 00	Kennebunkport		
do	Eagle Rock House	J. D. Wells	Kennebunkport, Me	75	2 00	8 00 to 14 00	Kennebunk B'ch		
do	Grove Hill House	J. F. Paul	Kennebunkport, Me	125	......	......	Grove Station		
do	Dirigo House (Long I.)	I. Perry	Portland, Me	80	1 50-2	7 00 to 9 00	Portland		
do	Granite Spring Hotel (Long Island).	E. Ponce	Portland, Me	100	1 50-3	10 00 to 20 00	Portland		
do	Casco Bay Ho. (Long I)	C. E. Cushing	Portland, Me	65	1 50-2	7 00 to 9 00	Portland		

Atlantic Coast	Old Orchard House	E. C. Staples	Old Orchard Beach, Me.	500			Old Orchard Bch		
do	Imperial	D. H. Swan	Old Orchard Beach, Me.	400			Old Orchard Bch		
do	Hotel Fiske	C. H. Fiske	Old Orchard Beach, Me.	300	$3 00	$14 00 to 21 00	Old Orchard Bch		
do	Seashore House	F. G. Staples	Old Orchard Beach, Me.	300	3 00	14 00 to 21 00	Old Orchard Bch		
do	Lawrence House	J. H. Horne	Old Orchard Beach, Me.	150	2 50	9 00 to 15 00	Old Orchard Bch		
do	Gorham House	C. W. Gorham	Old Orchard Beach, Me.	100	2-2 50		Old Orchard Bch		
do	Aldine House	Samuel Haines	Old Orchard Beach, Me.	125	2-3 00	10 00 to 16 00	Old Orchard Bch		
do	Hotel Belmont		Old Orchard Beach, Me.	125	1 50-3	15 00 to 30 00	Old Orchard Bch		
do	Irving House	G. S. Googins	Old Orchard Beach, Me.	100	1 to 2	7 00 to 10 00	Old Orchard Bch		
do	Montreal House	Mrs. A. B. Blanchard	Old Orchard Beach, Me.	100	2 00	10 00 to 15 00	Old Orchard Bch		
do	Revere House	L. A. Pillsbury	Old Orchard Beach, Me.	100	2 50	14 00	Old Orchard Bch		
do	Hotel Everett	Mrs. M. F. Porter	Old Orchard Beach, Me.	150	2 to 3	10 00 to 15 00	Old Orchard Bch		
do	Chapman H'se (Peak's Island).	Miss May Chapman	Portland, Me.	100	2-2 50	10 00 to 15 00	Portland		
do	Union H'se (Peak's Isl.)	Mrs. E. A. Jones	Portland, Me.	75	1 50-2	10 00 to 12 00	Portland		
do	St. Julian	R. W. Underwood	Portland, Me.	125	2-2 50	8 00 to 15 00	Portland		
do	Bay View H'se (Peak's I.	J. T. Sterling & Son	Portland, Me.	75	1 50-2	10 00 to 12 00	Portland		
do	Valley View H'se "	W. S. Trefeathen	Portland, Me.	75	1 50-2	10 00 to 12 00	Portland		
do	Pillsbury House	J. W. Pillsbury	Pine Point Beach, Me.	40	2 00	10 50	Pine Point Beach		
do	Falmouth Hotel	J. K. Martin	Portland, Me.	400	3 to 4	20 00 to 30 00	Portland		
do	Preble House	J. C. White	Portland, Me.	200	3-3 50	14 00 to 30 00	Portland		
do	United States Hotel	Foss & O'Connor	Portland, Me.	150	2-2 50	14 00 to 30 00	Portland		
do	Adams House	Joshua Taylor	Portland, Me.	100	1 50-2	6 00 to 12 00	Portland		
do	Atlantic House	S. B. Gunnison	Scarboro, Me.	125	2 50	14 00	Scarboro Beach		
do	Jocelyn House	F. B. Libby	Scarboro, Me.	125	2 50	12 00 to 18 00	Scarboro Beach		
do	Kirkwood House	Otis Kaler	Scarboro, Me.	125	2 00	8 00 to 12 00	Scarboro Beach		
do	Island H'se (Mt. Des'rt	H. H. Clark	South West Harbor, Me.	150	2 00	8 00 to 12 00	Bar Harbor		
do	Ocean House	A. Allen	South West Harbor, Me.	75	1 75	8 00 to 12 00	Bar Harbor		
do	Stanley House	Miss E. B. Stanley	South West Harbor, Me.	150	1 75	8 00 to 10 00	Bar Harbor		
do	Sea Wall House	D. S. Mooney	South West Harbor, Me.	100	1 75	8 00 to 10 00	Bar Harbor		
do	Eastern House	K. & H. Richards	Squirrel Island, Me.	200	2 00	10 00 to 14 00	Bath		Steamer
do	Fort Point House	J. C. Ryder	Stockton, Me.	250	2 50-3	10 00 to 20 00			
do	Waukeag	F. E. Balch	Sullivan, Me.				Mt. Desert Ferry		
do	Marshall	E. S. Marshall	York, Me.	300	2 50-3	14 00 to 17 50	York Harbor		
do	Sea Cottage	C. A. Grant	York, Me.	100	1½-2½	12 00	Long Beach		
do	Hotel Bartlett	H. E. Evans	York, Me.	150	2-2 50	10 00 to 15 00	Long Beach		
do	Young's Hotel	J. F. Young	York, Me.	300	1 50-3	8 00 to 20 00			
do	Garrison	J. W. Sanborn	York, Me.	100			Long Beach		
do	Ocean House	Ellis & Co.	York, Me.	300	2 3 00	12 00 to 21 00	York Beach		
do	Atlantic House	G. E. Gordon	York, Me.	100	2-3 00	10 00 to 20 00	York Beach		
do	Donnell House	B. G. Donnell	York, Me.	100	2-2 50	8 00 to 15 00	Long Beach		
do	York Harbor House	G. A. Goodell	York, Me.	100	2-2 50	10 00 to 14 00	York Harbor		
do	Harmon House	J. H. Vorrell	York, Me.	100	2-2 50	12 00 to 15 00	York Harbor		
Maine Hills	Mansion House	H. Ricker & Son	South Poland, Me.	75	2 50-3	10 00 to 17 00	Danville Junc. or		Stage
do	Poland Springs H'se (Poland Springs).	H. Ricker & Son	South Poland, Me.	500	4 50	18 00 to 28 00	Poland Sp's Junc.		Stage
do	Mount Kineo House	O. A. Dennen	Kineo, Me.	400	2-3 50	10 50 to 25 00	Greenville, Me.		Steamer
do	Bangor House	H. C. Chapman	Bangor, Me.	250	2-2 50	12 00 to 17 00	Bangor, Me.		
do	Penobscot Exchange	G. F. Hill & Co.	Bangor, Me.	200	2-2 50	10 00 to 17 00	Bangor, Me.		
do	Bangor Exch'ge Hotel	G. W. Stearns	Bangor, Me.	100	2 00		Bangor, Me.		
do	Windsor	F. W. Durgin	Bangor, Me.	100	2 00	10 00 to 14 00	Bangor, Me.		
Berkshire Hills	West Brook Cottage	Mrs. N. W. Mason	Cheshire, Berkshire Co., Mass.	150	1 50	7 00 to 9 00	Cheshire	½m	Carriage
Atlantic Coast	Pavilion	F. H. Sawyer	Gloucester, Mass.	140	3 00	10 00 to 20 00	Gloucester		
do	Webster	Nathaniel Webster	Gloucester, Mass.	75	2 00	7 00 to 10 00	Gloucester		
do	Gloucester	J. A. Herne	Gloucester, Mass.	100	1 50-2	8 00 to 12 00	Gloucester		
do	Mason	E. E. Saville	Gloucester, Mass.	100	1 50-2	8 00 to 12 00	Gloucester		
do	Belmont	A. Powell	Gloucester, Mass.	70	1 00-2	7 00 to 10 00	Gloucester		
do	Bass Rock	W. E. Forbes	Gloucester, Mass.	250		12 50 to 21 00	Gloucester		
do	Delphine	Simpson Lyle	Gloucester, Mass.	70	2-2 50	12 00 to 15 00	Gloucester		
do	Lancaster	S. T. Fuller	Lancaster, Mass.	50	1 50-2	5 00 to 14 00	Lancaster	1-5m	

LIST OF SUMMER HOTELS AND BOARDING HOUSES.

REGION.	Name of Hotel.	Proprietor.	Post-Office Address.	Room Capacity.	Rate per Day.	Rate per Week.	Nearest Railroad Station.	Dist. from R. R. Sta. in miles.	How Reached from Railroad Station.
Atlantic Coast	Ocean Side	George A. Upton	Magnolia, Mass.	200	$3-3½	$15 00 to 25 00	Magnolia		
do	Willow Cottage	E. Foster	Magnolia, Mass.	100	2 00	8 00 to 12 00	Magnolia		
do	Hesperus	Mrs. O. Page	Magnolia, Mass.	200	3-5 50	15 00 to 25 00	Magnolia		
do	The Blynman	W. F. Knowlton	Magnolia, Mass.	150	2 50	12 00 to 15 00	Magnolia		
do	Masconomo (Manchester-by-the-Sea)	J. J. Sullivan, Mg	Manchester, Mass.	300	5 00	30 00 to 40 00	Mancheste		
do	Turk's Head Inn	G. A. Keeler	Rockport, Mass.	200	2 00-4	10 00 to 20 00	Rockport		
do	Pigeon Cove	W. H. Wingate	Pigeon Cove, Mass.	125	3 50	15 00 to 17 50	Rockport	1¼m	Carriage or barge
do	Ocean View	Mrs. S. A. Lougee	Rockport, Mass.	120	2 00	12 00	Rockport		
do	Linwood	James Hurd	Rockport, Mass.	120	2 00	12 00	Rockport		
do	Central House	Jas. A. Reed, Mgr.	Provincetown, Mass.	50	2 00	8 00 to 10 00	Provincetown	½m	
do	Mayo Cottage	Mrs. A. M. Mayo	Provincetown, Mass.	25	1 25	8 00	Provincetown	1m	Carriage
do	Wiley Cottage	Mrs. Jesse Wiley	Provincetown, Mass. (P. O. Box 240.)	30	1 00	7 00	Provincetown	1m	Carriage
do	Dunham House	J. A. Dunham	Provincetown, Mass. (P. O. Box 254.)	20	1¼ 1½	9 00	Provincetown	near	Walk
do	Highland House	Willard M. Small	North Truro, Mass.	40	1¼ 1½	7 00 to 10 00	North Truro	1½m	Carriage 50c.
do	Negansett House	S. H. Cowen	North Falmouth, Mass.	20	1-2 00	7 00 to 15 00	North Falmouth	½m	Barge; fare 25c.
do	Hotel Columbus	Vincent Bros.	Stonington, Conn.	30	2-2 50	10 00 to 20 00	Stonington		
do	Algonquin	Albert Miller	St. Andrews, N. B.	300	3 00-5	12 00 to 30 00	St. Andrews		
do	Kennedy's Hotel	—— Kennedy	St. Andrews, N. B.	150	2 00-4	10 00 to 20 00	St. Andrews		
Ottawa River	Bellevue	Mrs. C. Thomas	Carillon, Que.	15	1 00	6 00	Carillon	near	Walk

* According to location of rooms.

STAGE. CONNECTIONS

LIST OF PLACES REACHED BY STAGE FROM R., W. & O. R.R. STATIONS.

Railroad Station.	Stage Destination.		Distance.	Fare.	Leaves Station.	
Adams	Belleville	N.Y.	6 m.	$0.50	11.00 a.m., 7.30 p.m.	Daily.
do	Lorraine	“	6 m.	.50	1.30 p.m.	Daily.
do	Worth	“	9 m.	.75	1.30 p.m.	Daily.
do	Worth Centre	“	13 m.	1.00	1.30 p.m.	Daily.
do	Roberts' Corners	“	5 m.	.40	4.00 p.m.	Daily.
do	Henderson	“	9 m.	.75	4.00 p.m.	Daily.
do	Henderson Harbor	“	10½ m.	.75	4.00 p.m.	Daily.
Adams Centre	Rodman	“	4 m.	.25	8.15 a.m., 7.00 p.m.	Daily, except Sunday.
Alder Creek	Alder Creek	“	1 m.	.10	Arrival of train	Daily, except Sunday.
do	Forestport	“	3 m.	.25	Arrival of train	Daily, except Sunday.
Alexandria Bay	Redwood	“	7 m.	.50	7.00 a.m., 3.00 p.m.	Daily, except Sunday.
Boonville	Leyden	“	4 m.	.25	8.30 a.m., 7.30 p.m.	Daily, except Sunday.
Brockville, Ont.	Spring Valley	Ont.	4 m.	....	8.25 a.m.	Daily, except Sunday.
do	Glen Buell	“	9 m.	....	8.25 a.m.	Daily, except Sunday.
do	Elbe	“	12 m.	....	8.25 a.m.	Daily, except Sunday.
do	Westport	“	45 m.	1.50	7.30 a.m.	Daily, except Sunday.
do	Athens	“	15 m.	....	10.30 a.m.	Daily, except Sunday.
do	Soperton	“	22 m.	....	10.30 a.m.	Daily, except Sunday.
do	Delta	“	25 m.	....	12.30 p.m.	Daily, except Sunday.
do	Phillipsville	“	29 m.	....	12.30 p.m.	Daily, except Sunday.
do	Forfar	“	33 m.	....	12.30 p.m.	Daily, except Sunday.
do	Singleton	“	36 m.	....	12.30 p.m.	Daily, except Sunday.
do	Newboro	“	40 m.	....	3.30 p.m.	Daily, except Sunday.
Brownville	Dexter	N.Y.	5 m.	.25	Arrival of 4.20 p.m. train	Daily, except Sunday.
Camden	East Florence	“	4 m.	.25	2.05 p.m.	Daily, except Sunday.
do	Florence	“	9 m.	.50	2.05 p.m.	Daily, except Sunday.
do	Osceola	“	14 m.	.75	2.05 p.m.	Daily, except Sunday.
Canton	Buck's Bridge	“	7 m.	.25	8.00 a.m.	Daily, except Sunday.
do	Morley	“	5 m.	.25	8.00 a.m.	Daily, except Sunday.
do	Madrid	“	10 m.	.50	8.00 a.m.	Daily, except Sunday.
do	Russell	“	12 m.	.75	1.00 p.m.	Daily, except Sunday.
do	Crary's Mills	“	5 m.	.25	2.00 p.m.	Daily, except Sunday.
do	Pyrites	“	6 m.	.50	2.00 p.m.	Daily, except Sunday.
do	Pierrepont	“	10 m.	.50	2.00 p.m.	Daily, except Sunday.
do	Colton	“	14 m.	.75	2.00 p.m.	Daily, except Sunday.
Carlton	Point Breeze	“	2½ m.	.25	9.40 a.m., 1.25 p.m.	Daily, except Sunday.
do	Oak Orchard	“	3 m.	.25	10.30 a.m., 7.30 p.m.	Daily, except Sunday.
Carthage	Copenhagen	“	7 m.	.50	10.30 a.m., 7.30 p.m.	Daily, except Sunday.
Castorland	Jerden Falls	“	17 m.	1.00	10.30 a.m.	Daily, except Sunday.
do	Belfort	“	11 m.	.70	10.30 a.m.	Daily, except Sunday.
do	Indian River	“	14 m.	.85	10.30 a.m.	Daily, except Sunday.
do	Naumburg	“	1 m.	.10	10.30 a.m., 4.00, 8.15 p.m.	Daily, except Sunday.
do	Beaver Falls	“	5 m.	.35	10.30 a.m., 4.00, 8.15 p.m.	Daily, except Sunday.
do	Croghan	“	7 m.	.50	10.30 a.m., 4.00, 8.15 p.m.	Daily, except Sunday.
Clay	Euclid	“	2½ m.	.15	On arrival trains 1 and 2	Daily, except Sunday.
Chaumont	Depauville	“	7 m.	.35	9.29 a.m., 7.07 p.m.	Daily, except Sunday.
Clayton	Thurso (by boat)	“	6 m.	.....	10.30 a.m.	Tuesday, Thursday and Saturday.

LIST OF PLACES REACHED BY STAGE FROM R., W. & O. R.R. STATIONS.

Railroad Station.	Stage Destination.		Distance.	Fare.	Leaves Station.	
Deer River	Deer River	N. Y.	1 m.	$0.10	On arrival of Mail train	Daily, except Sunday.
DeKalb Junction	Hermon	"	4 m.	.50	8.00 a.m., 1.00, 6.30 p.m.	Daily, except Sunday.
do	Russell	"	10 m.	.50	11.00 a.m.	Daily, except Sunday.
Edwards	South Edwards	"	5 m.	.35	7.00 p.m.	Daily, except Sunday.
do	Fine	"	10 m.	.75	7.00 p.m.	Daily, except Sunday.
Evan's Mills	Pamelia Four Corners	"	3½ m.	.25	Arrival of Mail trains	Daily, except Sunday.
Fulton	Mt. Pleasant	"	5 m.	.10	12.00 m.	Wednesdays and Saturdays.
do	Volney Centre	"	3 m.	.15	1.00 p.m.	Daily, except Sunday.
do	Palermo	"	8 m.	.40	1.00 p.m.	Daily, except Sunday.
do	Clifford	"	9 m.	.45	1.00 p.m.	Daily, except Sunday.
do	Vermilion	"	11 m.	.50	1.00 p.m.	Daily, except Sunday.
do	Butterfly	"	14 m.	.65	1.00 p.m.	Daily, except Sunday.
do	Mexico	"	17 m.	.75	1.00 p.m.	Daily, except Sunday.
do	Bowen's Corners	"	5 m.	.25	2.20 p.m.	Daily, except Sunday.
do	South Hannibal	"	8 m.	.35	2.20 p.m.	Daily, except Sunday.
do	Hannibal Centre	"	11 m.	.45	2.20 p.m.	Daily, except Sunday.
do	Hannibalville	"	14 m.	.50	2.20 p.m.	Daily, except Sunday.
do	Dexterville	"	4 m.	.25	4.00 p.m.	Daily, except Sunday.
do	Gilbert's Mills	"	6 m.	.25	4.00 p.m.	Daily, except Sunday.
Glendale	Dannatburg	"	5 m.	.25	8.00 a.m.	Daily, except Sunday.
do	Chase's Lake	"	7 m.	.30	8.00 a.m.	Daily, except Sunday.
do	Greig	"	3 m.	.25	10.00 a.m.	Daily, except Sunday.
do	Brantingham	"	7 m.	.50	10.00 a.m.	Daily, except Sunday.
Gouverneur	Somerville	"	6 m.	.25	1.00 p.m.	Daily, except Sunday.
do	Wegatchie	"	8 m.	.40	1.00 p.m.	Daily, except Sunday.
do	Ox Bow	"	10 m.	.50	1.00 p.m.	Daily, except Sunday.
do	Rossie	"	17 m.	.75	1.00 p.m.	Daily, except Sunday.
do	Hammond	"	25 m.	1.00	1.00 p.m.	Daily, except Sunday.
do	Natural Dam	"	1 m.	.15	1.45 p.m.	Daily, except Sunday.
do	Elmdale	"	5 m.	.25	1.45 p.m.	Daily, except Sunday.
do	Brasie's Corners	"	10 m.	.50	1.45 p.m.	Daily, except Sunday.
do	Pope's Mills	"	16 m.	.75	1.45 p.m.	Daily, except Sunday.
do	Homestead	"	4 m.	.25	1.00 p.m.	Tri-weekly.
do	Osbornville	"	5 m.	.25	1.00 p.m.	Tri-weekly.
Hailesboro	York (Fowler P. O.)	"	4 m.	.20	2.00 p.m.	Daily, except Sunday.
do	Fullerville	"	7 m.	.35	2.00 p.m.	Daily, except Sunday.
Hamlin	Hamlin Centre	"	½ m.	....	10.00 and 11.00 a.m.	Daily.
do	Oak Island Orchard	"	3 m.	....	Arrival of trains	Summer Season only.
Hammond	Gouverneur	"	22 m.	1.00	7.00 a.m.	Daily, except Sunday.
Hannibal	Fairdale	"	2 m.	.15	7.00 a.m.	Daily, except Sunday.
do	Dexterville	"	5 m.	.25	7.00 a.m.	Daily, except Sunday.
do	Granby Centre	"	7 m.	.40	7.00 a.m.	Daily, except Sunday.
do	Oswego Falls	"	8 m.	.50	7.00 a.m.	Daily, except Sunday.
do	Fulton	"	8 m.	.50	7.00 a.m.	Daily, except Sunday.
do	Hannibal Centre	"	2 m.	.10	7.30 a.m.	Daily, except Sunday.
do	South Hannibal	"	4 m.	.20	7.30 a.m.	Daily, except Sunday.
do	Bowen's Corners	"	8 m.	.35	7.30 a.m.	Daily, except Sunday.
do	Oswego Falls	"	10 m.	.50	7.30 a.m.	Daily, except Sunday.
do	Fulton	"	11 m.	.50	7.30 a.m.	Daily, except Sunday.
do	Kinney's Four Corners	"	3 m.	.10	7.30 a.m.	Daily, except Sunday.
do	Southwest Oswego	"	6 m.	.25	7.30 a.m.	Daily, except Sunday.
do	Fruit Valley	"	9 m.	.25	7.30 a.m.	Daily, except Sunday.
do	Oswego	"	11 m.	.25	7.30 a.m.	Daily, except Sunday.
Hastings	Hastings Village	"	1¼ m.	.10	8.10 a.m., 2.00, 7.00 p.m.	Daily, except Sunday.

Heuvelton	Kokomo	N. Y.	5 m.	$0.25	2.00 p.m.	Daily, except Sunday.
do	Edenton	"	9 m.	.50	2.00 p.m.	Daily, except Sunday.
do	Pope's Mills	"	14 m.	.65	2.00 p.m.	Daily, except Sunday.
do	De Peyster	"	5 m.	.25	2.00 p.m.	Daily, except Sunday.
do	Hickory	"	9 m.	.50	2.00 p.m.	Daily, except Sunday.
do	Macombe	"	15 m.	.60	2.00 p.m.	Daily, except Sunday.
Holland Patent	East Floyd	"	2 m.	.25	2.00 p.m.	Daily, except Sunday.
do	Steuben	"	6 m.	.25	2.00 p.m.	Daily, except Sunday.
do	Steuben Valley	"	9 m.	.25	2.00 p.m.	Daily, except Sunday.
do	Big Brook	"	12 m.	.25	2.00 p.m.	Daily, except Sunday.
Kasoag	Ricard	"	3 m.	.15	9.30 a.m.	Daily, except Sunday.
Lafargeville	Omar	"	5 m.	.35	10.30 a.m.	Daily, except Sunday.
do	Fisher's Landing	"	7 m.	.50	10.30 a.m.	Daily, except Sunday.
Lakeside	Lakeside Village	"	2 m.	.15	10.35 a.m., 7.30 p.m.	Daily, except Sunday.
Lewiston	Youngstown	"	6 m.	.25	10.30 a.m., 5.25 p.m.	Daily, except Sunday.
do	Fort Niagara	"	7 m.	.50	10.30 a.m., 5.25 p.m.	Daily, except Sunday.
Limerick	Dexter	"	2 m.	.25	Arrival of trains	Daily, except Sunday.
do	Perch River	"	3 m.	.25	9.30 a.m.	Daily, except Sunday.
do	Stone Mills	"	8 m.	.25	7.15 p.m.	Daily, except Sunday.
Lowville	Martinsburg	"	4 m.	.50	9.00 a.m., 3.00 p.m.	Daily, except Sunday.
do	Croghan	"	12 m.	.50	4.00 p.m.	Daily, except Sunday.
do	Rector	"	12 m.	.50	1.30 p.m.	Daily, except Sunday.
do	Gardner Corners	"	10½ m.	.50	1.30 p.m.	Daily, except Sunday.
do	New Bremen	"	4 m.	.50	1.30 p.m.	Daily, except Sunday.
Lyndonville	Ridgeway	"	4 m.	.40	9.00 a.m.	Tuesdays, Thursdays and Saturdays.
do	Medina	"	7 m.	....	9.00 a.m.	Tuesdays, Thursdays and Saturdays.
Lyons Falls	Collinsville	"	......	....	Arrival of all trains except No. 528	Daily, except Sunday.
do	Turin	"	3 m.	.25	Arrival of all trains except No. 528	Daily, except Sunday.
do	(From Turin) Houseville	"	4 m.	.25	About 10.00 a.m.	Daily, except Sunday.
do	Constableville	"	5 m.	.50	Arrival of all trains except No. 528	Daily, except Sunday.
do	Lyonsdale	"	2½ m.	.25	About 8.00 p.m.	Daily, except Sunday.
Massena Springs	Massena	"	1 m.	.10	Arrival of trains	Daily, except Sunday.
Mexico	Union Square	"	4 m.	.50	Arrival of trains	Daily, except Sunday.
do	Fulton	"	17 m.	.75	6.00 a.m.	Daily, except Sunday.
do	Wellwood	"	3½ m.	....	3.30 p.m.	Daily, except Sunday.
do	Texas	"	5 m.	....	2.45 p.m.	Daily, except Sunday.
do	Parish	"	7 m.	....	3.00 p.m.	Daily, except Sunday.
Newfane	Lockport	"	10 m.	.40	7.50 a.m.	Daily, except Sunday.
Norwood	Norfolk	"	3 m.	.25	1.30 p.m.	Daily, except Sunday.
do	Raymondville	"	6 m.	.50	1.30 p.m.	Daily, except Sunday.
do	Louiseville	"	11 m.	.75	1.30 p.m.	Daily, except Sunday.
do	Louiseville Landing	"	16½ m.	1.00	1.30 p.m.	Daily, except Sunday.
Ogdensburg	Waddington	"	18 m.	.75	3.00 p.m.	Daily, except Sunday.
do	Edwardsville	"	14 m.	.50	2.30 p.m.	Daily, except Sunday.
Ontario	Ontario Centre	"	1¾ m.	.25	Arrival of trains	Daily, except Sunday.
Oswego	Scriba	"	6 m.	.15	11.00 a.m.	Daily, except Sunday.
do	South New Haven	"	7 m.	.25	11.00 a.m.	Daily, except Sunday.
do	Sala	"	8 m.	.25	11.00 a.m.	Daily, except Sunday.
do	Vermilion	"	12 m.	.25	12.15 p.m.	Daily, except Sunday.
do	South Scriba	"	4½ m.	.15	12.15 p.m.	Daily, except Sunday.
do	North Volney	"	9 m.	.25	12.15 p.m.	Daily, except Sunday.
do	Fruit Valley	"	3½ m.	.15	3.30 p.m.	Daily, except Sunday.
do	Kinney's Four Corners	"	5 m.	.15	3.30 p.m.	Daily, except Sunday.
do	Southwest Oswego	"	4 m.	.15	3.30 p.m.	Daily, except Sunday.
do	Hannibal	"	11 m.	.25	3.30 p.m.	Daily, except Sunday.
Parma	Parma Centre	"	......	....	7.00 a.m., 2.00 p.m.	Daily, except Sunday.
do	Parma Corners	"	......	....	7.00 a.m., 2.00 p.m.	Daily, except Sunday.
do	Spencerport	"	7 m.	.25	7.30 a.m., 2.30 p.m.	Daily, except Sunday.
Phœnix	Hinmanville	"	3 m.	.50	10.00 a.m.	Daily, except Sunday.
Pierrepont Manor	Ellisburg	"	4 m.	.25	9.00 a.m., 7.15 p.m.	Daily, except Sunday.

LIST OF PLACES REACHED BY STAGE FROM R., W. & O. R.R. STATIONS.

Railroad Station.	Stage Destination.		Distance.	Fare.	Leaves Station.	
Pierrepont Manor	Woodville	N. Y.	7 m.	$0.50	8.00 a.m.	Daily, except Sunday.
do	Rural Hill	"	9½ m.	.75	8.00 a.m.	Daily, except Sunday.
Potsdam	Parishville	"	9 m.	.75	2.00 p.m.	Daily, except Sunday.
do	Colton	"	9 m.	.75	2.00 p.m.	Daily, except Sunday.
do	South Colton	"	15 m.	1.00	2.00 p.m.	Daily, except Sunday.
do	West Potsdam	"	7 m.	.50	2.30 p.m.	Daily, except Sunday.
Prescott, Ont	Maynard	Ont.	......	....	2.30 p.m.	Wednesdays and Saturdays.
do	Centre Augusta	"	......	....	2.30 p.m.	Wednesdays and Saturdays.
do	Throoptown	"	......	....	2.30 p.m.	Wednesdays and Saturdays.
do	North Augusta	"	16 m.	.50	2.30 p.m.	Wednesdays and Saturdays.
do	Domville	"	......	....	2.30 p.m.	Tuesdays, Thursdays and Saturdays.
do	Roebuck	"	......	....	2.30 p.m.	Tuesdays, Thursdays and Saturdays.
do	Garretton	"	......	....	2.30 p.m.	Tuesdays, Thursdays and Saturdays.
do	Bishop's Mills	"	16 m.	.50	2.30 p.m.	Tuesdays, Thursdays and Saturdays.
do	Cardinal	"	9 m.	....	3.00 p.m.	Tuesdays and Saturdays.
Prospect	Prospect Village	N. Y.	1½ m.	.15	All trains	Daily.
do	Hinckley	"	3½ m.	.40	6.35 and 9.10 a.m., 2.00 and 6.37 p.m.	Daily, except Sunday.
do	Grant	"	6½ m.	.50	6.35 and 9.10 a.m., 2.00 and 6.37 p.m.	Daily, except Sunday.
do	Ohio	"	11½ m.	.75	9.10 a.m.	Daily, except Sunday.
do	Wilmurt	"	18 m.	1.25	9.10 a.m.	Daily, except Sunday.
do	Morehouseville	"	25 m.	1.50	9.10 a.m.	Daily, except Sunday.
do	Northwood	"	10 m.	.75	9.10 a.m.	Daily, except Sunday.
Pulaski	Port Ontario	"	3 m.	.50	10.00 a.m.	Daily, except Sunday.
Ransomville	Hickory Corners	"	11 m.	.40	3.45 p.m.	Tri-weekly.
do	Warren Corners	"	11 m.	.40	3.45 p.m.	Tri-weekly.
do	Cambria	"	9 m.	.30	4.30 p.m.	Daily, except Sunday.
do	North Ridge	"	4 m.	.20	5.30 p.m.	Daily, except Sunday.
Red Creek	Westbury	"	3 m.	.50	4.30 a.m.	Daily, except Sunday.
do	Victory	"	5 m.	.50	4.30 a.m.	Daily, except Sunday.
do	Cato	"	10 m.	.50	4.30 a.m.	Daily, except Sunday.
do	North Victory	"	4 m.	.50	8.30 a.m.	Daily, except Sunday.
do	Martville	"	6 m.	.50	8.30 a.m.	Daily, except Sunday.
Redwood	Plessis	"	3½ m.	....	10.30 a.m., 5.45 p.m.	Daily, except Sunday.
do	Alexandria Bay	"	7 m.	....	10.30 a.m., 5.45 p.m.	Daily, except Sunday.
Richland	Orwell, N. Y	"	3 m.	.25	8.00 a.m., 3.00, 8.00 p.m.	Daily, except Sunday.
Richville	Richville Village	"	1½ m.	.20	All trains except No. 3	Daily, except Sunday.
Rome	Lowell	"	6 m.	.25	2.45 p.m.	Daily, except Sunday.
do	Plains	"	8 m.	.25	2.45 p.m.	Daily, except Sunday.
do	Lee	"	8 m.	.30	2.45 p.m.	Daily, except Sunday.
do	Northwestern	"	12 m.	.70	2.45 p.m.	Daily, except Sunday.
do	Point Rock	"	16 m.	.70	2.45 p.m.	Daily, except Sunday.
do	Constableville	"	25 m.	1.50	2.45 p.m.	Daily, except Sunday.
Rose	Rose Valley	"	......	.25	7.10 a.m., 12.09 p.m.	Daily, except Sunday.
do	Huron	"	......	.25	1.00 p.m.	Daily, except Sunday.
do	North Huron	"	......	.50	1.00 p.m.	Daily, except Sunday.
do	Lummisville	"	7 m.	.50	1.00 p.m.	Daily, except Sunday.
do	Port Glasco	"	3 m.	.50	12.00 m.	Daily, except Sunday.
do	Clyde	"	7 m.	.50	7.10 a.m., 12.08 p.m.	Daily, except Sunday.
Rosiere	St. Lawrence	"	5 m.	.25	10.00 a.m.	Daily, except Sunday.
Sackett's Harbor	Smithville	"	5 m.	.25	8.30 a.m., 6.00 p.m.	Daily, except Sunday.
Sandy Creek	Greenborough	"	11 m.	.50	1.00 p.m.	Tuesdays, Thursdays and Saturdays.
Sodus	Joy	"	4 m.	.25	2.00 p.m.	Daily, except Sunday.
Sterling	Sterling Village	"	2 m.	.20	10.00 a.m., 6.00 p.m.	Daily.
do	Sterling Valley	"	4 m.	.30	10.00 a.m.	Daily, except Sunday.

Sterling	North Sterling, N. Y.	6 m.	$0.40	10.00 a.m.	Daily, except Sunday.
Stittville	Floyd "	3 m.	.15	6.20 p.m.	Daily, except Sunday.
do	Camroden "	5 m.	.25	6.20 p.m.	Daily, except Sunday.
Taberg	Taberg Village "	2½ m.	.15	All trains	Daily, except Sunday.
do	Glenmore "	7 m.	.40	All trains	Daily, except Sunday.
Three Mile Bay	Three Mile Bay Village "	1 m.	.15	All trains	Daily, except Sunday.
do	Point Peninsula "	12 m.	.50	3.00 p.m.	Daily, except Sunday.
Trenton	Trenton Village "	¼ m.	.10	All trains	Daily, except Sunday.
do	South Trenton "	4 m.	.25	6.30 p.m.	Daily, except Sunday.
do	Trenton Falls "	2 m.	.25	9.16 a.m., 6.30 p.m.	Daily, except Sunday.
do	North Gage "	5 m.	.40	6.30 p.m.	Daily, except Sunday.
Trenton Falls	Trenton Falls "	1 m.	.25		Daily, except Sunday.
Union Square	Mexico "	4 m.	.50	All trains	Daily, except Sunday.
Waterport	Gaines "	4 m.	.25	8.30 a.m.	Daily, except Sunday.
do	Kuckville "	4 m.	.25	4.00 p.m.	Daily, except Sunday.
do	Lakeside "	4 m.	.25	4.00 p.m.	Daily, except Sunday.
do	Kenyonville "	2½ m.	.25	4.00 p.m.	Daily, except Sunday.
Watertown	Barnes' Corners "	14 m.	.75	3.01 p.m.	Daily, except Sunday.
do	Burr Mills "	4 m.	.25	3.01 p.m.	Daily, except Sunday.
do	East Rodman "	10 m.	.50	3.00 p.m.	Daily, except Sunday.
do	South Champion "	12 m.	.75	3.00 p.m.	Daily, except Sunday.
do	South Rutland "	9 m.	.50	3.00 p.m.	Daily, except Sunday.
do	East Watertown "	3 m.	.15	3.00 p.m., 4.15 p.m.	Daily, except Sunday.
do	Rutland "	5 m.	.25	3.00 p.m., 4.15 p.m.	Daily, except Sunday.
do	Copenhagen "	14 m.	75	4.15 p.m.	Daily, except Sunday.
Williamson	Pultneyville "	4 m.	25	11.33 a.m., 7.03 p.m.	Daily, except Sunday.
Williamstown	Amboy Centre "	5 m.	.50	2.30 p.m.	Daily, except Sunday.
do	West Amboy "	7 m.	.50	2.30 p.m.	Daily, except Sunday.
do	Redfield "	9 m.	.50	2.30 p.m.	Daily, except Sunday.
Wolcott	Rose Valley "	.....	....	6.30 a.m.	Daily, except Sunday.
do	North Wolcott "	6 m.	.50	2.00 p.m.	Daily, except Sunday.

THOUSAND ISLAND STEAMBOAT COMPANY'S STEAMER "ST. LAWRENCE," LARGEST, FASTEST AND HANDSOMEST STEAMER IN INLAND WATERS.

THE THOUSAND ISLANDS.

Hubbard House,

CLAYTON, N. Y.

The Home of the Fisherman. *Open from May to October.*

A first-class commodious Hotel, situated in the immediate vicinity of the far-famed fishing grounds of the St. Lawrence River; convenient to all Railroad and Steamboat lines. An addition of sixty rooms, many with parlors and baths attached, has been completed during the past winter. The table is supplied daily with fresh fruits, vegetables and cream from the celebrated Hubbard House Farm. For terms, descriptive circulars, etc., address

MRS. ELEANOR M. HUBBARD,
PROPRIETRESS.

C. R. NOTT,
MANAGER

Frenchman's Island

Situated in Oneida Lake, five miles from Brewerton, one and one-half miles from South Bay.

A MOST BEAUTIFUL SPOT. THE SURROUNDING WATERS ARE THE FISHERMAN'S PARADISE. ∴ A LARGE, COMMODIOUS HOTEL WITH PLEASANT ROOMS AND CUISINE PERFECT. ∴ ∵ ∴ ∵ ∴ LARGE POOL ROOMS AND BOWLING ALLEY. ∴ ∴

Thirty acres of shaded lawn, swings, tables, and dancing pavilion for picnic parties. Good boats with efficient oarsmen will be in constant attendance. A home for those wishing quiet and rest.

AMPLE PROVISION WILL BE MADE FOR CAMPING PARTIES. THERE IS ROOM FOR ALL.

The island is surrounded by a splendid Bicycle Track and there is also a fine Ball Ground.

The large and commodious steamer "Maple Bay" is owned by the managers, and will run from Brewerton in connection with all trains on the R., W. & O. R.R. from Syracuse. It will also make daily trips to Constantia, South Bay and other points of interest on Oneida Lake.

REDUCED RATES.

By procuring return tickets parties can secure reduced rates to the island with a Sunday excursion rate.

The ideal place in which to spend a day or a month.

Liberal inducements will be offered to picnic or excursion parties.

Hotel Rates: $2.00 per Day, $8, $10 and $12 per Week.

REDUCTION TO LARGE PARTIES.

WILEY & CAMPBELL,

MANAGERS.

FRANK WILEY. JOHN CAMPBELL.

NEW HOTEL PORTER,

NIAGARA FALLS, N. Y.

One of the most pleasantly located hotels at Niagara Falls is the NEW HOTEL PORTER, only a few steps from the New York Central Station and two blocks from the State Reservation and the Falls. This hotel is nearly new and is one of the best furnished hostelries in the State. Robert P. Murphy, the genial proprietor, is one of the youngest and most successful hotel men in the country, and prides himself on having built up his reputation by paying particular attention to the culinary department and making his guests feel that there is at least one place at the world-famed Niagara where parties can get first-class accommodation at moderate charges. The rates at this hotel are $2.00 to $3.00, and the house will hold 150 people comfortably, and is open all the year round.

Parties intending to visit Niagara Falls will do well to write the Hotel Porter to reserve rooms in advance.

"ST. LAWRENCE INN."

On the line of the R., W. & O., about 125 miles north of Syracuse and eighteen miles from the St. Lawrence River, is the beautiful village of Gouverneur. This place is so situated on the western edge of the Adirondacks, in the midst of river, lake and mountain scenery, as to make it an *ideal summer resort*, and just the place to drive dull care away and enjoy, to the fullest extent, the beauties of Nature. Here has been built, at a cost of upwards of $100,000, the beautiful "*ST. LAWRENCE INN.*" This magnificent hotel is of native marble and is one of the most imposing hotels in the State outside of New York City. It is furnished throughout with latest styles of furniture, tapestries, and polished hardwood floors, covered with Turkish rugs. No expense has been spared in construction to make this the most complete hotel in the State. There are forty rooms with baths and toilets so arranged as to allow suites for families and large parties. The house is lighted by 700 electric lights and furnished with an electric elevator. Telephone connection in each room with the office. The house fronts on a beautiful park with fountains and band stand, which is the property of the hotel and for the exclusive use of its guests. There will be music in the park every evening during the summer season. In the vicinity of Gouverneur are many beautiful drives, and the proprietor, besides having a livery stable in connection with the house, has purchased one of the famous World's Fair Tally-Ho Coaches which will make tri-weekly trips to Black Lake and weekly trips to Alexandria Bay and the Thousand Islands. The rates of this house are especially low considering its advantages, $2.00 to $3.00 per day, with special rates to families and summer parties. The owner, Robert P. Murphy, who also owns the famous Hotel Porter at Niagara Falls, will give the house his personal attention, and invites correspondence from all parties who wish to find a quiet spot amidst charming surroundings in which to spend their vacation.

THE Delaware & Hudson · Railroad ·

"THE LEADING TOURISTS' LINE OF AMERICA."

. . . TO . . .

The Adirondack Mountains,

Lake Champlain, Lake George, Ausable Chasm, Saratoga Springs, Round Lake, Howe's Cave, Sharon Springs, Cooperstown, The Gravity Railroad.

"It may be questioned whether there is a railway journey in the world which gives in one day a variety and splendor of landscape to equal that which is enjoyed by the traveller taking the morning express by this line between Montreal and New York."—*Scottish Review.*

"The Hotel Champlain"

Three Miles south of Plattsburgh, N. Y.

All Trains Stop at the Hotel Station.

The Superb Adirondack and Lake Champlain Resort.

The Natural Stopping Over Point for Tourists Through Lake Champlain. All Boats Land at the Hotel.

Unrivalled Panoramic Views of Adirondacks and Green Mountains.

. . . AND TO THE . . .

"HOTEL CHAMPLAIN,"

THE FINE SUMMER RESORT ON LAKE CHAMPLAIN.

The Shortest Route between New York and Montreal.

NEW YORK CITY TICKET OFFICE AND INFORMATION BUREAU, 21 CORTLANDT ST.

Enclose six cents in stamps for illustrated descriptive hand-book of the line to

H. G. YOUNG,	**W. H. HENRY,**	**J. W. BURDICK,**
Second Vice-President,	*Ticket Agent,*	*General Passenger Agent,*
ALBANY, N. Y.	143 ST. JAMES ST., MONTREAL, QUE.	ALBANY, N. Y.

MICHIGAN CENTRAL

From Chicago and Detroit

TO THE——THOUSAND ISLANDS AND THE
RAPIDS OF THE ST. LAWRENCE,
MONTREAL, QUEBEC AND OTHER CANADIAN POINTS,
THE ADIRONDACKS,
GREEN AND WHITE MOUNTAINS,
NEW ENGLAND SEA COAST,
SPRINGS AND OTHER RESORTS OF THE
NORTH AND EAST.

SEND TEN CENTS POSTAGE FOR A Summer Note Book.

"THE NIAGARA FALLS ROUTE" from Chicago and Detroit to New York, Boston and all Eastern Points.

TO MACKINAC ISLAND
and the delightful resorts of
Northern Michigan, Alma, St. Clair
and other points.

L. D. HEUSNER, City Passenger and Ticket Agent, 119 Adams Street, opposite Post-Office, Chicago.

ROBERT MILLER, General Superintendent, DETROIT.

O. W. RUGGLES, General Passenger and Ticket Agent, CHICAGO.

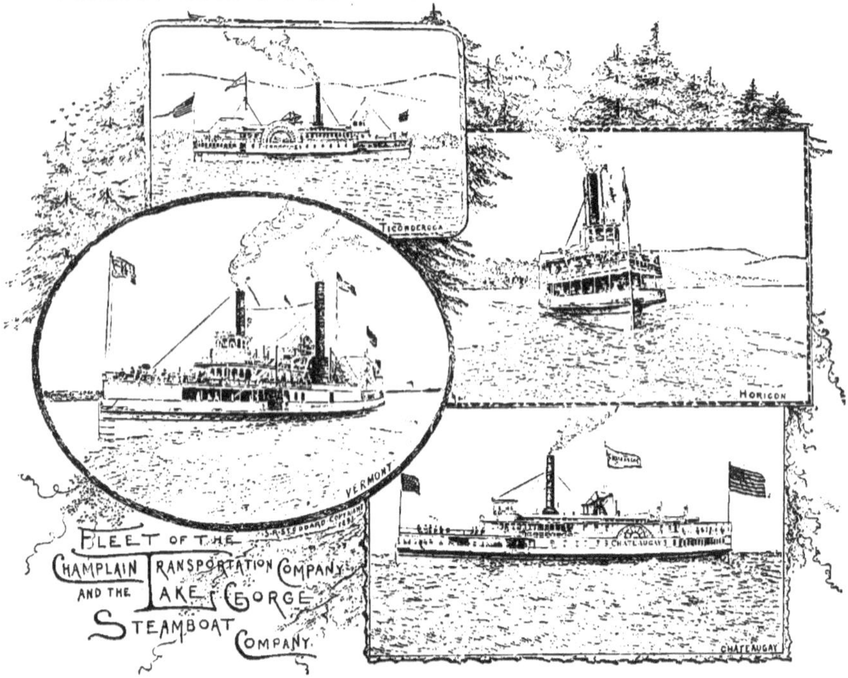

Champlain Transportation Co.

Lake George Steamboat Co.

THE GATEWAY OF THE COUNTRY.

Through the picturesque and historic Lakes George and Champlain to the famous summer resorts in the Green, Adirondack and White Mountains, Montreal, Saratoga and Ausable Chasm.

BEAUTIFUL LAKE AND MOUNTAIN SCENERY.
UNRIVALLED FOR GRANDEUR AND BEAUTY.

The popular pleasure route between all points in the Northern Country. Touching at the Hotel Champlain four times daily. The magnificent side-wheel steamers "Vermont" and "Chateaugay" on Lake Champlain and "Horicon" and "Ticonderoga" on Lake George.

MAIN AND CLOSE CONNECTIONS with all trains on the Delaware & Hudson Canal Company's Railroad at Fort Ticonderoga and Caldwell for Saratoga, Albany, New York and points south.

At Plattsburg for Thousand Islands, Ogdensburg, Montreal and Quebec. At Plattsburg with the Chateaugay Railroad for all points in the Adirondacks. At Burlington with the Central Vermont Railroad for White and Green Mountain resorts. At Port Kent for AUSABLE CHASM.

Meals served on board. The morning trains from the north have no boat connections on Lake Champlain. Take afternoon train and lodge at Plattsburg. Staterooms can be had on board steamer if desired. Parties using staterooms night before can have use of same during the passage through Lake Champlain.

GENERAL OFFICES:
BURLINGTON, VT.

GEORGE RUSHLOW, GENERAL MANAGER.

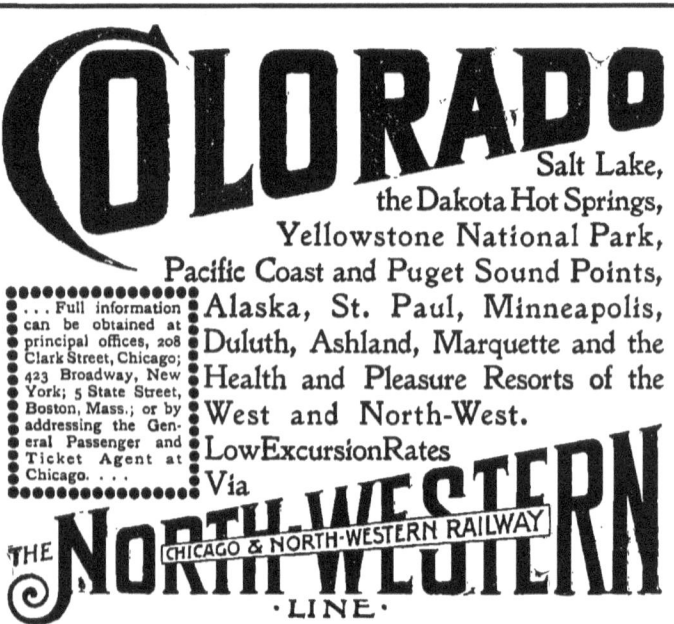

WATKINS GLEN AND GENEVA.

CLOSE CONNECTIONS WITH TRAINS ON THE N. C. R.R., N. Y. C. & H. R. R.R., LEHIGH VALLEY AND MIDDLESEX VALLEY RAILROADS.

Special attention given to Excursion Parties.

E. N. SQUIRES,
General Passenger Agent.

W. B. DUNNING,
General Manager.

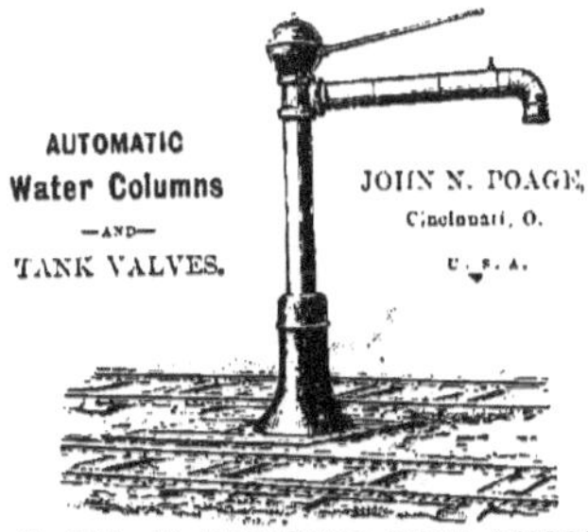

THE R. W. & O. R.R. IS EQUIPPED WITH THESE MACHINES.

J. B. McMURRICH,

OSWEGO, N.Y.,

SHIPPING AND SALES AGENT

DELAWARE AND HUDSON CANAL CO.,

DEALER IN

BITUMINOUS COAL AND COKE.

SHIPMENTS BY
BY WATER
FROM OSWEGO.

SHIPMENTS BY RAIL
DIRECT FROM
MINES AND FROM OSWEGO.

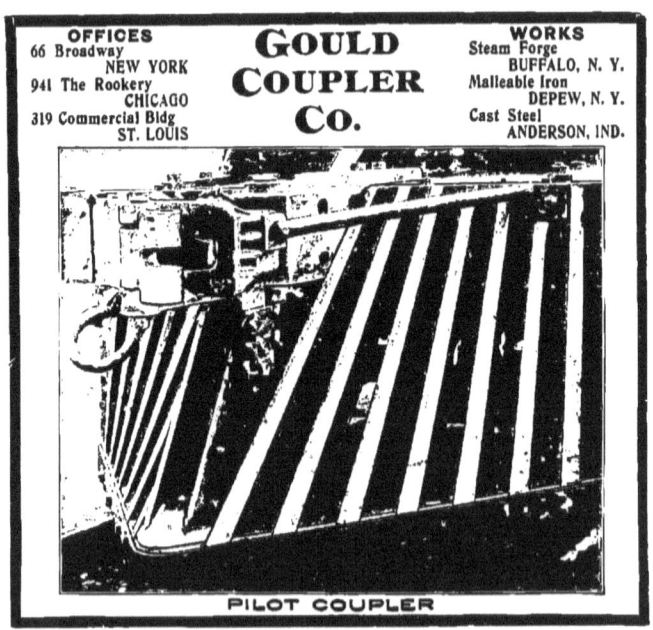

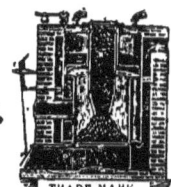

CAUTION.

Although the A B C PATHFINDER RAILWAY GUIDE is the oldest and best Guide in America, it is not the only one; "there are others," any one of which will make your vacation SEEM long.

If you can have a good time with a lame horse, a leaky boat, a sunny attic room and a feather bed you will have no use for the PATHFINDER.

We are gunning for tourists who are on time, up to date and will have nothing but the best. If you belong to that class, send 25 cents in stamps to the New England Railway Publishing Co., 67 Federal Street, Boston, Mass., and a copy of the PATHFINDER will be sent to you by return mail.

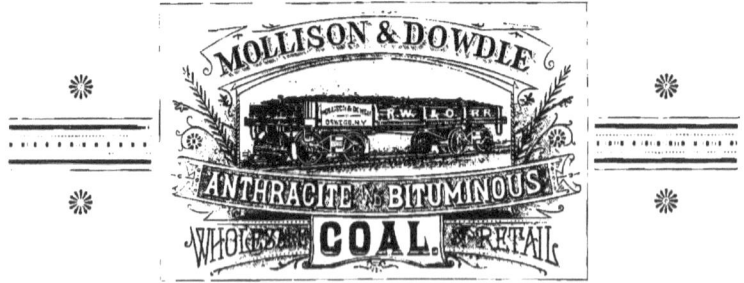

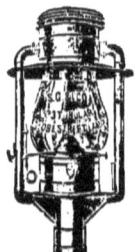

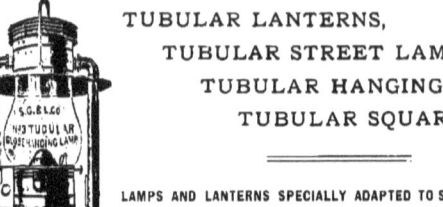

THE WHIRLPOOL AT NIAGARA FALLS.

THE TOURIST'S IDEAL ROUTE.

Tourists and pleasure seekers will find the Rome, Watertown & Ogdensburg Railroad to be pre-eminently the Route for Tourist Travel, and it was constructed with that end in view. It is the great highway and favorite route for fashionable pleasure travel. It reaches direct, and by its own lines, all of the Summer Pleasure Resorts in Northern New York, the Western and Northwestern Adirondacks and along the St. Lawrence River, and by its direct and immediate connections furnishes the shortest and most desirable route to the Lower St. Lawrence, the Saguenay, the White Mountains, the Sea-shore Resorts of New England and the Maritime Provinces. The system, under its new progressive management, has been greatly improved, as noticed on page 5. It was leased to the New York Central & Hudson River R.R. in March, 1891, and its road-bed and track have been raised to trunk line standard and are carefully maintained. The new motive power and the new equipment are of the best and latest designs; the new passenger coaches have Wagner Vestibules and are mounted on steel wheels. Their seats are very comfortable and are upholstered in blue figured plush. These cars are models of comfort and are provided with all latest improvements and many new devices.

During the summer season the fast train service, avoiding stops, is a feature greatly appreciated by the pleasure travel. Solid trains, magnificently equipped, are run by the New York Central and R., W. & O. from their principal western and southern terminals to the distributing points in Northern New York and along the River St. Lawrence. The Palace Sleeping Cars and Drawing-Room Cars running on this route all have Wagner Vestibules and are of the Wagner Palace Car Company's latest and most elegant design. The officials and employees of the Company will be found polite and attentive, and a trip over the line will convince one that nothing is omitted which can in the least conduce to the comfort or pleasure of its patrons.

INFORMATION EN ROUTE.

Tourists desiring reliable information regarding time schedules of different transportation lines, connections, places of interest, hotels, etc. along the different portions of the tour while en route, will please apply to the undermentioned gentlemen, who will cheerfully give such information:

Mr. M. C. ROACH..............413 Broadway, New York
Mr. O. E. JENKINS, G. W. P. A., R., W. & O. R.R. 95 Clark Street, Chicago, Ill.
Mr. L. D. HEUSNER......119 Adams Street, Chicago, Ill.
Mr. F. M. BYRON..........180 Clark Street, Chicago, Ill.
Mr. E. H. HUGHES.........103 Clark Street, Chicago, Ill.
Mr. N. C. KEERAN.........97 Adams Street, Chicago, Ill.
Mr. L. L. CAUFY.....85 Wisconsin St., Milwaukee, Wis.
Mr. H. S. BARLOW......139 Biddle St., Milwaukee, Wis.
Mr. H. H. MARLEY......Union Depot, Kansas City, Mo.
Mr. B. P. HUMPHREY....727 Maine St., Kansas City, Mo.
Mr. F. D. GILDERSLEEVE, Ticket Agent, "Big 4," St. Louis, Mo.
Mr. E. H. COFFIN, Wabash R.R..........St. Louis, Mo.
Mr. J. E. HULL......154 East Third St., St. Paul, Minn.
Mr. W. L. WYAND...170 East Third St., St. Paul, Minn.
Mr. J. F. ROLF, Ticket Agent, "Big 4," Cincinnati, Ohio
Mr. J. L. MILLER, Ticket Agent, "Big 4," Dayton, Ohio
Mr. E. M. SELTZER, Tick. Agt," Big 4," Columbus, Ohio
Mr. JAS. RHINES..........................Detroit, Mich.
Mr. M. TAYLOR...N. Y. C. & H. R. R.R., Albany, N. Y.
Mr. H. IRVING FAY.........................Utica, N. Y.
Mr. J. D. BROWN, City Agt. L. S. & M. S. R'y, Cleveland, Ohio
Mr. WM. GATES............................Toledo, Ohio
Mr. B. B. DENISON, No. 6 Cataract House, or N. Y. C. & H. R. R.R. Station, Niagara Falls, N. Y.
Mr. E. J. WEEKS, No. 1 Exchange Street, Buffalo, N. Y.
Mr. J. C. KALBFLEISCH, City Agent N. Y. C. and R., W. & O. R.R., East Main Street, Rochester, N. Y.
Mr. W. E. BROWN........Larned Block, Syracuse, N. Y.
Mr. H. F. DEWEY, Agent.................Clayton, N. Y.
Messrs CORNWALL BROS.........Alexandria Bay, N. Y.
Mr. GEO. W. BRASH..................Ogdensburg, N. Y.
Mr. J. E. PARKER..........................Ottawa, Ont.
DEPOT TICKET AGENT, B. & L. R.R....Fabyan's, N. H.
ALL ST. JAMES STREET TICKET OFFICES. Montreal, P. Q.
All Canadian Pacific and Grand Trunk R'y Offices, Quebec, P. Q.
Mr. GEO. H. THOMPSON, M. C. R.R. (Depot) Portland, Me.
Mr. WM. F. FERNALD, Agt. B. & M. R.R., Old Orchard Beach, Me.
TICKET AGENT, Maine Central R.R....Bar Harbor, Me.

Letters asking for information should be addressed to THEO. BUTTERFIELD, G. P. A., Syracuse, N. Y., or to O. E. JENKINS, General Western Passenger Agent, 95 Clark Street, Chicago, Ill.

For large parties special rates will be made for any of the tours herein named and a guide furnished, if desired. Special arrangements will also be made for hotel accommodations at reduced rates.

TABLE OF CONTENTS.

MAPS.

ILLUSTRATIONS.

INDEX.

ROUTES AND RATES.

INDEX TO ADVERTISERS.

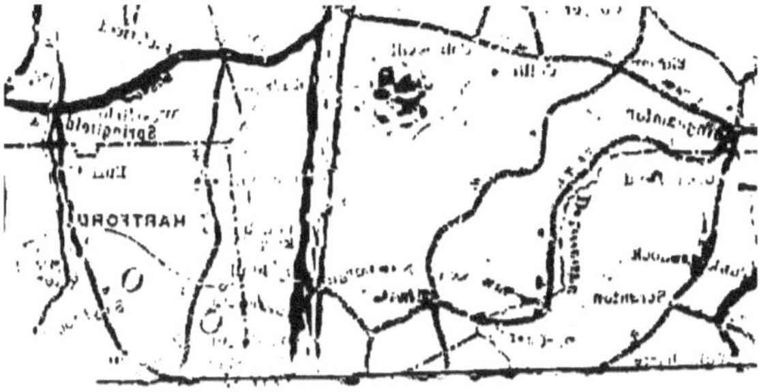

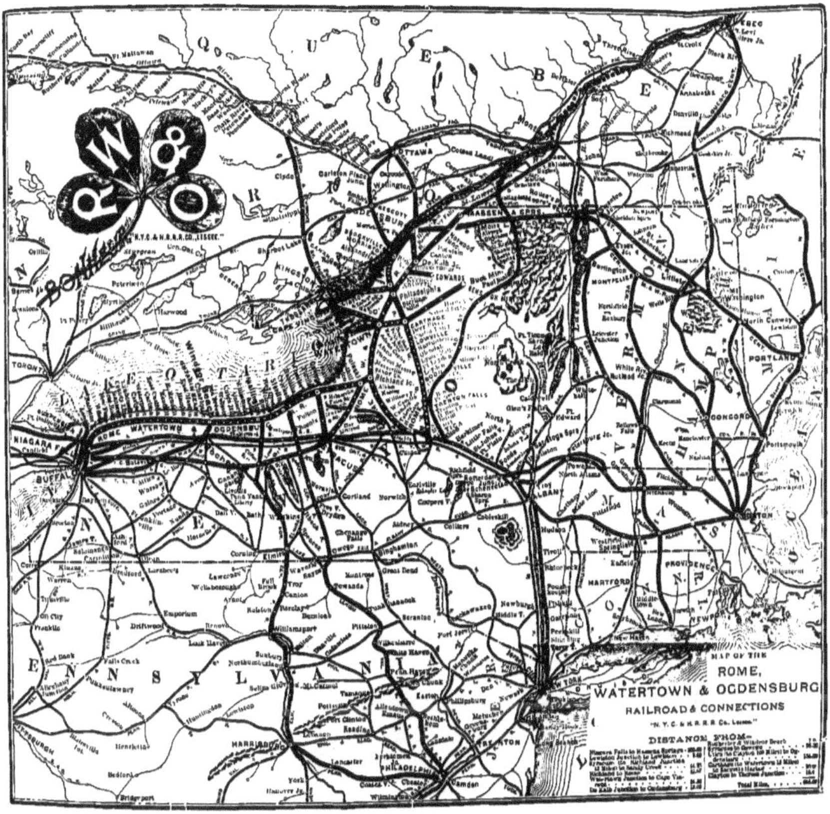
MAP OF THE
ROME,
WATERTOWN & OGDENSBURG
RAILROAD & CONNECTIONS
"N.Y.C. & H.R.R.R. Co. Lessee."
DISTANCE FROM
"N.Y.C. & H.R.R.R.CO.,LESSEE."
LAKE ONTARIO
PENNSYLVANIA
NIAGARA FALLS
BUFFALO
TORONTO
KINGSTON
OTTAWA
BOSTON
PORTLAND
CONCORD
PROVIDENCE
HARTFORD
NEW YORK
PHILADELPHIA
HARRISBURG
TRENTON
ALBANY
MONTPELIER
Binghamton
Williamsport
Cortland
Norwich
Emporium
Camden

www.ingramcontent.com/pod-product-compliance
Lightning Source LLC
Chambersburg PA
CBHW032149230426
43672CB00011B/2502
* 9 7 8 3 3 3 7 1 4 5 4 6 0 *